Y0-AZE-262

Your Money & Your Life

Your Money & Your Life

How to Plan Your Long-Range Financial Security

C. Colburn Hardy

amacom
A Division of American Management Associations

Library of Congress Cataloging in Publication Data

Hardy, C   Colburn.
  Your money & your life.

  Bibliography: p.
  Includes index.
  1. Finance, Personal. I. Title.
HG179.H29   332'.024   79-16972
ISBN 0-8144-5529-8

© 1979 AMACOM
A division of American Management Associations, New York.
All rights reserved. Printed in the United States of America.

This publication may not be reproduced, stored in a retrieval system, or transmitted in whole or in part, in any form or by any means, electronic, mechanical, photocopying, recording, or otherwise, without the prior written permission of AMACOM, 135 West 50th Street, New York, N.Y. 10020.

First Printing

Preface

In this guide, every effort has been made to ensure the accuracy and timeliness of the explanations, tables, charts, statistics, and examples. If there are differences, it is probably because information came from different sources at different times.

The text has been checked by competent authorities, but if there are errors or omissions, I apologize and repeat the advice which runs throughout the book: Do not make any major decision without consulting a knowledgeable adviser, preferably a lawyer. This is a *guide,* not a source of definitive information on financial planning.

A work of this scope requires the assistance of many people. I've tried to give credit in the text, but special thanks go to Emory Kates, lawyer; John Halper, real estate broker; Steven Glenn, certified life underwriter; Michael Stolper, financial planner; Richard Blackman, stockbroker; and John Winthrop Wright, professional money manager.

I'd also like to add special thanks for permission to quote copyrighted material from publications: *Barron's, Better Homes & Gardens, Business Week,* College Entrance Examination Board, *Dun's, Forbes, Money,* Moody's Investors Service, New York Insurance Department, New York Stock Exchange, *Physician's Management, Standard & Poor's, The Wall Street Journal,* and Wright Investors' Service. Thanks too to the publishers of books I've written, collaborated on, or edited for: Thomas Y. Crowell Company, Funk & Wagnalls, McGraw-Hill Book Company, *Medical Economics,* Prentice-Hall, and Simon & Schuster.

C. COLBURN HARDY

Contents

1	Introduction to Financial Planning	1
2	Staying Ahead of Inflation	8
3	A Millionaire in Every Family	15
4	Lifestyle and Financial Planning	19
5	The Importance of Net Worth and Personal Budgeting	28
6	The Mechanics of Money	46
7	Coping with College Costs	68
8	Planning for Retirement	84
9	The Role of Real Estate in Financial Planning	110
10	How to Invest for Maximum Total Returns	135
11	Special Investments and Speculations: Handle with Care	182
12	How to Use Life Insurance in Financial Planning	192
13	Don't Go Overboard to Save Taxes	222
14	Tax Shelters: Best for the Wealthy, Good for the Wise	239
15	Using Trusts for Financial Planning	247
16	Estate Planning to Reduce Taxes and Protect Property	259
17	The Importance of a Will	275
18	Choosing Your Advisers	282
19	Executive Incentives and Perks	296
20	Do It Yourself: Working Out Your Financial Plan	302
	Appendix I: What to Do When You Lose Your Job	312
	Appendix II: The Living Costs of Moving	319
	Bibliography	320
	Index	327

1 Introduction to Financial Planning

The idea of this guide to financial planning stems from real-life situations:

• A 45-year-old executive, with a $45,000 salary, realizes that he's over halfway through his working life and that, if inflation continues at a 6% rate, his annual income must rise to $144,000 just to have his present purchasing power when he retires at 65. After age 60, that increase will be over $500 every month!

• A 35-year-old business owner, after several years of struggling, is finally in the black and is now able to set aside, directly and through his company, $10,000 a year. He wants to learn how to judge the best buys in insurance, a retirement plan, and investments.

• A 55-year-old physician who has lived a full life (two divorces and five children) wakes up one morning to find that he has only $47,000 in his retirement plan and that, unless he changes his lifestyle, he'll have to work to age 75 to be able to afford to retire comfortably.

• A 40-year-old professional hits the jackpot with a top corporate position which pays a salary of $150,000 plus substantial fringe benefits and stock rights. His new job doubles his income; but in his drive for success, he's been spending more than he's been earning, and now he finds it difficult to curtail his expenditures. His wife is smarter and more realistic than he is. She points out that, even though he could be earning over $600,000 in his final year of employment (with raises for inflation), his after-work income will be inadequate unless he's lucky, profits from his stock rights, or starts financial planning now.

To some degree, most executives and professionals face similar problems. They earn quite a lot of money but are still concerned about steps to take to provide for the future because of inflation, expanding needs, and ever more onerous taxes. There's no one answer, but almost all those situations can be eased, if not eliminated, by wise financial planning. All that takes is knowledge, common sense, and self-discipline. This book is designed to provide the information, but the rest is up to you.

HOW YOUR SALARY CAN GROW

As you are well aware, the biggest single future factor in financial planning is inflation. For working people, the ever rising costs of living are offset by boosts in pay. For readers of this guide—executives and professionals—future salaries can be expected to increase at an average annual rate of 8%. Of that, at least 5% can be attributed to inflation, because the projections do not consider merit raises.

As a starter, let's make projections five years hence and lasting until ten years from now. (See Table 1–1.) That's about as far ahead as most people can predict with reasonable accuracy. If you're making $30,000 now, your anticipated earnings five years from now will be $43,800—the factor 1.46 multiplied by $30,000. In ten years, you'll be making $64,800 (2.16 × $30,000). That is welcome news, but with inflation at 6% the raises will be worth much less, as shown by these typical projected costs:

	Today	10 Years from Now
College (annual)	$6,000	$10,740
Automobile	5,000	8,950
Monthly electric bill	26	47
Hamburger	1.20	2.15

Obviously, it will be difficult to improve your standard of living substantially unless you start to organize yourself and your family for the accumulation, conservation, and distribution of your wealth. The purpose of this guide is to show you how to do that, how to plan your finances (and expenditures) to overcome the threat of inflation, understand alternative choices, and take actions which will help you reach your goals of security for your family and enjoyable retirement for yourself and spouse.

It's convenient to discuss the future in dollars, but remember that money is only a medium of exchange. Its value may decrease, but the real world stays: the earth and seas with all their resources, the houses, factories, office buildings, schools, colleges, museums, automobiles, airplanes, communication systems, and so on. Most important, people will be living longer, living better, and becoming even more dependent on one another. As men and women have adapted in the past, so they will adapt in the future.

Like most fears, the worrying is more awesome than the facts. The world is not about to end, and individuals who are willing to spend time and effort to develop long-term plans will find their future rewarding.

PAST CHANGES

It's easy to forget the changes which occur in a lifetime. When I started to work, in the early 1930s, I was lucky to be paid $1,200 a year for 5½ days per week of labor—plus a week's annual vacation and a few minor employee benefits. Today almost every college graduate starts off at $12,000, gets at least two weeks' vacation, and works about 35 hours a week. There are added benefits such as unemployment insurance, employer-paid health and life insurance, and pension plans to supplement Social Security.

True, costs were lower: a family could buy a week's groceries for $8 and a new car for $600. But few expenses have risen the ten times of salaries, and the values of property—real estate and common stocks, for example—are 20 to 30 times what they were half a century ago.

This book will show you how to plan to cope with economic change and how to use your resources more effectively. Financial planning is a never-ending

Table 1–1. Projecting your salary.

Years	Multiple of Present Salary (at Annual Salary Increase of 8%)
5	1.46
6	1.59
7	1.71
8	1.85
9	1.99
10	2.16

SOURCE: Adapted from David Thorndike, ed., *The Thorndike Encyclopedia of Banking & Financial Tables* (Boston: Warren, Gorham & Lamont, 1977).

process which should start as soon as you have a job—and even earlier if you are fortunate enough to have monetary help from your relatives.

In the chapters that follow, you will learn how to take advantage of the many opportunities offered by our free enterprise system, how to utilize tax benefits, and how to blend the preservation of capital with the gains possible from judicious investments. Success will not be easy, but it can be achieved by almost everyone who thinks things through, considers the alternatives, and recognizes that, historically, mankind has always been able to improve the quality of life and individual standards of living.

DO IT YOURSELF

When I started to plan this book, I envisioned that I would include examples of successful financial planning as developed by experts in the field. As I moved deeper into various areas and reviewed proposals by professional counselors, I discovered that case histories, although sometimes interesting, were seldom really helpful. Each individual has different resources, lifestyle, and goals. What might be appropriate for one would not be practical for, or acceptable to, another.

That's why this is a do-it-yourself book: a listing and explanation of various aspects of financial planning and money management with few specific recommendations. I have tried to explain techniques, outline the pros and cons of viable approaches to common problems, and provide data from which you can make your own decisions. If you have the knowledge and skill necessary to become a successful executive or professional, you can learn how to do your own financial planning. Or if you prefer to hire counsel, you will know the questions to ask and be better able to monitor and judge the value of the professional service.

RECURRENT THEMES

In this guide, there are several recurrent themes:

1. *Life in the United States, socially and economically, is constantly improving.* I believe it will continue to do so.

Throughout our history, there have been dramatic breakthroughs in industry, medicine, professions, and government programs. At the outset, they benefited only a handful of people, but over the decades the new products, services, and programs became available to most people.

My brother-in-law uses automobiles as an example. He points out that what first appeared as an extra on a Cadillac—power steering, power brakes, air conditioning—soon became standard on a Chevrolet. In much the same way, what was once confined to the rich is now enjoyed by nearly every family: vacations abroad, sailing, skiing, stereos, microwave ovens, and, in the financial area, pension plans, stock purchase opportunities, and profit-sharing programs.

The advances have become more inclusive with government action: unemployment and disability insurance, educational aid, Social Security, and, probably in the near future, expanded health care coverage. The significance of those programs does lessen with the rise in personal income, but there are scores of benefits which were not available, at reasonable cost, to our parents. There will be many new ones for our grandchildren.

Unemployment still is a nagging problem, but more Americans are working than ever before: an astounding 92 million in 1978 and 100 million soon.

2. *Americans have an amazing capacity to adapt:* to find solutions to what at first appeared to be insurmountable problems.

Take education. When costs of advanced study started to soar, we developed community colleges, work-study program, trimesters, loans, grants, and apparently soon, tax credits. When we believe something has merit, we find ways to make it available and workable.

3. *What has happened before is likely to happen again.* That is especially true of investments, the prices of which zoom to unjustified highs and fall to absurd lows. One of the most important roles of financial planning is to arrange your finances so that you can recognize such patterns. Then you can sell when properties become overvalued and buy them back when they become bargains again. In a similar way, an individual may suffer setbacks, but time and again the qualities responsible for early success become effective again.

4. *Things seldom work out as anticipated.* They are neither as rewarding as your hopes nor as detrimental as your fears. Few investments appreciate as far and as fast as projected; in home and career, what first appeared to be a harsh blow turns out to be the start of good fortune. When there are reverses, they often stop at a level higher than that from which they started; in the stock market, it's called the 50% rule.

5. *You can rarely have it both ways.* It's hard to have a carefree life while you work and after you retire. The longer you delay a logical decision, the less the chance of ultimate achievement. If you act now, you can have a better future. But if you are unwilling or unable to change your lifestyle now, you may be forced to change it later. Usually the change will be for the worse. The more and better you plan now, the less you will have to worry in the future.

6. *It is harder to get out than to get in.* That applies primarily to investments,

but it's also relevant to such personal decisions as getting married, taking a job, and choosing a career. Regardless of how tempting any opportunity may seem, always think ahead five or ten years and try to determine where you will be, whether you will be in a position to quit (sell) if things do not work out and whether your profits—in prestige, pleasure, or dollars—can be taken with you.

7. *Rewards must be balanced against risks.* If you choose a position with a major enterprise, whether business or government, the risks may be small but you will usually have to settle for security, ample benefits, and slow progress. The rewards will be hard to come by, and they will involve personal sacrifices and often frustration.

If you prefer to work with a small firm, the rewards may come more quickly and be greater but there will be the added risks of corporate failure, personality clashes, and opportunities limited by the size, capability, and resources of the enterprise and its management.

If you choose a profession or your own business, the rewards will be the pride in and pleasure of being your own boss but the risks will be the pressures of decisions, inadequate capital, competition, and, at times, seemingly overwhelming responsibilities and headaches. And you may have no reasonable way to get out!

So too with investments: the realistic rewards should always be double to triple the probable risks. Balance is important in life and in financial planning.

8. *Consider alternatives.* Most people tend to follow routines and shy away from, if not disregard, new approaches. They consult the old family lawyer even after they move far from their hometown; they put their savings in the bank used by their father; they buy straight life insurance because "that's what Dad left, and Mother is well fixed." And so on.

Reliance on familiarity is commendable, but it may not always be wise. When you discuss any major decision, consider the alternatives: other services and other means to reach the same goals. The necessity for choice applies to all established patterns, especially when there's the opportunity for a significant change: a new job, new home, investments, or altered family responsibilities. For example, you should not rule out a different type of insurance just because you have been paying premiums on straight life policies for 20 years. Instead, explore the same protection at lower cost or with the cost shared with your employer.

But do not make changes of any kind lightly. Careful review may convince you it's best to stand pat.

9. *Consistency and patience are important.* Financial planning is a lifelong process. Success takes time. The best illustration is the magic of compounding: earning income on reinvested income. (See Table 1–2.) With investments, progress is slow in the first few years but speeds up at an amazing rate in about 20 years.

Keep Table 1–2 in mind in all your financial planning and in all your investing. At an average rate of return of 8%, your savings will double every nine years.

Table 1-2. The magic of compound interest: How long it takes to double your capital at different rates of interest, compounded annually.*

Rate of Return	Approx. No. of Years	Rate of Return	Approx. No. of Years
1%	69⅔	6½%	11
2	35	7	10¼
2½	28	7½	9½
2¾	25½	8	9
3	23½	9	8
3½	20¼	10	7¼
4	17⅔	11	6⅔
4½	15¾	12	6⅛
5	14¼	13	5⅔
5½	13	14	5⅓
6	12	15	5

SOURCE: C. Colburn Hardy, *Dun & Bradstreet's Guide to Your Investments* (New York: Crowell, 1978)
Note: A simple way to get the exact number of years it takes to double your money at any assumed rate of return is to divide 69.3 by rate of return and add .35. Conversely, to determine rate required to double money over any period of years, divide 69.3 by years minus .35.
*Quarterly compounding would reduce required time.

And with wise management you can raise your total returns to 10% and thus double your assets 21 months earlier. Over a working lifetime of 45 years, the first investment will grow 64-fold! Even small sums will become very rewarding with consistency and patience.

A handy way to find how many years it takes $1 to become $2, at various rates of return, is the rule of 72. Divide 72 by the percentage of return: at 6%, doubling takes 12 years (72 divided by 6); at 10%, 7.2 years. Again, quarterly compounding would reduce the time required.

Note: In many examples and projections in this book I use an annual average rate of investment return of 10%. That, I believe, is realistic for the careful, intelligent money manager. Here is my reasoning:

1. Since quality bonds, which require no management, can yield 8.5% to 9%, why is it not possible to earn 1% to 1.5% more with a little research, supervision, and common sense?

2. Over many decades, the average return of all common stocks listed on the New York Stock Exchange was 9.3%. Obviously, selection of the best stocks, on the basis of quality and value, was more rewarding.

3. A return of well over 10% is possible with such a conservative investment as the common stock of AT&T. It can be had by taking advantage of automatic reinvestment of dividends. In 1978, "T" stock was selling at 60. The $4.60 per share dividend provided a 7.67% yield. Since the reinvested dividends could buy new shares at a 5% discount, the cost per share was 57. That raised the return to 8.07%. You also had a 5% "profit," since each share was worth 60 in the marketplace. Result: a 13.07% return on your money.

4. Compounding—earning income on income, as shown in Table 1-2—is one of the wonders of the financial world. With prompt reinvestment, an 8% return,

compounded annually, will grow to over 12% in three years: $126 on the initial $1,000. And that percentage of return will continue to grow.

A more familiar example of compounding is the high yield advertised for long-term savings certificates. The interest rate remains the same 5¼%, but with daily reinvestment of interest, it compounds 8.17% in eight years.

It is true that only a few professional money managers have averaged 10% on their portfolios, but their net results are reduced by fees and other costs. Also, because of the size of their holdings, the advisers are seldom able to move fast enough to get the best prices when buying or selling.

Anyway, if you prefer to count on only an 8% average annual rate of return, the projected results will take a little longer.

2 Staying Ahead of Inflation

Inflation appears to be here to stay and must be taken into account in all financial planning. There's little you can do about controlling its cause, but there is much you can do to ease the impact. To start off, be realistic and recognize that inflation is not all bad. As my brother-in-law, who is retired and living on a more or less fixed income, says, "Inflation is rough on us old-timers, but there must be something good about it because so many people seem to enjoy it."

If you are like most people, you growl and your spouse laments when you come across old bills for a new suit for $100 or for a ball gown for only $125 plus $20 for dancing slippers. That's history, and only one side of it. That house you bought in 1962 for $18,000 is now worth (or at least will sell for) about $56,000. And the job which once paid you a handsome $15,000 is now classified at $35,000 to $37,000. Life goes on.

Let's assume that inflation continues at an average annual rate of about 6%.* Projections are guesses at best, because there are so many variables and hypotheses and society makes unexpected adjustments. As you know from your own experience, most things which were awesome fears are now accepted, unalarming facts. Take all predictions, especially those involving money, with a grain of salt.

To provide a frame of reference for understanding the prospects of inflation, Table 2–1 presents some statistics on what happened between 1962 and 1977 and what may occur in 1987 and 1997. (The numbers are rounded off for

Table 2–1. The prospects of inflation.

	What Things Cost		What They May Cost	
	1962	1977	1987	1997
One-family house	$18,000	$54,000	$115,000	$245,000
Intermediate-size car	2,600	4,900	7,600	12,000
Private college (year)	2,650	7,060	13,000	26,000
Social Security taxes	150	965	3,046	5,888
Gasoline (gallon)	.31	.64	1.00	1.70
Auto insurance premium	90	250	500	1,000
Hamburger	.60	1.20	1.90	3.00
First-class postage stamp	.04	.13	.29	.63

SOURCE: Based on a consensus of predictions and projections from the U.S. Department of Health, Education, and Welfare, the U.S. Department of Labor, Octameron Associates (Alexandria, Va.), and experts in various fields.

*In making projections and comparisons, some authorities assume that inflation starts at the end of each year. Thus, in effect, the figures disregard the first 12 months. In this guide, the data are usually higher, and therefore more pessimistic, because inflation is calculated from January.

convenience.) If you've sold or bought a house lately, you can accept these nightmares, but it's difficult for most people to think that, in less than 20 years, a first-class postage stamp may cost 63¢. Yet the prospective figures, with some modifications, must be kept in mind in your financial planning. Your income and expenses are caught up in a powerful flood.

Still, there are reasons for optimism. That $18,000 house, bought in 1962, will be paid off, in 1987, with greatly depreciated dollars, and a new mortgage, at only 50% of the new value, will provide $57,500. Table 2–2 shows how earnings have soared in the past and can be projected into the future for an average executive and production worker.

THE INFLATION FACTOR

Most folks will find it an exercise in futility, but to calculate what's ahead, in theory anyway, use Table 2–3. The table shows the inflation factor at different rates over different time spans. In similar forms, the same information is repeated throughout this guide because it's the reference point for financial planning. It's the barrier you must breach.

The table is easy to use with your desk calculator. Let's start with a business example—an accountant with an established practice who spends a little time on his own future planning. This year the accountant has expenses of $30,000. To find out how much he'll be paying out for similar operating costs in five years, at an average 6% inflation rate, he multiplies the $30,000 by the 1.33 factor to get $39,900.

Next he uses the same table to project the value of his investments, which, he knows, will earn total returns of 8%. In ten years, the $50,000 in a bond fund, yielding 8%, will grow to $108,000 ($50,000 × 2.16)—assuming that the rate of interest stays about the same.

Use Table 2–3 for all projections for which you have base figures, time periods, and factors of return or increase.

INFLATION PLUS TAXES

Now let's be negative and see, in Table 2–4, how inflation erodes an 8% raise,

Table 2–2. Working income: past, present, and future.

| | What They Earned || What They May Earn ||
	1962	1977	1987	1997
Corporate or government executive				
Gross earnings	$16,000	$38,000	$69,000	$122,000
After-tax earnings	12,800	27,000	40,500	64,400
Production worker				
Gross earnings	$6,000	$13,000	$20,500	$37,000
After-tax earnings	5,100	10,700	16,000	26,300

Note: Married couple, joint return, two dependent children, standard deductions, little change in tax structure at federal, state, and local levels, estimated Social Security. Figures do not include what appear likely to be expanded fringe benefits such as life and health insurance and pension plans.

Table 2–3. Inflation factors for calculation of growth and income.

Years	Inflation Factor at Annual Rate of			
	6%	7%	8%	10%
5	1.33	1.40	1.46	1.61
6	1.42	1.50	1.59	1.77
7	1.50	1.61	1.71	1.94
8	1.59	1.72	1.85	2.14
9	1.69	1.84	1.99	2.36
10	1.78	1.97	2.16	2.59
15	2.40	2.76	3.17	4.18
20	3.20	3.87	4.66	6.73
25	4.29	5.43	6.85	10.83
30	5.74	7.61	10.06	17.45

SOURCE: David Thorndike, ed., *The Thorndike Encyclopedia of Banking & Financial Tables* (Boston: Warren, Gorham & Lamont, 1977).

which can be considered average for most corporation executives. The table includes taxes (at 1978 rates).

OUTLOOK FOR INFLATION

Before you begin to wonder how you can possibly survive with inflation, keep in mind that rising costs do not affect every budget item. Over the years, there will be offsetting factors.

1. Some major expenditures are fixed: monthly payments for the mortgage and installment loans and premiums for life insurance policies.

2. Costs of some items are declining: air fares, electronic products, and, in some states, real estate taxes.

3. Inflation may not remain high. No one can be sure, but many economists predict the rate will decline to 4% soon.

4. Adjustments will be made by society, and by individuals, to secure services at lower costs through government programs, subsidies, and new types of financing and greater cooperative use of facilities such as a clubhouse pool instead of a pool in every backyard.

Table 2–4. How taxes and inflation erode an 8% raise.

Adjusted Gross Income		After-tax Income		Effective Tax Rate*	After-tax Income Adjusted for 6.5% Inflation*
Last Year	This Year	Last Year	This Year		
$25,000	$27,000	$21,335	$22,833	15.43%	$21,439
35,000	37,800	28,636	30,531	19.23	28,668
45,000	48,600	35,850	37,743	22.34	35,439
55,000	59,400	41,981	44,813	24.56	42,078
65,000	70,200	47,382	50,738	27.72	47,641
75,000	81,000	53,731	57,229	29.35	53,736

SOURCE: Joint Committee on Taxation, U.S. Congress, 1977.
*If state and local income taxes are included, the tax rate will be higher and the adjusted income lower.

5. More employee benefits will be fully or partly financed by the employer: health and dental care, tuition for job-related courses, and unemployment or retirement plans.

6. Social Security checks will be higher. By 1990, they may amount to $10,000 a year for two people.

Right now, a 6% inflation rate seems to be generally regarded as the minimum for the immediate future. But such a projection is not accepted by some thoughtful people. There are, of course, pessimists who insist that continued inflation will force an end of the free enterprise system as we know it. But there are also optimists who argue that the worst of inflation is past, that the big thrust came from the sudden rise in the cost of energy and that, now that oil prices are more stable, the pressures for higher prices will lessen. They view the dollar's decline as temporary and, to some extent, justified and look for consumer prices to level off at average annual gains of 4%. That will soften future wage demands and lower the overall rate of inflation to 4.5% to 5%.

To support their views, the optimists note that prices of some foodstuffs and raw materials are trending downward, that some crops have been cut back because of depressed farm prices, and that developing countries, hard-pressed to finance oil deficits, are no longer boosting the prices of sugar, cotton, and many minerals. Add the new oil production from the North Sea and Alaska and, to the optimists, the outlook for lower inflation is brighter than at any time in the past decade even though there may be temporary rises.

Then they add some clinchers. Once inflation dips below 6% a year, there will be a domino effect. (1) With greater spendable income and more people working, consumption will rise, factories will become more fully utilized, productivity will improve, and price increases will be minimal. (2) New capital spending will be more constructive; it will provide more efficient plants rather than pay for unproductive environmental controls.

And do not sell the free enterprise system short. It may not be working too well, but it's far better than the alternatives. Take the long view of five or ten years, because that's what must be considered in financial planning.

One area in which gloom for the future is rising is in housing. According to a study by the MIT/Harvard Joint Center for Urban Studies, only three of ten families can afford a median-priced house, which was recently defined as one that cost about $53,000.

But let's look at a rebuttal from American Standard, Inc., a major manufacturer of plumbing supplies:

The single-family house is still affordable by 60% of American families, and its cost represents an ever-lower percentage of family income: 29% in 1965, 19% in 1975. . . . In that period, the number of homes sold doubled while there was only a 17% increase in family formations. The home is one of the few consumer investments that keeps rising in value while being used. The leverage effect of small down payments and rising home values plus tax benefits have made a well-located, single-family home an outstanding investment in good times and bad.

LOOKING AHEAD

In setting financial objectives, it's wise to have some idea of the type of world in which you and your family will be living 25 or 50 years from now. For most people, society will be only slightly different from what we have today. In a complex, structured world, change is slow. Only rarely will there be the dramatic new products, services, and benefits predicted by scientists anxious to create headlines or columnists and commentators pontificating to fill space and time. True, there will always be movement and improvement, but most of the activity will be centered in small areas and will take years to have a broad impact. If there are breakthroughs, their benefits will require years of development.

For practical purposes, prepare your financial plans on the basis of today's conditions but keep them flexible enough to catch significant shifts in monetary policies, investment outlooks, and public preferences. The world of the twenty-first century will have much the same type of housing and education and improved versions of familiar products and services. The changes will be primarily in taxes and the form of compensation and benefits. The taxes may be on different bases, but they will be greater because, despite Proposition 13, the overall cost of government shows little sign of declining. Wealthier individuals may take home fewer dollars, but they will also be able to count on government, and their employer, to assume a larger share of the costs of personal and family protection.

It will still be important to recognize the big, slow trends, but it will be far more useful to catch the small shifts. It's like timing investments: you want to sell when the chart shows a confirmed downtrend and buy when the stock is clearly moving up.

Population Trends

One important, and often overlooked, broad force is the makeup of the United States population. It will have a strong effect on legislation.

For the first two centuries in our country, people had large families to till fields, tend looms, and support parents who managed to live long. As James Tobin, chairman of the Department of Economics at Yale University, points out, "Historically, institutions were refreshed with new blood . . . for 200 years, the prevalent expectation was upward mobility. Parents were optimistic that their children would be better off, have better educations, and secure more rewarding jobs."

Now that the nation seems to be on the way to zero population growth, the old upward mobility will be limited, consumer demands will lessen and/or will shift, and the median age will rise to about 35 at the end of this century.

Already, the shift has caused greater emphasis on security: unemployment benefits, disability insurance, Social Security, and, recently, personal retirement plans and guaranteed corporate pensions. In broad terms, those are nonproductive costs of business and government; they add to the price of products and services and, in effect, redistribute wealth. The trends will continue, so that more types of protection will be government-paid or -sponsored and will not have to be paid for directly by the individual.

It's easy to forget how such social changes have been viewed during their development. In the presidential campaign of 1936, a vocal minority alleged that Social Security would be the death of the American system. A quarter of a century later, fiscal conservatives insisted that Medicare would destroy the nation. But those programs are here to stay, and there will be others like them. They work and benefit millions of men, women, and children.

It's wise to be skeptical of new proposals, but it's not wise to fear them. Change is inevitable and, in a democratic society, usually constructive—at least to the majority. In your financial planning, do not let your personal views or prejudices affect your decisions. Your job is to protect yourself and your family under real-world conditions. The United States will continue to move ahead and provide an even better life for most people. That may sound Pollyannish, but it's been true in the past and will, I believe, continue to be true in the future. That's what democracy is all about.

Again and again the robustness of the free enterprise system has been underestimated. Real growth today is faster and more pervasive than ever before. In 1928, before the Great Depression, Joseph Schumpeter, Harvard economist, predicted that, by 1978, aggregate real income would be 2.7 times what it would be in 1929. By 1970, the gross national product, *corrected for inflation,* was 3.6 times what Schumpeter projected!

Even after the erosion of inflation, the real standard of living, for the average American, can be expected to double over the next quarter of a century. Many economists anticipate an annual growth rate of 8.8% with a mix of 4.5% inflation and the balance due to higher physical production. They expect the change to be slow and gradual but sure.

Part of the problem of comprehension of such gains despite the persistently high unemployment rate is what Herman Kahn, Director of Hudson Institute, calls "a change in definition." He points out that "People may not be working but they have income: from government aid or savings. Most out-of-work is short-term and not a threat to our society or system."

Equally important in understanding what's happening, and is likely to happen, in the United States is the new mobility: almost everyone can pick up and move to where the jobs are. There are still pockets of perenially un- or underemployed, but many of those people stay by choice more than by necessity. The former anthracite coal miners still prefer depressed Pennsylvania to bustling Texas. In this country, no one *has* to be unemployed for long, as indicated by the record number of people at work.

People's Capitalism

The drive for security is also bringing about a major change in investments. Ian MacGregor, chairman of Amax, Inc., an international mining and resource company, notes that most industrial corporations are setting aside at least 10% of their payrolls for retirement plans. He predicts that allocation will double in the next decade.

Pointing out that "these allocations represent the major savings of many people," MacGregor predicts that as much as $300 billion of such capital "will be concentrated in securities of financially strong, growing, profitable corporations and thus assure a solid base for economic expansion. This people's capitalism will lessen the distinction between managers and workers and will strengthen the individual's interest in success of corporations generally and the employing corporation specifically."

That trend is one reason why the rate of individual savings, in the United States, lags behind that of other nations and, some observers feel, presages an inability to raise the capital needed for future corporate expansion.

The prospect of assured retirement income is already starting to change attitudes toward the work ethic, union-management relations, and worker autonomy in the selection of jobs and hours. The traditional Puritan insistence on the value of hard work and accumulation of money is giving way to a lifestyle that emphasizes personal pleasure, a more relaxed approach to employment, less striving to get ahead, and more concern with personal satisfaction away from the plant or office.

But that does not mean you can neglect your own financial planning. Even with the addition of Social Security (which is becoming integrated in an increasing number of plans), pensions will not be sufficient for most people to meet retirement needs, let alone hopes. You still have the responsibility to make wise use of at least 50% of your income (after deductions for taxes, Social Security, and so on). Whether your make your own decisions or turn your money over to someone else, proper financial planning is the only sure way to personal and family security. The longer you delay implementing a program, the harder it will be to achieve your goals. You will not only have insufficient resources but also lose the greatest benefits of compounding.

Those comments are background for what will be repeated throughout this guide: Despite the erosion of inflation, there's a better, more rewarding, more challenging world ahead. Wise financial planning can help you find ways to enjoy your life, protect your family, and achieve your goals more surely and more quickly.

Now, let's see how every family can have a millionaire: you or your spouse if you're young enough; your children if you're older.

3 A Millionaire in Every Family

This chapter discusses the results rather than the background and methods of financial planning. It is up front in order to make two very important points:
1. The value of an early start with a savings and investment program.
2. The impact of higher investment returns over the years.

Few people understand the power of time or money. They fail to recognize that money is a machine which has the capability of working 365 days a year. When properly managed, it can be the nearest thing to perpetual motion in that its returns can compound to ever-greater values. If you grasp that concept and develop your financial plans accordingly, you or someone in your family can be a millionaire! The goal is easy for those under age 25, not too hard for those in their forties, difficult, but not impossible, for those in their fifties. For those who have relatively few working years left, it can be achieved through gifts to children, grandchildren, or both.

To be a millionaire in your own right, you do not have to have much money; but you must start early, and you must save, invest, and reinvest consistently. A regular contribution of $1,265 a year to a personal retirement plan will accumulate, tax-free, to $1 million in 45 years at an average annual rate of return of 10%. Yet the actual dollars will be small: a total of only $56,925.

To simplify the calculations, let's see what happens to savings of $1,000 a year. At an average rate of return of 6%, in 20 years you will have about twice the amount you invested: $38,990. Over the next 20 years, the accumulation will be $164,040—four times your total cash outlay. (See Table 3–1.) At 10% return, the difference is far greater. In two decades, the $20,000 will grow to $63,000; in four decades, the $40,000 will become a whopping $486,850.

To put it another way, assume an executive who adheres to his financial plan to invest $100 a month ($1,200 a year) starts his plan at age 25 and puts his money in shares of a fund paying 8%. At age 65, he will retire with $335,736.

Another executive, who spends every dollar he makes to buy the house, car, furniture, furnishings, and recreation he and his spouse want, does not start his financial plan until age 40. At that time, he invests $200 a month. Despite the fact that he sets aside double the savings of the first executive and gets the same 8% return, he will have only $189,480 when he retires. (These investments won't make millionaires, but it's easy to multiply $100 units and refer to the table).

The buildup is slow in the first years, starts to roll after 15 years, and grows at an astounding rate thereafter. At an easy-to-calculate 10% annual return, the value of each $100, between the tenth and fifteenth year, rises a modest $1,742;

Table 3–1. The power of compound interest.

A Regular Investment of $100 per Year Invested at	\multicolumn{9}{c}{Will, Compounded Annually, Grow to the Sum Shown After}
	5 Years	10 Years	15 Years	20 Years	25 Years	30 Years	35 Years	40 Years	45 Years	50 Years
5%	$580	$1,321	$2,266	$3,472	$5,011	$6,976	$9,484	$12,684	$16,768	$21,981
6	598	1,397	2,467	3,899	5,816	8,380	11,812	16,404	22,551	30,776
7	615	1,478	2,689	4,387	6,767	10,107	14,791	21,361	30,575	43,498
8	634	1,565	2,932	4,942	7,895	12,234	18,610	27,978	41,743	61,967
9	652	1,656	3,200	5,576	9,232	14,857	23,512	35,820	57,318	88,844
10	671	1,753	3,495	6,300	10,818	18,094	29,812	48,685	79,079	128,030

SOURCE: C. Colburn Hardy, *Dun & Bradstreet's Guide to Your Investments* (New York: Crowell, 1978)

Note: To get the corresponding total for any other annually invested amount (*A*), multiply the dollar total given above for the interest rate and number of years assumed by *A*/100. For example, you plan to invest $75 per month, or $900 per year. What capital sum will that provide after 35 years, at 7% compounded annually? Check where the lines cross for 7% and 35 years. The answer is $14,791 × 900/100 = $133,119.

between the twentieth and twenty-fifth year, it's up $4,518; and, between the thirtieth and thirty-fifth year, a big $11,718—mostly from compounding.

MAKING THAT MILLION IN A CORPORATE PENSION PLAN

Garnering that $1 million with a corporate pension plan is more difficult but not impossible. The set-asides are related to your salary; but if you are permitted to add to the company's contributions, that goal can be achieved over 40 years. Not many people stick with one employer that long, but with the probability of portable pensions, it can work out.

At age 25, Bill B. has worked long enough for his company to be enrolled in its pension plan. Let's set the annual contributions at round figures and assume that they are met by the company alone or with voluntary payments by Bill.

The set-asides, keyed to Bill's ever-rising salary, graduate from $1,500 annually for the first ten years to $3,500 for the next five years to $5,000 for the next five years to $7,000 for the next ten years and to $9,000 for the last ten years to age 65.

At a 6% annual average return (about as well as most professionally managed funds perform), the accumulation, at retirement, will be just under $1 million. To make your own calculations, get the estimated contributions from your corporate benefits office and use Table 3–1.

MAKING THAT MILLION WITH A PERSONAL RETIREMENT PLAN

Bill's brother, a physician, doesn't start his personal retirement plan until age 35. For the first five years, he's strapped, so he sets aside $1,000 annually. Then he boosts his contributions to $3,000 and, at five-year intervals, to $4,000, $5,000, and $7,500 for the last fifteen years until he stops work at age 70.

Because he can choose his own investments (or investment adviser), Dr. Harry gets annual average returns of 10%. Over the 35 years, the higher income and gains will boost his $133,500 tax-free contributions to over $1 million.

Those examples are oversimplified. They assume that (1) all income and appreciation are promptly reinvested, (2) there are no current taxes because these are retirement plans, (3) there are no costs for commissions and fees, and (4) all savings and investments are made early each year. Still, they show the framework for successful financial planning.

FOR OLDER PEOPLE: CHILDREN AND GRANDCHILDREN CAN BE THE MILLIONAIRES

To older people, without a long base of retirement savings, that $1 million goal will be difficult of attainment for themselves. It's *possible* with hefty set-asides in special types of personal pension plans (Chapter 8). It is *certain* for their children and/or grandchildren if they make annual gifts of as little as $2,500 for as few as ten years or establish a one-time trust fund of $8,800 or more (Chapters 8 and 15).

For maximum returns and minimum taxes, the money should be invested for growth rather than for income. Under a plan calling for an annual gift of $2,500 for ten years and investments in shares of growth stocks paying 3% dividends, the child will pay no taxes until the eighth year and then start paying at a low 14% rate.

Let's say you begin your gift program when the child is eight years old and the total returns from the investments are 10% (3% income and 7% appreciation). By age 18, the nest egg will be worth almost $44,000. Now the real growth starts, as shown in Table 3–2. By age 51, the $25,000 will reach the magic million mark if all income taxes are paid from outside earnings.

Another approach is to start a trust fund when the child is born. If the fund

Table 3–2. A trust fund to make a child a millionaire, starting with $44,000.

Year	At 8%	At 10%	At 10% after Paying Taxes from the Fund*
5	$ 64,650	$ 70,640	$ 63,169
10	94,992	114,988	90,687
15	139,790	183,741	130,194
20	205,514	295,916	179,779
25	301,967	476,576	248,095
30	443,688	767,530	316,841
33		1,021,582	
35	651,924		404,378
41	1,034,553		541,905

SOURCE: *Physician's Management,* July 1977.

*Taxes paid at 25% for the first 15 years; 33% for the next 10 years; then 50%.

is sizable enough and is properly invested, there'll be no need for added contributions and the child will be a millionaire solely by the magic of compounding.

A natal gift of $8,800, and a modest 8% return from bonds, will grow to over $1 million in 30 years—again when taxes are paid from other income. Of course, if you can add more money periodically, the goal will be reached sooner.

To repeat: There can be a millionaire in every family if someone is able to start a regular savings and investment program through a trust or personal retirement plan! Get out your desk calculator and see for yourself. Granted that, in the years ahead, the $1 million will buy less and, perhaps, your heirs will not want such a vast sum. It's still a worthwhile goal, and most youngsters will appreciate the security that money can provide. If you can't be a millionaire on your own, it's nice to have one in the family.

The earlier you start, the easier and surer your goal. Success will take discipline, and you will have to tailor your lifestyle and financial planning while you are still young. Unfortunately, too many people wait until their fifties to think seriously about managing their resources. When they have so few working years to go, there's almost no way they can catch up. It comes down to this: without proper planning, you will have to change your lifestyle sometime, now or after you retire. You cannot have it both ways—unless you receive a large inheritance, win a lottery, or make a big hit with stocks or real estate.

Now let's see how to develop that all-important financial plan.

4 Lifestyle and Financial Planning

Financial planning cannot stand alone. It must be part of your overall lifestyle: what you want out of life today while you are working and tomorrow after you retire. It should be the framework against which all income, savings, insurance, investments, and planning should be judged.

The key to successful financial planning is the ability to project the use of your money in total terms of your lifestyle: today and tomorrow. What you do today will determine what you can or cannot do in the future. As will be repeated throughout this guide, the earlier you start and the longer you hold to a sound financial plan, the more likely you will be to attain the lifestyle you want in your working years and after retirement.

How you choose to live is a personal decision; it must reflect priorities in your financial planning. Unless you inherit wealth or get rich quick, you will not have enough money to do everything you and your family want—at least at the time. But most people can achieve most of their goals (if their goals are not changed too radically or too frequently) with patience, persistence, planning, and a little luck. Over a lifetime of 40 or 50 working years, a successful executive will earn between $1.5 and $2 million. Those dollars can buy a lot of things, and pleasures, even after taxes and even with inflation.

If you start later, at age 35 or 45, your goals may be modified but are still attainable. If you delay until the fifties, success, in monetary terms anyway, will be difficult and usually impossible. It's the old story of the grasshopper and the ant. The grasshopper may have a glorious time in the summer, but the ant will be the one who survives the winter.

That sounds pedantic and patronizing, but it's realistic. You may know it from examples in your own family: happy-go-lucky Uncle Ed earned a lot of money and had an exciting working life. But he failed to plan ahead and was so confident of making "one big hit" that he saved little. Now he has to be subsidized by his children. That's not a very satisfactory lifestyle for most people.

Consciously or unconsciously, everyone sets his own lifestyle. Ideally, you and your family should define broad future goals early in your career. They should reflect your present lifestyle but be flexible enough to be changed as conditions and income permit or dictate.

For financial planning, the immediate emphasis should be on things of lasting value: a home, college for the children, hobbies, collections, and personal pleasures such as a boat, summer cottage, or travel. For the longer term, the goals should be broader and less tangible: early retirement for a second career or regular worry-free retirement.

That suggests a warning that seems obvious but is too often scorned by aggressive, on-the-way-up executives: *Never let money dominate your life.* Money can buy goods, but you can drive only one car at a time. And, as is evident throughout our society, being worth a million dollars is no assurance of happiness. Adequate assets are important and will create a feeling of security for yourself and your loved one, but you can overdo it!

At all times and in all planning, recognize that you cannot have everything at once. There must be trade-offs. If you want to live in an expensive home, complete with ten acres, babbling brook, and horses, you will have to sacrifice somewhere else: take vacations at home or drive a ten-year-old car.

With rare exceptions, the lifestyle you set today will determine that of tomorrow. Seldom can you have it both ways. If you're a grasshopper, you will probably not be able to retire at age 65. And if you are too much of an ant, you'll have a lot of money at retirement but may not know how to enjoy it.

CHANGING CONCEPTS

When I was growing up in the 1920s and 1930s, the prevailing wisdom was to:

- Keep six months' pay in a savings account for emergencies.
- Never spend more than 25% of income for housing.
- Save at least 10% of your salary directly by purchase of straight life insurance.
- Never borrow more than 1½ times your *monthly* salary.
- Pay all debts as promptly as possible.
- Patch it up and make it do before buying anything new: clothes, appliances, furniture, and so on.

All those aphorisms have some validity today, but few still apply in toto. To a certain extent, yesterday's heresy is today's gospel. With inflation, for example, debt can be beneficial and purchases made today will be less expensive than if delayed until next year.

It's still important to set aside savings, but now you can count on greater basic protection through unemployment compensation, severance pay, health insurance, and disability coverage through Social Security.

The biggest change is the attitude toward debt. While you are young, it almost always pays to borrow as much as you can. You will be paying off with depreciated dollars, and the value of many goods you buy with borrowed funds will increase at a rate faster than the interest on the debt you incur—all because of what appears to be inevitable inflation.

These days, a successful executive can afford to owe double or triple his salary if the loan is used to acquire appreciating assets. That original $50,000 mortgage on a $60,000 house will be modest when the value of the real estate soars to $100,000 or more. And with ever-higher taxes, the interest on the loan will become a more useful tax deduction.

The same "borrow now, pay later" concept applies to many other major expenditures; that new porch may seem a big item at $8,000, but in two years it will cost $10,000 or more. And that second car, now priced at $5,500, will set you back $7,000 in the near future. Prudent borrowing will not only save you money but give you extra years of enjoyment. That does not mean that you should go overboard and pile up greater debts than you can reasonably handle. It does mean that your financial planning should be flexible and adaptable to your lifestyle, especially when you are young and are capable of ever-higher earnings.

Your parents may disagree, but forget about the old rules of thumb. If the house you and your family want requires 35% of your income (and you can get the mortgage), buy it. Realize, however, that you must set priorities different from those of the past and probably those of your neighbors. Make your decision judiciously without eliminating some of your basic responsibilities for family protection: life insurance and savings.

As with all monetary expenditures, it's easier to get into debt than to get out. Inflation is an aid, not a cure-all. Always weigh the risks against the rewards. A new, expensive home won't be fun if you and your spouse are worried about meeting the payments, losing your job, or paying devastating medical bills.

Before you sign the purchase agreement for any major expenditure, take a second look at the negatives. You could be fired; your company could skip the year-end bonus; or your stock options could become worthless (as happened frequently in the early 1970s). Just because you landed a better job last year is no guarantee of similarly rewarding progress next year. It's fine to spend some of your new-found income, but it's a lot smarter to put some of it away for the future.

That take-it-easy approach applies especially to aggressive young executives who continue to live beyond their means—like the 40-year-old lawyer who became legal vice president for a medium-size NYSE-listed corporation at $150,000 a year plus stock options. Previously, he had been spending far more than his $75,000 salary: a big house, vacation condominium, a Cadillac and a Continental, membership in an exclusive downtown club and two expensive country clubs, private schools for both children, frequent entertaining, and so on. He felt that his lifestyle helped him to get the big job so, when the break came, he plunged even deeper: (1) divorced his wife, leaving the old house to her and the kids, (2) married a younger woman, (3) bought a new, bigger house, and (4) showered the bride with gifts and credit cards. He was confident that, within a few years, he would become president of the company at $250,000 plus perks and better stock options.

The sad truth is that he blew it because he refused to consider the risks. As it was, one of the three other vice presidents, all of whom had greater experience and seniority, got the nod; his resources were drained away by alimony and the extravagance of his new wife; the stock options faded under new tax laws; and his financial woes so affected his work that his job was in jeopardy. The end of the tale is that he is divorced again, is all but bankrupt, and is glad to be working for his brother-in-law at $40,000 a year. He may come back. If he does, he will base his financial planning on a more realistic projection of his future.

CHANGING WORLD OF BUSINESS

Your choice of lifestyle should concentrate on the *now*, but it should not disregard significant changes in our business society, notably the new role of women. Traditionally, women of affluent families were not supposed to work. A college girl became a secretary, worked long enough to attract a man, got married, had children, ran the household, and became involved in community and social activities. Most career women were teachers, social workers, or entertainers.

That was the accepted role until World War II. Then it became patriotic to work and, with husbands away, many wives took jobs. They found that they could compete in the business world; they relished the pay; and they discovered that, with the help of relatives, they could raise their children.

Well, you know the rest. It was what Columbia University economist Eli Ginzburg called "A revolution . . . which had greater impact than the rise of communism and the development of nuclear energy. Now the problem is 'How do you keep 'em down on the farm once they've seen Paree?'"

Important as are the social implications, the shift is even more vital for the national economy and for personal financial planning. American business and government could not withstand the withdrawal of women from the workforce. Once families get used to two incomes, it is difficult to get them back to living on one salary. Few men can support their families, in the style to which they have become accustomed, on their own earned income. That's why it is wise, in financial planning, to set aside a substantial portion of the extra income in savings. It is especially important when the wife may have to interrupt her career to bear and raise children. Once a solid base of reserves has been established, the extra dollars can be used for luxuries and the fulfillment of dreams.

The change in the workforce is taking place at a faster rate than most people realize. In 1976, the Bureau of Labor Statistics predicted that by 1980, 48.4% of women over 16 would be working. By September 1977, 48.9% of that group had outside-the-home jobs! The results have been, and will be, significant:

• *More women marrying later*. Many women are able to build a financial base and learn skills which will make it possible for them to return to the labor market after their children are grown.

• *Fewer children*. Generally, fewer children will mean there will be greater job opportunities for the competent, regardless of sex or race. Specifically, the family income will stretch further: for more extensive advance education, for a better home, more elaborate furnishings, or greater recreation and travel.

• *More divorce with greater individual independence*. One of the major causes for legal separation, according to Georgia Dullea in *The New York Times* (November 29, 1977), is that most men still do not like the idea of a working wife.

- *More professionals.* In college, women students already outnumber males; in law and medical schools, they now represent 25% of enrollees. According to Eli Ginzburg, in his role as chairman of the National Committee for Manpower Policy, that will create greater competition in fields traditionally dominated by men.
- *Greater social and personal problems.* So far there's not been time to know whether or to what extent children who see much less of their mothers will be as well off, better off, or worse off than their ancestors. Older people assume that women who work neglect their children, but there's no certainty that is true. And what will be the ultimate reaction of both males and females when they become adults?

It's true that women still earn less than men, even for the same job, but the gap is narrowing and, as business and government accept women in supervisory and executive positions, there is a gradual trend toward parity. Already, that has made a change within the family. The once-dominant male can no longer assume that, just because he is the primary wage earner, he can make all the decisions.

The impact in lifestyle is extraordinary. In some families, the male is assuming traditionally female chores such as shopping, preparing meals, and caring for the children. In others, the career of the woman is becoming more important than that of the man. More and more frequently, male corporate executives turn down promotions rather than move and lose their wives' income.

In both personal and financial planning, it is essential for each individual to reexamine his or her role and goals and to do so in partnership. If you fail to do that now, you will have to do it later when changes are more difficult emotionally and economically. In all financial projections, compilations of assets, and budgeting, consider both husband and wife. That means adding in the spouse's income, counting on two pensions, and considering delaying retirement until both partners are ready to quit work.

OTHER EMPLOYMENT CHANGES

Along with the revolution in lifestyle has come one in corporate attitudes. Back in the 1960s, any executive who was seeking to relocate was considered too old at the age of 50. Now such men, and occasionally women, are in demand. Business is hiring for experience rather than for training. The difference is due to the fact that there is a shortage of competent executives and many top officers are nearing retirement.

Many medium-size and some large corporations are willing to hire older, work-tested individuals. The recruits may work only for five or ten years, but that's long enough to complete the training and seasoning of younger executives. If you have reached a dead end at threescore years, do not lose hope of landing a top job! You may be able to take early retirement and still enjoy the challenge—and income—of a responsible new position.

The future beneficiaries are the young executives in their late thirties and early forties. Many of them were student activists in the 1960s. As they rise in business ranks, they are presenting unusual challenges to their bosses: demands for increased personal attention, intensive career planning, and openness with information and a determination to enjoy their personal lives.

As a result, nonconformity is no longer openly discouraged; in some smaller organizations, it may even be fostered. To the new generation, the quality of life is more important than how fast the move up the corporation is. As the vice chairman of a major bank put it,

> In management today, whether it's business, government or education, the older group respects patriotism, Judeo-Christian morality, prudence, thrift and loyalty; the younger, on-their-way-up managers value creativity, energy, sensitivity, and candor. If they do not get present-day satisfaction, they will not stay. As far as they are concerned, the future is "now."

All of which emphasizes that, in most cases, the individual can, and does, choose his own lifestyle. That is not always true in specific situations, but to attract competent personnel, almost all larger employers already recognize that performance, not appearance, is what counts.

It's easy to attribute the trend toward personal freedom to changing social mores, but there's more to it than that:

1. *The development of government and corporate benefits.* Social Security, unemployment compensation, group life, health, and auto insurance, and all-inclusive retirement plans have become so integral a part of most paychecks that, in many families, personal protection through individual payments is a supplementary rather than a primary responsibility. Now the employee has fewer fears and expenses, and so he is not afraid to be himself on the job and at home.

2. *One-time luxuries that are now necessities.* Automobiles, air conditioning, college education, and annual vacations are no longer dreamed-of goals; they are basic essentials. They still vary widely in cost, but their purchase and maintenance are an accepted part of budgets and no longer represent discretionary spending.

3. *Public acceptance of individual tastes and lifestyles.* Time was when anyone who refused to live in standard style, dress in a standard manner, spend according to a standard budget, or conform to community standards of morality was not considered executive material. Today nobody is average or standard anymore. That's why the charts and tables in this guide should be considered "typical" and should be used only as a framework for your own lifestyle.

How and where you and your family (if any) live is your personal business. Being happy is the main thing, but you should also be judicious. The world, especially of large organizations whether business or government or academic, is slow to change.

If you work for a conservative organization that wants all its executives to wear white shirts and dark suits, conform on the job and let loose at home. As long as you accept a paycheck, you have some obligation to abide by your organization's standards.

Most major employers will tolerate some deviations if you do your job well. But you must recognize that, all too often when promotions are being considered, your independence will probably not place you at the head of the list.

Cool it. Before you get angry, in public anyway, weigh the potential rewards against the almost certain risks. Then think back to similar situations in the past. You may find that what appeared to be important then is almost forgotten now. You can make changes when you get that policy-making position. A little compromise now may pay big dividends in the future.

FINANCIAL PLANNING

So much for background. Lifestyle considerations, to varying degrees, should be taken into account before you start your financial planning. That is the point at which the emphasis should be when you think of what is ahead and your and your family's specific objectives. Without goals, no program can be logical or effective.

You can start out with a plus: most executives and professionals have far more wealth than their predecessors. But because of work or social pressures, they may not have, or be willing to devote, enough time to personal financial affairs.

To a surprising degree, the successful individual is not well informed about his assets, does not keep up with ever-changing concepts of money management, taxation, and estate planning, and has no well-defined, well-thought-out program for personal and family security. He never quite catches up with his financial planning. The failures are not only personally frustrating; they subject families to unnecessary risks and, on occasion, interfere with jobs and careers.

As of most problems, the solution is relatively simple: to break financial resources and needs into small units and, step by step, organize them into an intelligent plan of spending, saving, and investment to achieve certain goals.

Successful financial planning is partly a process of trial and error; it is usually a reflection of individual lifestyle; and it is always the result of a reasonable amount of knowledge and a lot of common sense. There is no one plan to fit every individual. A program that is ideal for Bill Smith may be totally unsuitable for brother Joe even though Bill and Joe hold similar positions and have generally similar goals. But the fundamentals remain the same: developing a plan, disciplining yourself and your family to follow agreed-upon procedures, and being willing to change tactics over the years. The simpler, the more direct, and the more workable your financial plan, the greater its chance of being fulfilled.

There is nothing complicated about financial planning. In most cases it's easier to develop and implement than to devise a marketing program for a new product, arrange for corporate financing, manage a department, or conduct a successful professional practice. Advisers can be helpful, but later. At the outset, do it yourself if only to learn the rules of the game, be able to judge the recommendations of others, and explain your efforts to your spouse and children. In most cases, outside experts tell you to do what you should have sense enough to do yourself. Usually they provide confirmation and set up disciplines which

Table 4–1. Goals and implementation of personal financial planning.

	What You Want	How You Get It
Where you are	Analysis of your present financial situation and selection of areas for improvement.	By preparing a net worth statement and personal budget and discovering your strengths and weaknesses.
Investment analysis	To make sure your investments are appropriate and are consistent with your financial goals.	Making a detailed analysis of all holdings to determine whether, and how, each investment can, or will, aid attainment of your financial needs and wants.
Opportunities for capital appreciation	To find the best opportunities for maximum total returns: income plus appreciation.	By measuring present returns against accepted standards, by reviewing alternatives, and by projecting rewards and risks for each area of your portfolio.
Maximum tax savings	To take full advantage of tax savings in a manner that is consistent with the sleep-well points of yourself and your spouse and with your overall financial goals.	Using an expert to help you review your tax returns, suggest tax-saving programs (personal retirement plans, real estate, and so on), or, when affluent, utilize tax shelters.
Optimization of assets	To determine if you are receiving the fullest value from each asset you own.	Analyzing all personal property, real estate, insurance, business interests, employment fringe benefits, government benefits, and so on.
Coordination of assets	To integrate all property owned within your family group into a total financial plan that will provide present security and future personal and family benefits.	By determining the best strategy for coordinating your resources with your financial objectives. Outside counsel can be helpful primarily when you have substantial assets or feel you are, or will be, in trouble.

SOURCE: Based on data from the Oakland Financial Group, Aptos, Cal.

you accept because you feel that's what you are paying for. Counsel is fine if you need reassurance, but it can be an unnecessary expense until you have accumulated substantial assets.

Table 4–1 is a digest of the approach used by Oakland Financial Group, a counseling firm retained by major corporations to advise top executives. Use it as a reference point in your own program. It provides the framework for this book.

Table 4–1. (continued)

	What You Want	How You Get It
Preservation of capital	To make certain that all your assets are protected during your own lifetime and, when passed to heirs, are not subject to unnecessary costs.	Consulting (1) an attorney to prepare a proper will and, if justified, to set up trusts and other arrangements for the easy, inexpensive passage of your estate, (2) a tax and investment adviser to help you preserve present and future capital.
Cash flow	To understand your total income, taxes, and expenses now and in the immediate future so that you can anticipate shortages or surpluses.	Preparing a personal budget and projecting for five years with allowances for inflation, educational costs, and other extra expenses.
Financial steps to take	To know what financial moves to consider in order to achieve your short- and long-range goals in the easiest way at the lowest cost.	By keeping a running record of all financial gains and losses and by developing a systematic program to take necessary steps to curtail losses and increase profits.
Enjoy life now	To find ways to make life more enjoyable now and to minimize the stress and worry about personal finances.	By compiling a short- and long-term plan to be sure you and your family fully understand what you have now and what must be done to achieve your financial objectives.
Getting ahead financially	To know what's probably ahead financially and to be certain that you are doing everything necessary to plan wisely for the financial security of yourself and your family.	By preparing an annual review to keep posted on progress and to point up additional steps needed as your financial situation improves and objectives change.

5 The Importance of Net Worth and Personal Budgeting

There are two basic tables in successful financial planning: *net worth* and *personal budget*. They provide the framework for understanding the growth of your assets and the amounts and sources of your income and expenditures. Both are essential in targeting your financial goals, monitoring your progress (or lack of it), and building retirement for yourself and an estate for your family.

Net worth is what you own in dollars: your assets minus your liabilities. Personal budget is a running record of income and expenditures. Net worth is calculated annually, but it should be reviewed when there are significant changes in assets or liabilities. Personal budget starts as an annual projection but must be revised monthly.

Since even the best plans can be dented by unexpected expenditures (and, occasionally, income), some people prefer to set up a moving average. For example, they record net worth data over a five-year period, add the total, and divide by five to get an average. Then, when the information for the sixth year is added, the first-year totals are dropped and a new average is calculated.

As you become more familiar with financial planning, you can introduce your own form of flexibility. Most of the time, your net worth will probably lag behind your projections; but if any item grows much faster than anticipated, don't get puffed up. It may be more a sign of luck, or caution, than skillful money management. At all times, be hard-nosed and keep asking yourself (1) where some of your funds could be working more productively and (2) whether some expenditures can be cut in view of new circumstances.

With most people, past is prologue. Established habits will persist unless strong efforts are made to change in the ways necessary to reach specific goals. To know where you are going with your money, you must know where you have been. If you fail to increase your net worth according to plan, you will have constantly greater difficulties in the future. At the outset, discipline will be difficult; but once you have set a pattern, everything will tend to fall into place.

NET WORTH TABLE

There are three parts to a net worth calculation (Worksheet 1): what you had last year, what you have this year, and what you hope to have next year. Those figures quickly reveal whether your assets are growing sufficiently to meet your established objectives. Your net worth should increase every year by a percentage great enough to provide the total resources you want for your family's security and your own retirement.

It seems easy enough to say, at age 25, that "I want to be able to retire, at age 65, with an income of $40,000 a year plus Social Security. All I'll need is $500,000, which I can get by saving $1,450 a year and investing at an 8% annual rate of return [at 10%, you'll need only $1,040]. With such small savings, I can afford to skip planning for a few years and make it up later."

It does not work out that way. Failure to develop discipline in the early years will compound. Each year of delay will make it more difficult to catch up. Suddenly, at age 45, you will realize that you have only 20 more working years—about the same as you've already put in—to make it. Worse yet, inflation will have made that $500,000 look puny.

I could quote some figures to show the net worth you should have at various ages, but it will be more dramatic, and effective, if you do your own calculations. With an average annual rate of inflation of 6%, your net worth will have to double about every 12 years just to keep pace with the loss of purchasing power. At age 37, you will have to up that retirement goal to $1,000,000; at age 49, to $2,000,000; and so on. Obviously, you will have to earn more, spend less, save more, and make your money work harder *or* lower your target. (Of course, if inflation abates, the goals will be easier to attain.)

Even if the figures given here are mind-boggling and appear impossible to achieve, you have to start somewhere, and that's with your net worth. Few people will reach their financial goals in the same ways as anticipated at the beginning of their planning. But society, like individuals, has a way of working things out so that what seems impossible today will be routine tomorrow. With proper financial planning, you can make most of your dreams come true. Without it, you won't have a chance unless you are unusually smart and lucky or come from a wealthy family.

How to Do It

Step 1, which financial counselor Michael Stolper calls the "doomsday approach," is to assume that your doctor has just told you that you've signed your last tax return and it's time to get your affairs in order.

1. Assemble all records, including checkbooks, bank passbooks and savings certificates, list of securities, and mortgage statements.
2. Ask your insurance agent for the current cash value of all life insurance policies.
3. Check with your employer's personnel, industrial relations, and employees benefit department to get your *vested* interest in the corporate retirement plan.
4. Write the Social Security Administration for a statement of your account (and spouse if qualified): Baltimore, MD 21235.
5. If you own limited partnership interests, ask the general partner for an estimate of how much you would realize if you sold out.

Worksheet 1
Keeping Track of Net Worth

	Last Year	This Year	Next Year
Assets			
Cash or Equivalents			
Checking account (his)	_____	_____	_____
Checking account (hers)	_____	_____	_____
Savings account	_____	_____	_____
Cash value of insurance	_____	_____	_____
Current value of annuities	_____	_____	_____
Money market funds	_____	_____	_____
Debts owed to you	_____	_____	_____
Other	_____	_____	_____
Investments			
Common stocks	_____	_____	_____
Preferred stocks	_____	_____	_____
Bonds	_____	_____	_____
Stock mutual funds	_____	_____	_____
Bond mutual funds	_____	_____	_____
Sideline business	_____	_____	_____
Vested interest in pension (corporate, Keogh, IRA)	_____	_____	_____
Partnership interest: oil, timber, cattle	_____	_____	_____
Stock options	_____	_____	_____
Country club certificate	_____	_____	_____
Other	_____	_____	_____
Real Estate			
Home	_____	_____	_____
Vacation home	_____	_____	_____
Land	_____	_____	_____
Apartments (share)	_____	_____	_____
Commercial buildings (share)	_____	_____	_____
Other	_____	_____	_____

Worksheet 1
(continued)

	Last Year	This Year	Next Year
Possessions			
Automobiles	_____	_____	_____
Appliances and equipment	_____	_____	_____
Jewelry	_____	_____	_____
Antiques	_____	_____	_____
Furs	_____	_____	_____
Collections	_____	_____	_____
Other valuables	_____	_____	_____
Total Assets	_____	_____	_____
Liabilities			
Bills payable	_____	_____	_____
Credit cards payable	_____	_____	_____
Notes payable	_____	_____	_____
Margin account	_____	_____	_____
Insurance loans	_____	_____	_____
Balance of mortgages			
Home	_____	_____	_____
Vacation home	_____	_____	_____
Land	_____	_____	_____
Apartments (share)	_____	_____	_____
Commercial building (share)	_____	_____	_____
Pledges to charities	_____	_____	_____
Estimated personal and real estate taxes payable	_____	_____	_____
Other debts	_____	_____	_____
Total liabilities	_____	_____	_____

Net worth: Assets $ _____ − Liabilities $ _____ = $ _____

6. Calculate the redemption value of your series E or H bonds.
7. Check your safety deposit box and dresser and desk drawers to make sure that you have not missed anything.

Step 2. Check Worksheet 1 against your assets and liabilities and change the categories to fit your situation. For example, delete "sideline business" if you have no such operation and add a line for collections if you own valuable stamps or coins.

Step 3. Make a realistic appraisal of all of your properties. *For your house* set a price that is halfway between the evaluation set by the assessor's office and what you believe you would realize, after commissions, if you sold your house now. *For your car* set the market value, not the trade-in price. Ask your banker what the *Blue Book* quotes. *For securities and shares of mutual funds* set the year-end market value, not cost. If you feel you have to fudge a bit to boost your own (and your spouse's) morale, use the redemption worth of short- to intermediate-term bonds when the bonds are selling below par. For example, when AT&T 2¾s, '80 are quoted at 92 ($920), list their value at 100 ($1,000) because they will be paid off at that price soon. But under no circumstances set stock values at what you hope to sell the stock for. Even the top-quality stocks fluctuate in value.

Step 4. With the help of your spouse, inventory the valuable contents (those that can be easily sold for more than $100) of your home: sterling silver, fur coats, furniture, or whatever. Be realistic. If the washer is five years old, it may be worth $75. On the other hand, your wife's wedding ring is probably worth at least double what you paid for it.

When in doubt, call in a professional appraiser and get a signed statement of his estimates. Use his values to update the rider to your homeowner's insurance policy so you will be able to receive proper compensation in case of loss, theft, or fire.

Step 5. On your worksheet, leave room at the end of each grouping for future acquisitions such as a new painting, your share of the proceeds of the sale of the family farm, or gifts from relatives.

Step 6. Be just as accurate with your liabilities: list all credit card charges, your three-year pledge to the alumni fund, and even that note which you cosigned for your sister-in-law.

How Do You Stack Up?

To give you a frame of reference, Table 5–1 shows how other people's assets are allocated—on the average.

There will be differences according to location—more real estate in smaller communities, more securities in big cities—but if you find you are way low or high in any category, take a second look at your holdings. Maybe there could be a better balance.

Now that you know where you are, let's see how to use the information in your future planning. Your net worth is based on money, so it should be projected

Table 5–1. Allocations of net worth.

Net Worth (000 Omitted)	Cash	Stocks	Bonds	Life Insurance	Notes and Mortgages	Real Estate	Possessions
$ 100–150	18.9%	21.2%	3.8%	2.1%	4.3%	36.4%	13.3%
150–250	16.8	25.0	4.9	4.9	5.1	31.7	11.6
250–500	13.4	34.2	6.1	6.1	4.8	25.3	10.1
500–1,000	8.6	43.5	7.1	7.1	4.2	19.4	10.1
1,000–5,000	4.7	47.2	11.0	11.0	2.8	14.0	9.3

SOURCE: *Personal Finance Letter*, July 29, 1974.

in the same terms: how large you want your assets to be in the years ahead. Granted that, when you are under 40, the target will be a guesstimate, you have to start somewhere.

Set Goals

Your dollar target should be the total value of what you want to own, free and clear, at some future date. The most convenient date is retirement, at which time, you assume, you will be able to get along comfortably on two-thirds to three-quarters of your last working year's income.

Or you may prefer to choose a fixed sum for your living expenses, say, $25,000 a year. For a rough estimate of how much you'll need to produce such an amount, use an annuity as your base: $1,000 annual income for each $10,000 in money-earning assets. That is, for that $25,000 a year as long as you and your spouse live, you will need $250,000. Note that "money-earning," because many of your resources—automobiles, home, furniture, and jewelry—do not provide dollar yields until they are sold and the proceeds are invested. A $500,000 net worth consisting of $100,000 in furs, paintings and furnishings, and insurance will be more productive than a $600,000 net worth consisting of $200,000 in antiques, $200,000 in raw land, and the rest in securities.

How Much Growth?

Figure 1 shows how much your current assets must grow to reach your target. The chart enables you to estimate the growth of each $1,000 at various rates of return over different periods of time. In year 1 (1978), you invest $1,000 at a consistent rate of return. By 1995, that will grow to about $2,900 at 6%, to $4,000 at 8%, and so on. Figure 1 also enables you to find the needed growth rate by working backward. Follow the year line to where it intercepts the dollar line, and then look down to find the yield.

EXAMPLE: You have $135,000 in 1978 and want $500,000 by 1995. Divide 500 by 135 to get 3.7. Every $1,000 today must, 17 years from now, be worth $3,700. For the growth rate to reach that goal, follow the 1995 line to $3,700, and then drop down to find a 7.5% rate of return.

So far, no problems. But now comes the sad news: *inflation*. Table 5–2 shows that, in the next 17 years, with inflation at 6%, that $500,000 will have to be

Figure 1. Growth of net worth.

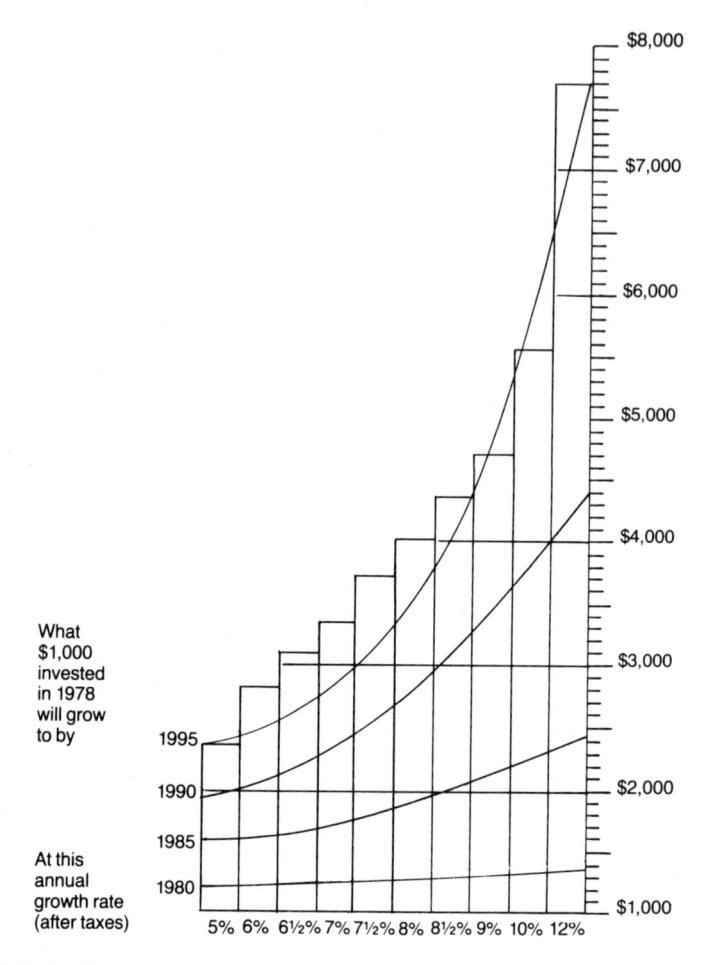

What $1,000 invested in 1978 will grow to by

At this annual growth rate (after taxes): 5%, 6%, 6½%, 7%, 7½%, 8%, 8½%, 9%, 10%, 12%

SOURCE: Medical Economics, November 7, 1977.

multiplied by 2.69, and your goal will be a whopping $1,345,000. To reach that huge sum, your assets must grow by about 13% annually: 7.5% return plus 6% inflation with a "discount" due to the benefits of compounding. That's not easy, but it is possible with shrewd investing or, better and more likely, a combination of modest yields and regular savings. If you're conservative, that can be the result of 4.5% after-tax investment returns plus 8.5% annual savings. If you're aggressive, make it 8% total after-tax yield and growth and about 5% added money each year.

For many people, the prospect is crucial. They must decide whether they can achieve their goal on their own or through a professional investor, can afford such substantial savings and still maintain their present lifestyle, or must modify

Table 5–2. Inflation and your retirement income goal.

Years to Retirement	6% Inflation Factor	Years to Retirement	6% Inflation Factor
1	1.06	14	2.26
2	1.12	15	2.40
3	1.19	16	2.54
4	1.26	17	2.69
5	1.33	18	2.85
6	1.42	19	3.03
7	1.50	20	3.21
8	1.59	21	3.40
9	1.69	22	3.60
10	1.78	23	3.82
11	1.90	24	4.05
12	2.01	25	4.29
13	2.13		

SOURCE: David Thorndike, ed., *The Thorndike Encyclopedia of Banking & Financial Tables* (Boston: Warren, Gorham & Lamont, 1977).

Note: To calculate how much of a nest egg you will need to offset the erosion of inflation, find the factor that applies to the number of years until retirement. Multiply that by your retirement income goal. For example, if you plan for $25,000 a year in retirement and have 20 years to go, you'll need $80,250 ($25,000 × 3.20) a year instead to offset inflation.

their retirement goal. They must make the choice *now* before it's too late to recoup and catch up. Again, what you do or do not do today will determine what you can do or cannot do in the future.

Once you have gotten over the first shock, you'll find the goal is not as difficult, or as distant, as it may appear. We started on the assumption that the $500,000 might be used to purchase an annuity. The payout is guaranteed for life, which, actuarially, will be about 15 years past the 65 retirement age. With a straight annuity, there will be nothing left for your heirs. With a refund annuity, the annual payment will be less but the remaining principal, after death, will go to your heirs.

The good news is that if you become a skilled investor, you should be able to set up your own annuity program and make your funds last longer. And, for extra protection, you can always start to utilize part of the principal. (See Table 5–3.) With a 2% annual withdrawal of $22,900 per year at the outset and less thereafter, you'll be absolutely safe beyond any known lifespan. You won't be able to leave as much to your children, but you will have an estate far greater than if you had bought an annuity. For further information see the chapters on insurance and retirement.

Worksheet 2 shows the net worth of a typical middle-income family which has developed sufficient discipline to plan and operate effectively: to set aside $1,000 a year for future educational expenses, add $5,000 to a retirement plan, and invest $5,000. Overall, their net worth rose a hefty $28,900 from $176,000

Table 5–3. How long assets will last with withdrawals.

Annual Withdrawal	Number of Years Assets Will Last at Annual Growth Rate of							
	5%	6%	7%	8%	9%	10%	11%	12%
5%								
6	36							
7	25	33						
8	20	23	30					
9	16	18	22	28				
10	14	15	17	20	26			
11	12	13	14	16	19	25		
12	11	11	12	13	15	18	23	
15	8	8	9	9	10	11	12	14

SOURCE: C. Colburn Hardy, *Funk & Wagnalls Guide to Personal Money Management* (New York: Funk & Wagnalls, 1976).

to $204,900, a 16.5% annual gain. At that pace, there will be no difficulty in building a substantial estate.

But that is overly optimistic (though it happens to be an actual case history). There are no major expenditures for health care, a new car, purchase of appliances and furniture, and so on. Hopefully, those extras will be met by added income. If they are not, there's always the surplus built up in "good" years.

Broadly, problems arise when the net worth increase is less than 10% a year. In a bear market, for example, total investment returns will be small or negative unless you're smart enough to shift to bonds or sell short. When gains are under 10% annually, it becomes imperative to start tightening quickly: to finecomb every expense and seek ways to boost investment and other income.

PERSONAL BUDGET

The companion table to net worth is a personal budget. It shows what you took in and what you spent and, in the second column, what you plan for the coming year. You can buy a handy printed form, but it's usually better to tailor your own. Normally, the budget is projected only for the next year, but if you like to work with figures, add a third column for projections three or even five years ahead.

For convenience, break all your expenditures down into two categories: *fixed* and *variable*. To most people, some expenses seem more fixed than variable, but experience will show that a surprisingly large number of outlays can be curtailed or expanded according to family resources. If you and your spouse argue about what "must" be spent, set priorities and delay or reduce payments for items at the bottom of the list. It's surprising how quickly needs can become wants when you examine them closely.

Here's a list of how most budget items can be classified:

Fixed expenses (must be paid every month or so; amounts may vary):
    Housing: rent, mortgage payments

Worksheet 2
Successful Net Worth Planning

	January 1	December 31
Assets		
Current assets		
Cash and checking accounts	$ 3,000	$ 2,500
Savings	1,000	1,500
Education account (mutual fund shares)	2,000	3,000
	$ 6,000	$ 7,000
Investments		
Bonds and stocks (including company stock)	$123,800	$133,800
Insurance cash value	5,000	5,500
Vested pension plan	17,700	31,500
	$146,500	$170,800
Fixed assets		
Home	$ 75,000	$ 80,000
Personal property	17,000	21,000
	$ 92,000	$101,000
Total assets	$243,500	$278,800
Liabilities		
Notes payable	$ 12,500	$ 11,500
Mortgage	55,000	52,400
Total liabilities	$ 67,500	$ 63,900
Net worth	$176,000	$204,900

Taxes: federal, state, local, and Social Security
Utilities: electricity, gas, water, telephone, fuel, sewerage, and garbage collection
Installment payments: automobile, appliances, furniture, charge accounts, credit cards, personal loans
Insurance: life, auto, health, fire and theft
Education: tuition, room and board, books
Transportation: auto license, registration, commutation, parking
Personal allowances for children
Personal improvement: music and dancing lessons
Membership dues: clubs, professional associations, unions
Contributions: church, charity, college
Subscriptions: newspapers, magazines

Variable expenses (can be decreased, increased, or omitted):
Food: at home, meals out
Clothing: new clothing and accessories, laundry, dry cleaning
Household equipment: new appliances, new furniture, repairs, renovation
Home improvement: maintenance, remodeling, expansion

Household help: maid, sitter, yard care
Gifts: birthdays, weddings, anniversaries, showers, illness, graduation
Transportation: gasoline, repairs, car insurance, and bus, train, taxi, and air
Health (not covered by insurance): medical, dental
Personal care: beauty parlor, barber, grooming aids
Entertainment: theater, hobbies, sporting events, clubs, parties
Recreation: hobbies, sports equipment and fees, vacation
Miscellaneous: periodicals, books, postage, stationery, tobacco

Some people feel that savings should be a fixed expense. I agree in theory, but in practice savings are usually what's left over. A really successful personal budget will make, and keep, savings and investments a *fixed* item.

The next step is to set down specific budgets, as shown by Worksheets 3 and 4—real-life examples of families with $35,000 and $75,000 annual incomes. Once you have set down your own budget for the year past and the year ahead, the planning really starts. When you find that your proposals call for spending more than you expect to take in, there are obvious solutions: keeping one of your cars for another year before trading it in, scheduling one week of your three-week vacation at home, or curtailing recreational and social activities. Make the solutions tentative, because a more effective answer may be supplied by such businesslike approaches as setting up a capital spending budget or zero-base budgeting (ZBB).

Capital Spending Budget

A complete spending budget is simple and easy to put into operation. The projections should cover at least three years and should concentrate on major expenditures; see Table 5–4. Note that the table lists the monthly amounts to be saved. In real life, you won't be able to set aside such specific amounts every month, so always plan on an annual basis and review and revise every six months.

Try to meet each monthly schedule. If you fail to do so, add to the fund when you have extra money from a tax refund, gift, or capital gain. If you do not

Table 5–4. Capital spending (based on 1979 budget).

Objective	Amount Needed	Target Date	Months to Save	Amount to Save Monthly	Annual Savings
New car: down payment with balance financed and old car traded in	$1,000	7/79	6	$167	$1,000
Major appliance	600	1/80	12	50	600
European vacation	3,600	7/81	30	120	1,440
House remodeling	2,400	1/81	24	200	1,200

Worksheet 3
Personal Budget: $35,000 a Year

	Last Year	This Year
Income		
Salary	$30,000	_____
Bonus	2,000	_____
Interest, dividends, and net gains	3,000	_____
Total	$35,000	_____
Less taxes		
Federal and state	$ 7,000	_____
Social Security	1,070	1,404
Total	$ 8,070	_____
Personal disposable income		
Fixed expenses		
Housing and utilities	$ 6,000	_____
Transportation	2,500	_____
Medical	750	_____
Debt repayment	1,200	_____
Household repairs	1,000	_____
Insurance	1,000	_____
Total	$12,450	_____
Variable expenses		
Food, liquor, and household supplies	$ 3,000	_____
Clothing and cleaning	2,750	_____
Recreation	2,750	_____
Household furnishings	1,000	_____
Contributions	1,000	_____
Education and publications	500	_____
Savings and retirement plan	1,750	_____
Investments	1,000	_____
Other	1,730	_____
Total	$15,480	_____
Total annual expenditures (without taxes)	$27,930	_____

SOURCE: C. Colburn Hardy, *Funk & Wagnalls Guide to Personal Money Management* (New York: Funk & Wagnalls, 1976).

Worksheet 4
Personal Budget: $75,000 a Year

	Last Year	This Year
Income		
Salary and bonus	$50,000	_____
Rental income	5,000	_____
Interest, dividends, and net gains	15,000	_____
Other sources (trust fund)	5,000	_____
Total	$75,000	_____
Less taxes		
Federal	$18,000	_____
State and local	2,500	_____
Social Security	1,070	1,404
Total	$21,570	_____
Personal Disposable Income		
Fixed expenses		
Housing and utilities	$ 8,000	_____
Transportation	3,000	_____
Medical	750	_____
Debt repayment	3,400	_____
Household repairs	1,500	_____
Insurance	3,000	_____
Total	$19,650	_____
Variable Expenses		
Food, liquor, and household supplies	$ 4,600	_____
Clothing and cleaning	3,600	_____
Recreation	5,500	_____
Household furnishings	2,000	_____
Contributions	2,500	_____
Education and publications	3,000	_____
Savings and retirement plan	5,000	_____
Investments	5,000	_____
Other	2,780	_____
Total	$33,980	_____
Total annual expenditures (without taxes)	$53,630	_____

SOURCE: Based on data from Stolper & Co., Inc., San Diego, Cal.

have nearly enough the month before the target date, postpone the expenditure or get ready to borrow the money. If you delay too long, there is sure to be trouble ahead—not only financially but within your family. The idea of a budget is to plan ahead realistically!

Zero-Base Budgeting

Zero-base budgeting (ZBB) has become popular as the result of the emphasis given it by the Carter administration. It may not always work, but it's a worthwhile approach.

In conventional budgeting, you start with last year's expenses, estimate next year's income, and tailor your budget to fit by clipping a little here and adding more there. You assume that last year's priorities were correct, and you focus primarily on new money to increase or reduce spending. In zero-base budgeting, you start from scratch and examine each item separately by (1) projecting the minimum level of spending to meet basic needs and (2) setting down, and evaluating, the options that will require additional money.

With transportation, for example, your options might be (1) keeping the old buggy, (2) buying a new luxury model by paying cash or financing, or (3) buying a less expensive car. The final decision must be related to the total available funds and all priorities, which can be checked by such designations as (A) costliest and (B) least expensive. In each case, try to list the probable costs on the basis of (1) purchasing everything outside; (2) financing all or part; (3) the money needed if you do most of the work yourself.

The priorities apply only to discretionary spending: items above those of housing, food, utilities, and taxes. Itemize each category and cost alternative on a card and then assign priorities in a family discussion. The inevitable arguments will help to develop a better picture of all alternatives.

Here's an example of a family—husband and wife and two teen-age children—with an annual after-tax income of $47,000. Their basic expenses are $23,000, so there's $24,000 discretionary money. Now the arguments begin, but, for illustration, let's say that everyone agrees that a top priority is a sailboat. A new one will cost $18,000 plus $3,000 for maintenance and berthing. The alternatives are to:

- Buy a used boat at a total cost of $16,500.
- Set up a savings fund for future purchase, say, $4,500 a year. That would mean a long delay and, probably, a higher price.
- Finance the purchase: $2,500 down, $4,000 annual payments, and $3,000 for upkeep. That would involve a long-term commitment and thus lower funds available for other items. The $4,000 is 16⅔% of the $24,000 kitty, which is below the 20% usually considered maximum for debt service.

ZBB can be especially useful when spending decisions are complicated by an extraneous factor such as a change in career or a sudden need to help an aged parent. The system of setting priorities also makes it possible to time expenditures so that the most important ones are made early in the year. If, in the spring, son

Larry has to have costly dental work, the new porch can be postponed. Or if father Al gets an unexpected bonus, the living room redecoration can be started at once.

ZBB is sure to result in temporary pouting. It can clarify choices and put expenditures in perspective, but it can never eliminate the need for compromise. Worksheet 5 illustrates the process.

Children's Allowances

Budgeting, as a part of financial planning, should extend to all members of the family. At an early age, children should be informed of the value and use of money. Making them aware should be a regular, planned program because youngsters become aware of money sooner than most people think: from family conversations, arguments, TV, school arithmetic, and their friends. What they learn will influence their adult habits. The single most important points to make are that although money is not a goal in itself, it is one of the resources of living and that wise money management is a key to a happy, meaningful life.

A child learns by example and experience. He begins to understand basic economics when he finds that his wants must be tailored to his resources and that money management requires financial priorities. One of the best investments of time that parents can make is to help their children use money wisely: to make choices and to promote security and confidence—and that in turn to build independence.

Some families are free and loose about allowances; others play it tight and hold the kids accountable for every dollar. Both approaches work as long as they are in line with family income and mode of living and are applied consistently.

The trouble comes when allowances become hit-and-miss, spur-of-the-moment allocations. A regular, logical plan is important because most children tend to do with pennies what you do with dollars. Give your children reasonable allowances, help them to plan their spending, let them be disappointed and joyful with their own decisions, and keep stressing the wisdom of money management and savings.

Scheduling Allowances

Allowances should start no earlier than age 5 with payments of a quarter once or twice a week but no more than can be managed easily. By age 10, there should be a weekly allocation, perhaps $2.50 to $3.00. That will permit a surplus so the youngsters can have spending options and be able to start some sort of savings program. At 13, make it a monthly payment and start a budget. At 15, bring the children into family budgeting councils, but not too deeply, especially when there are financial problems. Anxiety can be harmful.

It's wise to keep allowances in line with those of their friends, but don't go overboard. If the children get too much money, they may become wasteful and feel guilty. If the allocation is too frugal, they can be resentful and troubled. Remember, they are *not* adults.

Worksheet 5
Zero-Base Budgeting

Priority Rating	Item and Options	Costs Option A	Option Selected	
1	Music and art lessons for Connie (A) Both, $800 (B) One, $400	$ 800	A	$ 800
2	Camp for Larry (A) Four weeks, $700 (B) Two weeks, $400	700	A	700
3	Dining out (A) Once a week, $1,300 (B) Three times a month, $800	1,300	A	1,300
4	Family gifts (A) Maximum, $1,600 (B) Minimum, $1,000	1,600	B	1,000
5	New appliances (A) Stove, refrigerator, $1,200 (B) Refrigerator, $700	1,200	A	1,200
6	Sailboat (with upkeep) (A) New, $21,000 (B) Used, $16,500 (C) New, financed, $9,500 (D) Savings fund, $4,500	21,000	C	9,500
7	Country club (A) Full membership, $1,500 (B) Limited membership, $800	1,500	A	1,500
8	Household help (A) Weekly, $1,200 (B) Biweekly, $600	1,200	A	1,200
9	Tractor for father Al (A) Buy, $800 (B) Hired help, $300	800	B	300
10	Fur coat for wife Lois (A) Mink, $2,500 (B) Fun fur, $800	2,500	B	800
11	Family vacation (A) Summer, $4,000 (B) Spring, combined with association meeting, $3,000	4,000	B	3,000
12	New car (with trade-in) (A) Outright purchase, $3,500 (B) Two-year financing, $1,900	3,500	B	1,900
13	New porch (A) As planned, $1,600	1,600		None
14	Living room redecoration (A) With new furniture, $1,800 (B) Redecoration and upholstering, $800 (C) Do it yourself, $200	1,800	B	800
Totals		$43,500		$24,000

Once the youngster is past the candy and gum stage, help keep a record of necessary expenses: school lunch, bus fare, Scout dues, sunday school contribution, and so on. Then add a reasonable sum for extras such as ice cream, gifts to grandma, and, hopefully, a savings account. Review the budget every few months and be ready to grant increases for both needs and wants. In the early teens, add a clothing allowance. That will make it possible for the children to do their own shopping (with mother's assistance), and they will be ready to be on their own by college time.

The most difficult time, for the child and parents, will be the mid-teens, when most children will want more than they (and you) can afford. If their plans include expensive items such as a stereo, stamps, and weekend trips, make them prepare a schedule: savings of $x with the balance to be "borrowed" from future allowances. Do not make the "loan" deductions too large, because that would diminish the value of the training. If there are emergencies, be willing to advance the money with the understanding that repayment will be made from earnings or gifts from relatives.

At every age:

Do provide help by setting good examples, showing how to plan and budget, and, gently but firmly, forcing them to stick to their programs.

Do be consistent, yet flexible. If you agree to a fixed sum of money policy, hold fast. But be willing to relax a bit when there are extenuating circumstances.

Do try to keep them realistic by projecting their plans and pointing out false premises.

Do respect individuality. Each child differs in temperament, rate of development, ability to learn, and approach to money.

Do encourage earnings. Outside income is always more significant than an allowance or gift. At home, pay for chores which you would have to hire someone to do, but not for routine chores.

Be careful you do not force the youngsters to place extra income above fun, sleep, school, and family responsibilities. Children underestimate their family's ability to cope with financial problems and overestimate their own ability to engage in a number of activities.

Do encourage an understanding of money by motivating them to participate in school fund-raising projects, join Junior Achievement, take special Scout courses in money management, shop for food, and so on.

When they become old enough to qualify for a charge account or to use family credit cards, discuss the pros and cons in a family session. If installment sales are involved, make sure that the child makes prompt payments for his or her share.

Do suggest new approaches. If a child tends to be a "big spender," help him or her consider alternatives as well as consequences.

Do praise when a plan works well.

Don't threaten. Never use money as a disciplinary measure unless the offense is directly related to the use of the allowance.

Don't use money as a reward, except on a matching basis. If sister wants a new bicycle, make a deal whereby an improved report card warrants a bonus to match her after-school earnings.

Don't criticize except constructively. Learning by doing is always a trial-and-error process.

Handling Problems

When something goes wrong with money management, there will be anger and tears. Your role is to find out what happened, suggest solutions, and help develop preventative measures. If it's a loss or theft, be ready to replace funds for essentials but not for extras. And if your son went on a spending spree, pay the bills and, jointly, work out a schedule for repayments.

At every age, teach your children to respect money, manage it for their personal goals, and recognize that, as a medium of exchange, it carries with it certain responsibilities to the spender, to the family, and to society.

The money-handling habits and standards you set and monitor will affect your children all their lives. Start wise financial planning early and you will have no future fears.

6 The Mechanics of Money

In a way, this chapter is a mishmash of information about money: types and costs of mortgages, the importance of credit, whether it is better to rent or buy, and other information that is valuable in financial planning but did not fit easily into other chapters. The examples are typical rather than inclusive. They were selected to help you understand how to handle your money *now* so you will have more *later*. In most cases, they illustrate concepts and procedures that can be applied to other areas of money management. For example, appliances and office equipment, as well as automobiles, can be either leased or bought.

Some of the information may seem elementary, but a retired banker who checked the text suggested that, based on his experience, it was important to start with A when discussing areas where the consumer-customer has options. Corporate VPs may be whizzes with a multimillion dollar budget for a new building or for marketing a new product, but they, and their wives, have a lot to learn about simple subjects such as mortgages, credit cards, and car loans. They seldom know, let alone consider, the alternatives.

As background, let's remember that, although it is a medium of exchange, money is also the "product" sold by financial institutions. When you borrow, directly or indirectly, you must pay a service charge in the form of interest, fees, or points or sometimes all three. Conversely, when you lend money, you expect to receive income. If you invest for a 6% return, someone else must make 12% or more.

The terms of loans depend somewhat on your collateral but primarily on your credit standing. If you build a record of prompt repayment, money will become more readily available and often at lower cost. But if you are unable, or reluctant, to pay your bills on time, the lender will have extra costs that will, to some degree, raise the interest rate on your future borrowing (if you can still get a loan). Money is a product which should be treated with respect, handled with care, and used constructively.

CREDIT

The modern business world is built on credit. That is increasingly true of consumer spending: retail stores encourage charge accounts; banks promote worry-free checking which permits overdrafts paid by temporary loans; and restaurants, airlines, and car rental companies advertise "Enjoy now and pay later."

Credit can provide convenience and immediate satisfaction, but the loss of credit can be disastrous. It can disrupt family life, hamper a business or professional career, and destroy financial planning. It's often wise to use credit for leverage, but never borrow more than you can afford to repay comfortably.

The Costs of Credit

The trouble is that credit seems so easy and inexpensive. From every side, the public, and especially the affluent, are pressured to demean cash and extol credit. But as you have probably learned by sad experience, debt is easier to get into than out of.

This guide is no place to lecture on the importance of credit. If you do not accept the concept by now, you will not learn much in the pages which follow. Debt can be a powerful force in financial planning, but the radio jingle makes sense—"Never borrow needlessly." And, it should be added, "Unless you *know* how you are going to make repayment on time."

With credit, act your age. Forget about those well-promoted, well-publicized tricks to delay bill payments and sneak in a few extra pennies by timing or taking advantage of the float—the days it takes for your check to clear. Few of those sleight-of-hand efforts are worth the effort and expense, and their benefits are greater for the authors than for the readers of the books on the subject.

Borrowing small sums through charge accounts, credit cards, or automatic overdrafts is expensive. Regardless of advertising claims, the true interest rate on such unsecured loans runs from 15% to 18% a year. That's more than the cost of a standard loan, but it's not too much to pay if you get caught in a temporary bind. To keep the cost in perspective, remember that, if you invested the same amount of money, your return would be half as much.

If you or your employer is a good customer, a bank will be lenient with late payments on modest loans, but usually the interest meter starts quickly. The literature may promise a 30-day grace period but, between slow mail and fast computers, the effective starting date for interest is about 25 days after you receive the statement. And remember that, once the extra charge is billed, a correction can cost you more, in postage and phone calls, than the savings you're trying to make.

Do not assume that every lender has the same regulations. Terms may appear to be similar in advertising, but there can be significant differences in the small print. A good example is the variety of conditions which banks set on ready-credit, revolving-credit plans which permit an automatic overdraft:

Bank 1: Minimum, instant loan of $100. Thus if you write a check for $25 more than your balance, the interest and repayment will be on $100. *This can be expensive.*

Bank 2. Minimum monthly repayment of $10 or one-twentieth of the outstanding balance of the overdraft plus interest from the day of the deficit. *This is a fair deal.*

Bank 3: All new deposits are used to offset the loan balance, which bears immediate interest charges. *Unless you keep an accurate balance in your checkbook, this can be troublesome and costly.*

Bank 4: A bill is issued for the overdraft and interest regardless of the amount deposited later. *This nudges your memory but can be expensive if you forget to make prompt payment and have to pay postage.*

Still, the cost to the borrower will probably be less than the $4 charge for each bounced check. Certainly it's a good deal for the lender: one credit application, lower processing costs (typically $39 versus $59 for an installment loan), higher yields on the debt, and no grace period.

With credit, as in all areas of money use, it pays to investigate *before* you make a commitment.

What to Do When You Have Credit Problems

Even with the best money management, there will be periods when you owe more than you can afford to pay. Don't be overly alarmed, but don't hope that the problem will disappear if you throw the bills in your desk drawer. These are legal obligations and they should be handled with respect. Also, you should recognize that the bank, store, or credit card company is more concerned with payment than with controversy.

Never let the payment date slip by in silence. It may be embarrassing, but call the credit manager and explain your problem. That will show you are not trying to dodge your responsibility. The lender will probably suggest partial payment or a stretch-out. Take action early before the computer gets the bad word. Once there is a serious blemish on your credit file (which will be checked frequently by local business firms), you will not only have difficulty in getting back into financial favor but you may not pass routine queries in connection with a major purchase or even a new job.

If you feel there's been an error and your reputation has been sullied, visit the local credit agency. For a fee, you can update and correct information. By law, you will be able to present your side of the difference of opinion for future reference by creditors. Above all, do not despair. With few exceptions, all adverse reports will be deleted after seven years.

Credit Cards

Credit cards are so widely used that they need little comment other than the observation that there are significant differences in their cost and coverage. As Table 6-1 shows, bank-issued cards are generally free (but that may change). In many states, the bank can (1) take money, for overdue credit card charges, from your checking account without your knowledge or approval or (2) charge an "insufficient funds" fee if other checks bounce because of credit card payments or withdrawals. Good advice, then, is to *not* keep your checking account in the same bank as your credit card.

So much for small loans. Now let's take a look at what, for most people, is their biggest monetary commitment: the purchase of a house.

BUYING A HOUSE

The American dream calls for a house of your own. That may be an impossible dream for you because of your lifestyle, your financial obligations (a youngster

Table 6–1. How major credit cards stack up.

	American Express	Carte Blanche	Diners Club	Master Charge	VISA
Cost	$25*	$20*	$20**	Generally free	Generally free***
Countries used	138	120	150	90	120
Places used	350,000	300,000	400,000	2,600,000	2,400,000
Credit limit	No preset	No preset	No preset	$1,000	$1,000
Cash advance	Gold card****	No	$100	To credit limit	To credit limit
Service charge	No	No	$4	No	No
Interest rate (annual)	12%	18%	12%	12–18%	12–18%
Extended payments	Airline tickets; travel packages	Airline tickets	Airline tickets	Yes	Yes

*$10 for additional cards.
**$7.50 for additional cards.
***Set by banks; some banks charge 50¢ per month even if the card is not used.
****With gold card, $100 in cash; $500 in travelers cheques every 7 days in United States and Canada; $1,000 every 21 days abroad.

who needs special medical care or parents who require your help), or your own present and anticipated resources.

The purchase of a house is an emotional as well as a financial decision. It requires commitments which may be greater than you are willing to make. As a starter, think of a house the mortgage on which is double your earned income: a $60,000 debt with a $30,000 salary. You can go higher if you have other resources or a secure job and prospects of steady raises. A larger down payment will cut the monthly obligations, but never use all of your reserves just because you, and your spouse, are entranced with the house.

As a rule of thumb, the cost of owning a house should not exceed 25% of a family's yearly income. By custom, that is gross income, not net after taxes. You may have a little leeway if you have extra tax deductions because of higher-than-average charitable gifts, medical expenses, or veteran's exemptions. When the total payments for mortgage, property taxes, and home insurance are 30% of pretax income, go slow. At 35%, you'll be lucky to get a mortgage from an institutional lender.

Realistically, however, you won't make the decision. You and your spouse may be impressed with your combined salaries, but the banker knows, from harsh experience, that the birth of a child, illness, or loss of a job can make it very difficult to meet those monthly payments. Before you blow your top over a mortgage refusal, put yourself in the banker's chair.

With a house, it's not just the purchase price which should be considered, it's the upkeep, especially in the first years of ownership. When you are ready to buy, check all figures carefully and then boost home-related budget items by 10% a year for the next three years. If you and your spouse are not willing, or able, to spend time on cleaning, painting, repairs, and lawn and garden care, make that a 15% annual rise.

Always consider the alternatives. If you are a handyman and your wife likes to redecorate, it may be wise to forget about a new house in the suburbs and take a look at older houses in the city. They are larger, better landscaped, and cheaper. On the other hand, the costs of heat, repairs, and maintenance (especially if contracted out) can be double or triple those of new houses. For a conventional loan, you may have to come up with more cash and pay a higher interest rate, but if you can get the owner to take back a mortgage or can find a neighborhood-minded savings and loan association, the older dwellings, in stable areas, can be bargains.

Note in Table 6–2 how the prices of houses shifted in just one year: for older houses, +21% in Los Angeles, +18% in San Francisco, and +31% in St.

Table 6–2. Advantages of older house, showing percentage change in price and mortgage interest rate over one year (1976–1977).

Area	New House Price	New House Interest Rate	Older House Price	Older House Interest Rate
Atlanta	$58,900	9.12%	$49,400	9.14%
	+5.2%	−.75%	+9.1%	−.33%
Baltimore	56,900	8.69	52,000	8.85
	+5.2	+.58	+15.8	−.14
Chicago	61,100	8.90	59,600	8.92
	+14.2	−.56	+14.8	−.45
Dallas–Ft. Worth	60,200	9.07	52,400	9.15
	+3.4	−2.1	−7.4	−1.8
Denver	69,200	9.24	55,200	9.26
	+3.4	+2.1	+12.4	−.22
Detroit metro	59,000	8.76	45,700	8.96
	+16.8	−2.4	+7.8	−6.1
Houston	54,500	9.22	55,800	9.34
	+1.4	−.32	+1.8	−.64
Los Angeles metro	74,900	9.44	76,100	9.46
	+4.5	+.11	+21	−.85
Miami metro	49,900	8.93	53,700	8.98
	−1.6	−.11	+3.1	−2.1
Minneapolis–St. Paul	55,900	9.02	48,700	9.03
	+8.5	+4.2	−4.9	+4.4
New York metro	71,200	8.48	60,200	8.58
	+16.9	−1.7	+2	−.69
Philadelphia metro	51,500	8.70	42,400	8.94
	−5	−.68	−3.4	−1.1
St. Louis	64,400	8.74	40,800	9.10
	+6.4	−1.0	+31	−.11
San Francisco Bay	82,000	9.31	80,200	9.35
	+20	−.32	+18	−2.0
Washington metro	66,400	8.93	70,300	9.02
	+11.4	−3.6	+12	−1.7
Nationwide	62,290	8.97	55,200	9.08
	+9.2	−.75	+9.3	−1.14

SOURCE: *Personal Finance Letter*, November 17, 1977.

Louis; for new houses in the same areas, +4.5%, +20%, and +6.4%, respectively. Always check the trend of prices first.

Buy or Rent?

Once you have a good idea of the costs of owning a single-family house, take time to review the financial factors in other types of housing: owning a condominium or co-op or renting an apartment. Calculate total costs, now and in the future, of community recreation facilities versus country club dues and fees, and growth of equity versus the returns on investments of money which would be used for down payment and so on.

There will be regional differences, but to set up your own Worksheets 6 and 7, use the comparisons given there. They are for a family of four paying average federal taxes (before the rise in Social Security deductions) and living in a medium-size community. Here are the other assumptions:

1. 7½% annual appreciation in property value.
2. 9¼%, 25-year mortgage.
3. 20% down payment and closing costs of about 3% of the purchase price.
4. The rental family invests funds which would have been used for down payment and closing costs at a 10% rate of return.

Explanation

The areas of difference between buying and renting are these:

1. *A house can be a profitable investment.*
   (a) The tax deductions for interest and taxes are important; for the $70,000 house, over ten years, they are at least $72,540.
   (b) The home buyer can get a 50% return on his cash outlay. When the value of the $70,000 house rises 10%, that's a 10% "return" on the $13,000 down payment.
   (c) Equity, which is defined as the money value of the property in excess of claims or liens against it, continues to grow steadily. At the end of 15 years, with appreciation, the equity will be greater than the original purchase price: $72,000 compared with $70,000.
   On the other hand, some of the pluses will be offset by:
   (a) The costs of the pride of ownership: $2,000 or more annually if you landscape the grounds, add rooms, update the kitchen, or make all the changes described in shelter magazines.
   (b) Commutation costs. Most homes are located at a considerable distance from the office or plant. Transportation, by car, rail, or bus, can add up in dollars and time.
2. *The condominium is a good financial compromise.* You get the tax deductions and appreciation in equity. But there can be social problems with the neighbors and, over the long term, extra costs when equipment, machinery, and materials, such as air-conditioning systems or the roof, have to be replaced.

Worksheet 6
Rent vs. Buy—Income, $50,000; House, $70,000

	When You Buy			
	House	Condominium	Co-op	When You Rent
Your tax deductions				
Exemptions and miscellaneous	$ 6,625	$ 6,625	$ 6,625	$ 6,625
Mortgage interest	5,154	5,154	5,576	0
Real estate tax	2,100	2,100	2,100	0
Total	$13,879	$13,879	$14,301	$ 6,625
Federal tax bill	$ 9,214	$ 9,214	$ 9,038	$12,704
Your living costs				
Homeowners' Insurance	$ 220	$ 220	$ 220	$ 100
Real estate tax	2,100	2,100	2,100	0
Maintenance	600	300	300	0
Maintenance charges	0	840	3,080	0
Utilities	900	750	750	840
Heating	1,680	1,120	1,120	0
Rent or mortgage payment	5,754	5,754	6,106	6,600
Total	$11,254	$11,084	$13,676	$ 7,540
Total costs (taxes and living expenses)	$20,468	$20,298	$22,714	$20,244
How your equity increases:	End year 1	+$ 4,420		0
	End year 5	+$25,000		0
	End year 10	+$49,400		0
	End year 15	+$72,000		0

3. *The co-op provides tax benefits and equity buildup but is a riskier investment.* You buy a share in a building corporation; if other tenants default, you will have to pay more and could lose the property. That's why the interest charges are higher. In addition, the maintenance is expensive because each tenant must pay a share of the costs of fixing a leaky faucet, tending the grounds, and so on.
4. *The rental apartment offers far lower living costs.*
    (a) Your living costs are $7,540 versus $11,000 to $13,000 for the owned properties. Thus you have more ready cash—the money you did not have to use for a down payment and closing costs and the taxes, maintenance charges, and, possibly, heating and utility costs, which may be included in the rent. When invested, these savings can earn money: the $13,000 down payment, at 10%, will yield $1,300 a year—more when compounded.
    (b) You cannot benefit from the ever-higher values of the owned properties, which, in all likelihood, will bring higher rents in the future.

Worksheet 7
Rent vs. Buy—Income, $70,000; House, $100,000

	When You Buy			When You Rent
	House	Condominium	Co-op	
Your tax deductions				
Exemptions and miscellaneous	$14,000	$14,000	$14,000	$14,000
Mortgage interest	7,364	7,364	7,966	0
Real estate tax	3,000	3,000	3,000	0
Total	$24,364	$24,364	$24,966	$14,000
Federal tax bill	$12,989	$12,989	$12,700	$18,565
Your Living Costs				
Homeowner's insurance	$ 275	$ 275	$ 275	$ 150
Real estate tax	3,000	3,000	3,000	0
Maintenance	720	350	350	0
Maintenance charges	0	1,200	6,080	0
Utilities	960	800	800	960
Heating	1,680	1,120	1,120	0
Rent or mortgage payments	8,221	8,221	8,724	9,000
Total	$14,856	$14,966	$20,349	$10,110
Total costs (taxes and living expenses)	$27,845	$27,955	$33,049	$28,675
How your equity increases:				
	End year 1	+ $ 7,450		0
	End year 5	+ $ 41,900		0
	End year 10	+ $ 84,400		0
	End year 15	+ $126,000		0

The decision as to which course to follow depends on the stability of your job, your lifestyle, your ready cash, and your willingness to be tied up with a long, heavy debt obligation. The figures given here are optimistic in that they project a rise in property values. But in the 1930s, many a home was worth less and less, yet the mortgage and tax payments had to be met.

THE MORTGAGE

Now let's assume that you choose to buy a house. Such a large purchase will require a mortgage that will represent 50% to 95% of the acquisition price.

Mortgages can be obtained from a savings and loan association, a bank, or an individual—occasionally a professional lender, a friend or relative, or, with older houses, the seller. By shopping, you may save some money and you will probably get more flexible terms, but few people have the time or patience to do it. They know that, over the 25 years or more of the loan, the monthly savings will be small, and they will usually prefer to accept preset provisions or deal with a familiar lender. Still, it's a good idea to check at least two lenders and discuss the offers with your banker or real estate agent.

If it's a new house in a development, the builder will probably offer a package plan with low closing costs. If it's a resale, there can be some leeway: lower interest rate, small down payment, and a longer payout. And don't forget the seller, especially when you are dealing with an older person who may want income. He or she may be willing to take back a mortgage. There will be no points and fewer fees. On the other hand, an institution will probably be more flexible, will offer alternative plans, and will give you the privilege of refinancing—an important factor when the value of the house is likely to rise over the years.

Types of Mortgages

Four types of traditional mortgages are available from the institutional lenders, which are primarily savings and loan associations and savings banks. Terms will vary with the cost of money, local housing demand, competition, quality of dwelling, and resources of the borrower.

Lenders boast that a mortgage is "the cheapest way for an individual to borrow money," but as you'll learn when shopping, there can be an amazing number of extra costs. So view these terms as the starting point:

Conventional. Down payment of 20% to 25% of purchase price, median interest (in 1978, 8¾% to 9¾%), and a 15- to 25-year payout.

Insured conventional. Lower down payment and longer term when there is full or partial insurance by a private firm. The cost of this coverage is about $500 per $100,000 plus 0.25% per year on the balance.

With both conventional and insured conventional mortgages there will almost always be *points:* extra initial payments, to the lender, at the rate of 1% of the total mortgage: $10 per $1,000.

Federal Housing Administration (FHA). Low down payment, an extra one-half of 1% interest for the insurance premium, and the total payable over 25 to 40 years. The purchase can be financed with a down payment of 3% of the first $25,000 plus 5% of the balance to $60,000. The closing costs can become part of the total mortgage.

Veterans Administration (VA). No or low down payment, long term (30 years or more), and low interest (recently, under 9%). VA mortgages are available to veterans who served on active duty for 90 days. There's no limit to the size of the loan by a lending institution, but the VA guarantee applies to only the first $17,500. The loan cannot be over 97% of the first $25,000, plus 90% of the next $10,000, plus 80% of the balance. Veterans who have previously taken out such a GI loan can get another if the earlier mortgage has been paid off.

With both FHA and VA mortgages there can be no points. For that reason FHA and VA mortgages are not readily available for resales and are most widely used with development houses.

As shown in Table 6–3, mortgages involve the trade-offs which are so important in all financial planning: what you do today will benefit you tomorrow, or vice versa. On the conventional mortgage, the down payment is large but the

Table 6–3. Typical terms for mortgage for $55,000 house.

Type of Mortgage and Interest Rate	Down Payment (with Closing Costs and Fees)	Monthly Payment	Estimated Annual Income Required
Conventional (8¾%)	$13,750	$323	$21,700
Conventional with private mortgage insurance (9¼%)	5,768	412	26,000
Federal Housing Administration (FHA) (8½% plus ½% insurance premium)	10,500	362	23,500
Veterans Administration (VA) (8½%)	550*	423	26,500

SOURCE: American Savings & Loan Association, Miami, Fla.
*Also possible to arrange for no down payment.

monthly charges, and thus the required annual income, are relatively small. On the VA mortgage, the cash layout is tiny but the monthly payments, and thus the earnings, must be substantial. If those terms seem beyond your means, talk to the loan officer anyway. He wants to lend money, and most institutions are flexible within broad frameworks.

Note in Table 6–4 how much of the early-year payments of long-term mortgages goes for interest and how little for amortization. For the 20-year debt, they come into balance at about the twelfth year. Table 6–4 can also be used to determine the tax deductions for interest payments; the deductions are high at the outset and decrease steadily over the years.

Mortgage Payments

With Table 6–5 you can calculate interest rates; with Table 6–6 you can determine the savings possible with a lower rate of interest; and with Table 6–7 you can keep track of the year-end balance of your debt.

Once you get a ballpark figure for the monthly mortgage payments, add 60% for insurance premiums, real estate taxes, maintenance, and utility costs by multiplying by 1.6. Thus the monthly payment on that $50,000, 25-year mortgage at 9.5% should be $699.20 (0437 × 1.6).

Then see your lending institution to get exact data. Compared with other types of personal loans, mortgages are an inexpensive way to borrow (interest of 8.5% to 9.5% versus 12% to 18% for standard loans). But over the years, that interest mounts up and that $50,000 loan will require payment of $131,100!

How Much Do You Still Owe on Your House?

The amount of principal to be paid off on your mortgage at different periods and at different rates of interest is given in Table 6–7. The data are for each $1,000 of the original loan. To get the full amount, multiply the appropriate

Table 6–4. Mortgage amortization schedule: $10,000 loan.

Year	Monthly Payment	Annual Allocation Interest	Annual Allocation Principal	Year-End Balance
At 8½% for 10 Years; Annual Constant: 14.88				
1	$123.98	$824.55	$ 663.72	$9,337
2	123.98	765.93	721.90	8,615
3	123.98	702.12	785.71	7,829
5	123.98	557.08	930.75	6,043
10	123.98	66.30	1,421.53	—
At 8½% for 20 Years; Annual Constant: 10.42				
1	86.78	842.36	199.02	9,801
5	86.78	762.11	279.28	8,803
10	86.78	614.84	426.55	6,999
15	86.78	389.82	651.47	4,230
20	86.78	48.40	994.98	—
At 8½% for 30 Years; Annual Constant: 9.23				
5	76.89	816.61	106.08	9,549
10	76.89	760.68	162.02	8,860
15	76.89	675.25	247.45	7,808
20	76.89	544.76	377.93	6,202
25	76.89	345.48	577.22	3,748
30	76.89	41.11	881.58	—

SOURCE: David Thorndike, ed., *The Thorndike Encyclopedia of Banking & Financial Tables* (Boston: Warren, Gorham & Lamont, 1977).

sum by the face amount of the mortgage. Thus on that $50,000 loan, multiply by 50. After 15 years on a 25-year loan, at 9.5% interest, the balance would be $33,750 ($675 × 50).

Keep Table 6–7 handy when you make projections for your financial plan. It can be used to calculate the part of your net worth which represents your house. Take the base cost of your house; use Table 2–3 to determine the appreciated value of the property; and then deduct the balance of the mortgage due to discover the worth of the asset at the time.

Table 6–5. Interest payments.

Years of Loan	8.5%	8.75%	9.0%	9.25%	9.5%
5	.0244	.0245	.0247	.0248	.0250
10	.0147	.0149	.0150	.0152	.0154
15	.0117	.0119	.0120	.0122	.0124
20	.0103	.0105	.0107	.0109	.0111
25	.0096	.0098	.0100	.0102	.0104
30	.0091	.0093	.0095	.0098	.0100

Interest Factor for Each $1,000 Borrowed at

SOURCE: Adapted from David Thorndike, ed., *The Thorndike Encyclopedia of Banking & Financial Tables* (Boston: Warren, Gorham & Lamont, 1977).

Note: To use this table, multiply the amount of the mortgage by the factor for the years of repayment. For example, with a $50,000, 25-year loan at 9.25%, the monthly payment would be $510.

Table 6–6. Mortgage payments.

Length of Mortgage, Years	\$8%	8.25%	8.5%	8.75%	9%	9.25%	9.50%	9.75%
20	$8.37	$8.53	$8.68	$8.84	$9.00	$9.16	$9.33	$9.49
25	7.72	7.89	8.06	8.23	8.40	8.57	8.74	8.92
30	7.34	7.52	7.69	7.87	8.05	8.23	8.41	8.60

Monthly Payments per $1,000 Borrowed with Interest at

SOURCE: American Savings & Loan Association, Miami, Fla.

Note: Use this table to estimate monthly costs of owning your house. The data include amortization. On a 25-year, $50,000 loan at 9.5%, check the second line to find the $8.74 base. Multiply by 50 ($50,000) to get a monthly payment of $437. That's the start, because you must also add payments for insurance, real estate taxes, maintenance, and utilities—roughly, another 60%.

EXAMPLE: The ten-year appreciated value of a $60,000 home, at 6% annually, will be $106,800 (factor of 1.78 × $60,000). With that 9.5%, 25-year loan, the $50,000 mortgage would be paid down to $41,850 ($837 × 50), so the net worth of your home will be $64,950 ($106,800 minus $41,850)—more than ten times the $10,000 value with which you started ($60,000 minus $50,000 mortgage).

New Types of Mortgages

So far we've described more or less conventional mortgages for which there's a set monthly payment for a set number of years. There are alternatives with lower early-year payments that make home ownership possible for those who have limited cash but who can hope for rising future income. With some of the alternatives you are "mortgaging your future," but that's the price you may have to pay if you want to own your own home. The newer types of mortgages

Table 6–7. Mortgage principal due.

Terms of Loan, Years	Years Elapsed	8%	8.5%	9%	9.5%
20	5	$875	$881	$887	$893
	10	689	700	710	720
	15	413	423	433	444
25	5	923	928	933	937
	10	808	818	827	837
	15	636	649	662	675
	20	251	392	404	416
30	5	951	955	959	962
	10	877	886	894	902
	15	768	781	793	805
	20	605	620	635	650
	25	362	375	388	400

Principal Due per $1,000 Loan with Interest at

SOURCE: Adapted from David Thorndike, ed., *The Thorndike Encyclopedia of Banking & Financial Tables* (Boston: Warren, Gorham & Lamont, 1974).

can be valuable in specific financial situations, but they should be studied carefully. When you borrow large sums, there's no free lunch!

Among the most widely available "special" mortgages is the *graduated payment mortgage* (GPM). It is a loan keyed to upward income. Instead of the traditional level payment, the interest and amortization start low and increase with family fortunes.

One of the GPMs is called FLIP (an acronym to denote its flexibility). Suppose a young family, with $5,000 cash, wants to buy a $50,000 house. With such a small down payment, they would need an income of $22,656 (if they could find a willing lender). That's not enough to be sure of meeting the monthly payments. Next year, when they have saved $1,000 more, the price of the house could be $55,000 and they still would not qualify.

With FLIP, the $5,000 goes into an escrow account whose principal and interest are used to supplement the monthly payments for the first five years. With the lower costs, their income can be as little as $18,132 a year. At the end of five years, when they will presumably be earning more, the deposit will be nearly exhausted but they will be able to afford the higher payments.

With a $45,000, 30-year, 9% mortgage, monthly payments on a standard loan would be $362.25 (45 × 8.05, Table 6–6). Under FLIP, they could be from $267.75 at the outset to $397.08 in the sixth year. (See Table 6–8.) The total payments would be about 10% greater for the GPM than for a conventional mortgage. Over the three decades, however, the value of the home can be expected to double or more, so what's a few dollars extra interest if you could not own the house otherwise?

Other variations of GPM escalate early and then level off:

- Monthly payment increases of 2½% to 7¼% for the first years.
- Annual increases of 2% to 3% for ten years and level payments thereafter.
- Rising interest rates; that is, 9% in the first year, 9¼% after two years, 9½% after two more years, 9¾% for two years, and 10% from the seventh year.

Table 6–8. Graduated payment mortgage: $50,000 house, $5,000 cash, 9% interest.

Year	Traditional	FLIP 4%	FLIP 5%	FLIP 6%
1	$362.09	$292.64	$280.01	$267.75
2	362.09	310.14	300.33	290.76
3	362.09	328.24	321.65	315.12
4	362.09	347.27	344.05	340.91
5	362.09	366.95	367.56	368.20
6–30	362.09	387.43*	392.25*	397.08*
First-year income needed	$22,656**	$19,296**	$18,720**	$18,132**

SOURCE: FLIP Mortgage Corporation, Newtown, Pa.
*Principal and interest payment throughout loan, supplemented by the pledged account in early years.
**Assuming typical taxes, insurance, and a five-year supplementary period.

Some lenders are reluctant to offer GPM plans because the home owner has less money invested in the early years. But with competition, you can probably find a GPM lender in your area.

With the *variable rate mortgage* (VRM) the interest rate shifts with the cost of money as measured by a money market index outside the lender's control. If you believe that interest rates will drop over the years, the VRM can result in worthwhile savings. So far, however, interest rates have risen more often than they have declined, so there's been no benefit.

In California, VRMs are offered one-fourth of 1% below the institution's fixed mortgage rate and are guaranteed for the first year. Thereafter, the rate can be boosted every six months but by no more than one-fourth of 1% at a time. There's no limit on the decrease. There's an added advantage. If the house is resold, the lender can continue the loan at the going rate and there's no penalty for prepayment.

The *balloon mortgage* can be useful when your present income is limited but you expect to have considerably more money in a few years. It's a commercial type mortgage which starts with a low monthly payment figured on a 25-year basis. Full payment is due at the end of five or ten years.

EXAMPLE: Newly married Dr. Wilkins buys a $40,000 condominium with $10,000 down and a $30,000 balloon mortgage at 8½%. In 60 months, his $241.75 monthly payments will reduce the loan to about $28,000, fully payable at that time. By then the property is worth $50,000, so he can either sell and pay off the mortgage or get a new loan on terms he can afford at his higher income level.

Balloon mortgages can be great if you're young and confident, but they can become a heavy burden if the full repayment date comes at a time when you're financially strapped.

Those Pesky Closing Costs

One thing that will startle first-time house buyers (and those who are moving to a new area after retirement) is the amount of closing cost. Lenders and taxing authorities are taking full advantage of the desire for home ownership. The extra charges may be included in the mortgage, but they will usually require cash on the barrelhead. If you argue hard enough and you are a good depositor or customer, you may be able to cut them a bit. Some items, however, are mandated by law and others are what are euphemistically called "customary."

Closing costs can be as much as 7% of the total commitment—$3,500 on the $50,000 mortgage—because lenders want to keep their returns at what they consider competitive rates. In addition, there will probably be extra levies for the credit report, legal fees, stamps, mortgage tax, and title search, as the example of a Florida mortgage in Table 6–9 shows.

Checkpoints in Getting a Mortgage

Take your time. A mortgage is a big, long-term commitment. Review all financial terms and project their future impact against your financial plan. That dream

Table 6–9. Those pesky closing costs: $30,000 mortgage, 15 years, 8.75% interest.

Item	Amount
Points (2)	$ 600.00
Prepaid interest	116.88
Credit report	21.50
Legal fees (lender's attorney)	300.00
Payable to county	
Stamps	45.00
Tax on mortgage	60.00
Recording	
Mortgage	8.00
Deed	4.00
Affadavit	4.00
Stamps on deed	138.00
Surtax on deed	50.60
Recording	30.00
Title search	124.00
Property insurance	139.00
Legal fees (buyer's attorney)	300.00
Total	$1,940.98

could become a nightmare if you cannot meet the payments. No home can be happy when it is burdened with monetary fears.

Get the biggest loan possible if you are under 50 years of age. You will be paying off with ever-depreciating dollars, and you can count on ever-rising value for the house—at least until there's a depression or you buy the wrong house in the wrong location.

When you are over 50 years of age, consider that, if you retire at age 65, the mortgage payments will have 10 to 15 years to go. You better be sure that the future value of the home will be enough to justify refinancing when your income drops.

Know your costs. To the regular monthly payment, add insurance premiums and taxes. Also, in your budget, provide for maintenance. A good rule of thumb is to add 5% of the annual mortgage payment and more if the house is old.

Arrange for open-end financing. Provision for open-end financing allows you to borrow part of the paid-off principal against the appreciation. That will eliminate the costs of a new mortgage and closing, but you will probably have to agree to pay the new, current rate of interest on the full loan.

Insist on prepayment without penalties. This is part of all FHA and VA commitments. With conventional loans, prepayment without penalties is usually OK after several years of prompt payments.

Never pay a kickback or referral fee. This may be necessary for a commercial mortgage but not for home loans. In most areas, you will find plenty of willing lenders.

Ask if the title policy on a previously occupied house can be reissued. If it can be, you can save up to 40% of the cost of a new title search. The coverage will, however, apply only to the old value. The cost is about $3.50 per $1,000 for additional protection based on the higher resale price.

Have the house checked for structural faults and termite damage. Once you're the owner, the responsibility is yours unless you can prove fraud or negligence.

Plan ahead. If you have a GPM or balloon mortgage, make certain that you have a savings program, or other future assets, which can meet the extra costs.

Prepaying the Mortgage

After about 25% of the mortgage has been paid off and when there's extra cash from an inheritance, bonus, or profitable investment, someone in the family will bring up the idea of prepaying part of the mortgage. Prepayment may be psychologically beneficial, but it seldom makes sense financially unless the original mortgage was at a very high rate of interest.

Your tax deduction, for the interest on a lower balance, will be less but not much less. With most mortgages, but not with FHA and VA loans, the prepayment will be limited to 20% of the original loan. On a $50,000 mortgage, that's $10,000. A 1% lower interest rate will mean a savings of $100, and the tax benefits will be less.

If yours is a low interest rate mortgage, the suggestion for early payment of the full mortgage will probably come from the lender, who sees a chance to make more money. He'll offer to settle at a discount. Bring out your calculator to show your mother-in-law that the deal is probably better for the lender than for the borrower.

EXAMPLE: John Smith has a $17,000 5¾% mortgage with six years to go. The savings and loan association offers a 10% discount for prepayment so the deal can be made for $15,300, a savings of $1,700.

If John invested that $15,300 in a 9% bond, he would earn $8,262 until the mortgage was paid off under the original terms. If he keeps paying the mortgage, his total outlay will be $19,400 and his total wealth will be $23,562. He will be $4,162 ahead by refusing to refinance.

Refinancing Your Mortgage

There may be times when refinancing your mortgage is profitable. A house with a modest mortgage and substantial appreciation represents nonworking capital. A higher loan will provide extra money for income-producing investments.

EXAMPLE: Three years ago, Ed Stern bought a $90,000 house for $50,000 cash and a $40,000 mortgage. His monthly payments have been $500. The house is now worth $125,000, so he refinances with a $60,000 mortgage. With the higher interest, the payments are $700 per month.

He invests the $20,000 at 9% to get $1,800 annual interest: $150 per month. In effect, that reduces his new mortgage payments to $550 per month, only slightly more than he paid before. When he deducts the extra interest on his tax returns, he's ahead of the game and has an extra $20,000 hard at work.

Actually, the benefits are exaggerated a bit because his investable funds will be reduced by costs for a new appraisal, title insurance, legal fees, and, in some states, transfer taxes.

If the property owner understands real estate, he can use the extra money to buy a new house and rent the old one.

EXAMPLE: In 1970, Sam Kass bought a house for $50,000. By 1977, it was worth $110,000 and the 6½% mortgage was down to $25,000. He refinanced the mortgage with a new $80,000, 30-year commitment at 9%. After repaying the first mortgage, he had $54,000 for a down payment on a new home.

Next he rented his first house for $800 a month to cover carrying charges and taxes. He was able to deduct, from his income tax return, the costs of repairs, interest, and improvements on his now-investment property. He swapped one small 6½% mortgage for two large mortgages at 9% because he realized the importance of real estate appreciation. He did what every smart financial planner should do: kept all of his money working at worthwhile returns.

AUTOMOBILES

So much for your home. Now let's discuss other areas in which an understanding of the mechanics of money can effect economies. Take your car, for example. It's a major investment. Careful planning and common sense can save money in operating costs, financing, and insurance. Those concepts can be applied to other areas of financial planning also.

Car Operating Costs

Keep your car longer but not too long. The typical figures in Tables 6–10 and 6–11 show why. On the average, a new car driven 10,000 miles a year has

Table 6–10. Operating costs: intermediate car, 10,000 miles per year (1977).

Nature of Cost	Operating Cost per Mile of Car Acquired When					
	New, at $5,211		1 Year Old, at $4,846;	2 Years Old, at $4,676;	3 Years Old, at $3,934;	4 Years Old, at $3,493;
	Used 3 Years	Used 10 Years	Used 3 Years	Used 3 Years	Used 3 Years	Used 3 Years
Depreciation	.1328	.0511	.1277	.1262	.1062	.0943
Licenses and fees	.0048	.0048	.0046	.0046	.0043	.0040
Insurance	.0560	.0462	.0445	.0342	.0327	.0310
Interest and financing	.0308	.0129	.0302	.0331	.0246	.0203
Fixed Costs	.2244	.1150	.2070	.1981	.1678	.1496
Maintenance	.0212	.0293	.0208	.0191	.0182	.0177
Gas and oil	.0551	.0557	.0531	.0546	.0520	.0344
Variable costs	.0763	.0850	.0739	.0737	.0702	.0521
Total	.3007	.2000	.2809	.2718	.2380	.2017

SOURCE: Hertz Corporation, New York.

Table 6–11. Cost per mile of operating a passenger car 15,000 and 25,000 miles per year (1977).

Car Use, Years	Subcompact 15,000	Subcompact 25,000	Intermediate 15,000	Intermediate 25,000	Standard 15,000	Standard 25,000
1	.1816	.1310	.2399	.1724	.2664	.1987
2	.1796	.1309	.2339	.1702	.2659	.1964
3	.1734	.1277	.2259	.1661	.2573	.1919
4	.1600	.1200	.2119	.1581	.2387	.1813
5	.1493	—	.1951	—	.2260	—

SOURCE: Hertz Corporation, New York.

operating costs of .3007¢ per mile. A four-year-old automobile, also driven 10,000 miles per year, costs 20.17¢ per mile. The difference represents the higher prices at purchase, for insurance, and for gasoline.

Depreciation is the single largest element of car ownership. Most of it takes place in the early years. It is calculated from the purchase price (ever-rising) less the eventual trade-in or resale value divided by the number of months of ownership.

In the example cited by Hertz:

- The purchase price assumes a 12% discount from list price plus 5.1% state and local taxes: $5,634 cost less $676 discount for a net cost of $4,958 plus $253 in taxes.
- Sale or trade-in when the car has been driven 45,000 miles over three years and is worth $1,225. That is based on a 2.125% per month depreciation.
- If the car is driven less, the fixed costs will be higher; they will be lower if it is driven over 15,000 miles annually.
- The insurance is $500,000/$1,000,000 liability and $100 deductible comprehensive collision, fire, and theft policy at a cost of $560.

The above figures are typical but variable, especially when consideration is given to the objective of the survey: to show that it is more economical to lease than to buy.

Cheaper to Buy or Lease?

The answer to the buy or lease question depends on many factors: availability of funds, type of car, driving habits, annual mileage, maintenance charges, insurance premiums, and interest costs. Hertz Corporation (not exactly an impartial source) concludes that, in many cases, leasing is better and cites the example of an intermediate-size car driven 15,000 miles annually and a non-maintenance, closed-end lease. The survey shows that the lease savings can be over $200 in a three-year period.

Those are ideal figures. They project that, if cash were used for the purchase, there would be an adjustment for the earnings on the money if it instead remained in the bank while the car was leased. At 5.57% interest, with withdrawals of one thirty-sixth of the money each month to apply to lease payments, the cash buyer would lose about $160 a year in compound interest over the three years. That "loss" adds about one cent per mile to ownership costs.

If the buyer finances the purchase, the pretax interest amounts to about $202 a year based on borrowing two-thirds of the purchase price and paying a 10.5% interest on the unpaid balance. An increase of 1% adds $35 a year in before-tax costs. If insurance also is financed, that will boost the costs still more.

Conclusion: With a closed-end nonmaintenance lease, the cost for a three-year, 45,000-miles-use vehicle will be $2,170 versus $2,244 for ownership.

Which Lease?

The type of lease is important. With an open-end lease, the person renting the car takes any gain or loss in the car's resale value at the end of the contract. If the car commands a higher-than-example price, the customer gets the additional dollars. If the vehicle is sold for less, he loses the difference.

With a closed-end lease, usually more expensive, the leasing company takes the gain or loss on the resale value.

Advice: If you anticipate high, hard mileage, get a closed-end lease. If you expect low, light-driving mileage, an open-end arrangement is probably better.

Worksheet 8 shows how Hertz calculated ownership versus leasing for a 1977 Ford LTD II with numerous options over a three-year contract.

Under all conditions, do your calculations first and remember that it is *always* cheaper to pay cash and *usually* less expensive to borrow from a bank than to sign up for a long-term lease. Basically, leasing is a form of financing in which the company makes part of its profit from the difference between the cost of the money it borrows and the amount you pay over the length of the commitment.

Your monthly payments may be less than those under an installment loan, but at the end of the contract your will not own anything. All you will have left are options: to return the vehicle or equipment, to buy at a pre-agreed-upon price or fair market value, or to sign a new lease for a later, improved model.

The real dollar pluses of leasing are conservation of capital, improved cash flow, and elimination of the costs, and bother, of trade-ins. You pay for the car, typewriter, or machine as it is used and, hopefully, it helps you to generate income. Forget about tax advantages. Except under unusual circumstances, IRS uses the same test for both owned and leased items: how much of the use is related to your business or profession.

To summarize, leasing:

1. *Saves cash.* If your credit is good, you pay only the monthly charge. Even with an installment sale from Friendly Fred, you will have to put down at least 10%, and probably 25%, of the cost.

If you want to use your money for another purpose, leasing frees cash. Conversely, it eliminates the need to sell securities or real estate, possibly at a loss.

Worksheet 8
Ownership vs. Leasing of an Automobile

	Ownership (Finance Purchase)	Nonmaintenance Open-End Lease	Nonmaintenance Closed-End Lease	Closed-End Maintenance Lease
Automobile expense				
Retail price*	$ 5,634			
Less discount	676			
Sale price	4,958			
Purchase price	5,211			
Less future trade resale	1,225			
Net cost—total 3 years	3,986			
Per year cost	$ 1,328			
Costs per mile at 15,000 miles a year				
Fixed charges	Per Yr.	Per Mi.			
License and insurance**	$ 608	$ .0405			
Depreciation	1,328	.0885			
Subtotal	1,936	.1290			
Time purchase***	308	.0205			
Total fixed costs or annual lease payments	$2,244	$ .1495	$ 2,203 or $ .1468 a mile	$ 2,170 or $ .1447 a mile	
Variable charges				
Maintenance, repairs, tires, etc.	$ 318	$ .0212	$ .0212	$ .0212	
Gas and oil	827	.0551	.0551	.0551	.0551
Total variable costs	$1,145	$ .0763	$ .0763	$ .0763	$ .0551
Grand total—per year	$3,389	$ .2258 or $ 3,389	$ .2231 or $ 3,347	$ .2210 or $ 3,315	$ .2280 or $ 3,420
Grand total—3 years		$10,166	$10,040	$9,945	$10,528
Cost differences per mile			− $ .0028	− $ .0049	+ .0021
Ownership vs. leases per year			− $ 42	− $ 74	+ $ 31
3-year total			− $ 126	− $ 221	+ $ 93
Percentage difference to total			− 1.2 %	− 2.2 %	+ 0.9 %

SOURCE: Hertz Corporation, New York.

Note: Slight variations due to rounding.

*1977 Ford Ltd II base list $4,785 + options: V8 engine std.; auto. trans. std.; power steering and brakes std.; radio $72; air cond. $512; tinted glass $55; freight and delivery prep. $210. Total: $5,634. Discount 12%; sales tax 5.1%.

**License $48; insurance $560.

***Use 10.5% on $3,475 as two-thirds unpaid balance + 5.75% on remainder. Total: $924 by 3 years. For all-cash purchases, use $159.

THE MECHANICS OF MONEY 65

2. *Permits a more expensive car.* For the same monthly outlay, leasing permits you to drive a Cadillac rather than own a Chevrolet.

3. *Gives you a better balance sheet.* If you are planning to ask for a major loan—for business or a new home—the lease arrangement will not appear on your financial report, and so it won't alarm your banker.

4. *Gives you a lower price.* In some states, car-leasing companies are exempt from sales taxes on automobiles. That can save several hundred dollars, which will be reflected in lower monthly payments.

Still, be cautious. Leasing terms vary widely, so:

1. Deal with an established, reputable leasing firm.

2. Shop around for the best value. In 1978, advertisements for leasing a Chevrolet Caprice quoted prices from $166 to $189 per month. That $23 spread can add up to $552 or $828 in the two or three years of a rental arrangement.

3. Read the fine print of the contract. With open-end leases, you are responsible for keeping the car in good condition, "ordinary wear and tear excepted." That's a tough phrase to define if you have three young children.

4. Check with your accountant and make sure that the figure proposed by the leasing company is applicable to your financial needs and resources. Leasing can look better on paper than it actually is. But it is an alternative—always important in financial planning.

Longer Car Loan Can Make Sense

With automobiles and other big-ticket items, a few dollars in savings can add up over a period of time. For those in a high tax bracket, even interest charges can become significant because of the tax deductibility. It may pay to take a 48-month car loan rather than a conventional 36-month one, but the benefits will be marginal when you're in a lower tax bracket. Comparative data are given in Table 6–12.

SAVINGS WITH SELF-INSURANCE

A savings area which most people neglect is self-insurance. With all types of casualty insurance, on your home, car, or boat or your wife's furs or jewelry,

Table 6–12. Three- vs. four-year loan costs.

	3-Year Loan	4-Year Loan
Typical interest rate	13.38%	11.40%
Amount borrowed	$6,007	$6,007
Life insurance premium	74	99
Total amount financed	6,081	6,106
Total interest	1,335	1,526
Total to be paid	7,416	7,632
Monthly payment	206	159

SOURCE: Citibank, New York.

the idea is to provide protection against *major* losses: those whose replacement or repair will severely dent your budget. Do not overinsure.

On automobiles, for example, the annual insurance premiums can run up to $1,000. Since the cost of uninsured repairs is deductible on your federal income tax return, there's a gray area which should be carefully checked. With a new car, it's wise to carry full coverage with a $100 deductible: you pay the first $100 and then the insurance company takes over. As the car grows older, boost that deductible possibly after three years and certainly after five years. You will have two factors working for you: the car's depreciation and the tax benefits, which obviously are greatest for those in the high tax brackets. The after-tax gains and losses in self-insuring a Chevrolet worth about $5,000 are given in Table 6–13.

The same commonsense approach applies to items which are no longer needed, can be done without, or can be replaced at modest cost. If your spouse's five-year-old fur coat is stolen, you can afford to buy a new one. Chances are you will have to anyway because the old one will be out of style. But with that new mink stole, call your insurance agent.

Those examples point up the importance of examining *all* costs and benefits of every major purchase. In all financial planning, project your total expenditures and make comparisons of the various methods of payment, including the possible tax savings.

Cash is almost always the cheapest means of acquisition, but there are times when, for convenience or for the pleasure (not necessarily the dollar benefits) of cutting taxes, other methods may be more rewarding. As with investments, investigate *before* you buy or charge and *after* you have made a commitment and are in a position to consider a change. That's what financial planning is all about.

Table 6–13. Savings from self-insurance of automobile.

Collision and Comprehensive Premiums Saved Annually		Gain (Loss) When Taxable Income, Joint Return, Is		
		$20,000	$35,000	$50,000
$200	A:	($2,655)	($1,999)	($1,550)
	B:	(1,655)	(999)	(550)
300	A:	(2,155)	(1,400)	(1,050)
	B:	(655)	1	450
400	A:	(1,655)	(999)	(550)
	B:	345	1,001	1,450

SOURCE: Based on Internal Revenue Service tables, 1978.

Note: The after-tax gain or loss (in parentheses) is computed by subtracting from $5,000 the $100 deductible on income tax casualty loss deductions, the reduction in income taxes created by the $4,900 net casualty loss, and the total amount of insurance premiums saved. Car is destroyed or stolen for complete loss at (A) end of 5 years, (B) end of 10 years.

7 Coping with College Costs

Paying college costs is one of the great challenges of financial planning. You must balance that obligation against your responsibility for family security and retirement resources. Fortunately, for most people, the tough task is eased because the sacrifices are largely unselfish and, whether through masochism or pride, most people are more willing to discipline themselves to benefit others than to aid themselves.

One bright note is that, although the scrimping will limit some pleasures and many purchases, you should be in an enviable position once you've paid the last college bill. That tight lifestyle will be so ingrained that savings will begin to pile up. There will, of course, be deferred expenditures, but once you have bought a new car, modernized the kitchen, or added a porch to the house, you will have the resources to build a bigger nest egg. With 15 to 20 years to retirement, those savings can compound to a welcome sum.

Do *not* factor that "surplus" into your planning. Continue to program your savings and investments as you have been. The time to decide how to handle the extra money is *after* the money is in the bank.

COLLEGE IS WORTH THE COST

Sending your children to college, if they want to go, will be worthwhile not only for the pride of parents and the broadening of the outlook and skills of the students but also because of the monetary rewards. A college education is a requirement for many positions, especially in government; and although it is no guarantee of financial success, it does provide a solid base for greater achievements.

It's true that some tradesmen and a few groups of relatively unskilled, organized workers do earn more than teachers, but surveys show that college-trained individuals lead a more enjoyable, meaningful life, contribute more to their community, and, on the average, receive greater financial rewards. The modern world requires the kind of knowledge, insight, and mental discipline that advanced education can provide.

New Approaches to Meeting the Cost

There are many reasons to anticipate that future college costs will be lower than projected and that family financing will be easier and possibly less expensive. Colleges are streamlining operations; the federal government seems likely to establish tax benefits; and loans are becoming more widely available from both public and private sources. In the next few years, there will be:

1. *Lower costs.* Typically, Yale University, faced with a $23 million deficit, is redesigning its Cadillac education so that it can be run with greater fuel economy. As the result of a detailed study of financial conditions, Yale is trying to coordinate academic and financial management and install a system for long-range planning. That will mean the elimination of many special courses, the merging of departments, and greater cooperation with nearby educational institutions. Yale's new president, A. Bartlett Giamatti, believes that it won't be long before that same "business" approach will be adopted in secondary and even elementary schools.

One look at Table 7–1, which does not include expenses for graduate school, and most parents are ready to have their children become dropouts. But the situation is not as overwhelming as it may appear. With their usual ingenuity, Americans are finding ways to meet the skyrocketing costs of higher education.

2. *More efficient use of facilities and staff.* That will include (a) the expansion of work-study programs to enable students to combine regular employment with late afternoon and evening classes, (b) greater flexibility in the form of years off for work, travel, and military service, (c) increased use of trimesters, (d) special programs offering special degrees in nontraditional time and work spans, and (e) greater emphasis on mechanical, impersonal, inexpensive methods of teaching such as TV, correspondence schools, and on-the-job instruction.

Table 7–1. College cost projections.

Present Age of Child	4-Year Cost When Child Reaches College Age	
	State University	Private University
1	$35,520	$59,200
2	33,480	55,800
3	31,560	52,600
4	29,160	48,600
5	28,200	47,000
6	26,520	44,200
7	24,720	41,200
8	23,040	38,400
9	21,720	36,200
10	20,400	34,000
11	19,320	32,200
12	18,120	30,200
13	17,280	28,800
14	16,560	27,600
15	15,600	26,000
16	14,760	24,600
17	13,920	23,200
18	13,080	21,800

SOURCE: Oakland Financial Group, Aptos, Cal.

Note: Based on costs of $3,000 a year for a state university and $5,000 for a private one, assuming an inflation rate of 6% annually.

3. *Federal guaranteed loans, subsidies, and grants.* Under 1978 legislation, the Federal Student Loan Program was revised so that the government pays all interest on loans made to eligible students by private lenders—banks, savings and loan associations, credit unions, and pension plans. The base interest rate of 7% is supplemented by an allowance that is keyed to the average Treasury bill rates. In late 1978, this was 4⅛% and was estimated to be worth $400 to the average borrower. There's no longer a ceiling on the income of the family of the recipient.

Loan limits: for undergraduates, up to $2,500 a year to a maximum of $7,500; for graduate students, up to $5,000 a year to a maximum of $15,000 including money borrowed as an undergraduate.

All loans are guaranteed by the combined backing of the Department of Health, Education, and Welfare and state-supported higher education loan authorities. *With higher interest rates, some institutions may be reluctant to make these loans, so shop around your community and ask the college student aid office for suggestions of potential lenders.*

Also under 1978 legislation, the Basic Educational Opportunity Grant program was extended. This provides annual grants of from $200 to $1,800 to students of families with incomes up to $25,000 a year. The financial aid is given automatically to eligible applicants.

4. *More private loans to be paid over a longer period of time.* Yale has pioneered in this area; it has established a system that permits the student to repay loans after graduation according to financial resources. Other colleges are developing similar study now, pay later programs.

5. *Greater use of community colleges.* The community colleges have lower operating costs; and although their courses may be limited, they can be adapted to area educational and training needs.

There are also savings from living at home. The arrangement may not be ideal for either the child or the family, but on the average, the costs for commuting students are about $500 a year less than those for on-campus residents.

Clearly there will be major changes in the form and financing of advanced education. Once again, America's dedication to knowledge is too strong to be set back solely by lack of money. There is no question that, in the years ahead, there will be workable programs to aid every individual who wants to go to college. Still, it's a good idea to set up your financial plan without reliance on such extra benefits. If and when the benefits become available, you can make the welcome adjustments.

Paying the Bills Now

Except for buying a home, college costs are the single largest expenditure for many families. With few exceptions, they place a heavy responsibility on parents. Almost every family unit must make sacrifices either by reducing standards of living or by going into debt. Success will take careful planning, family teamwork, discipline, and, usually, outside aid. No matter how dismal the outlook may be when you're young, keep the faith. You can, and will, make it. The one excuse for not sending your children to college should never be financial inability. With higher education, when there's a will, there's a way.

Now let's see how you can cope. To provide a frame of reference, check the table. With three youngsters, now ages 6, 8, and 10, you will have to come up with, roughly, $120,000. That's not such a bundle when spread over 30 years, which will be the time span between marriage and the last graduation. Sure, $4,000 a year is staggering when you are earning only $20,000, but it's not awesome when you are earning $40,000, especially since you can be benefiting from the returns on early investments.

That $4,000 per year should be a target written large on your financial planning sheets. When the children are old enough, it should be emblazoned on the bulletin board to remind every member of your family of personal responsibility to reduce it by savings, work, grants, loans, and wise investments. Planning and saving should start early: preferably right after the maternity bills have been paid and certainly no later than age 5. The longer you delay implementing a program, the greater the ultimate strain and, probably, the lower you'll have to set your sights.

To get more accurate, up-to-date information when the youngsters are in their early teens, send $3.50 to The College Board, 888 Seventh Avenue, New York, NY 10019. For it you will get expert counsel based on worksheets of College Scholarship Service. The worksheets contain 18 questions on the family and its financial situation. The answers form the basis for a confidential 20-page financial planning guide.

At this point, let me add a caveat which I delivered to a neighboring young couple. No matter how anxious you may be for your children to attend your alma mater or a prestigious university, be realistic on two points:

1. *His or her ability and desire.* If your son wants to be a blacksmith, persuading him to go to law school will probably backfire. And if sister has neither the marks nor the will to go beyond high school, relax and look forward to enjoying your grandchildren. It's their life and, like it or not, they are going to make up their own minds.

2. *Your own financial resources.* If you have to support a parent or pay heavy medical bills, set up a flexible program so that you will not become overburdened with "must savings."

SOURCES OF FINANCIAL AID

There are a surprising number of opportunities for financial assistance: from the college, government, industry, foundations, and service organizations. On the average, 60% of students in private colleges receive some sort of monetary or service supplement. You can get details from the student aid bureau, but look around your own community. Getting grants or scholarships may not be a part of orthodox financial planning, but success makes fulfillment of your plan much easier.

The first place to start is within your own family. Find ways to add income with the help of your children and better use of your assets. Here are some areas to check:

Student Earnings

Part-time and summer work can provide both money and experience. It's OK to give your children some job leads, but let them do their own searching—with the aid of the college staff. At the outset, discuss with each child how much extra money will be needed. Keep the figure flexible, and do not skimp on personal expenses. Youth is still a time for fun and excitement.

Student earnings vary with opportunities, time, and ability. Roughly, the average total of summer and in-school work income will be about $1,000 a year. Now you can cut that bulletin board figure to $3,000.

College Programs

Every educational institution has some sort of financial aid: grants, scholarships, work-study programs, and loans. Get detailed information from the student aid department. Do not be embarrassed to ask. Most students receive some sort of help, and most colleges insist on parental involvement.

One new development is the lump-sum-in-advance payment pioneered by Washington University in St. Louis. By prepaying the full tuition bill, you can freeze your costs for the next four years—no small saving with inflation. Since interest is tax deductible, it may pay some families to borrow the money.

State Programs

Many states provide financial aid to students: flat grants for tuition, special training incentives, scholarships, and tuition-equalization plans. Aid is based on need, but marks and achievements are always a consideration.

Each state sets its own criteria and amounts of allocations. Missouri has grants of up to about $500 for students at either public or private colleges in the state; California provides $1,000 to $1,200 for attendees at four-year colleges within the state and, in some cases, for students at local two-year institutions. For information in your area, contact the department of education in the state capital.

Other Federal Programs

As shown in Table 7–2, Uncle Sam also provides aid through Social Security benefits, work-study programs, and scholarships. Social Security payments are available for unmarried children, aged 18 to 22, of deceased or disabled parents. The monthly allocations, set by formula, are substantial. (See Chapter 8.) Work-study programs, involving on- and off-campus employment, are open to financially hard-pressed students, usually on the basis of family income. And if your child is interested in a government career, ask about special loans for law enforcement or scholarships through the Truman Scholarship Foundation.

Table 7–2A. Federal aid programs—unrestricted.

Program	What It's About	Eligibility and Application
Basic Educational Opportunity Grant	Maximum of $1600. Average award $850.	Based on need. Pick up application forms after December 1. U.S. Office of Education will determine eligibility from financial aid data you provided on FAF or FFS forms for need analysis.
National Direct Student Loan	Loan. Maximum: $5000 over four years. Repayment starts nine months after graduation. 3%. Various remission features.	Administered by colleges as part of financial aid package. Generally reserved for lower-income applicants.
Supplemental Educational Opportunity Grant	Grant. From $200 to $1500 per year.	Reserved for exceptional financial need. Administered by colleges as part of financial aid package.
College Work-Study Program	On- and off-campus employment.	Reserved for student with great financial need. Administered by colleges as part of financial aid package.
Guaranteed Student Loan	Loan. Private lenders. Up to $2500 per year for total of $7500. Federal government pays interest until loan is due. Repayment begins 9–12 months after graduation; 7% interest.	Contact your local HEW office or the loan officer at your local bank. Programs may vary in states.

Family Contribution

The dollars available from each family are a key factor in grants and scholarships. The final allocations are based on the parents' assets and income with subtractions for normal federal income tax deductions and taxes plus allowances for family size, employment, and assets protection. The balance is then multiplied by a "taxation rate." Estimates of family contributions to a child's education are given in Table 7–3. They are based on a two-parent family with one parent working and one child in college. They are ballpark figures derived from averages, so they cannot be used to find a family's exact need.

As a rule of thumb, the student's share is about 35% of savings and other assets, and it is assumed that the youngster earns $500 each year. There is leeway when several children are in college at the same time. For up-to-date information, get the booklet *Meeting College Costs* from your high school or prep school counselor. Note that, with few exceptions, the family is expected to chip in something.

Table 7-2B. Federal aid programs—specific career fields.

Career Field	Program	Eligibility and Application
General	Social Security Benefits—Title III	Unmarried sons and daughters, 18–22, of deceased, disabled, or retired parent(s). Almost 800,000 participants. $1.3 billion in annual benefits. See Social Security office.
Law enforcement	Law Enforcement Education Program	Loans up to $2200 for students committed to obtaining employment in criminal justice. Program administered by colleges. Send for booklet, "LEEP—a Step Ahead," from Office of Criminal Justice Education & Training, LEAA—Dept. of Justice, Washington, DC 20530.
Nursing	Nursing Student Loan Program: $2500 per year for maximum of $10,000. Ten-year repayment, 3% interest. Nursing Scholarship Program: $2,000/academic year.	Nursing student loan and scholarship programs are administered by schools and colleges. Principal criterion: need. Names of participating schools can be obtained from HEW-PHS, Bureau of Health Manpower, Student Assistance Branch, Bethesda, MD 20014
Nursing, mental health	Psychiatric–Mental Health Nursing Trainee Stipends	Administered by schools and Colleges. Get list from Alcohol, Drug Abuse & Mental Health Admin., Public Health Service—HEW, 5600 Fishers Ln., Rockville, MD 20852
Public service careers	Harry S. Truman Scholarship Foundation: Top scholars. $5,000/year. At least one recipient per state.	Nominated by colleges. Not for freshmen, but freshmen should begin thinking about this major opportunity. Information from Truman Scholarship Foundation, 712 Jackson Place, NW, Washington, DC 20006.
Special education	HEW provides grants to schools and agencies to prepare people to work with the handicapped.	For participating schools, write Division of Personnel Preparation, Bureau of Education for the Handicapped, U.S. Office of Education, Washington, DC 20202.

SOURCE: Adapted from information from Octameron Associates (Alexandria, Va.), American Legion Education and Scholarship Program, and the U.S. Department of Health, Education, and Welfare.

Table 7-3. Formula for determining need.

Income Before Taxes	Family Contribution per Year	
	One Child	Three Children
$16,000	$1,180	$ 570
18,000	1,530	850
20,000	1,950	1,170
25,000	3,350	2,170
30,000	4,740	3,540
35,000	6,040	4,880

SOURCE: College Scholarship Service, The College Board, New York.

ESTIMATING THE FAMILY'S CONTRIBUTION

Another way to discover your probable financial costs is to use Table 7-4. Again, the figures are broad and are subject to interpretation and modification by college authorities. If the institution needs students, it will probably be more understanding.

Private Aid

And don't forget to look for help from private sources, both national and local. Generally, the grants and scholarships are small, but any amount can be helpful, especially when more than one student is involved. For information, check the high school guidance counselor and look for organizations like those listed in Table 7-5.

PLANNING

Once you have a good idea of the probable costs and your own resources, start planning ahead. Explore every possibility and use every available asset.

Insurance

If you're worried about death before the children finish college, ask your insurance agent about special life policies. Basically, such policies are forced-savings vehicles the premiums of which are set high enough to provide an assured sum at the end of a predetermined number of years. Compared with a term policy, they are an expensive form of protection, but as long as you keep up the payments (and they can be guaranteed against disability for a small extra cost) the money will be available whether you live or die.

EXAMPLE: At the birth of a son, John Keogh, age 30, buys $20,000 coverage for an annual premium of $390. In 18 years, he will have paid in $7,020 and the policy will have a cash value of about $8,300. It can be used as collateral for a loan if extra funds are needed.

If $390 is too great a burden and Mr. Keogh is worried about early demise,

Table 7-4. The family's contribution to education.

Family Size	Number in College	Gross Adjusted Income	Family Assets	Expected Contribution per Year
3	1	$30,000	$45,000	$7,280
4	1	24,000	30,000	3,490
4	2	27,000	40,000	2,875 each
	1	31,000	50,000	5,975
6	3	36,000	60,000	3,795 each

SOURCE: Octameron Associates, Alexandria, Va.

he can buy term life for the same face value at a much lower, though rising, cost. There will be no savings or assets to use as collateral, but he's sure of protection.

Savings and Investments

The subject of savings and investments is covered in detail in Chapter 10. Broadly speaking, these are avenues:

1. *Set up a daily interest savings account and make regular additions.* This is convenient but little more. The total returns will be under 6% until you accumulate enough money to buy a long-term certificate of deposit so that your savings will compound to a return of just over 8%. Taxes and inflation will reduce the real return, but it's safe.

2. *Buy bonds which mature in the years of college.* For a child born in 1970, redemption dates should be 1988, 1989, 1990, and 1991. Unless you buy the bonds at a discount, there'll be no appreciation, but you'll be sure of getting full face value—more if you reinvest the interest promptly. Again, the value will be cut by taxes and inflation.

3. *Buy shares in the company for which you work through a payroll deduction plan.* If the company chips in, your money will grow faster. Be sure there are provisions for withdrawal when college starts or when you leave for a better job. This should be separate from your pension plan.

4. *Invest in stocks of profitable, dividend-boosting companies which automatically reinvest income.* The best bets are those which offer new shares at a discount, for example, AT&T.

5. *Sign up for a stock purchase, dividend-reinvestment plan at a local bank.* This is similar to (4), but it permits a choice of companies. You approve a monthly deduction from your bank account ($20 minimum, $500 maximum), pay a service charge of $1 to $2 per transaction, and have the advantage of the lower commissions paid on large-volume purchases.

With (3), (4) and (5), if the corporation prospers, chances are that the dividends will be increased and the value of the stock will rise. Such a regular investment could pay most or all of the college bills, thanks to the magic of compounding.

Table 7–5A. Private aid—unrestricted.

Program	Description	Eligibility and Application
Elks Foundation Scholarship Award	Long-time program. Awarded $650,000 to 926 students in 1977.	Scholarship, leadership, need. Apply to Lodge Foundation Chairman of the B.P.O. Elks Lodge in your city. Deadline: February 10.
I.O.F.	Loans after first college grading period. Maximum $5,000. 4% interest. Repayment starts 3 months after graduation.	Executive Secretary Educational Foundation, I.O.O.F. PO Box 214 Connersville, IN 47331
Mensa Scholarship Fund	Last year: 18 grants ranging from $100 to $350. Applicants are required to prepare 500-word essay on career, academic, goal directions.	Dr. Abbie Sainy 143 River Dr. Elmwood Park, NJ 07407 By April 15.
National Merit Scholarship Corp.	National competition based on PSAT/NMSQT scores. 1000 nonrenewable $1000 awards.	National Merit Scholarship Corp. 990 Grove Street Evanston, IL 60201.
Pickett and Hatcher Educational Fund	Loans. $1,500 per year to maximum of $6,000. Interest: 2% while in school, 6% thereafter.	Pickett and Hatcher Educational Fund PO Box 2128 Columbus, GA 31902
AFSA Scholarships	Merit awards and financial aid grants for children of active, deceased, or retired foreign service officers.	AFSA Scholarship Program 2101 E Street, NW Washington, DC 20037
Merit Scholars	1325 renewable scholarships ($250 to $1500 per year) sponsored by 300 corporations for Merit Program finalists who are children of employees (some scholarships reserved for other purposes). List of companies in Student Bulletin.	Ask for Student Bulletin in guidance office or write to National Merit Scholarship Corporation 990 Grove St. Evanston, IL 60201
Motor Carriers	Booklet Scholarship Programs of Motor Carrier Companies and Associates lists programs of 27 companies—some for employee children, some for specific schools or localities.	Write for booklet to Public Relations Dept., American Trucking Assn. 1616 P Street, NW Washington, DC 20036

Special Bank Loans

Tuition-aid loans against which you can write checks for specific college expenses are available. At National Shawmut in Boston the amount and term of the loan is keyed to your credit standing. Since interest is paid only on the

Table 7–5B. Private aid—specific career fields.

Career Field	Program	Application/Information
Accounting	Scholarships. Generally $500.	By February 28 to Scholarship Foundation Nat. Society of Public Accountants 1717 Pennsylvania Avenue, NW Washington, DC 20006
Art and architecture	Competitive scholarships, renewable, valued at $2700/year.	Dean of Admissions Cooper Union 51 Astor Place New York, NY 10003
Dental hygiene	Assistance based on need.	By April 15 to American Dental Hygienists Association 211 E. Chicago Chicago, IL 60611
Dental lab technology	About 30 scholarships per year, $500 to $600 for students enrolled or planning to enroll in accredited DLT program.	By June 1 to American Fund for Dental Health 211 E. Chicago Chicago, IL 60611
Dietetics	Awards, loans, scholarships, fellowships. Write for summary sheet of programs.	The American Dietetic Assn. 430 N. Michigan Ave. Chicago, IL 60611
Earth and mineral sciences	Extensive freshman scholarship program ($400 to $2000).	Dean, College of Earth and Mineral Sciences The Penn State University 116 Deike Building University Park, PA 16802
Graphic arts	Numerous scholarships.	National Scholarship Trust Fund GATF 4615 Forbes Ave. Pittsburgh, PA 15213
Health careers (audiology, nursing, occupational therapy, physical therapy, speech pathology)	March of Dimes Health Career Awards, $100 to $500/year. Announcement reaches Guidance Office in February.	By April 15 through HS Guidance Office
Hotel management	Club Managers Association maintains undergraduate scholarships at schools offering hotel, restaurant, institutional management courses. Write for list of schools.	Club Managers Association of America 5530 Wisconsin–Suite 705 Washington, DC 20015.

Table 7–5B. (continued)

Career Field	Program	Application/Information
Journalism	Excellent booklet listing $2 million in journalism scholarships. Write for Scholarship Guide.	The Newspaper Fund, Inc. PO Box 300 Princeton, NJ 08540
Journalism	Several awards under $1000.	By April 15 to Scripps-Howard Foundation 200 Park Avenue New York, NY 10017
Journalism	Many competitive awards.	William Randolph Hearst Foundation Suite 218–Hearst Building Third & Market St. San Francisco, CA 94103
Librarianship	Compendium of scholarships available for library technical assistant and librarian. Ask for booklet Financial Assistance for Library Education; include fifty cents.	Library Education Division ALA 50 East Huron St. Chicago, IL 60611
Petroleum fields	Write for list of schools teaching accredited petroleum or petroleum-related programs.	American Petroleum Institute 2101 L Street NW Washington, DC 20037
Petroleum land management	American Association of Petroleum Landsmen maintains several scholarships at U. of Colorado, U. of Texas, and U. of Oklahoma.	Apply through schools.
Photography	Two $750 scholarships at Rochester Institute of Technology and Brooks Institute of Photography. Apply after acceptance.	Photographic Art & Science Foundation 111 Stratford Rd. Des Plaines, IL 60016.
Planning	Charles Abrams Scholarships. $2000. At Columbia, Harvard, MIT, New School of Social Research, and U. of Pa.	Apply through schools.
Statistics	Write for list of schools with accredited majors in statistics.	American Statistical Assn. 806 15th Street, NW Washington, DC 20005
Theology	Directory of 199 theological schools, their programs and scholarship opportunities. Send $1.50.	American Theological Society Box 396 Vandalia, OH 45377

SOURCE: Adapted from information from Octameron Associates (Alexandria, Va.), American Legion Education and Scholarship Program, and U.S. Department of Health, Education, and Welfare.

money spent, total costs are less than those of a regular bank loan. Each loan is protected by life insurance, and monthly payments start after you sign the first check to the college.

Similar plans are offered by insurance specialists. In the *extended repayment plan* there is no limit to the size of the loan and interest is 12% on the outstanding balance with six years to repay. There is a $25 returnable application fee, and insurance, for life and disability, is 60¢ per $1,000 per month to age 55.

Under the *prepayment plan* you pay a monthly sum from which the agency pays college bills. There is a $25 application fee and a 50¢ per month service charge. Insurance is 80¢ per $1,000 monthly. There is a credit of 5% monthly interest on all money held on deposit.

Custodian or Trust Accounts

Custodian or trust accounts can be set up by parents or relatives in several ways. Their format should be discussed with an attorney and tax adviser to keep taxes at a minimum for both donor and donee.

The capital in such an account can come from a single gift or from small, consistent donations. As explained in Chapter 3, compounding is the magic ingredient. A gift of $5,000 invested at the time of the child's birth will, with a modest 8% return, grow to $19,980 by age 18. Regular annual savings of $1,000, with a 10% yield, can swell to $63,000 in the 20 years before the last tuition bill is due.

Even if you can afford to set aside only $100 in the first year, $200 in the second, $300 in the third—to a maximum of $1,700 by college starting time—you will have a fund of $27,336 with an average annual 8% rate of return under a tax shelter or when taxes are paid from other income.

TAX SHELTERS

At the risk of repeating some information of Chapter 14, here's a quick summary of the most widely used legal formats which permit the tax-free accumulation of savings for college costs.

Uniform Gift to Minors

The money, securities, or real estate is given to the child under the custody of an older relative or friend who has broad powers of investment. Ideally, there should be one gift, but it's permissible to make annual additions.

The child will pay no tax until the unearned income is over $1,000 a year ($100 more if that sum comes from dividends). Even when the tax starts, it will be at the low 14% rate.

The child owns the property, so that at maturity, age 18 in most states, he or she has sole responsibility for its disposition. Your son could blow it all on a new sports car or your daughter could take off, with her unemployed boyfriend, for Europe. But those sad situations seldom occur.

Short-Term Trust

A short-term trust provides more control because you can name yourself as custodian. If you die before termination, however, the money could become part of your estate. Short-term trusts, are excellent for gifts from other members of the family: grandparents, uncles, aunts, and so on. In 18 years, $3,000 a year will grow to $93,000 even in a puny-paying 5¼% savings account. That's enough to pay for three or four college students.

A variation is the *living trust*. It is a temporary arrangement which must last for ten years. It is most valuable when donors are in a high tax bracket because of the one-time deduction for the gift and the continuing benefit of not having to pay taxes on the extra income. The money in the trust accumulates tax-free, and at termination it reverts to the original donor.

EXAMPLE: Mr. O'Loughlin, who earns $35,000 a year, inherits property worth $26,000. The property provides $1,800 annual income on which he pays income taxes of $615.

Son Robert is nine years old. To finance his education, Mr. O. sets up a living trust with the inheritance and names Robert as income beneficiary. Even when the income taxes are paid by the trust, the net income of the college kitty will swell to around $25,000. At the end of the decade, there's money for college bills, the trust is dissolved, and the property goes back to Mr. O. That's a great deal *if* you can afford to lose income for 10 years!

MAKE EDUCATION A FAMILY RESPONSIBILITY

If you are lucky enough to belong to a family which believes enough in higher education to make its financing a joint responsibility, start discussing the subject before, during, and after the arrival of the first child. Grandpa may be willing to set up a living trust with those bonds he's been keeping to buy a boat on retirement. He can get along without the interest for ten years.

Or widowed Aunt Lil, rather than waiting until her death, could set up a tax-free trust with the gift of a share of the apartment house she inherited. Most families have resources which are not fully utilized or whose income is not fully needed. What better way "to give while you live" than to aid the education of loved ones?

Caution: In the enthusiasm of the arrival of the first child, don't let the gift arrangements be too inflexible. There may be brothers and sisters who will want to go to college, too. The family lawyer can suggest some steps to take to be fair to everyone.

For Emergencies

Some families, of course, will never be able to acquire enough money or assets to pay tuition bills, even with careful financial planning. Even when you have exhausted your cash and checked all avenues of aid, do not despair. There are still ways to come up with the necessary cash by borrowing:

Refinancing your home mortgage. You may be able to swap your original $50,000 loan, now down to $35,000, for a new $60,000 commitment. The carrying costs will be higher and the payout longer, but as long as property values keep rising, that can be a worthwhile use of your resources.

Taking out a second mortgage. You can take out a second mortgage of, say, $10,000 for five years. It will be expensive, probably at 15% interest; but if you can afford the extra payments, it can be a convenient way to ease the pressure.

Borrowing on life insurance. You can borrow against the cash value of straight life policies. The interest rate will be modest, but your heirs will receive less if you die before you are able to make repayment.

Borrowing against savings account passbook. Usually you can borrow up to 95% of your deposit. Your savings will continue to earn interest, so the net cost will be small. But be cautious. A passbook loan will deplete your rainy day reserves.

Borrowing against securities. Currently you can borrow up to 50% of the value of stocks and up to 90% of the value of bonds, notes, and bills. Here again, you hope to benefit from the returns on assets used as collateral: income plus appreciation. But that can be risky in a down stock market.

All the above suggestions add up to one idea: to use every available resource to a reasonable limit, which is roughly 25% below the maximum loan limit. Your plan should call for educational loans to be repaid while you are working. Interest compounds to a tidy sum over the years when there's no amortization. Hopefully, the terms of the loan will enable you to do that with the surplus funds which will no longer be needed for college costs. But never dig so deeply into your savings that you will not be able to handle such unexpected crises as illness, loss of job, or severe financial setbacks.

CORPORATE EDUCATION AIDS

An increasing number of companies provide financial aid for children of their employees. Large corporations offer scholarships; smaller ones set up trusts; both may have low-interest loans. Educational benefit trusts can be established to aid children of certain key employees. They are a fringe benefit; they can be made available on a selective basis; and they can pay varying sums or percentages of college costs.

The corporation makes contributions to the trust and tax-deducts its contributions as business expenses. The money in the fund is invested, and the earnings are taxed as trust income at lower rates than are paid by the corporation or the favored employee. When the money in the trust is paid out, it is taxed in different ways, depending on the type of plan. Here are the most widely used formats:

EDUCO, an organization in Lake Forest, Illinois, sets up its plans so that the payouts are scholarships for the employee's children. EDUCO contends that the money is not taxable, and after several court cases it seems to be winning its point. Its argument is that the arrangement is a legitimate fringe benefit for highly paid employees whose children cannot get scholarships.

CO-ED, a Dallas group, arranges for payouts to be taxed as part of the child's income, still a considerable tax break.

Other plans allow for taxes on distributions to be paid by the corporate employee at the time of payment. That is more beneficial to the corporation than to the employee.

Educational benefit trusts are worth checking if you are employed by a small company or a professional corporation or are a member of a partnership. Be sure to consult a smart lawyer, and do not be discouraged if the local IRS office says no. Higher federal authorities have approved these guidelines:

- Children must be selected by the employer.
- The money must be used for annual college expenses: tuition, fees, room, board, books, and so on.
- Funding must be by semiannual corporate contributions according to an actuarily determined schedule based on the child's age.
- Money must be allocated, at the trustee's discretion, to the college or the student, not to the employee.
- There must be restrictions to require that the student maintain academic good standing.

If your boss is concerned about the possible tax limitations, try to arrange for low-cost loans. You should be able to save 3% to 5% in interest charges.

Financing college costs for your children will not be easy, but it can be done with wise financial planning, strict family discipline, full cooperation of everyone, and willingness to spend time to locate sources of assistance. Start early; save regularly; invest wisely; ask for family help; and say a few prayers. *No child should be denied the opportunity of a college education just because of financial stringency.*

8 Planning for Retirement

The time to start planning your retirement income is when you are young, preferably when you get your first job. That is not easy. In their twenties, most people have trouble balancing their budgets and saving enough to buy life insurance and furniture. They do not have time or money enough to worry about retirement fund contributions which they will not be able to enjoy for 40 or 50 years. And being starry-eyed and optimistic, they delay starting a personal pension plan, or joining a corporate one, in hopes of an inheritance, a big gain from investments, or a much larger paycheck.

That attitude is foolish, and it can be expensive. It's hard to catch up when you're older even though you may become more affluent. If you start your retirement plan savings early, you will have little trouble in reaching your goal of adequate after-work income provided you save consistently and take advantage of the magic of compounding. The longer your delay, the more difficult will be the accumulation of the money you need to assure a retirement free of cares about money. Also, in the meantime you lose substantial tax advantages. With a personal plan, immediate deductions can be made for current contributions. With all types of retirement programs, you have the long-term benefits of tax-free accumulation of income and appreciation until withdrawal. *Start your pension plan now even if it means scrimping and postponing purchases or pleasures.*

PERSONAL RETIREMENT PLANS

For illustrative purposes, the emphasis in this chapter is on personal retirement plans under which the individual controls the amount of savings and can direct investment policies and ultimate benefits. A pension plan where you work is easier and more convenient, but you will have little to say about its operation. Everything is packaged. Your contributions and benefits are set by formula, usually with little leeway. Generally, it's a good idea to sign up unless you do not expect to stay long. When you leave your job, you can always withdraw your own savings. After five years, you will own part of the corporate contributions, although usually it will not be available until you retire.

If the company has a noncontributory plan, you'll be getting the equivalent of extra, tax-free income. If the plan is contributory, you'll be forced to save. When your money is matched, you will do OK even if the investment performance of the fund is mediocre.

When you join a corporate or government pension plan, none of your income from that employer can be used to contribute to another retirement program. But if you had a plan prior to your corporate employment, the original plan can continue and grow with allocations from outside income: fees as a director of another corporation, from free-lance writing, and from weekend consulting. Or you can set up a new plan with part of those extra, outside earnings. A pension plan can be one of the most tax-beneficial, rewarding forces in successful financial planning.

Now let's get back to personal retirement plans. The examples given here are keyed to retirement at age 65. If you prefer to work until 70, you will have five more years for savings, income, and appreciation to reach your monetary target. And that much less time to enjoy your savings.

How Much You Will Need

As a rough rule, you will need 66% to 75% of your last working year's income for a reasonably comfortable retirement. The amount will vary according to your anticipated lifestyle. If you pull up stakes and head for a South Sea isle or a Maine village, your expenses will be lower than if you had chosen a populated area. If you splurge in travel, you'll need more money. The amount will also vary with your responsibilities—financial aid to your children or relatives, hospital costs, and so on. Nor do the figures take into account the ever-debilitating effect of inflation. Most folks need at least a year of adjustment before they settle down to a fairly stable budget and lifestyle.

Despite all the caveats and fears, achieving adequate retirement income is easy. Most corporations and all governments have pension plans. Also, under the Employment Retirement Income Security Act (ERISA), almost every individual can build a satisfactory sum by withdrawal time, generally permissible at age 59½ and mandatory at 70½. It's the oft-stressed plan of consistent savings and compounding.

Before your spouse insists that she cannot live on less, at any age, point out that, at retirement time, the mortgage will probably be paid off, you will need less life insurance, and the children should be on their own and, possibly, be able to help a bit by letting you use their vacation cottage or paying for airplane tickets for visits.

In your retirement planning, be sensible and flexible. If you remarry at age 50 and have children, you probably won't stop work until 70 or more. And if your parents outlived the actuarial tables, you may have to help them out. That's why it is important to review your plan frequently.

First, of course, set down your objectives and time schedule from a checklist like this:

At what age do you plan to retire?
What type of retirement plan do you have?
How much income will you need at retirement?
What do you plan to do after retirement?
Do you plan to live elsewhere? One home? Two homes?
How much do you project your retirement income to be now?
How much do you project your ultimate retirement income to be on the basis of inflation, higher income, and so on?

86 YOUR MONEY & YOUR LIFE

The answers to those questions may not make much sense now, but over the years they will form the pattern which you will need in your financial planning. To guesstimate how your present assets will grow if compounded, use Worksheet 9. It can also show you how much growth you will need to counteract inflation.

EXAMPLE: A single investment, at an annual compound rate of return of 8%, will grow to $21,600 in ten years: $10,000 multiplied by the compounding factor of 2.16 (see Table 8–1).

To determine the effects of inflation, use the Table 8–1 data with your current nest egg. If you have $100,000, expect to retire in 20 years, and believe inflation will be at 5%, multiply $100,000 by 2.65 to get $265,000, the amount you'll need to have the same purchasing power in two decades.

Worksheet 9
Estimating Retirement Expenses

	Annual Expenditures This Year (1)	After Retirement —% of (1) (2)	Inflation Factor (3)
Housing (taxes, maintenance, utilities)			
Food and liquor			
Clothing and cleaning			
Insurance			
Transportation			
Recreation and hobbies			
Travel and entertainment			
Contributions and charities			
Medical and dental			
Household (new and repairs)			
Miscellaneous			
Total			
Inflation allowance (column 3)			
Income taxes*			
Annual retirement income goal			

*20% of combined totals for expenses and inflation—more if in high income bracket. Subtract Social Security benefits; then calculate tax on balance.

Table 8–1. Projecting growth of assets and inflation.

Years to Go	Compounding Factor at Inflation Rate of				
	5%	6%	7%	8%	9%
1	1.05	1.06	1.07	1.08	1.09
2	1.10	1.12	1.14	1.17	1.19
3	1.16	1.19	1.23	1.26	1.30
4	1.22	1.26	1.31	1.36	1.41
5	1.28	1.33	1.40	1.46	1.54
6	1.34	1.42	1.50	1.59	1.68
7	1.41	1.50	1.61	1.71	1.83
8	1.48	1.59	1.72	1.85	1.99
9	1.55	1.69	1.84	1.99	2.17
10	1.63	1.79	1.97	2.16	2.37
15	2.08	2.40	2.76	3.17	3.64
20	2.65	3.21	3.87	4.66	5.60
25	3.39	4.29	5.43	6.85	8.62
30	4.32	5.74	7.61	10.06	13.27

SOURCE: C. Colburn Hardy, *Dun & Bradstreet's Guide to Your Investments* (New York: Crowell, 1978).

You can use the data in Table 8–1 to project retirement expenses. If you expect to spend $6,000 for housing and look for inflation to average 6% for the next two decades, multiply the $6,000 by 3.21 to get $19,260. The difference of $13,260 is the inflation factor to be entered in column 3 of Worksheet 9.

Don't panic if those future, inflation-factored expenses seem high. Chances are that you will be making much more money by then and, with wise investments, your assets can grow at a faster-than-inflation rate. To find monthly income, use Table 8–2.

Of course, when the gap between projected retirement income and expenses becomes too wide, make revisions. (1) Set arbitrary limits for future expenses, for example, a flat $3,000 for travel and entertainment and $2,000 for transportation. Those are only guesstimates, and they will be changed frequently over the next 20 years. (2) Boost your savings to increase your future assets.

Don't forget taxes based on the income you expect to have after subtracting Social Security income.

Table 8–2. Capital-to-income conversion.

Amount of Capital	Monthly Income at Rate of					
	5%	6%	7%	8%	9%	10%
$ 10,000	$ 42	$ 50	$ 58	$ 67	$ 75	$ 83
20,000	83	100	117	133	150	167
30,000	125	150	175	200	225	250
40,000	167	200	233	267	300	333
50,000	208	250	292	333	375	417
75,000	312	375	438	500	562	625
100,000	417	500	583	667	750	833

SOURCE: C. Colburn Hardy, *Dun & Bradstreet's Guide to Your Investments* (New York: Crowell, 1978).

WELCOME SOCIAL SECURITY

And now some good news: extra income from Uncle Sam in the form of monthly Social Security checks. The checks can be substantial: over $6,000 a year for the primary beneficiary and over $3,000 more if the spouse also is eligible. By law, all payments will be increased periodically. In 1978, based on average annual earnings of $10,000, the primary benefit was $502 and the spouse benefit was $251, both at age 65. That's a total of $753. However, the maximum earnings covered by Social Security were lower in preceding years and must be included in figuring average earnings. The highest total may not always be payable. Also, at age 62, the spouse can start drawing benefits at a rate that is roughly 25% less.

Benefits are adjusted automatically in every year that there is a significant increase (a rise of 3%) in living costs. Thus, my own Social Security check, which was a net (after deductions for Medicare) of $452.10 in 1978, was $456.80 in early 1979 and will be higher after July 1979.

Recent changes have been made in the amount of money that can be earned without losing benefits. Before 1978, beneficiaries could receive full benefits for any month in which their wages were below the allowed limit or in which they were not actively self-employed—no matter how high their total yearly earnings. In 1979, the non-work limit on earnings was $375 per month for those age 65 or older and $290 per month for those under 65. You will not lose benefits if your annual earnings are under $4,500 in 1979, $5,000 in 1980, $5,500 in 1981, and $6,000 in 1982. And, starting in 1982, those over 70 will receive full monthly benefits regardless of earnings.

If you're under 45 years of age, consider Social Security payments as an extra. If you're older, add them in only when you need them to reach your goal. Over the years, watch for changes in payouts and other benefits.

If you like to work with a calculator, you can estimate what you will receive from Social Security by using Worksheet 10, which is based on data prepared by the government. Your check will be based on your average earnings over a period of years.

Historically, retirement benefits have risen as the result of pressure from organized bargaining units. With inflation, however, more companies are taking the initiative and improving both the terms and dollars of their agreements. Over the next several decades, it's probable that many corporate pension plans will consider Social Security and include some sort of automatic benefit increases for both present and future retirees.

On the other hand, some smaller companies, overwhelmed by costs, reports, and red tape, are abandoning their retirement programs and urging employees to set up individual plans.

Advice: Again, if your company has a pension plan, join it as soon as you are eligible. If it's contributory, add as much as you can as often as you can, especially when your savings are matched. A retirement plan is one of the most important tools of successful financial planning. It can save you taxes when you contribute, assure after-work income for you and your spouse, and provide protection for your family after you're gone—usually but not always.

HOW MUCH YOU MUST SAVE

Still puzzled by how much you will have to save to meet your after-work money goal? Get out your calculator and use Table 8-3. It provides a handy way to guesstimate the percent of your salary you will have to set aside to obtain the pension you want. Note that it applies primarily to personal retirement plans, because the terms of most corporate programs limit contributions.

On the average, to get 50% of your pay after retirement, you will need a fund equal to 10 times your annual earned income. If you never get a raise, calculations are easy, as shown in column 1. When you have 30 years to work, the rate of savings will be 1.5% to establish the needed sinking fund, assuming an investment return of 5% annually. Since you need 10 times that sum, the factor becomes 15%: $15 on every $100 of income.

To get the rate for intermediate years, interpolate with an average rate of increase; for 29 years to retirement, average the 30- and 35-year sinking fund data. The difference is .6; divide it by 5 to get .12 annually. Add that to the 1.5 to get 1.62%, which, multiplied by 10, means an annual rate of savings of 16.2%.

The problems come with projections involving raises. Every time your salary increases, you must boost not just the amount but also the percent of savings. To find the constant percent of salary to be set aside, use column B. It assumes a 5.75% annual increase in salary. For 30 years, the factor is 36%: 3.6 × 10, again when savings yield 5%. For in-between years, use averages.

Table 8-3. Set-asides necessary to obtain desired pension (5% return).

Years to Retirement	Set-aside Necessary from Level Salary	Salary Increased by 5.75% per Year
5	18.1%	19.8%
10	8.0	10.1
15	4.6	6.8
20	3.0	5.2
25	2.1	4.2
30	1.5	3.6

SOURCE: Based on data from Peat, Marwick, Mitchell & Co., New York.

Note: The percentages represent the portion of yearly salary, when invested at a 5% yield, that must be set aside to create a fund equal to the final year's earned income. Column 1 assumes that you never get a raise. Column 2 is more realistic in that it assumes a 5.75% annual increase in salary. When retirement income is 50% of the last working year's income, you will need a nest egg 10 times that annual total. To get the real rate of savings, then, multiply by 10. For 30 years, the percent of salary to be saved will be 15% with no raise, 36% with annual raises.

Worksheet 10
Estimate of Social Security Benefits

Table 1		Table 2		
Year You Were Born	Years Needed	Year	A	B
1913	19	1951	$ 3,600	_____
1914	20	1952	3,600	_____
1915	21	1953	3,600	_____
1916	22	1954	3,600	_____
1918	24	1955	4,200	_____
1920	26	1956	4,200	_____
1925	31	1957	4,200	_____
1930 or later	35*	1958	4,200	_____

*Maximum number of years that count.

1. In Table 1, find the number of years needed and write it here:_____.

2. In Table 2, column A shows the maximum earnings covered by Social Security. List your own earnings in column B: 0 if you made no money, but the maximum shown even if you earned more. For future years, estimate earnings, including those for years worked after age 65. Stop the year *before* you retire.

3. Cross off the years of lowest earnings until the number of years left is the same as the number of years needed, as shown in Table 1.

4. Add the earnings left in Table 2 and write the total at the bottom of the table and here: _____.

5. Divide the total in (4) by the number of years in (1) to get the average yearly earnings covered by Social Security: _____.

6. Compare the figure in (5) with the average yearly earnings closest to it in Table 3. Then check the benefits column to find out how much you can look forward to. If you have an eligible spouse or child, the check will be larger. Note that past earnings, which were lower, must be computed for the average, so the benefits will not be as great as given in the table until future years.

Year	A	B
1959	4,800	_____
1960	4,800	_____
1961	4,800	_____
1962	4,800	_____
1963	4,800	_____
1964	4,800	_____
1965	4,800	_____
1966	6,600	_____
1967	6,600	_____
1968	7,800	_____
1969	7,800	_____
1970	7,800	_____
1971	7,800	_____
1972	9,000	_____
1973	10,800	_____
1974	13,200	_____
1975	14,100	_____
1976	15,300	_____
1977	16,500	_____
1978	17,700	_____
1979	22,900	_____
1980	25,900	_____
1981	29,700*	_____
Total		$

*The maximum amount of annual earnings that count for Social Security will rise automatically after 1981 as earnings levels increase. Because of this, the base in 1982 and later may be higher than $29,700.

Obviously, such a high rate of savings—from 15% to 36%—is difficult unless you live frugally, get additional financial help from your employer (probably only if he's your father-in-law), or obtain higher returns on the investment of your pension funds.

Once again, these examples point out why you must make a choice as to your lifestyle. If you want a *big* pension, you must save more than the average family and thus curtail your present expenditures. Or if you feel you cannot save more now, you must prepare yourself to get along on less when you retire. But in both cases, wise investing, as explained in Chapter 10, can be mighty helpful.

Worksheet 10 (continued)

Table 3

Benefits Can Be Paid to	\$923 or Less	\$3,000	\$4,000	\$5,000	\$6,000	\$8,000	\$10,000*
Retired worker at 65	\$121.80	\$251.80	\$296.20	\$343.50	\$388.20	\$482.60	\$534.70
Worker under 65 and disabled	121.80	251.80	296.20	343.50	388.20	482.60	534.70
Retired worker at 62	97.50	201.50	237.00	274.80	310.60	386.10	427.80
Wife or husband at 65	60.90	125.90	148.10	171.80	194.10	241.30	267.40
Wife or husband at 62	45.70	94.50	111.10	128.90	145.60	181.00	200.60
Wife under 65 with one child in her care	61.00	133.20	210.00	290.40	324.00	362.00	401.00
Widow or widower at 65 if worker never received reduced benefits	121.80	251.80	296.20	343.50	388.20	482.60	534.70
Widow or widower at 60 if sole survivor	87.10	180.10	211.80	245.70	277.60	345.10	382.40
Widow or widower at 50 and disabled if sole survivor	61.00	126.00	148.20	171.90	194.10	241.40	267.50
Widow or widower with one child in care	182.80	377.80	444.40	515.40	582.40	724.00	802.20
Maximum family payment	182.70	384.90	506.20	633.80	712.10	844.50	935.70

Average Yearly Earnings After 1950 Covered by Social Security

SOURCE: U.S. Department of Health, Education, and Welfare.

*Maximum earnings covered by Social Security were lower in past years and must be included in figuring your average earnings. This average determines your payment amount. Because of this, amounts shown in the last column generally won't be payable until future years. The maximum retirement benefit generally payable to a worker who is 65 in 1978 is $489.70.

PENSION PLANS

Now that you have an idea of what you will need and the income you may have, let's discuss the regulations which make retirement income possible. As the result of ERISA, there are standards which apply to all pension programs. Here's a summary of the major provisions:

1. *Eligibility* must be extended to:
   - Persons 25 years of age with at least one year's employment.

- Newly hired workers unless they are within five years of the company's normal retirement age.
- Part-time workers with over 1,000 hours of employment in one year.
2. *Vesting* has these minimums:
   - After 5 years, 25% of accumulated benefits.
   - After 10 years, 50% of accumulated benefits.
   - After 15 years, 100% of accumulated benefits.

Or under the rule of 45, when age and years of service add up to 45 years after five years of service, vesting is 50% with 10% increases for each additional year to a maximum of 100%.

When your plan is fully vested, it's all your money. A few plans permit you to withdraw everything if you leave your employing company, but most plans do not permit any take-out before retirement. Full payment is made at age 65 and lesser benefits at age 60.

Corporate Pension Plans

There are so many formulas used to compute corporate pension benefits that we'll have to generalize. The better programs provide an annuity equal to one-third to one-half of final compensation or of the average of the last three, or highest-income, years.

Because individual employees have little to say about corporate pension plans, I am suggesting questions to ask. And in the examples, I have eliminated Social Security payments in computations and considered them as welcome extras to bridge an income gap. But do not take that for granted. Increasingly, corporations are including Social Security benefits as part of their projections of total retirement packages.

Income at Retirement

First, let's list some of the questions to ask. If you cannot find the answers in the employees' handbook, contact the corporate benefits office. You may find that you have better protection than you expected.

Is income at retirement determined by salary, years of employment, or both?
If salary, is the pension based on final compensation? Or the average of the last five years?
How many days of annual work are required to assure credited coverage?
Does coverage start immediately, or is there a waiting period?
Can you leave the company and return without losing your pension benefit?
If so, for how long and for what reasons? (Maybe you'll have a chance to take a leave of absence to serve in government for a year or two.)
Will Social Security payments be added to or deducted from your pension income?
Is there provision for benefits to be adjusted for inflation?
Is the plan contributory or noncontributory? The best bet is contributory, because returns on your savings accumulate tax-free.

Beneficiaries

How much will your survivors receive for how long?
Will the survivor provision mean a lower pension payout for you?
When must you make the survivor benefit choice? (Usually, one year before actual retirement.)
If you die before retirement, what will your heirs receive? Generally, the greater the protection provided after death, the lower the retirement income as long as you live. You may have these options: (1) To receive pension income as long as you or your beneficiary lives. (2) To take full income while you live and leave 50% to 75% of income to your survivor.

Disability

How is disability defined? By whom?
Does the period of disability count as "credited service" toward retirement benefits?
Must you be vested to receive disability payments? This is an area in which the individual seldom has much to say. The contract with the insurance company is made at a high level. It spells out specific definitions and terms and leaves little room for exceptions.

Early Retirement

At what age can you retire and with what benefits?
Is there a requirement of years of service?
How much will benefits be reduced? Generally, early retirement (before age 65) is available with a reduction of benefits: from 4% to 6% of annual income for each year before normal retirement date. As an example, suppose an employee scheduled to get $15,000 at age 65 quits at 60. He ends up with between $10,500 and $12,000 a year. Some plans require a minimum age of 60 or 55 if you've had 15 years of vested service.

Profit-Sharing Plans

How soon after starting work can you participate?
How much of your annual income can you invest? Does that include just salary or salary plus bonus?
Will the company match? To what limits?
Does matching depend on corporate profits?
What options do you have for investments: corporate stock, growth fund, fixed income holdings, or a combination?
Can you withdraw all or part of your savings or just income? Or must you wait until you leave the company?
Will there be a penalty for early withdrawal?

Profit sharing or matching is the area of greatest divergence in company policies. Generally, smaller corporations are more liberal. But most major firms permit you to save a fixed percent of your salary, up to 10%, and will match you dollar for dollar up to a preset limit. In some cases, however, the corporate contributions will depend on annual profits. Now and then, they may be made only when profits are above a minimum figure.

Calculating Corporate Benefits

In most companies, the retirement income is based on a combination of salary and years of employment (credited service). Typically, it provides for 1.25% of salary or wages of the last year of work multiplied by the years of credited service, less 1⅔% of the Social Security benefit for each year of employment to a maximum of 50% of the Social Security payment.

EXAMPLE: Bob Blumenthal, who has worked for Controlled Cosmetics for 30 years, is retiring. He is making $75,000 a year. At his age of 65, his Social Security benefit will be $6,024. Here are the calculations:

$$30 \text{ years} \times 1.25\% = 37.50\% \times \$75,000 = \$28,125$$
$$1.67 \times 30 = 5.01 \times \$6,024 = \$3,018$$

Since $3,018 is above the 50% of Social Security, deduct only 50% ($3,012) to get an annual pension of $25,113. That is about one-third of Bob's last year's earnings—a modest but not overly generous benefit for his many years of service.

Another type of plan, used by the U.S. Post Office, does not include Social Security. Here is the formula: 1.5% of the average pay of the "high three" years multiplied by service up to five years, plus 1.75% of the same high three multiplied by five additional years of service, plus 2% of the high three average pay years, multiplied by all service over ten years. Thus Mr. Morison, with 30 years service and a high-three average pay of $36,000 would get $20,250:

1.5% of $36,000 × 5 years =	$ 2,700
1.75% of $36,000 × 5 years =	3,150
2.0% of $36,000 × 20 years =	14,400
Total	$20,250

Voluntary Contributions

Some companies pay all pension costs; others require employee contributions; still others permit voluntary additions, usually under a profit-sharing plan. With that benefit, an employee may add savings on an advancing scale (2%, 4%, 6%) to a maximum that is seldom over 10%. Then the corporation may match such savings. Thus an individual earning $50,000 can have as much as $10,000 in the plan each year: $5,000 of his own funds and $5,000 from the corporation. In many cases, corporate contributions depend on annual profits and may be limited, in total, to 6% of annual profits.

If you can make voluntary contributions, do so because your money will accumulate tax-free. If there's a match, try to set aside the maximum. With compounding, your savings will grow rapidly over the years, and you can always take at least your contributions, plus earnings, if you leave for another job. For a typical corporate pension plan see Table 8–4.

Table 8–4. Typical corporate pension plan.

If You Are	Eligibility	Vesting	Benefit Accrual	Termination Insurance
Not yet enrolled.	Usually, eligible to join as soon as you have completed one year of service and are 25 years old.	After you join, service credit for vesting for all years of continuous employment since age 22.*	Start as soon as you join and have two years continuous employment.	
Enrolled but not yet vested in company plan.		After 5 years, 25% of accumulated benefits; after 10 years, 50%; after 15 years, 100% or rule of 45 (when age and years of service total 45 after 5 years' service: 50% with 10% increase for each additional year to maximum of 100%.)	Previous benefits continue to accrue.	Vested benefits insured by U.S. government (some exceptions until 1981) up to $750 per month.
Enrolled and already vested in plan.		Benefits must meet federal standards.	Previous benefits continue to accrue.	Normally, vested benefits insured by U.S. government up to $750 per month.
Leaving job where enrolled in plan.		Unless paid out in lump sum or transferred to another plan, vested benefits belong to you.**		Same as above.
Working for former employer or rehired by one in future.	May have to wait one year to join plan.	If rehired before 1976, company is not required to restore previously accrued benefits. Thereafter, benefits can be restored if previously vested.		Same as above.

*If plan is contributory, you need not be given credit for years in which you declined to contribute.
**If you receive lump-sum distribution of vested benefits, you must restore sum to plan if you are rehired and are anxious to retain benefit credits.

When to Check a Corporate Pension Plan

Most corporate pension plans are safe. When they are inadequately funded, however, it is possible that, in the future, retirement payments could be delayed, reduced, or even eliminated. There is a federal guarantee, but that's limited to $750 per month and it comes into effect only when the company goes broke or, under certain conditions, moves or is merged. Collecting can be a long, slow process.

There are two occasions when it pays to be cautious about a company that has substantial unfunded pension commitments: (1) when you are considering a new job, have a choice between two companies, and are at an age when retirement is not far away and (2) when you are investing in the securities of the corporation.

Under ERISA, pension liabilities can be a legal claim against corporate assets rather than just against the pension fund. That means that if a retirement plan is terminated and the corporate pension reserves are inadequate, the government can go after company assets, up to 30% of net worth. Legally, the liabilities have the status of tax liens, which makes them senior to claims of other creditors.

As to investments, the point is that, when there are substantial unfunded benefits, the company may have to boost annual contributions. That leaves less money for shareholds and for productive investment for corporate growth. ERISA requires amortization of unfunded prior last service costs against earnings over a 30- to 40-year period. The effect of that mandate will become apparent in the near future, and it could be a strong deterrent to ownership of stocks in debt-heavy, marginally profitable concerns.

Getting accurate information on pension plans is difficult because such data are seldom included in the annual report. A *Business Week* survey indicates a wide variation of assumptions used to determine the value of future pension obligations: actuarial rates as low as 4% and as high as 8%, salary or wage growth rates of 2% to 8%, and so on. The study also shows that unfunded vested benefits, as a percent of corporate net worth, range from 89% for Uniroyal to 1% for IT&T. A high ratio doesn't mean the company is in financial trouble, but it can indicate future problems.

TYPES OF PERSONAL RETIREMENT PLANS

With personal retirement plans, you have a wider choice and can maintain greater control. You can select and, within limits, direct the plan to best suit your financial abilities while saving and at withdrawal.

Most personal retirement plans are sold as package prototypes offered by banks, thrift institutions, investment companies, brokerage firms, and insurance companies; they take your money and handle all details. But as with all investments entrusted to others, your returns may be less than can be obtained under your own direction. As stressed throughout this guide, there will be off-the-top costs: sales commissions, management fees, and operating expenses.

You are, however, legally allowed to do it yourself: that is, you can deal with your stockbroker, who names a bank as trustee/custodian and permits you to make your own investment decisions. The three basic types of plans are individual retirement account (IRA), Keogh plan, and professional corporation. Before choosing one of them, investigate the pros and cons to find the best-for-you, long-term plan. You may be able to have more than one personal retirement plan, so can make changes as your income rises or your needs shift. Early withdrawals are subject to substantial penalties, so it's best to retain a plan even if you are not able to make additional contributions.

All three plans have characteristics that are similar to those of corporate pension plans: (1) they must be qualified by IRS; (2) annual contributions are tax-free when made; (3) all earnings, from interest, dividends, and capital gains, accumulate tax-free until withdrawn; (4) they are subject to ERISA standards of eligibility, vesting, and prudent investing.

The major differences lie in the limit of contributions, withdrawal dates, eligibility, and types of investments.

Limit of contributions:
- IRA: 15% of gross earned income to a maximum of $1,500 a year for individuals, $1,750 when a nonworking spouse is included, and $7,500 when paid by a company for the benefit of an individual.
- Keogh plan: 15% of earned income to a maximum of $7,500, with modest additions under special arrangements.
- Professional corporation: Up to 35% of salary. Greater contributions are possible to provide ultimate retirement benefits of as much as $90,050 a year with future increases to offset inflation.

Withdrawal Date
- IRA and Keogh: Optional at age 59½, mandatory at 70½.
- Professional corporation: Any time.
- Earlier or illegal withdrawals are subject to nondeductible penalties and may cause cancellation of the pension plan.

Eligibility
- IRA: (1) Part-time workers who do not earn enough to justify a Keogh or corporate plan. This includes executives who receive fees for consulting, free-lance writing, or serving as a director of a corporation other than their principal employer. (2) Individuals who do not choose to join or continue the pension plan where they work. (3) Individuals who withdraw lump sum retirement benefits early.
- Keogh plan: Self-employed individuals and proprietors and employees of small companies. All contributions are vested. The percent of salary contributions is the same for all full-time employees who have worked three years or longer, unless a special program is adopted.
- Professional corporation: All employees have vesting in accordance with ERISA guidelines: full vesting after ten years, progressive vesting after five years, and the rule of 45.

When employees leave before retirement, nonvested funds are forfeited and are added to the remaining funds or are used to reduce corporate contributions.

Types of Investments
- IRA: Limited to thrift accounts in a bank savings and loan association or federally insured credit union, mutual fund shares, common trust funds, corporate and U.S. government bonds, stocks rated B or better, an annuity contract, retirement income or endowment life insurance, U.S. government retirement bonds.
- Keogh and professional corporation plans have wider latitude and can own real estate, art, stamps, coins, and so on.

All investments must be prudent; they must not involve a conflict of interest; and they must provide sufficient income to meet commitments and withdrawals.

Trustees

All personal pension plans require a trustee and custodian.

Special Provisions

Under both Keogh and professional corporation plans, arrangements can be made to permit the principals to make larger contributions and/or reduce the savings made for employees.

The *defined-benefits plan* (DBP) requires that the retirement benefit and the annual contribution be set at the outset. It assumes specified rates of return on investments and permits annual savings up to the amount needed to provide a predetermined pension benefit.

The DBP is most advantageous with a professional corporation because there's no limit to the annual contributions as long as the ultimate retirement income is not over $90,050 a year (with future increases to keep pace with inflation). As a practical matter, IRS will probably question any savings more than 50% of annual compensation.

EXAMPLE: Dr. Moore, age 45, earns $60,000 a year. Under his Keogh plan, his regular contribution has been $7,500 a year, but with his children out of college, he feels he can afford to increase it. By setting his DBP at $3,000 a month and referring to an IRS approved formula, he can boost his annual allocation to $9,300.

Under the *defined-contributions plan* (DCP) the same number of dollars must be saved in lean years as in prosperous ones. An exception is when a corporation uses a profit-sharing plan which limits the contribution, per employee, to 15% of compensation. Once the annual allocation is set, the actuary determines the ultimate monetary benefits by adding the savings and income at an anticipated rate of return. Permissible contributions vary with the type of plan, but the maximum allocation, at this time, is $30,050. There is provision for increases to keep pace with inflation.

With a money-purchase plan (such as an annuity), the limit is 25% of compensation. With profit sharing, the amount is variable up to 15% of distributed money. With a combination of both money purchase and profit sharing, the maximum is 25% of compensation, partially fixed, partially variable. The money-purchase total is set at 10% to 15%, and each year the amount put into profit sharing can be shifted up or down.

It's also possible to have a combination DBP and DCP.

When you become involved in any type of personal retirement plan involving substantial sums, consult experts: an actuary, an accountant, and a lawyer. Regulations change frequently, usually as the result of legal action, and local IRS offices often interpret rules differently. The several retirement plans are compared in Table 8–5.

Keogh Plan or Professional Corporation?

At this point, it might be well to contrast personal retirement plans under Keogh and a professional corporation. First, let's recognize that the corporation does have other financial advantages such as substantial fringe benefits: payment (with pretax dollars) of premiums for life, health, and disability insurance and, if the directors are willing to take the chance of trouble with IRS, even educational costs (Chapter 7).

Second, the annual contributions to retirement plans can be greater. Under a qualified profit-sharing plan, they can be up to 15% of salary, which with individual contributions can be 25% of compensation. Under a defined benefits plan, the annual pension contribution can be as much as is needed to provide after-work income equal to 100% of salary to a maximum of $90,050. Future annual adjustments will be made to offset inflation. In effect, that means an older physician who had outside income could set aside a very high percentage of his salary.

Third, there's an estate tax break. When the participant's share of the retirement fund is paid in a lump sum to a named beneficiary other than his or her estate, there's no estate tax. The beneficiary qualifies for a $5,000 death benefit exclusion, and he can avoid a heavy capital gains tax by arranging for averaging the income over ten years.

Offsetting those pros are several major cons: higher organization and setup costs, from $1,500 to $2,500; requirements for regular corporate meetings and minutes; substantial expenses for accounting, legal counsel, and, possibly, investment advisory service; costs and bother of numerous reports; and added taxes to both federal and state authorities.

Here is some advice from Charles H. Walsh, president of Associated Professional Consultants, Elmhurst, Illinois:

If you incorporate, have your accountant or business adviser analyze the financial aspects of both Keogh and corporate pension plans. With higher deductions for Social Security alone, corporate costs will continue to soar. On the average, at this time, it costs $3,000 per employee to keep a corporation. With a Keogh plan, you'll be able to cut that figure in half.

On the other hand, the pension set-asides of a corporation can be greater. Check these, too. Many physicians are contributing too much to their pension plans. They will end up with over $1,000,000 at age 65, more if they work until 70. These millions are

Table 8-5. Comparison of personal retirement plans.

Plan	Contributions	When Employee Leaves	Investment Earnings or Losses	At Retirement, Participant Gets
Keogh Plan				
Defined-contributions plan	15% of compensation to $7,500 a year.	Takes entire amount.	Added to or subtracted from account balance.	Balance of account.
Defined-benefits plan	Based of IRS tables; can be about 25% more than $7,500 depending on age and years paid.	Takes entire amount	Annual contribution adjusted to reflect.	Predetermined amount based on age at start, generally under $50,000 annual income.
Corporate Plan				
Defined-contributions plan	Up to 25% compensation to maximum of $30,050* fixed in advance.	Corporate contributions cut by amount of forfeited funds.	Added to or subtracted from account balance.	Balance of account.
Profit sharing	Varies annually, up to 15% of compensation to maximum of $30,050.*	Forfeited funds added to remaining account balances.	Added to or subtracted from account balances.	Balance of account.
Combined money purchase and profit sharing	To 25% of compensation (part fixed, part variable) to maximum of $30,050.*	Forfeited funds reduce corporate contributions if maximum; otherwise, added to profit-sharing accounts.	Added to or subtracted from account balance.	Balance of account.
Defined-Benefits Plan				
Fixed benefit	Amount needed to fund predetermined benefit.	Corporate contributions cut by amount of forfeited funds.	Annual contributions adjusted to reflect.	Predetermined amount to 100% compensation to maximum of $90,050.*
Target benefit	Amount needed to fund predetermined benefit to maximum of 25% of compensation or $30,050.*	Corporate contributions cut by amount of forfeited funds.	Added to or subtracted from account balances.	Predetermined amount to 100% compensation to maximum of $90,050,* plus or minus investment gains or losses.
Combined Plan				
Money purchase	To 10% of compensation as fixed in advance.	Corporate contributions cut by amount of forfeited funds.	Added to or subtracted from account balances.	Balance of account.
Fixed benefit	Amount needed to fund predetermined benefit, no maximum.	Corporate contributions cut by amount of forfeited funds.	Annual corporate contribution adjusted to reflect.	Predetermined amount to 100% compensation to maximum of $90,050.*

SOURCE: Based on data in C. Colburn Hardy, *ABCs of Investing Your Retirement Funds* (Oradell, N.J.: Medical Economics, 1978).
*Adjusted annually for inflation.

impressive and, even after 50% taxes, will provide a lifetime income of $100,000—with some invasion of capital. At an advanced age, most people will have a tough time spending that sum every year. After all, how many times can you go around the world and how many Cadillacs will you want to own?

Still, that bugaboo inflation will have a major impact. In 20 years, each Cadillac could cost $50,000 or more.

PENSIONS FOR EMPLOYESS OF NONPROFIT INSTITUTIONS

Special retirement plans are available for people who work for nonprofit institutions such as hospitals, social service agencies, and foundations. You are allowed to set aside 20% of your salary with the advantages of other personal pension plans: no tax when you put it in, and no tax on earnings and appreciation until you take it out.

The plans can be used by employees who are paid a regular salary. They are nonforfeitable after one year, and they can be set up for direct contribution or under an agreement whereby the participant takes less salary and has the savings invested, usually in a trusteed savings fund managed by an insurance company. From the tax standpoint that can be a good deal; from the investment standpoint, it's marginal because the results of most such funds leave much to be desired. Usually they involve life insurance, which, as we point out below, is not the best use of retirement savings. Always check to be sure that there are no other benefits which will be of sufficient value to justify the lower returns or non-maximum use of your savings.

LIFE INSURANCE IN PERSONAL RETIREMENT PLANS

Life insurance protection is permitted with all three types of plans. It is not the best use of tax-free savings because:

1. The sales charge is high, so you have less money accumulating tax-free.
2. The portion of the contribution used to buy life insurance is not tax-deductible.
3. The mathematics are unfavorable.
4. The primary purpose of a personal pension plan is to build retirement income for yourself, not protection for your family in case of your early death.

For illustrations, let's stick with IRAs because, with small sums, the problems are exacerbated.

Under an IRA, life insurance must be "incidental" to the basic accumulation: the value of the policy can be no more than 100 times the monthly retirement income. With their usual merchandising skill, life insurance companies issue a retirement income insurance policy (RIIP) that provides $1,000 of immediate protection for each $10 of monthly income at retirement. As the cash value increases, the amount of insurance decreases. If the individual lives, the insurance is eliminated and the cash value becomes the death benefit.

EXAMPLES: Betsy Booth, age 45, starts an IRA under a RIIP. She can count on a full death benefit of $10,000 or the cash value, if it is greater, and a retirement income of $100 a month. At age 55, the cash value of the policy is $6,030, so the pure insurance is $3,970. By age 60, the cash value is $10,400, so there's no insurance. That is not exactly a smart way to build after-work income.

Gordon Smith, age 40, starts his IRA with $1,500 and continues that contribution for 25 years. Half is used to buy shares in a mutual fund; half is for straight life insurance. At age 65, the fund shares are worth $66,838 and the guaranteed cash value of the life insurance is about $30,374.

Sounds great? Well, if the same $1,500 had been placed in a 7.5% savings certificate or bond, the total would be $114,595. There is greater insurance coverage in the early years, but that advantage is overcome by about year 12 by the growth of the compounding of the fixed-income holdings. Taxes won't be due until withdrawal.

Because of the larger amounts involved in Keogh and corporate plans, the difference is far greater. Buy life insurance for protection; contribute to a retirement plan for future income, not current protection.

INVESTING RETIREMENT SAVINGS

Investing funds of Keogh and corporate retirement plans is important because, for many people, those savings *are* the investment portfolio; the investors may have comparatively few assets other than their houses and life insurance. Whether you direct the investments yourself or turn them over to others, follow the principles of quality, value, and timing as outlined in Chapter 10. A difference of 2% in returns, over 25 years, can mean thousands more after-work dollars.

When participants in multimember plans have different philosophies, consider earmarking: permitting each individual to control the investing of his or her funds. The 55-year-old can choose bonds for safety and income; the 40-year-old may prefer real estate; and the 30-year-old may opt for growth stocks. Just be sure that each transaction is authorized, preferably in writing, so that there will be no complaints if the investments turn out poorly.

Generally, investments can be made in almost anything prudent and, in total, income-producing. It's OK to put some money in coins if you can prove, to IRS, that you are an experienced numismatist. But there must be a balance of assured income and sufficient liquidity if any participant wants to withdraw funds early.

Under ERISA, there are strict rules to ban self-interest deals, which can become a temptation when substantial sums are involved. *These are fiduciary funds, so do not try to be cute.* Here's a summary of "cannots" as outlined by financial writer Abner A. Layne. A principal or trustee cannot:

1. *Use plan assets for his own account or interest.* Dr. Wilson needs $100,000 to complete a business deal. With a properly structured plan, he can borrow from his share of the corporate pension plan, but he cannot pledge all fund assets

as collateral for a loan from a third party. Such a transaction is subject to a penalty of $5,000 plus the possibility of an additional payment equal to the full value of the transaction.

2. *Act in any capacity involving a pension plan in behalf of a party whose interests are adverse to those of the plan.* Dr. Webster, a close friend of the owner of a small medical publishing company, arranges for a lease, at less-than-market rental, of space in an office building owned by the pension plan. The physician is liable for the difference between the agreed-upon price and the fair rental value.

3. *Cause the plan to engage in any transaction benefiting a "party in interest."* That prohibits any actions, direct or indirect, that aid anyone involved in the pension plan by (1) sale, exchange, or lease of property, (2) loan of services or facilities, (3) furnishing of goods, services, or facilities, (4) transfer of assets to, or use by, the party of interest.

4. *Cause the plan to acquire property in violation of the special rules applicable to real estate, securities, and so on.* No longer can the corporation or any pension plan participant sell an office building to the retirement plan and lease it back. It's still possible to borrow from fund assets, but the same privilege must be extended to every participant. Then all dealings must be at arm's length, bear a reasonable rate of interest, and require additional collateral if the loan is for more than the vested amount.

All self-interest transactions are dangerous; and despite an original IRS approval, they can be upset in a post-audit review. If you are the type who likes to play games with money, isolate yourself from all decisions regarding pension plan investments by appointing an outside trustee.

Other Uses for IRAs

Executives who are already covered by a corporate pension plan can use IRAs for both personal and family advantage. When money from another pension plan is involved, the transfer must be made within 60 days, and it can be made only once every three years.

An IRA can be a *temporary parking place* when you are switching jobs and are waiting for eligibility in a new pension plan.

Young Charlie Collins takes a job with another company. He receives a lump-sum distribution of $15,000 from the corporate pension plan. He puts the money in an IRA, pays no tax, and has a full tax shelter. The IRA can continue to grow until he is ready for retirement even if he joins a pension plan at his new job.

An IRA can be used as a *rollover* when substantial money is withdrawn at early retirement. You can roll your savings over into an IRA regardless of the sum. Thus you can keep your money working, tax-free, until withdrawal.

Clark Kent, a top-ranking corporate officer, takes early retirement at age 60. He has three options with his pension:

1. Start a $19,000-a-year pension with half payments to his widow should

be predecease her. When both die, there will be nothing for his heirs. Since the plan is noncontributory, annual payouts are taxable as ordinary income—at a high rate if he takes another high-paying post.

2. Take a lump-sum payment of $255,000 and invest it promptly. After taxes, he'd have a lot less capital and, unless he bought municipal bonds, he would have to pay taxes on the investment income.

3. Roll the $255,000 over into an IRA trust in which new investments can be made to provide an annual income for 24 years under IRS tables for joint life expectancy.

Taxes would be modest because part of the income would be a return of principal. At Mr. Kent's death, his widow's income would be less, but it would still be more than that available under the corporate pension.

Mr. Kent chose plan 3 and then structured the portfolio to yield 8.5% from a mix of bonds and high-dividend-paying common stocks. All money must be paid out at the end of 24 years, so if one of the Kents lives longer, he or she will have to rely on other income.

An IRA can be set up for working minor children. If your son or daughter works during vacations and after school, his or her earnings can be set up in an IRA. Here the 15% rules does not apply, because the annual contributions can be up to $750. With compounding, even small savings can grow to a sizable sum by retirement time.

IRAs also offer a federal tax advantage. If the owner of an IRA dies when there is still a balance in the pension plan, that balance can be estate-tax-free if the named beneficiary is someone other than his or her estate (a spouse or child). Then, the beneficiary must agree to withdraw the IRA balance in substantially equal periodic payments of a span of at least 36 months or life expectancy, whichever is less. The tax exclusion is available only for amounts attributable to deposits to the account that were tax deductible and/or rollover contributions.

How a Personal Retirement Plan Can Grow

Tables 8–6 and 8–7 can be used to make calculations in your financial planning. They are based on a Keogh plan, which represents a median between IRAs and

Table 8–6. Keogh plan fund increase.

Fund Earns	\multicolumn{5}{c}{Number of Times Your Current Fund Will Increase If the Number of Years to Retirement Is}
	10	15	20	25	30
6 %	1.81	2.44	3.29	4.43	5.97
7.5	2.10	3.05	4.42	6.41	9.29
9	2.43	3.80	5.93	9.25	14.44
12	3.26	5.80	10.64	19.22	34.71

SOURCE: David Thorndike, ed., *The Thorndike Encyclopedia of Banking & Financial Tables* (Boston: Warren, Gorham & Lamont, 1977).

Table 8–7. Keogh plan investment growth.

Fund Earns	What $1 Annual Investment Will Grow to If the Number of Years to Retirement Is				
	10	15	20	25	30
6 %	13.27	23.52	37.33	55.93	80.98
7.5	14.29	26.55	44.34	70.12	107.50
9	15.42	38.08	52.96	88.67	144.40
12	18.02	38.97	76.81	145.16	268.59

SOURCE: David Thorndike, ed., *The Thorndike Encyclopedia of Banking & Financial Tables* (Boston: Warren, Gorham & Lamont, 1977).

corporate plans. There are several variables, so if the bottom line isn't what you're hoping for, you can increase the amount put away under a defined benefits plan or invest for higher total returns.

Investment Responsibilities

All investments of all personal pension plans require trustees. Usually the trustee is a fiduciary: a bank, trust company, S&L, insurance company, investment company, or investment adviser. You can also do it yourself either directly or in cooperation with an institution. If you want to control the investments, name a bank or brokerage firm as trustee or custodian with the understanding that the role will be supervisory and will be for the primary purpose of keeping you out of trouble. Before you make such an arrangement, get a written schedule of fees. If the fees appear to be high for either custody or reports, shop around. Be sure you make arrangements for annual reports which must go to government agencies—always IRS and usually the Department of Labor. The reports must detail contributions, premium payments, investments, returns, profits, losses, and so on.

Fiduciaries of plans covering over 25 persons must be bonded at a cost of about $2.50 per $1,000 contribution per person per year. If you're nervous about dealing with large sums and worried about a suit by participants, buy fiduciary liability insurance. It is protection against mistakes, errors, and poor judgment. You may have to shop around for an agent who handles that type of policy, and it's not cheap—about $200 per year for coverage with a $1,000 deductible. Most policies provide recourse to trustees if the premiums are paid by the pension fund or corporation. If you use your own money, there's no such secondary liability.

Contribute Early Each Year

Try to make contributions to any pension plan early each year to take advantage of compounding. Over 25 years that $1,500 a year into an IRA, at a 7¾% annual return, will compound to $121,604 if contributed in January. If the payment is delayed until December 31, the total will be only $112,420.

Taking Your Money Out

At withdrawal, the funds accumulated in a personal retirement plan can be used to buy an annuity, reinvested after paying taxes, or swapped for U.S. retirement bonds if the savings are not already invested in those special securities. The bonds are available at Federal Reserve banks in denominations of $50, $100, and $500 to a maximum of a $10,000 purchase in any one year. They yield 6%, are not transferable, and cannot be used as collateral for loans.

When the bonds are redeemed after age 59½, interest is paid on the earlier of two dates: five years after death or the date on which the decedent would have reached age 70½. No interest accumulates after age 70½.

As investments either during the buildup of savings or as a parking place after formal retirement, the retirement bonds are no great shakes. Their yields are modest and their appreciation nil, but they are safe.

Use Worksheet 11 to estimate what you will have at retirement: the total dollars before and after taxes and annual income whether you opt to preserve or spend out your capital. The example is based on a 45-year-old professional who plans to quit work at 65, makes an annual contribution of $7,500 to a Keogh plan, and is smart enough to be able to achieve average annual total returns of 9% on investments. He expects to live 20 years after quitting work.

WHAT IF YOU DON'T HAVE SUFFICIENT INCOME?

Most older people worry that they will not have sufficient income to live in the style to which they have become accustomed or, if they are genuine 100% certified worriers, that they will go broke and have to rely on welfare. Such tragedies can happen, but they occur only rarely to those who make a sincere attempt to plan their finances.

Besides, homeowners have an untapped source of regular income: the reverse annuity obtained by borrowing against the value of their house. With the property as collateral, they receive a series of monthly loans for the next 10 to 15 years, depending on life expectancy of either or both. The total, plus interest, represents 50% to 60% of the value of the house.

If they die before the loan is paid out, the estate can repay the balance plus interest or forfeit the property. If they outlive the averages, they can sell the home, repay the loan, and live on what's left. Or if the value of the property has appreciated, they can negotiate a new reverse annuity based on the higher worth.

There are added advantages: the income is tax-free as a return of capital, and the interest is tax deductible on federal income tax returns. (See Chapter 20.)

HIGH TAXES ON RETIREMENT INCOME

Don't be fooled by advertisements of thrift institutions and insurance companies that stress that you'll be taking out your retirement income when you are paying taxes at a lower rate. That will *not* be true for many executives and professionals. The current trend of taxation and inflation is likely to continue so that you may

Worksheet 11
Calculating Retirement Income

	Sample	Your Own
1. Current value of pension plan	$ 30,000	_____
2. Number of years to retirement	20	_____
3. Estimated annual rate of return on investments	9%	_____
4. Growth factor (Table 8–1)	5.60	_____
5. Value of current fund at retirement (line 4 × line 1)	$168,000	_____
6. Annual contribution to fund	$ 7,500	_____
7. Growth factor of added money (Table 8–2)	51.16	_____
8. Value of added contributions at 65 (line 6 × line 7)	$383,700	_____
9. Total Keogh assets at retirement (line 5 + line 8)	$551,700	_____
10. Estimated lump-sum payout after taxes: 25% on first $250,000, 35% thereafter	$383,605	_____
11. Annual retirement income, preserving capital (line 10 divided by factor of 11.1 from Table 8–3)	$ 34,559	_____
12. Annual 20-year retirement income using capital (line 10 divided by factor of 10 from Table 8–3)	$ 38,360	_____

SOURCE: Adapted from material published in *Medical Economics*, November 7, 1977.

be paying taxes on after-work withdrawals at rates as high as or even higher than you paid while employed.

Remember: Mr. P, a 34-year-old employee who is now earning $30,000, will be making over $300,000 if his salary rises at an annual rate of 8%. Currently, he's in the 30% tax bracket and is putting aside enough to get, at age 65, half his final work year income: $150,000. This is an exciting prospect, but he forgets that, in all too few years, he'll move into the top tax bracket. Under present laws, when he starts to draw his pension, he'll be paying at the 50% tax rate. His projected $150,000 will be cut to $75,000 and, of course, will buy fewer goods and services each year. Table 8–8 shows that his retirement income, if taken out, will be subject to the maximum tax in 4 years.

Table 8-8. 50% tax rate on retirement income.

Current Salary and Tax Bracket	At this annual rate of salary increase		
	5%	7%	8%
	With this many work years ahead		
	31	22	20
	Your retirement income* will be subject to a 50% tax rate in this number of years		
$30,000 (39%)	23	16	14
40,000 (48%)	17	12	11
50,000 (50%)	12	9	8
60,000 (50%)	8	6	5
70,000 (50%)	5	4	3

SOURCE: Based on data from Professor Joseph A. Lavely, chairman of the Indiana-Purdue University Finance Department, Fort Wayne, Ind.
*At 50% of last working year's salary.

For Mr. Q, a 45-year-old, $70,000-a-year executive, the sad news comes faster. He's already in the 50% tax bracket, so his retirement income will be similarly taxed in three or five years, depending on the rate of annual raises. Says Professor Joseph A. Lavely, chairman of the Indiana-Purdue University Finance Department at Fort Wayne (who is responsible for these figures), "Don't assume that your tax bracket will ever be lower than it is now."

Municipal Bonds May Be Better

Normally, it would not make sense to invest in tax-free securities with already tax-free retirement savings, but it can pay off for a high-rate taxpayer. The interest will be less than that which could be obtained with corporate bonds or stocks, but the ultimate after-work benefits may be greater. At 6%, an annual $4,000 contribution will accumulate to $232,626 in 25 years and not be subject to taxes at withdrawal. The same sum in a retirement plan returning 9% will grow to $369,296 in the same quarter of a century. But at withdrawal, the larger sum will be cut to $234,648: the nontaxable return of $100,000 contribution plus $134,648 which would be left after paying a 50% tax.

Actually, that is somewhat of an overstatement, because (1) the income will be withdrawn over several years and, at some point, the taxes may be under 50%, and (2) the balance of the fund will continue to appreciate from the interest of the municipals and the income and capital gains of the diversified portfolio.

But do not become so enthralled with tax savings that you neglect your primary responsibility: to insure adequate resources for your family if you die and for yourself when you retire. Your employer could go out of business and you could be disabled or fired.

GLOSSARY

actuary. A professional trained in the mathematics of insurance and investments such as the calculation of premiums and reserves, a designer of financially sound pension programs.

annuity. A contract that provides income for a specified period of time, generally after retirement.

custodian. A fiduciary that holds securities or property for safekeeping.

defined-benefits plan. A Keogh or corporate retirement plan in which the annual contribution varies and the participant's retirement income is predetermined.

defined-contributions plan. A Keogh or corporate retirement plan in which the annual contribution is predetermined and the participant's retirement income is variable.

Employee Retirement Income Security Act (ERISA). The law that controls all private retirement plans. It sets rules for prudent investing, vesting of benefits, and reporting to the IRS and Department of Labor.

fixed-benefits plan. A Keogh or corporate retirement plan under which the participant's annual retirement income is fixed at inception and contributions are set by an actuary. Benefits can be up to 100% of the participant's average compensation, for the three highest consecutive years, to a current maximum of $90,050 that is adjustable upward for inflation. In a Keogh plan, contributions can go above the $7,500 a year maximum when based on a percentage of predetermined benefits.

fringe benefits. A service or monetary benefit granted by a corporation to its employee, such as the payment of insurance.

guaranteed-income contract (GIC). A lump-sum investment, for retirement plan assets, available from an insurance company. It guarantees a specific rate of return for a specified number of years.

HR–10. The legislative title to the bill that created Keogh plans.

Individual Retirement Account (IRA). An account that enables persons not covered by pension or profit-sharing plans to provide for their retirement. A participant may contribute 15% of his or her earned income to a maximum of $1,500 a year. If the participant's spouse is not employed, the maximum annual contribution can be $1,750. An employer can contribute up to $7,500 per participant.

Keogh plan (HR–10). A personal retirement plan for owners and employees of sole proprietorships and partnerships. A participant may contribute, tax-free, up to 15% of earned income to a maximum of $7,500, and a little more under special circumstances.

money-purchase plan. A Keogh or corporate retirement plan under which the employer's contributions are predetermined. Each participant's allocation is usually a percent of his or her compensation, and retirement income is based on the sums contributed.

vest. To give a retirement plan participant who has met certain requirements a right to all or some of the accrued retirement benefits, even though service with the employer may terminate before the participant's retirement.

voluntary contribution. Money paid into a personal retirement plan above the usual limit. The contribution is not tax deductible, but the income is tax-free until withdrawn.

years-certain annuity. An annuity that guarantees the number of years payments will be made even if the annuitant dies.

9 The Role of Real Estate in Financial Planning

Real estate can be one of the most important and effective forces in successful financial planning. Properly selected, wisely financed, and well-managed properties can provide excellent income, almost sure appreciation, and welcome tax benefits. Real estate is one of the best ways to beat inflation because, in recent years, its value has increased at a rate faster than the rate of loss of purchasing power.

But do not become too optimistic. Historically, real estate values have been subject to deflation, and some experts predict that this may occur again in the not-too-distant future. Most real estate should be considered a long-term investment. If you pay too much or time your purchase poorly, you will end up with a dwindling asset on which you must meet monthly payments of interest and amortization. Invest in real estate only for the long haul, usually a minimum of five and probably ten years. You have to be smart, and lucky, to be able to profit more quickly.

The best place to start to understand real estate is with your own house. Few investments have risen in value as much in recent years: 17% in 1977 and 1978! Typically, a house bought in 1948 for $15,000 was worth $50,000 in 1978—and more in some areas. If your house is in a good neighborhood and is well maintained, it's value is likely to continue to rise. That's more than can be said for almost any other kind of property. And, meantime, you enjoy its use.

It's great to know that you have such a "profit," but remember it's relative. If you sell, you probably will have to pay more for a new house and the proceeds will probably be reduced by taxes.

When you own your own house, you get income tax deductions for the interest on the mortgage and property taxes and, when you sell, credits for improvements. Under special situations, there are no taxes on part or all of the profits of a sale: (1) when, within 18 months before or after the sale, you purchase or start construction of another principal residence; (2) when the house is sold in connection with a new work location such as a company-forced move. In addition, there is a one-shot $100,000 exemption on gains when the owner is 55 or over and has lived in the house for three of the last five years.

For most people, a home is the best single investment. Whenever you have a choice between adding to the value of your home and using the same dollars for other kinds of investments, it's usually best to improve your home. But do not overimprove in hopes of getting a higher sales price. It's OK to add a pool or solarium for your own pleasure, but the new buyer may not be impressed and will settle for the house with fewer features down the street. Owning the "best" home in the neighborhood is better for pride than for profit.

With all real estate, plan ahead. Property, whether a home, apartment, commercial building, or industrial plant, is subject to factors over which the individual investor has little control: new highways that divert traffic onto once quiet streets; neighbors who fail to keep up their grounds; overcrowded schools; skyrocketing taxes; deteriorating surroundings; and so on. These shifts can come rapidly and dent, if not destroy, your investment. You'll be lucky to be able to sell at a profit, and you will probably have to take back a big mortgage and wait for your monthly check.

One more important point: unlike the stock market, in which all shares of the same company have the same market value, parcels of real estate are never equal. Some properties will zoom in value; the worth of others will rise slowly; and the prices of still others will decline. Every major city has tax liens on once-valuable land and buildings. Real estate is an ever-changing investment that must be watched, cared for, and, usually, utilized and promoted.

The key to successful real estate investing is growth: added value as the result of greater demand, population movements, inflation, and, of course, the attractiveness of the property. Some people, however, like the tangibility; real estate is something they can see, touch, and walk over.

The drawbacks to real estate investments are lack of liquidity (in the inability to sell quickly and profitably), the frequent necessity for additional financing to protect your position, and ever-increasing taxes. At all times and with all types of investment real estate, never underestimate the risks. Remember that *it is more important to know how to get out than how to get in.*

As we'll see, it is always important to get all the facts and to weigh, carefully and realistically, the potential rewards against the possible risks.

THE IMPORTANCE OF LEVERAGE

The highest returns from real estate investments come with leverage: the use of borrowed money to magnify gains by paying 20% to 29% down and borrowing the balance of the purchase price. The simplest way to understand leverage is in connection with raw land, for there are no costs for maintenance, management, and so on.

EXAMPLE: You buy 12 acres of undeveloped land for $30,000: $10,000 cash and a $20,000 mortgage from the seller. If the value of the property rises to $50,000, you can sell, repay the mortgage, and enjoy a healthy $20,000 gain on a cash outlay of $10,000, before taxes.

Without leverage, the original $10,000 would have bought only four acres. With the same double-your-money gain, the sale would have brought $16,664: a comparatively modest 66% profit, again before taxes.

Leverage is even better when there's a small down payment and a large, long-term mortgage. But the carrying charges can be heavy, and there will have to be a cash flow, from some source, to meet the interest and, probably, amortization.

EXAMPLE: You buy a $100,000 building for $10,000 cash and a $90,000, 20-year mortgage. Five years later, you sell the property for $150,000, so you have a fivefold, $50,000 return on a $10,000 outlay—not counting taxes.

But leverage can work both ways. If you make a mistake and the property's worth remains constant, you'll be tying up a lot of money. If the value declines to, say, $80,000, you will lose your cash and be on the hook for the $10,000 difference between the debt and sale price.

The ultimate form of leverage is pyramiding: using currently owned property as the base for new loans to purchase additional holdings.

EXAMPLE: Tom Brown buys a small apartment house for $20,000 down plus a $60,000 mortgage. He paints and renovates and raises the rents so that the building's value rises to $100,000 (with a little help from inflation). Now he has an extra $20,000 in equity and he can (1) sell the property at a profit, (2) take a second mortgage on the basis of the higher value (expensive), or (3) refinance the mortgage to get extra cash (costs are dear and he will lose amortization).

With the new cash, he buys a second property and repeats the process. If all goes well, he pyramids his holdings without additional cash. The risk is overextension: greater debt that can be handled by the income, which can be decreased by vacancies, slow rental payments, higher-than-anticipated operating expenses, and so on. On a larger scale, that's how Bill Zeckendorf built, and destroyed, his real estate empire.

Here's a formula to determine how much income will be needed from the second property as outlined in *Investing in Real Estate*. (See Bibliography.) Let's assume that (1) you have built substantial equity in your house so that you can get a much bigger mortgage. You want to keep your money working, so you obtain a new mortgage at 9.5%. (2) You use the extra cash from the refinancing to make a 30% down payment on an office building. The balance of the purchase is covered by a 10% mortgage.

Purchase price of office building: 100%	
30% down payment with money borrowed on home from 9.5% mortgage: .30 × .095	.0285
10% mortgage on building at 70% of purchase price: .10 × .70	.0700
Minimum required earning rate on purchase	.0985 or 9.85%

Thus the new property must return almost 10% to be profitable.

Now let's see how good an investment this can be. If the building has a net income of $40 per $1,000 of purchase price after all mortgage payments, it earns:

70% mortgage at 10%: .70 × .10	.070
The equity of $300 per $1,000 (down payment) at an earning rate of $40 per $1,000: .30 × .40	1.20
Earning rate on purchase price	.190 or 19%

Since the 19% earning rate is sufficiently above the minimum to provide a cushion for vacancies, unexpected costs, and so on, the new building could be a good buy.

BEATING INFLATION

When you borrow heavily, for a long period, you win because the mortgage interest and amortization are paid with dollars that constantly decrease in value. At a 6% inflation rate, an annual $5,000 payment will be made with depreciating dollars worth $4,700 in year 2, $4,418 in year 3, $4,153 in year 4, and so on. Always try to get the biggest, longest loan you can on investments and your own home while you are young and are making money enough to be sure of handling the constant debt payments. Toward retirement, of course, you may prefer the mental security of freedom from debt.

WHERE TO LOOK FOR REAL ESTATE INVESTMENTS

The best place to find real estate investments is in a familiar area: near your home or vacation spot. You can do your research and watch developments—something that's almost impossible if you live in Peoria and put your money in Duluth.

The opportunities for profits are raw land, commercial buildings, multifamily dwellings, and, occasionally, single-family houses. You can get ideas by watching the ads in local newspapers, driving around the community, and talking with friends and business acquaintances. If you don't have time to do your own checking, get suggestions from a reputable real estate broker.

Raw Land

The best opportunity for long-term gains and for investment with money you will not need for several years is raw land. The income, if any, will probably be small, so you will have to plan to add money regularly for taxes, interest, and possibly amortization or to sell off portions annually. The property should:

• Be suitable for development: near highways, in the path of progress as indicated by population trends or commercial or recreational projects, and not too far from other new building.

• Be available with substantial leverage: no more than 30% down payment plus, hopefully, a mortgage by a seller who will ask only interest in the first three years and ask no penalty for prepayment. That type of installment sale helps the seller, too. He pays capital gain taxes only on the principal received each year. From your viewpoint, it's also worthwhile if only because the interest is a tax deductible expense.

• Have a potential of a 50% rise in value in three to five years. A somewhat lower target may be acceptable if there is assured income from rental to an outdoor club, camping group, or farmer.

• Have annual carrying charges of no more than 10% of the land value.

With inflation at 6%, you can afford to wait, but not for long—especially when taxes rise in a booming area.

To calculate how much your land must increase in value every year to offset costs and yield a profit, use this formula:

For each $1,000 investment:

Down payment: 20% on which you hope to earn 15%: .20 × 15	.030
Loan (from landowner) for 80% of purchase price at 10% interest: .80 × .10	.080
Property taxes at 2.5% of land value: .025 × 1	.025
Special taxes and assessments (roads, road maintenance, and so on) at 3% annually: .03 × 1	.030
Total costs	.165 or 16.5%

Thus, to make a profit, the land must appreciate by more than 16.5% each year. That's easily possible in a fast-growing area.

Timber

If you're the outdoors type, an investment in timber can combine a hobby or recreation with profit. There's possible income from federal subsidies, sure income from timber sales, which are taxed at the lower capital gains rate, and long-term appreciation in the value of the underlying land.

There's also inflation protection because the future price of timber is almost sure to rise. The major competitor, plastics, will continue to cost more because of the ever-rising price of petroleum. Also, as the trees grow, there will be more and better timber to sell.

Here's what to look for:

1. Land with a net cost of about $100 per acre. If you pay $300 per acre and the timber is worth $250, the land cost is $50.
2. Access to paved roads for inexpensive transportation.
3. A lumber mill within harvesting range, no more than 100 miles.
4. Units under 500 acres. There'll be government help to increase the timber yield of small areas: annual payments, to a maximum of $10,000, based on 50% to 70% of the cost of replanting and improving the trees.
5. Expert assistance to tell you the value of the timber, how to harvest, and how to prevent damage from fire, insects, and disease. The cost will be about $1 per acre. Check with the Association of Consulting Foresters, Box 6, Wake, VA 23176.

Even if the trees aren't ready to harvest, you can count on income to pay interest and maintenance expenses by (1) selective cutting of mature trees, (2) leasing hunting and/or fishing rights, (3) setting up a campground, (4) federal subsidies for fire and erosion control, (5) leasing the forest to a wood products company.

Investing in timber does take time and attention, but it's a profitable way to invest in real estate and have fun, too.

Farm Investments

Despite the sharp rise in the price of farmland, a well-chosen investment in a working farm should appreciate by 10% a year. Food supplies, worldwide, are in short supply; world population is growing; farmers are building greater political clout; and there's less farmland to develop.

The immediate attraction is the tax shelter from deductions for mortgage interest and depreciation of buildings, fences, equipment, and livestock. Straight profits are skimpy, seldom more than 5%, so you must either need the tax benefits, enjoy the idea of ownership, or be able to wait for long-term appreciation.

Since few people have the time or expertise to manage a working farm, it's best to hire a professional at a cost of 5% to 8% of gross income. For help, check with your banker or the American Society of Farm Managers and Rural Appraisers in Denver, Doane Agricultural Service in St. Louis, Farmers National Co. in Omaha, or Oppenheimer Industries in Kansas City.

The working farmer is paid either by a share lease or cash rental. Under a share lease arrangement you pay property taxes, insurance, and maintenance and the farmer provides labor and machinery. The costs of seed, fertilizer, and so on are split. The proceeds are divided, so the share lease is better when you anticipate higher crop prices. Cash rental is at a fixed sum for a fixed time. It is paid half at planting and half when the crop is in. That works well when you want assured income and fear that prices will decline. Look for:

1. Land which can bear multiple crops, is in an area with a long growing season, and has good drainage.
2. A small farm of 80 to 160 acres until you feel confident.
3. Land that can support a maximum debt of 50% of value. That should assure a cash flow sufficient to cover your debt burden, taxes, and other base costs. You can get an 85% mortgage through the Federal Land Bank, but carrying charges can be expensive.
4. Long-term appreciation—at least three and more likely five to ten years. Worthwhile profits take time.

Unless you are willing to accept losses, stop dreaming about the bucolic life. You are buying the farm as part of your financial plan. That means you should make money and should give little heed to tax benefits or fulfillment of childhood dreams. Farmland should be an investment, not a tax shelter.

COMPLEX ACCOUNTING

Before getting into a summary of income-producing real estate, it may be well to explain a bit about depreciation. Depreciation represents the losses of value from wear and tear, obsolesence, and so on. If it is on investment properties, the dollars can be used for tax deductions, and they are of greatest interest to individuals in high tax brackets. In most cases, however, depreciation provides a current tax shelter so that future profits will be subject to the lower capital gains tax rate.

Real estate accounting is difficult to understand, and it should always be reviewed with your accountant. Generally, the principles are similar to those applied by corporations to their buildings, machinery, equipment, and so on. The individual real estate investor has a chance to choose the schedule which will assure the greatest tax benefits over the anticipated period of ownership. Once established, the same system must be continued. Any change or early sale can involve the loss of all or most of the tax savings, as will be outlined later.

Here are the choices of depreciation accounting and some guides to their wise use:

Straight Line

In a straight-line depreciation a fixed percent of the price of the property is taken annually over the projected life. That is, if a $40,000 building has a 25-year expectancy, divide $40,000 by 25 to get $1,600, or a depreciation rate of 4% a year. That is the most conservative method.

Declining Balance

When the annual depreciation is accelerated as a percent of the straight-line deduction, the declining balance method is used. A 200% declining balance is double the straight-line allowance; for the $40,000 building it is 8% ($3,200) in the first year. In the second year, the depreciation is calculated by dividing $36,800 ($40,000 minus $3,200) by 24, the number of years left. By the tenth year, the write-off will be less than that of straight-line depreciation: 3.78% versus 4.0%. But the owner will have had the benefit of greater depreciation against income.

It's also possible to use a 150% or 125% declining balance schedule when either fits needs. After all, there's no sense in setting up deductions you cannot use. Once established, however, the original method must be continued.

Sum of Digits

In the sum-of-digits method a fraction instead of a percent is used. Over a 25-year life span, the digits used are 1,2,3,. . . . To find the denominator, add all those numbers to get a total of 325. For the first year, the numerator is the time factor, here 25, so the formula is $25/325$ times $40,000, or $3,077. The next year it's $24/325$ times $36,923, or $2,727. The method is more or less a compromise between slow and fast depreciation.

You won't have to do your own calculations, because there are handy printed tables. With the aid of your accountant, choose the method which is best for you and meets IRS regulations. Once you have taken depreciation, you have reduced your tax base for a future sale.

Type of Property	Depreciation Permitted
Apartments	Any one of the three
Old residential housing with useful life of 20 years	Straight line or 125% declining balance
Office buildings or nonresidential property	Straight line or 150% declining balance (with some exceptions)
Rehabilitation units for low- or moderate-income housing	Straight line over five years
All other used property	Straight line over the remaining useful life

Table 9–1 shows how depreciation alternatives might compare.

INCOME-PRODUCING PROPERTIES

Opportunities with income-producing properties usually involve ownership and always require good management. They include construction of new buildings, buying proven-profitable units, and renovating old structures. In most cases, the returns will be a combination of income, tax benefits, and capital gains. If you choose wisely, finance properly, and manage well, you'll boost your net worth and wallop inflation. But you must be patient; even with good income-producing properties you may need seven years or more to recoup the purchase price.

When you are dealing with small holdings, you can do it yourself at the outset, especially if you are handy with tools and a paintbrush and are willing to spend time on repairs, maintenance, and tenants. Later, when more dollars are involved, you will probably want to join with others.

Again, start looking in your own backyard and concentrate on areas and buildings with growth-in-value possibilities. That's what you want in your financial plan investments. In small towns, where business is rising, look for

Table 9–1. Depreciation alternatives.

Depreciation Method	Percent of Building Cost		
	Year 1	Year 5 Total	Year 10 Total
Straight line			
25 years	4.0 %	20.0%	40.0%
40 years	2.5	12.5	25.0
125% declining balance			
25 years	5.0	22.6	40.1
40 years	3.125	14.7	27.2
200% declining balance			
25 years	8.0	34.1	56.6
40 years	5.0	22.6	40.1
Sum of digits			
25 years	7.7	35.4	63.1
40 years	4.9	23.2	43.3

three or four vacant stores on Main Street. Depending on their condition, they should be available for $25,000 each, and if the present owner won't give back a mortgage, the local bank will probably be helpful if only because of its own future.

The renovation costs will run about $10,000 per store. In some communities, the money may be available under Federal Rehabilitation programs for 3% interest on a 20-year commitment. Such terms give you a lot of leverage, but there can be downside risks too. The community would not qualify for federal aid unless it was in real trouble. Plan ahead; use imagination in the remodeling; and try to line up a specific tenant, perhaps a neighboring retailer anxious to expand or add new lines. You can get a higher rent now and a better sale later.

In larger communities, watch for housing in turning-around neighborhoods. Small apartments, with four or five units, are best, because there'll be no rent control and you can be your own manager. It's easier if you move in, but most small buildings can be handled with the aid of a local superintendent to care for garbage and maintenance. You will have to be a rental agent, complaint department, repairman, and decorator, but if you pick an improving area, you can make out well. Your cash outlay should be about 20% of the cost. All interest, operating expenses (taxes, insurance, maintenance, advertising, and utilities), and depreciation are tax deductible, so an investor in a high tax bracket can save money even when the property seems to run at a loss.

EXAMPLES: In a fast-growing suburb, Richard and Rachel Jones joined a friend to buy four apartments for $160,000. The rents bring in $1,400 a month, just about enough to cover costs. Already, however, the property has appreciated in value, and income will rise with rent hikes.

In Hoboken, New Jersey, Dick and Ella Willenborg bought a brownstone for $120,000, rented six units, and kept the best apartment for themselves, practically rent-free.

If you want to go this route:

• Keep the cost at no more than 100 times monthly rent: that is, $50,000 for a building bringing in $500 a month. You may not find such buildings easily in big cities, but they are available in the suburbs and in the smaller communities.

• Ask yourself: Why is the owner selling? And how can I get out—eventually or in a hurry if there's a financial emergency?

• Pick a specific area and type of housing so you can become knowledgeable about tenants, maintenance, and values.

• Don't buy where there are rent controls. The houses may be bargains, but profits will be hard to come by.

• Don't buy in a city with a declining tax base. That means higher taxes and lower property values.

• Avoid areas where one employer hires more than 20% of the workforce. Look what happened to Youngstown when the steel mills shut down!

• Ban pets (or insist on a big deposit against damage). It's a heck of a job to remove odors and costly to replace carpets.

- Look for big houses. Their prices have not risen as much as those of smaller ones and there can be economies in operation (except for heat).
- Use your imagination. In a large Eastern city, Tom Evans bought a fine old house in a commercial area. Recognizing the attraction of its gargoyles, chandeliers, and fireplaces, he turned it into an elegant women's dress store. With the lease as collateral, he borrowed enough to make renovations and still had more than enough money to meet carrying costs.
- Be ready for constant crises: slow-paying tenants, middle-of-the-night complaints, damage from active children, and so on.
- Consult a lawyer before purchase to be sure you are protected against misrepresentation, and a lawyer and accountant when you sell in order to keep taxes at a minimum.

MAKING MONEY WITH A TWO-FAMILY HOUSE

One way young married couples can accumulate the cash needed for the down payment on a home of their own is by buying a two-family house, fixing it up, renting out one floor, and using the income, tax benefits, and appreciation to supplement their savings. With wise selection, a little upgrading, and a bit of luck, it's possible to obtain the down payment for that dream house in three years—five years sooner than would be possible through a regular savings program.

Here's an example from the files of Jack Ferrara, Mortgage Consultants, Inc., Rockaway, New Jersey. Bill and Marie are paying $3,720 rent for a one-bedroom apartment in a fashionable section of a medium-size city. Their dream house, in the suburbs, is on the market for $80,000. They have $10,000 in the bank and need to double that for the down payment.

Solution: Buy a two-family house for $50,000; get a $37,500 first mortgage from a savings and loan association and a $3,500 second mortgage from the seller. They spend $1,000 to paint the exterior, and Bill makes minor repairs while Marie spruces up the landscaping. Their cost: $5,940:

Mortgage payments	$4,510
Taxes	820
Insurance	110
Maintenance	500
	$5,940

They rent the downstairs apartment for $3,480 and save $860 a year in income taxes by taking deductions for real estate taxes and interest payments. Now their shelter costs are $1,240, so they can add $2,480 a year to their savings.

The house, in an older but stable neighborhood, appreciates at 10% annually. But their dream house is now selling at $106,480 and will require a down payment of $26,620 in just three years.

But Bill and Marie are ready to move up because the savings and the appreciation will provide more than enough for the down payment. Here's what happened over three years:

Normal savings	$ 3,750
Rent savings	7,440
Appreciation	16,550
Mortgage reduction	2,150
	$29,890

That's enough money to buy the new house, pay the closing costs, and buy some furniture!

If the young couple had followed the standard program and continued to rent and save, they would not have had the $20,000 for eight years. By that time, the dream house would have been worth $150,000 and the purchase would have required a far larger down payment.

The Bill and Marie approach takes some sacrifices and mental adjustments. A two-family house is not likely to be in the most fashionable area, and there will be plenty of weekend work; but you may be able to enjoy that new home five years sooner.

JOINING OTHERS

If you prefer to let someone else handle the headaches or want to invest on a larger scale, consider joining a group or building your own team. Joint ventures have the one thing that most promoters and builders want: *money*. Whether the dollars come from your own savings or your personal retirement plan, they give you, and your investing partners, an edge. Take advantage of that position. For example, if the money comes from a pension fund, use it to buy the land, because the fiduciary account cannot benefit from depreciation and should concentrate on income. Thus the fund can own the land, subordinate it to a mortgage, and have a flexible lease tied to rental income. The balance of the money can come from individual investors who can benefit from tax deductions and appreciations.

Usually, real estate joint ventures involve partnerships or syndicates, but occasionally they involve subchapter S corporations or a land trust (explained later in this chapter).

Limited Partnerships

The structure and operations of limited partnerships are set by law. As an investor, (1) your liability is limited to the amount you invest, (2) you cannot take an active part in the management, (3) you share in the profits and losses in relation to your investment, (4) you get all the tax advantages which you would have if you were the sole owner of the property, again on a proportional-to-investment basis, (5) you cannot get your money out unless you have a prior agreement for a buy-out.

Typically, a local partnership would consist of:

• A real estate broker: someone who knows local values, has broad contacts to find suitable properties, is well thought of by local financial institutions, and is able to administer the project directly or through a qualified manager.

• A real estate lawyer who has political savvy. He can expedite zoning

changes, be aware of future government plans, and be experienced in setting up a structure which will provide the greatest tax benefits.
• Friends or acquaintances who have extra funds for investing and are seeking goals similar to yours.

And if you want to become involved with new construction, add a reputable builder who is accepted by local bankers, is bondable, and is willing to risk his own capital.

Before getting into examples of how your local group can operate, a word of warning against another type of limited partnership which is promoted by some brokerage firms. In this type of real estate joint venture, you buy "shares" for $500 and $10,000 each. The sales pitch is that you can tax shelter as much as $6,000 for each $1,000 investment. That is possible when the deal involves rapid depreciation in the early years.

What you may not be told is that the tax benefits come at the expense of your equity, so that, in 15 years or so, the residual value of the property in which you have invested is only slightly greater than the mortgage. You bought a tax shelter which ends up with little or no assets. And the salesman pockets a hefty commission.

Typical Income-Producing Investments

Now back to the local limited partnership. The five to ten participants should be able to come up with $50,000 to $100,000 which, combined with a mortgage, can buy or build a property worth $400,000 to $1,000,000.

Generally, the same rules apply to the acquisition and ownership of both new and existing structures. You supply the capital and the professionals do the work: selection, financing, rentals management, and so on. Your target returns—from income, tax benefits, and capital gains when sold—should be 15% to 20% a year. You may not do as well in the early years, by you can reach, or surpass, such profits over the long term, especially when there's appreciation in value. That's why real estate should be included in financial planning. But never forget that there are risks, so, just as with securities, stick with quality and value and time your investments when the probable rewards outweigh the ever-present risks.

Here are examples of local building or investment opportunities as outlined by John B. Halper, New York real estate–mortgage consultant.

Apartment House

Look for a small apartment house (16 to 36 units) in an accessible location, attractively landscaped, well designed, and with on-site parking. The cash outlay should be about 20% of the first $1 million and 15% thereafter. For a 20-unit garden apartment, costs would run about $21,000 per unit: $2,000 for land and $19,000 for the building. That's a total investment of $420,000. It would be financed by $84,000 cash and a $336,000 mortgage with provision for prepayment or, in some cases, a short-term second mortgage.

With a small local partnership, there should be no trouble in raising that

$84,000 cash plus a few extra dollars for start-up expenses. The goals, as part of an individual's financial plan, should be modest income, reasonable tax benefits, and maximum capital gains through future refinancing or sale.

The size of the mortgage on an income-producing property depends somewhat on the value of the property but primarily on the annual income. The greater the income the larger the mortgage. The key, says Halper, is the constant factor of debt service—the percent of the original loan representing the interest and amortization over the life of the mortgage. "At 9.25% interest for 25 years, the constant for debt service is 10.28%, so the income should be $34,541 to justify the $336,000 mortgage."

For investors, the rental property should show net bottom line earnings, after debt payments, of at least 10% before depreciation: in the example, $8,400 on the $84,000 cash outlay. Many well-managed, well-located apartments are more profitable.

Here's a summary of what the investors anticipate per year (for details of a typical profit and loss statement, see the categories of Worksheet 12).

20 units rented, at $350 per month	$84,000
Less 5% vacancy	4,200
Gross income	79,800
Expenses	70,000
Net income	$ 9,800

On the $84,000 cash, that's an 11.6% return. Add tax deductions for interest, investment tax credit, and depreciation (depending on the accounting method used), and the effective returns are well over 15%. The big benefit comes later when, as the result of a successful operation, the rents can be raised and the property refinanced for an additional $100,000 or more.

Commercial Opportunities

Look around your community for new buildings which are needed: a strip shopping center or a free-standing building for a fast-food operation. The structures are standard and therefore comparatively inexpensive. In the right locations, they can be steady money makers.

A strip shopping center is a cluster of five to eight stores along a highway and close to a residential area. Hopefully, the anchor store will be a branch of a bank or savings and loan (which will also provide the mortgage). Other tenants might include a drug store, beauty parlor, superette or delicatessen, and hardware franchise—at least one of which has good, bankable credit.

For a $200,000 package, a small group should be able to borrow 75%, so it will need $50,000 cash. Since leases will be on a net-net basis (the tenant pays all taxes, repairs, maintenance, and so on), the annual cash income should be about $6,000 plus depreciation. And in a few years, a profitable deal can be sold or refinanced. Still, there are risks: a poor location, vacancies, tenant failures, and unanticipated expenses.

The same concept can be applied to a free-standing building for a fast-food or service franchise. The deal may give you a chance to do some bargaining to get: (1) the national firm to guarantee the first 20% of the rent on a 10- to 15-year lease and (2) the operator to add a percent of gross volume above a preset minimum.

Once the word gets around about the availability of money, you'll be offered scores of deals. The best bet, says Halper, is a package such that the developer plans, acquires the land, finds a builder, and signs good tenants. That approach gives the mortgage broker a viable package to present to potential lenders.

Syndicates

Broadly speaking, syndicates are king-size versions of limited partnerships. They involve large sums and a large property or properties. They occasionally invest in raw land but usually in income-producing real estate: an apartment house, office building, motel, or shopping center. They are professionally sponsored and managed.

Private syndicates often consist of a small group of wealthy individuals. Public offerings are designed for a large group of small investors. The operations and tax benefits of both types are similar to those of limited partnership: income, tax benefits, and hoped-for appreciation.

Public programs must be filed with the SEC, so all potential risks will be spelled out in the prospectus. *Even if you are dealing with your brother-in-law, read that prospectus.* By law, it must provide complete information on financial projections, management, operations, and investment perils.

In all joint ventures, the keys to success are the ability and integrity of the general partner. That individual should have a strong personal balance sheet and be liquid enough to have access to extra cash in case of cost overruns in building or cash flow problems in operations. Most important, he should have a proven record of competence and success.

Always be skeptical and cautious. With a new building, dribble out your money: check 1 at the setup of the deal, check 2 when 50% of the construction is completed, check 3 when the certificate of occupancy is issued, check 4 when the permanent mortgage is approved, and check 5 when the project is fully rented. You can, of course, do that only with private deals. Always consult your lawyer and tax adviser about terms and risks. Depreciation can cut taxes, but there can be serious trouble if the project fails or your have to get your money out.

On the average, half of the returns from income-producing properties will be the result of tax benefits, primarily depreciation. As a return of capital, that money is not subject to income taxes. Accelerated depreciation can be used with residential properties but not always with commercial or industrial buildings. Fast depreciation sounds attractive because of its bigger benefits at the outset, but that method of accounting can take away an extra chunk of profits when you sell, especially if you have to get out earlier than anticipated.

EXAMPLE: Sam Grossman, in the 50% tax bracket, puts $20,000 into a syndicate formed to build an apartment house. For the first four years, he takes tax deductions of $10,000 a year. Since he deducts half of those annually, he gets his money back quickly—on paper.

During the next 10 years, Sam continues to get smaller tax losses plus modest cash income. In 15 years, he can hope to average a 16% to 20% annual rate of return if there are no major problems.

But, stresses Halper, there are substantial risks. (1) If Sam has to sell soon after his investment, his profits may be taxable, and if the sale is at a loss (most likely), the total losses will probably be greater than the tax benefits. Under IRS regulations, if partners get out of a property within 8½ years (120 months on government-subsidized projects), they may have to pay taxes, at ordinary rates, on the difference between straight-line and accelerated depreciation. (2) Operating costs may be higher and/or rental income lower than projected. (3) More capital may be needed because of delays in construction, etc.

To repeat: *Real estate can be rewarding, but it can also be risky*. Keep that note at the top of your financial planning worksheet.

Other Types of Joint Ventures

The *subchapter S corporation* is a special legal format which enables an investor or shareholder to pass corporate income and losses directly to his personal income tax statement. Because it involves a corporation, individual liability is limited.

The arrangement is better in theory than in practice. It's complex and difficult to form; it requires someone to spend time in property management; and it must be conducted under restrictive rules. Financing is difficult because all shareholders must agree to assume liability as individuals. The loss pass-through cannot exceed the amount of the shareholder's basis plus any loans made to the corporation. That means the investor cannot claim a share of any mortgage to lever the total investment.

Subchapter S can be worthwhile if you are part of a family group, retain a skilled attorney, and have considerable experience in real estate investing.

A *land trust* is a convenient way to eliminate the necessity for 100% agreement among investors. The trustee makes all the decisions. Under the arrangement, the property is transferred into the land trust, so the investor owns an interest in the trust, not the real estate. Creditors cannot levy a lien and force a sale, but they can make a legal claim against the individual's joint ownership interest.

Land trusts are not legal in all states. They should be used sparingly, and then only with the counsel of an experienced lawyer.

GUIDELINES FOR PARTNERSHIPS AND SYNDICATES

1. *Deal only with established, reputable groups or individuals*. Check bank reference, credit standing, community involvement (with the local chamber of commerce and board of realtors), and, most important, past clients.

Beware of glib talkers, especially those who boast of never having had a loss. Even the best operators and promoters succeed only 80% of the time.

2. *Insist that the promoter put up some of his own money,* the more the better. Don't let anyone get a free ride.

3. *Review the agreement with an experienced real estate attorney.* For names of experts, contact the American Society of Real Estate Counsellors, 155 East Superior Street, Chicago, IL 60611.

4. *Watch out for complex details and obfuscating language you do not understand.* Some promoters use every legal loophole and tax dodge to use your money or get the most for themselves rather than all participants. There may be clauses which appear proper but can be costly. For example, part ownership of a lease is worth less than the equivalent ownership of a leased property.

5. *Judge every venture as a business venture, not as a tax shelter alone.* If there are no profits, you will be shelling out hard-earned dollars for little or no gain.

6. *Never invest cash which you will need in the next five to ten years.* Early withdrawal will probably mean a substantial loss in dollars and tax benefits. Real estate should always be considered a long-term investment.

7. *Concentrate on what you will make, not the size of the fees or the sales commissions.* Able management is expensive but worthwhile when the net returns are added up. You must be willing to pay for expertise. At the same time, be sure you get it.

8. *Look for cash flow, tax shelter, and equity buildup to total well above the prime bank rate:* a minimum of 12% on residential and commercial property and 20% on motels and so on.

9. *Look for a long-term first mortgage from a reputable lender;* it means that the financial institution has confidence in the project. You'll get excellent leverage and a better chance for profitable refinancing long before the maturity date.

10. *Be skeptical of all appraisals.* If you are putting up a lot of money, insist on two checks. Even a reputable firm can become overly enthusiastic if the broker is an important client. On the average, a fair valuation or purchase price is four times the annual rent for office buildings, ten times annual cash production for apartments, and nine times rent for a shopping center.

Remember that the loss of one major tenant, such as W. T. Grant in shopping centers, can cause havoc with realistic appraisals.

11. *Discount all projections by 20%, and double the years targeted for success.* There can be unforeseen events: delays in building, fires, new highways, and so on. Be conservative. If things work out well, you'll be that much richer and happier.

12. *Be wary of investing in a business rather than real estate.* If the tenant gets into financial trouble, there will be pressure from some investors to take over the operation of the bowling alley, motel, or whatever.

Any such operation requires skills and experience different from those of property management. In most cases, take your loss and relax. Otherwise, you may have to come up with more money.

13. *Monitor the management.* Watch for signs of trouble: vacancies, com-

petition from new buildings, poor maintenance, sloppy landscaping, and similar negatives. If your checks are late or the reports incomplete, start worrying. If the problems persist, you can be sure that the word is out and you'll be lucky to sell out at any price.

And one final caveat for all real estate investments in which you join with others. Be skeptical. Take nothing for granted. Investigate before, during, and after every deal. Few areas of business offer greater opportunities for fraud, misrepresentation, and petty finagling than real estate. The manager of an apartment house can lease furniture from his brother-in-law (at a high cost, of course); the broker can double-charge fees; the superintendent can pocket the rent and report a vacancy. Real estate is a business in which most operators have minimum capital and maximum hope—and nerve.

Get All the Facts

The same warning goes for all properties in which you have a chance to invest. Real estate agents are not noted for veracity or full disclosure. They tend to understate costs and overstate potential values.

Here's an example of a deal that, at first look, appeared very worthwhile: $5,631 net income a year, after depreciation, on a 50-unit apartment house. Cost: $500,000 with $100,000 down and a $400,000 mortage at 10% for 25 years. *But the facts were not so profitable;* see Table 9–2.

ANNUAL REVIEW

To keep your financial plan on line, it is essential to make an annual review of all of your real estate holdings: your home, summer cottage, condominium,

Table 9–2. Why you need to check all property data.

	What the Salesman Said	What the Audit Showed
Annual gross income	$120,000	$100,000
Operating expenses		
Real estate taxes	20,000	24,000
Insurance	4,800	7,500
Electricity, gas, heat	9,350	10,000
Water	2,300	2,500
Rubbish removal	1,000	1,200
Repairs and maintenance	2,100	9,000
Supplies	800	1,600
Legal, accounting, and advertising	2,100	2,400
Management	8,300	15,400
Total	$ 50,750	$ 73,600
Gross profit	69,250	26,400
Mortgage amortization	43,619	43,619
Net cash flow	25,631	(17,219)
Depreciation at 4%	20,000	20,000
Net after depreciation	$ 5,631	($ 37,219)

investments, and participations in partnerships or syndicates. You want to be sure that your holdings are profitable and, if they are not, that you are in a position to make them so.

There should be two checks: of operating costs and of appreciation. You may not be able to get exact information on joint ventures, but do the best you can. Whenever possible, keep accurate year-to-year records. They will be valuable for tax reports.

Operating Costs

Use Worksheet 12 to determine what each property is really costing you: the net after taxes and the tax savings. You should have the data for your home and vacation dwelling in your files. For investment properties, refer to the annual report of the manager or general partner. You don't have to be correct to the last penny, because the objective is to utilize the information in your overall financial planning. If you find that costs are out of line with projections, take action. Economize where you can; raise the rents on investment property; or consider selling.

Worksheet 12
Review of Operating Costs of Real Estate Properties

	Home	Vacation Dwelling	Commercial Investment	Apartment Investment
1. Property taxes	___	___	___	___
2. Mortgage interest	___	___	___	___
3. Improvements	___	___	___	___
4. Insurance	___	___	___	___
5. Maintenance	___	___	___	___
6. Utilities	___	___	___	___
7. Other costs	___	___	___	___
8. Total operating expenses	___	___	___	___
9. Rental income	___	___	___	___
10. Net operating costs (line 8 minus line 9)	___	___	___	___
11. Tax savings*	___	___	___	___
12. After-tax cost (line 10 minus line 11)	___	___	___	___

SOURCE: John B. Halper & Co., Inc., New York.

*For your home or vacation dwelling, line 1 plus line 2 multiplied by your tax bracket; for commercial and apartment buildings, line 10 plus depreciation multiplied by your tax bracket.

Appreciation

To help monitor and project your financial plans, it's necessary to know the rate of growth of your real estate investments. That is difficult unless you are working with a professional, who must keep such data, or are willing to pay for annual appraisal, which is probably not worthwhile until you have investments of over $1 million.

You can track progress with Worksheet 13 and Table 9–3. The current market value can be approximated by prices paid for similar properties, by the value assessed for tax purposes, and by offers from reputable agents. You are trying to find a rate of growth, so have some leeway in your figures. But always err on the low side. Most people have exalted ideas of the value of their properties.

Since real estate is a long-term investment, it's best to delay the check of appreciation until you have held the property for three years. Skip a year before updating. Use Worksheet 13 and determine the rate of appreciation by Table 9–3.

RELATE TO FINANCIAL PLANNING

As you review the preceding calculations and others that you may undertake for your own edification, keep in mind that, with the exception of your dwellings, real estate is just another investment which is supposed to help you reach your

Worksheet 13
Checking Real Estate Appreciation

	Your Home	Vacation Dwelling	Commercial Building*	Apartment Investment*
1. Purchase price	$50,000	$32,000	$150,000	$200,000
2. Capitalized improvements	5,000	1,000	11,000	16,000
3. Total invested capital (line 1 plus line 2)	55,000	33,000	161,000	216,000
4. Current market value**	93,000	42,000	255,000	380,000
5. Appreciation factor (line 4 divided by line 3)	1.69	1.27	1.58	1.76
6. Years held	7	5	3	9
7. Annual compound rate of appreciation (Table 7–3)	8%	6%	14+%	6%

SOURCE: John B. Halper & Co., Inc., New York.

*If jointly owned, divide by the number of partners.

**Take an average of estimates of real estate agent and bank's appraisal for refinancing and assessed value (project to full worth when on a percentage basis). Be sure to subtract possible sales commission and closing costs.

Table 9–3. Annual rates of appreciation.

Appreciation Rate	Rate of Appreciation for Number of Years Owned						
	3	5	7	9	11	13	15
6%	1.2%	1.3%	1.5%	1.7%	1.9%	2.1%	2.4%
8	1.3	1.5	1.7	2.0	2.3	2.7	3.2
10	1.3	1.6	1.9	2.4	2.9	3.5	4.2
12	1.4	1.8	2.2	2.8	3.5	4.4	5.5
14	1.5	1.9	2.5	3.3	4.2	5.5	7.1

SOURCE: John B. Halper & Co., Inc., New York.
Note: From Worksheet 13:
1. Find the years of property ownership, item 6.
2. Run down the year column of this table to find the figure closest to the appreciation factor, item 5.
3. Refer back to the first column of this table to get the appreciation rate over the years of ownership.

financial goals. *Do not fall in love with property.* The farmland may be beautiful for a twice-a-year outing, but if it has not appreciated in value or has no strong prospects of appreciating, sell it. Of course, you may be able to afford the luxury of an investment which is not fully productive.

Your objective with all your investment assets should be to get the greatest total returns without unnecessary risks. What you do, or do not do, today, will influence what you can, or cannot, do in the future.

RELYING ON PROFESSIONALS

Most explanations of real estate investments so far have involved, fully or partly, do-it-yourself projects. There are other areas in which professionals take full charge: exchanging properties, real estate investment trusts (REITs), and pooled, bank-managed funds. With all those you turn your assets, or savings, over to someone else and pay fees for services.

Exchanging Real Estate

When your real estate investments become substantial and you are in a high tax bracket, consider swapping properties. It's an excellent way to defer part or all of the capital gains taxes.

Under section 1031 of the IRS code, you can exchange "like properties." The term is broadly interpreted, so you can trade lakefront lots for apartments, stores for office buildings, condominiums for land, and so on. Eventually, when you do sell, you will have to pay taxes on the capital gains on all real estate swapped. In the meantime, you can (1) preserve your equity that otherwise would be lost in taxes and (2) set up an increased base for depreciation to shelter other income.

EXAMPLES: Janice Stevens has a $70,000 building on land worth $40,000, so the total value is $110,000. Since the land is not depreciable and she can use a higher depreciation base, she swaps for a $90,000 building on land worth $20,000. Now she has an extra $20,000 to use for tax deductions.

That's a deal you can handle yourself, but as you get deeper into the investment area, transactions can become more complex. Then they require the time, skill, and contacts of a professional. (For information, contact National Society of Exchange Counsellors, P.O. Box 5906, San Jose, CA 95150.) Here's a complex series of deals that took six months to complete, involved sizable commissions, and satisfied three different investors.

Mr. A owned a building purchased ten years ago and now worth $230,000 for a substantial gain. The mortgage is down to $110,000, so the equity is $120,000. Mr. A is in the 50% tax bracket, so he needs more depreciation to reduce his taxes.

B is ready to buy A's building for cash, but A prefers to swap.

C wants to unload his $550,000 building on any favorable terms.

In exchange for his building ($120,000 equity), $20,000 cash, and a note for $410,000, A acquires C's property. A now has a tax-deferred deal and a much bigger depreciation base.

To complete the swaps, C sells A's buildings for $120,000 cash. Everybody gets what he wants, and the real estate agent gets hefty commissions for his hard work.

If you are in a high tax bracket and can benefit from tax postponement and depreciation, swapping real estate can be an excellent technique in financial planning. But success requires expert counsel to be sure there is no slip in the transfers, because IRS agents almost always check such deals.

Real Estate Investment Trusts (REITs)

REITs are similar to closed-end investment companies. They sell shares to the public and pool the proceeds for investments in land and buildings.

Until 1974, REITs were among the most rewarding investments: they offered high yields and substantial appreciation. The principle is sound; the REIT is a way for the small investor to participate in the ownership of real estate. The practice, however, has left much to be desired.

In their battle to outperform competition, many REIT managers made stupid loans, were guilty of fraud and mismanagement, and rolled up overwhelming debts. Most of the funds have been reorganized with horrendous losses to investors and sponsors. Loans have been written off or stretched out at interest rates as low as 1%, and properties have been auctioned off at a fraction of cost.

There are a few well-managed REITs, but generally their operations have not justified inclusion in investment plans. If you want to speculate, you may make money. Shares are selling at up to 50% discounts below book value, and there's often a dividend, half tax-free, as a return of capital. That's not too bad a deal for savings you can afford to risk for a couple of years.

Pooled Bank-Managed Funds

Major banks set up pooled bank-managed funds to invest in, own, and in some cases operate income-producing real estate. Investments are made directly for large trusts, estates, and corporate pension plans and indirectly for small accounts through a commingled fund.

Mindful of their fiduciary responsibilities, managers of many of the bank-managed funds have been more conservative than their REIT counterparts. As a result, most of the bank funds have compiled long, consistent records of superior performance. Wachovia Individual Capital Management, associated with the Wachovia Bank in Winston-Salem, North Carolina, reported a compounded annual rate of return of 9.2% for the eight years ending December 31, 1977. Direct accounts, which could benefit from depreciation, had an extra return of about 3%, depending on the tax bracket of the investor. Both figures were net after deduction of an annual fee of 1% of the total market value as determined by outside appraisers.

To give you an idea of what to look for with a similar fund in your area, here are the Wachovia criteria:

- For direct investments, a minimum of $25,000 and one month's notice for withdrawal.
- For shares of commingled fund; a minimum of $2,000 and opportunity to sell shares to other participants.

The investment standards also are worth reviewing:

- *Quality.* Prime, income-producing properties in growing, stable areas: shopping centers, office buildings, warehouses. No residential holdings such as apartments, condominiums, hotels, or motels because they demand intensive day-to-day management.
- *Prudence.* Financing and lease arrangements designed to suit the needs of the purchaser. All properties are selected to provide protection against inflation and a competitive investment yield.
- *Diversification by geographic area and type.* Long-term objectives call for 40% to 50% in industrial or distribution centers and office or warehouse facilities in prime business and industrial parks, 20% in office buildings on the outskirts of major cities, 20% in medium-size shopping centers, and 10% to 20% in development land ready for immediate use—zoned and with water, sewer, and other utilities and, if possible, completed roads.

These standards can help you in your own selection of real estate investments. They are similar to the Quality, Value, and Timing for stock market success.

INVESTING IN MORTGAGES

In most real estate investments, you'll be the one borrowing money with a mortgage. But someone has to make those loans, and if you want security and better than thrift account returns for a long time, first mortgages can be worthwhile investments. And if you're willing and able to take extra risks, second mortgages can provide even higher income, although usually for a shorter period.

As has been stressed, long-term mortgages are more advantageous for the borrower than the lender because they are repaid with ever-depreciating dollars. Even more important for financial planning, there are few opportunities for appreciation: with home loans when the mortgage is bought at a discount; with commercial loans (which typically involve large sums) when there's a kicker such as a share of profits above a certain limit or part ownership of the building through stock, rights, or warrants. Still, some people find satisfaction in knowing they can get a monthly check, with a 9½% or 10% yield, for the next 20 or 25 years.

To most people, mortgages are most valuable toward the end of their financial planning when they want steady income during retirement. They sell the old homestead and take back a mortgage. During working years, however, mortgage investments should be made only when you are willing to tie up capital, accept responsibility for collections, and recognize the possibility of having to go to the bother and expense of foreclosure proceedings.

First Mortgages

If you are investing in first mortgages, set up a regular program, preferably with $50,000 and plans for regular additions. You can use your own savings or money from your personal retirement plan. With such a sum, you can diversify through loans on old houses, to new families, on homes in different areas, on commercial properties, and on apartments. Always deposit the monthly checks in a daily interest savings account so that you will build funds for new loans.

One way to start is to join with friends who have had considerable experience and have developed good contacts for leads. If money is tight, ask your banker about participations. With participations you take 20% to 30% of the loan and the bank provides expertise in selection of properties, screening borrowers, and administering details. Your returns will be slightly less than with a straight mortgage, but you won't be bothered with details. When you can invest $100,000 or more, contact a local mortgage broker about joint ventures. He will find new deals, handle collections, check insurance, and set up a tax escrow account.

Once you are fully committed, have substantial holdings, and do not need current income, consider setting up a trust to hold the mortgages. The tax savings will provide more money for new loans.

Discount Mortgages

When you become more confident and can count on readily available cash, watch for discount mortgages: those selling below face value because of their low original rate of interest. For example, a $20,000 mortgage at 6% might be bought for $15,000 when the interest rate is over 8%. You can count on competitive yields, capital gains at maturity, and extra security: the $20,000 was only 67% of the $30,000 home value; the $15,000 represents only 50% of the property's worth without appreciation.

Second Mortgages

As subordinated loans, second mortgages can be risky, but you will get interest of over 15% and relatively short payouts of five to ten years. Make certain that there is adequate equity in case the borrower defaults. On a $50,000 house with a $30,000 first mortgage, a second loan for $10,000 is OK. But that should be the limit. To minimize risks, make sure that the agreement includes:

1. *An acceleration clause* with the option of demanding full payment before the property can be resold.

2. *A priority clause* specifying no increase in the first mortgage until the second is paid. Otherwise, a fast operator could refinance his first loan, get back his down payment, and abandon the property. To protect yourself, you would have to take over the property.

3. *A notification clause* that, if there's a default on the first mortgage, you agree to continue payments only if notified in advance. Without such a provision, the property could be auctioned off and the first mortgage satisfied and there would be little or nothing left for your claim. With the clause, you can submit your agreement to the trustee and, if the sale price is too low, to protect your investment, you can bid more to cover the loan.

For bigger profits, and risks, check around for distress second mortgages, which can be bought at discounts of 25% to 40% because the holder needs the money fast. That is a rough area, however. You must be tough-skinned; you must make sure of prompt payments; and you must be willing to start legal action to protect your investment. There's no room for sentiment.

SUMMARY

To get an overview of the costs, risks, and potential rewards of real estate investments, Table 9-4 provides a summary of the major opportunities. Under the right conditions, real estate is one of the few investments that can provide triple benefits for financial planning: income, appreciation, and tax benefits. Most people would settle for two out of three.

Table 9–4. Real estate investments.

Type	Tax Shelter	Down Payment	Risk	Rates of Return
Apartment	Yes	20–35%	Moderate	8–15 %
Hotel or motel	Yes	25–40	High	15–20
Recreation home	Yes*	10–20	Moderate	0–20
Nursing home	Yes	25–40	High	10–15
Office building	Yes	20–25	Moderate	8–15
Shopping center	Yes	20–30	Moderate	15–20
Raw land	No			
Exurban		30–50	High	75–100
Suburban		20–50	Moderate	50–75
Urban		30–50	High	25–50
Warehouse	Yes	20–30	Moderate	10–15

SOURCE: C. Colburn Hardy, *Dun & Bradstreet's Guide to Your Investments* (New York: Crowell, 1978).
*Subject to strict IRS rules on personal use. Realistically, you'll make money only if the dwelling is rarely used for pleasure.

Your home is probably the best investment you'll ever make, and with a little hard work and a lot of common sense you can find profitable opportunities in your own community. If you enjoy, and understand, real estate and can allocate time for adequate research and supervision, give it a prominent place in your personal and pension plan portfolios. Concentrate your savings even at the expense of securities. Unless you are wealthy enough to hire professional management, you will not be able to watch both the stock and real estate markets.

The best time to learn about, and invest in, real estate is when you are in your forties, earning enough to be able to use the tax benefits, and expect to live long enough to reap long-term appreciation.

Above all, be conservative. For the past two decades, most real estate holdings have been very profitable, but there's no guarantee that, even with inflation, values will continue to soar. In planning ahead, remember that, whenever there are unusual rewards, there will also be greater risks.

GLOSSARY

amortization. The gradual extinguishment of a mortgage by periodic payments, usually at the same time as interest is paid.

depreciation. An accounting term used in the lowering of the value of property. For tax purposes, the most widely used forms are *straight line*—taking a fixed percent of the value each year over the life of the property: for example, 10% for 10 years; *declining balance*—speeding up the deductions at 125%, 150%, 200% of the rate of straight-line depreciation; *sum of digits*—using a fraction instead of a percent to calculate the annual deductions.

mortgage. A loan against property that is usually payable monthly by fixed sums including both interest and amortization. A *second mortgage* is a loan which is subordinate to the first mortgage. It is used by home buyers who lack adequate cash and by investors who are willing to take extra risks for higher-than-first mortgage rewards. A *reverse mortgage* is an arrangement whereby the homeowner borrows against the value of his house. The individual, usually an older person, receives a monthly payment for actuarial life.

net-net lease. A lease on commercial property under the terms of which the tenant pays rent plus all property expenses such as taxes and utilities.

partnerships. If a limited partnership, an investment entity managed by a general partner. The individual investor cannot take an active part in management, has liability limited to his investment, and shares in profits, losses, and tax advantages. A *syndicate* is similar, but it involves larger sums and more investors and may involve publicly traded securities.

tax shelter. An investment, such as a home, residential, or commercial property, that permits deductions against current income. Interest and, when there is income, depreciation and operating expenses are deductible.

10 How to Invest for Maximum Total Returns

Investing is an integral part of financial planning. Yet, to many people, management of savings is an afterthought—something to be turned over to someone else or to be learned later when resources are ample.

Nothing could be more foolish! Investing should start with the first few dollars earned after school. When you have a job, the first check you write every month should be to yourself for investment in some way: in a savings account, property, securities, a collection, or whatever. Wise investing is the core of every successful financial plan.

That is seldom the case with ambitious executives and busy professionals. They do not set aside time enough to develop a true concept of the power of money. They work hard to acquire wealth and then either set the wealth aside at minimal returns or throw it away on speculations. They fail to take advantage of their own skills and common sense to determine specific dollar objectives, establish disciplines, and manage their resources.

As pointed out earlier, one of the great forces of money making is reinvestment—the magic of compounding, earning income on income. In a working lifetime, every $100 invested at age 25 can be worth at least $6,400 when you retire. You will have to pay taxes from other sources unless the money is tax-sheltered, but even with small, consistent savings, you will be secure and, if you invest wisely, you can be rich. That's what financial planning is all about.

Unfortunately, most people learn the hard way: by stupid "investments" or foolish speculations. They try to make money in a hurry. It seldom works out that way. *The tortoise* did *beat the hare!*

That does not rule out risk taking; but when you speculate, recognize that you are bucking the odds. That is especially true of "growth stocks"—those shares of unseasoned companies which are touted as a new Xerox or Polaroid and whose values will "soar and, in a few years, provide all the money you will ever need."

Once in a while, of course, there are such bonanzas, and if you have personal knowledge of the products and personnel of a well-managed small company and have confidence in the persons' business (not promotional, technical, and sales) ability, buy the stock gingerly with extra savings you can afford to lose. Then, write at the head of the record sheet: *Only three of every ten new publicly owned companies survive and only one is successful.*

If you are lucky enough to pick a winner, add more money when there's a new stock issue or the company announces plans for listing on a stock exchange.

Better yet, borrow against the shares you own. If the bank is willing to lend against such collateral, you may be on your way to those dreamed-of profits. Even then, however, be wary of making a substantial commitment unless you are under 45 years of age and have time to recoup losses. Only when the company has a proven record of performance, at least five, and, preferably, ten years of strong, profitable growth, can such securities be regarded as investments.

So much for what not to do. Now let's get down to the fundamentals of stock market success: Quality, Value, and Timing (QVT).

Anyone who understands QVT, takes time to apply them intelligently, follows the rules, and is patient should be able to achieve average total annual returns (income plus appreciation) of 10%. With experience and/or professional assistance and a little luck, he can hope to boost the value of savings by 15% a year over a period of time when compounding can add so much.

This chapter will show you how to achieve such results. You won't get those rewards every year, but over a decade or so the goals are realistic as long as the U.S. capitalistic system survives. There is always competition for capital. The wise investor moves where the demand is greatest. If unmanaged investments, such as bonds or savings certificates, can yield 8%, it's logical to believe that properly managed accounts can do better. To me, it seems foolish to pay a professional such as a bank, insurance company, investment company, or investment adviser unless the results are substantially better than those you can obtain yourself.

As the result of the erratic, and generally disappointing, action of the stock market in the 1970s, many people are afraid of securities. They forget that managing money is a long-term process. Certainly, Wall Street is often puzzling, is usually frustrating, and frequently acts foolishly in the short term. That is understandable because the stock market is the end result of the fears and hopes of millions of people and involves billions of dollars. The temporary swings reflect rumors, headlines, excessive optimism, and dire pessimism. But over the long term, the stock market is always logical. The securities traded on major exchanges are the core of our economic life, and profit is the name of the game.

The reasons I believe in the money-making power of common stocks are summarized in two tables: Table 10–1, which shows how investments in American business, as measured by the Dow Jones Industrial Average (DJIA), have been profitable over the years, and Table 10–2, which illustrates how their total returns can be a hedge against inflation.

The long-term progress of the stock market has always been up, despite dips and plateaus. It's easy to forget that, in 1950, the DJIA was 235. Since then, it's moved over 1000 several times, and many analysts predict that it will be above 2000 by the year 2000. That means that any moderately successful investor will double his money in a little over 20 years. Add the returns of reinvestment of income and appreciation and an intelligent investor can do vastly better. Taxes are, of course, important but not nearly as much so as many people think.

That does not mean that one should always invest only in common stocks.

Table 10-1. Stock market performance, 1930 to 1979.

Year	Dow Jones Industrial Average High	Low	Last	Price/Earnings Ratio	Earnings	Dividends	Inflation
1930	294	158	165	27–12	$ 11.02	$11.13	−2.6%
1935	148	97	144	23–15	6.34	4.55	+1.0
1940	153	112	131	14–10	10.92	7.06	+1.6
1945	196	151	193	19–14	10.56	6.69	+2.6
1950	235	197	235	7.7–6.4	30.70	16.13	+4.3
1955	488	388	488	14–11	35.78	21.58	+2.0
1960	685	566	616	21–18	32.21	21.36	+1.9
1965	969	841	969	18–16	53.67	28.61	+1.7
1970	842	631	839	17–12	51.02	31.53	+5.3
1971	951	798	890	17–14	55.09	30.86	+3.5
1972	1036	889	1020	15–13	64.11	32.27	+3.7
1973	1052	788	851	12–9.1	86.17	35.33	+7.4
1974	892	578	616	9–5.8	99.04	37.72	+12.0
1975	882	632	852	12–8.4	75.66	37.46	+6.1
1976	1015	859	1005	10–8.9	96.72	41.40	+4.6
1977	1000	801	801	11–8.9	89.86	45.84	+5.7
1978	908	742	805	9.2–7.4	101.59	48.85	+7.4
1979*	879	807	836	6.7	124.10	51.73	+8.0

*May 1979. From Wright Investors' Service, Bridgeport, Conn.

As in all phases of financial planning, it is important to stay flexible, not to get locked in, and to *manage* your assets.

To be sure that we're all taking the same language, let's review the choices of security investments.

TYPES OF SECURITIES

Publicly traded securities can be classified in four broad groups: common stock, preferred stock, convertibles, and bonds. Each has a place in portfolios at different times. It matters little whether they are bought directly or through funds, trusts, annuities, or retirement plans.

Common Stock

Shares of common stock represent ownership in a business. If the corporation prospers, you gain by:

1. *Ever-increasing dividends* which, over the years, provide an ever-higher return on cost. Between 1967 and 1977, the 30 companies which make up the Dow Jones Industrial Average boosted payouts from $30.19 to $45.84 per share. Many individual corporations increase their dividends by 10% annually.

2. *Constantly growing underlying, tax-sheltered values.* Quality corporations reinvest half to three-quarters of their profits, tax-free, to increase the company's worth. The book value of Beatrice Foods, over ten recent years, grew from $4.87 to $13.16 per share.

Table 10–2. What you have left after inflation (at 6%) with various types of investments.

Investments	Time	Average Return	Net Return
Treasury bills	1 year	8.33%	+2.33%
Treasury notes	5 years	8.49	+2.49
Treasury bonds	20 years	8.63	+2.63
U.S. government agency bonds	10 years	8.77	+2.77
Municipal bonds	30 years	6.20*	+ .20
Passbook savings	No time	5.25	− .75
Passbook savings	90 days	5.75	− .25
Savings certificate	1 year	6.50	+ .50
Savings certificate	4 years	7.25	+1.25
CDs—$100,000	340 days	8.38	+2.30
Corporate bonds	20 years	8.95	+2.95
Common stocks	No time**	9.3	+3.30

SOURCE: C. Colburn Hardy, *Dun & Bradstreet's Guide to Your Investments* (New York: Crowell, 1978).
*Since there are no income taxes, the inflation applies to a higher effective rate of return: 12.4% for those in the 50% tax bracket.
**Historical rate. Quality stocks should average total returns of 12% or more.

3. *Long-term growth.* As corporate earnings rise, the prices of the stocks will increase. That may not be reflected immediately, but value will eventually out. In 1944, one share of American Home Products traded at $32. By 1977, an average investing lifetime, each share, after stock splits, had grown to 108 for a total worth of $3,300. If the alert investor had sold at interim highs and bought back at favorable lows, the profits would have been far greater.

4. *Greater total returns than any other type of security.* On such a stable stock as AT&T, the dividends in recent years have been over 7%. With a price gain of only 3% (1⅞) from the recent quotation of 60, the total annual returns will be higher than the 8% yield on well-rated bonds. On more volatile issues, the dividends will be lower but the potential appreciation will be greater.

5. *Protection against inflation.* In recent years the yields of fixed-income investments, such as savings accounts and bonds, have been high: from 8% to over 9% a year. Those returns are taxable at full income tax rates, so the true value of that interest is cut to 4.8% to 5.4% depending on the tax bracket. That's not enough to keep pace with 6% inflation.

With an average annual return of 10% from a well-managed portfolio of common stocks, the net returns will be higher because, although the taxes on the dividends are at the full rate, the taxes on realized capital gains are, for most people, half as much. At a 40% tax rate, the stock yield of 5% is cut to 3% but only 60% of the 5% long-term appreciation is taxed, so that net is 4.2%. The total return, therefore, is 7.2%.

Common stocks have two possible disadvantages: (1) Loss of capital if the corporation fails. Only rarely will there be assets left for distribution to common shareholders. Such a risk is practically nonexistent with quality companies, however. (2) Depletion of capital due to price declines when the company falters and you buy at the wrong time or fail to sell wisely. Fluctuations in market value are the price you pay for the liquidity of your investment.

Over the long term of financial planning, the rewards of quality common stocks can be substantial, but such stocks are not always the best investments. Far from it. They must be managed: sold when they become overpriced, when total returns do not meet your financial needs, or when there's a decline in the market and/or stock value. That is the time to put the proceeds in fixed-income holdings and wait until the economic outlook is brighter and stock market values are rising. Quality common stocks should be the core of any long-term financial planning investment program, but just as with all your assets, they should be sold and bought to achieve the greatest total returns. Note, in Table 10–3, that over the last 30 years, despite the loss of values incurred in some years, common stocks provided substantially higher returns than bonds did. They should do so in the future also.

Preferred Stocks: Better for Corporations Than for Individuals

Preferred stocks are hybrids; they are equity investments, but they do not have the full voting privileges of common stocks except when the company gets into financial trouble. They do pay fixed income, but they do not have the security of corporate bonds or the appreciation potential of common stocks.

As fixed-income securities, preferreds tend to move with the interest rate: *up* when the cost of the money drops and *down* when it rises. Their prices seldom reflect corporate profits unless earnings have been just enough to meet the fixed charges. Usually, the prices move within a narrow range. Most preferreds are issued to balance a corporation's capital structure. Utilities, for example, like to keep their mix about 50% to 55% debt, 30% to 40% common stock, and 10% to 15% preferred stock.

Table 10–3. Comparative investment returns: compound annual rate = appreciation + income, 1947 to 1977.

	Dow Jones Industrial Stocks			Dow Jones Corporate Bonds			U.S. Treasury Bills		
Year	Percent Return Annual	Percent Return Cumulative	Compound Annual Rates, Cumulative Average	Percent Return Annual	Percent Return Cumulative	Compound Annual Rates, Cumulative Average	Percent Return Annual	Percent Return Cumulative	Compound Annual Rates, Cumulative Average
1947	+ 7.61	+ 7.61	+ 7.61	- 4.27	- 4.27	-4.27	+0.59	+ 0.59	+0.59
1950	+26.40	+ 71.50	+14.44	+ 4.25	+ 10.27	+2.47	+1.22	+ 4.01	+0.99
1957	- 8.63	+ 357.40	+14.82	+ 1.73	+ 18.28	+1.54	+3.27	+ 19.31	+1.62
1960	- 6.13	+ 619.00	+15.13	+ 9.07	+ 29.00	+1.84	+2.95	+ 29.35	+1.86
1967	+19.16	+1245.31	+13.18	- 0.38	+ 57.93	+2.20	+4.34	+ 65.39	+2.42
1970	+ 9.21	+1298.94	+11.62	+16.92	+ 99.05	+2.91	+6.44	+ 97.84	+2.88
1971	+ 9.83	+1436.40	+11.55	+11.95	+122.83	+3.13	+4.34	+106.42	+2.94
1972	+18.48	+1720.28	+11.81	+ 8.38	+141.51	+3.45	+4.07	+114.81	+2.98
1973	-13.28	+1478.61	+10.76	+ 3.64	+150.29	+3.46	+7.02	+129.89	+3.13
1974	-23.58	+1106.45	+ 9.30	- 0.84	+148.19	+3.30	+7.85	+147.98	+3.30
1975	+44.75	+1646.35	+10.37	+14.53	+184.24	+3.67	+5.84	+162.46	+3.38
1976	+22.82	+2044.92	+10.76	+22.82	+249.11	+4.26	+4.90	+175.33	+3.43
1977	-12.84	+1769.42	+ 9.91	+ 5.54	+268.45	+4.30	+5.27	+190.08	+3.50

SOURCE: C. Colburn Hardy, *Dun & Bradstreet's Guide to Your Investments* (New York: Crowell, 1978).

For the average investor, the major advantage of preferreds is low price, normally $100 a share but, in recent years, as low as $25. Thus with the same dollars you can buy more shares of preferreds than bonds. With $5,000, you could own 100 preferreds versus five $1,000 corporate bonds.

Preferreds are excellent holdings for corporations because of the tax advantages. When any corporation, business or professional, buys them, it receives an 85% tax exemption on the dividends received—taxes are paid on only 15% of the income. A corporation in a fully taxable (46%) status would pay taxes equal to 6.9% of the dividend (.46 × .15 = 6.9%). Thus, on an $8.50 dividend, it could keep $5.86 per share, tax-free.

Watch out for new issues. There's little chance new issues will appreciate; and if they are low-priced, your broker may be pushing them because he gets an extra commission. Your best bets are old issues with low coupons or convertibles. When the interest rate is 8%, 4% preferreds will be selling at about 50. You'll get a good return, a chance of appreciation if the cost of money declines, and capital gains if the issue can be called or redeemed at a higher price. Convertibles assure steady income and have potential for appreciation if the related common stock moves up.

Straight preferreds are advisable for professional corporations (but not personal retirement plans, which already provide tax-free benefits); convertibles are advisable if you have only a modest sum and can afford to wait for gains. In either case, concentrate on preferreds selling at discounts well below face value.

Junior Preferreds

There are also junior preferreds; they are senior to common stock but junior to regular preferred stock. Usually, they are subject to gradual retirement by corporate repurchase. They are issued by public utilities whose financial condition does not permit new straight preferred or common stock.

EXAMPLE: Boston Edison, at 12½, pays a $1.17 dividend for a 9.4% yield. The company can retire the stock at any time and is required to repurchase 4% of the shares each year if the price drops below $10 in 1980.

Preferred Stock Fund

If you decide to let someone else manage your money in preferred stocks, take a look at qualified dividend portfolio II (QDP II), which uses the tax benefits of preferred stocks and regulated investment companies. Interest must be less than 25% of gross investment income.

A QDP II fund gets two tax benefits: (1) *as a corporation,* the 85% deduction for dividends from investments in preferred stocks, and (2) *as a regulated investment company,* because short-term gains can be treated as dividends when they do not account for more than 25% of investment income.

The fund can trade for short-term capital gains, take the profits, pay an effective tax of 7.2%, and, if the securities still look good, buy them back again. With a $200,000 investment in QDP II, the tax savings can be significant:

		Corporate Tax Rate	
Income Source	Amount	No QDP II	With QDP II
Dividends	$10,000	7.2% ($ 720)	7.2% ($ 720)
Interest	2,000	48.0 (960)	7.2 (144)
Short-term gains	6,000	48.0 (2,880)	7.2 (432)
	$18,000	($4,560)	($1,296)

With the tax shelter of a QDP II fund, the investor gets $3,264 more income: $4,560 with QDP versus $1,296 without QDP.

Convertibles: Preferreds and Bonds

Convertible securities (CVs) combine the fixed income of bonds and preferred stocks with the growth potential of common stocks. They pay a set income, and they can be swapped for the shares of the related common stock at specified ratios, usually until a specified date. For example, a $1,000 CV bond might be exchanged for 20 shares of common.

CV bonds, called debentures, represent debt of the issuing company. Like bonds, most are callable, but they are always more closely related to common stock than to bonds. They have two values:

Investment value is the theoretical worth of a CV as a conventional bond or preferred stock. Because that reflects the yield, prices move with the interest rate—up when the cost of money drops, down when it rises.

In theory, the investment value sets a floor below which the CV will not fall. In practice, that applies only to CVs of strong corporations. With small or marginal companies, the CV price will drop as far and as fast as the price of the related stock when there's a bear market or there are corporate problems.

Conversion value is the amount a CV would be worth if it were exchanged for shares of the common stock. That rises with the price of the stock when the stock is close to or above the conversion value.

CVs are issued by companies which do not have the financial strength or investor acceptance to float common stock. As debt, their cost to the corporation is low and the potential is great: the money received is expected to be used to boost earnings. Before the CVs mature, the value of the common stock will have risen so much that holders will be glad to swap.

In considering CVs for investment, deal with a knowledgeable broker and look for issues selling at discounts from par and at premiums up to 15% above conversion price. For example, when GAF $1.20 preferred, convertible to 1.25 shares of common stock, was selling at 18½ and the common was at 13½, the premium was about 10%. It's a good buy if you believe the price of the common will rise soon. Meantime, the yield is 6.5%.

Because CVs combine reasonable income and potential growth, they are excellent investments for money you want to leave to your children. You get regular income and, hopefully, your heirs will benefit from the appreciation.

Bonds for Safety and Comfort

When you buy a corporate bond, you are loaning your money to the corporation. You receive a fixed rate of interest and a promise that, at maturity, some 10 to 40 years hence, you will get back the face value of the debt. Bonds are rated according to the financial strength of the issuer and the assets back of the bond. Standard & Poor's rates bonds from AAA (gilt-edged) through AA (high quality) down to the Cs (speculative); Moody's Investors Service rates bonds Aaa, Aa, and so on. The higher the rating, the greater the safety and the lower the interest rate. Thus, an AAA bond might carry a 7⅞% coupon, whereas an A-rated bond, with similar maturity, would pay 8⅜%. *Never* buy any bond, for investment, rated below BBB (Baa).

Unlike the prices of stocks, which reflect supply and demand, the values of bonds move with the interest rate, but in the opposite direction. When the interest rate falls, the price of the bond rises; for example, a 4% 20-year bond, issued at $1,000, sold at 64 when the prime rate was 8.5%. With a drop in the interest rate to 7%, the bond traded at 73. When the price of money goes up, the values of bonds decline.

The trouble with bonds is inflation. Bonds can provide sure income, but they cannot maintain the purchasing power of either principal or income. In a 20-year period, with inflation at 6%, the real worth of a $1,000 bond will drop to about $321 in terms of goods and services that can be bought. And, of course, the interest is taxed at the full rate. But most bonds are safe. Unless the corporation defaults, you are sure of getting that twice-a-year check for interest and full value at maturity.

The prices of bonds will not fluctuate as much as those of common stocks but, unless the original interest rate is high (over 8%), there's little chance of worthwhile appreciation. In such cases, the bond may be called early and you will have to find new investments.

The greatest total returns from bonds come from buying outstanding issues at discounts. You get modest income plus sure appreciation; for example, from AT&T 4⅜'s '85 at 83 ($830), you will have a current yield of 5.3% plus $170 capital gains between now and 1985.

Bonds are best for investments when you want a set sum at a specific future date, as for college tuition, or a long-planned vacation. There's no such assurance even with the best common stocks, because there might be a bear market at that time and you might have to sell at a loss.

Just as from stocks, the best returns come with prompt reinvestment to benefit from compounding. Put the semiannual interest checks in a daily interest savings account and, when you have sufficient funds, buy more bonds. (A handy substitute is a bond fund in which the reinvestment of interest is automatic.)

Unless you have a sizable portfolio, it's difficult to manage bonds: to sell and buy according to anticipated changes in the interest rate. That's why bonds are best for people who place income and safety above growth. There's nothing wrong with getting a 9.6% return with AAA-rated debt. Such opportunities do not come often. Generally, when you invest in bonds, you do so to sleep well rather than to build capital to reach your financial objectives.

SELECTING SECURITIES

The single most important factor in successful investing is quality. It is an essential aspect of all securities. With quality stocks you are almost sure of better than average returns on your money: reasonable income plus substantial appreciation. You are following the leaders: the big, institutional investors which account for over 60% of all stock market transactions and who normally concentrate on quality investments.

In a corporation, quality is a combination of financial strength, fairly consistent high profitability and growth, and prospects of a comparable record in the future. Year after year, quality companies plow back a portion of their profits into research, more efficient equipment, new plants, new products, and new markets. Those investments boost corporate worth and provide the base for higher earnings which bring an advance in the prices of the company stocks.

The safest, surest way to stock market success is to buy quality stocks when the stocks are undervalued and becoming popular and to sell them when they become fully priced—before they start to decline.

Standard & Poor's *Stock Guide* (available from your broker or library) rates companies A+ (highest quality), A (high), and so on. For investment, select only stocks rated B+ or higher and then concentrate on the most profitable companies. Wright Investors' Service, a professional money management firm, relies on two fundamental yardsticks: earned growth rate (EGR) and profit rate (PR). Table 10–4 shows how they are calculated with top-quality Johnson & Johnson (J&J).

Earned Growth Rate

The earned growth rate (EGR) is the annual rate at which the company's equity capital per common share is increased by the net earnings after payment of the dividend. It is a reliable measure of investment growth because it shows the increase in the capital invested in the business: *your money*. The base is *book*

Table 10–4. Johnson & Johnson stock, A+.

Year	Book Value Beginning Year	Per Share Earnings	Per Share Dividends	EGR	PR
1967	$ 4.78	$ .76	$ .21	11.5%	15.9%
1972	11.10	2.15	.45	15.3	19.4
1974	15.10	2.80	.73	13.7	18.5
1975	17.29	3.18	.85	13.5	18.4
1976	19.83	3.53	1.05	12.5	17.8
1977	22.35	3.88	1.40	12.7	18.9
1978	25.28	4.23	1.70	13.1	19.8

SOURCE: Wright Investors' Service, Bridgeport, Conn.

value (also known as stockholders' equity): the net assets behind each share of stock after all liabilities, including bonds and preferred stocks, are subtracted from total assets. You can find the book value in every annual report and most financial summaries.

EGR is a measure of true growth, and it can be used with all types of companies from food processors to steel mills, from metal miners to computer component makers. You use the book value at the beginning of the year because that's the money you entrusted to corporate management.

Here's the formula to determine the EGR:

$$\text{EGR} = \frac{E - D}{BV}$$

where EGR = earned growth rate
       E = earnings per share
       D = dividends per share
       BV = book value per share (at the start of the year)

With J&J, for 1976:

$$\frac{3.53 - 1.05}{19.83} = \frac{2.48}{19.83} = 12.5\%$$

The value of each share of common stock grew 12.5% during 1976. The extra worth may not immediately be reflected in the price of the stock, but when continued, it will eventually bring a rise in value.

Profit Rate

The profit rate (PR) measures the ability of a company to make money with your money. It shows the rate of return on shareholder's equity capital at corporate book value: the profitability of the corporation. It is calculated by dividing the earnings per common share by the book value per common share, also at the beginning of the year. The formula is:

$$\text{PR} = \frac{P}{BV}$$

where PR = profit rate
       P = profit per share
       BV = book value per share (at the start of the year)

In 1976, for J&J:

$$\text{PR} = \frac{3.53}{19.83} = 17.8\%$$

By every standard, J&J is a top-quality investment. Its EGR of 12.5% was nearly double the 7.1% of the 30 DJIA stocks; its PR of 17.8% was almost half again as rewarding as the DJIA PR of 12.3%.

Table 10–4 shows the importance of a fairly consistently high EGR and PR. On an adjusted-for-splits basis (three for one in 1967 and again in 1970), the stock moved from 18 to 133 in 1972. Then came the stock market decline, but

J&J recovered and, in late 1977, was quoted in the 70s. In the same period, the per share profits rose from 76¢ to an estimated $3.88 and dividends jumped from 21¢ to $1.30. That's profitable growth!

Reference Points

Table 10–5 is a list of quality corporations which have had a ten-year average EGR of 6% and a PR of 6%; with a few exceptions, the corporations are primarily stable utilities and very large, financially strong companies. *For the best profits, buy the stocks of the best companies: quality corporations that make the most money.*

Table 10–5. Some basic information needed for analysis and projections.*

Company	P/E Ratio 1968–1977	Cash Dividend Yield	Earnings per Share (Last 12 Months)	Dividends per Share (Indicated)	Earned Growth Rate 1968–1977	Profit Rate 1968–1977
Aerospace						
Cessna Aircraft	12–6.9	4.0%	$ 3.71	$ 1.44	10.6%	16.2%
Apparel						
Blue Bell, Inc.	9.6–4.8	6.8	5.34	1.40	17.2	21.7
Interco, Inc.	12–7.7	4.7	5.79	2.00	9.3	14.0
U.S. Shoe	13–7.6	5.5	3.42	1.32	7.9	14.3
V.F. Corp.	14–8.4	6.7	2.88	1.20	10.3	16.6
Automotive						
Champion Spark Plug	14–9	6.6	1.52	.72	10.0	19.0
Dana Corp.	9.6–6.1	4.7	4.05	1.32	11.0	17.1
Eaton Corp.	11–7	6.1	6.48	2.25	8.8	14.8
Echlin Mfg.	22–13	2.5	2.50	.72	16.0	22.5
Ford Motor	8.5–5.9	7.7	13.99	3.60	8.0	12.9
General Motors	12–8.6	11.0	10.44	6.75	5.8	17.0
Beverages						
Coca-Cola	32–22	4.2	2.74	1.74	10.3	23.7
Dr. Pepper	35–20	3.6	1.03	.60	14.6	29.8
Heublein, Inc.	25–14	5.2	2.32	1.40	12.1	22.1
PepsiCo	21–14	3.4	2.21	1.00	12.4	19.5
Royal Crown	21–10	5.8	2.06	1.00	11.1	20.5
Chemicals						
American Cyanamid	14–9.4	5.2	3.02	1.50	6.0	13.4
Big Three Industries	20–13	1.7	2.53	.60	14.2	17.7
Colgate-Palmolive	21–13	4.8	2.10	1.00	8.6	15.5
Du Pont	19–14	5.1	12.06	5.75	5.0	13.4
Ethyl Corp.	8–5.4	5.1	3.79	1.10	12.5	16.4
Ferro Corp.	12–6.6	3.3	3.05	1.08	10.8	15.4
International Flavors	46–30	2.4	1.32	.56	13.8	22.0
Lubrizol Corp.	26–17	3.8	3.08	1.44	15.3	23.7
Nalco Chemical	27–17	4.2	2.46	1.24	14.2	23.8
National Chemsearch	34–20	2.9	1.71	.56	15.5	24.8
National Starch	21–13	1.7	4.16	1.18	12.5	17.7
Procter & Gamble	24–17	3.5	6.09	3.00	10.1	18.6
Purex Corp.	15–9.1	6.4	1.95	1.08	7.3	14.3
Rubbermaid, Inc.	27–15	2.6	2.18	.76	11.6	16.4
Stauffer Chemical	11–7.2	5.0	5.61	2.00	10.8	17.1
Union Carbide	11–8.1	7.4	5.95	2.80	7.3	13.6
Witco Chemical	11–6.7	5.8	4.62	1.80	5.3	15.0
Construction						
Caterpillar	16–11	3.2	5.40	1.80	12.5	19.9
Fischbach-Moore	16–12	4.4	3.62	1.30	11.6	17.5
Halliburton	19–12	2.2	6.24	1.40	18.1	22.5
Ideal Basic	12–8	6.6	2.73	1.40	5.2	11.9

SOURCE: Wright Investors' Service, Bridgeport, Conn.

*Figures are digested and do not contain explanations used in the original tables. These were the stocks on the Approved Wright Investment List in July 1978. All selections are subject to change when they no longer meet the requirements of quality and value. They should be considered *examples*, not specific recommendations, of stocks to consider for investment portfolios.

Table 10-5. *(Continued)*

Company	P/E Ratio 1968–1977	Cash Dividend Yield	Earnings per Share (Last 12 Months)	Dividends per Share (Indicated)	Earned Growth Rate 1968–1977	Profit Rate 1968–1977
Johns-Manville	14–8.8	5.9	4.91	1.80	5.7	10.5
Masco Corp.	25–14	1.9	1.97	.40	19.3	22.5
Masonite Corp.	21–13	3.7	2.61	.68	8.6	13.8
Stone & Webster	13–7.8	5.9	6.13	2.75	12.6	21.9
Vulcan Material	8.9–6.3	4.7	3.41	1.30	11.0	17.2
Weyerhaeuser	23–14	3.2	2.28	.80	11.6	17.7
Diversified						
Ametek, Inc.	14–8.2	4.9	3.40	1.60	9.2	17.4
Dart Industries	15–8.9	3.8	4.63	1.00	14.1	16.7
Diamond International	12–8.6	6.6	3.93	2.20	6.5	13.9
Eagle-Picher	10–6.7	3.0	2.57	.76	10.5	15.2
Koppers Co.	11–6.6	5.0	2.68	1.10	8.6	13.4
Minn. Mining	31–21	3.6	3.85	2.00	10.1	19.4
Drugs						
Abbott Labs	22–14	2.2	2.09	.72	11.3	17.5
American Home Products	28–20	4.6	2.00	1.30	12.9	30.0
American Hospital	37–24	2.4	2.11	.68	9.0	12.1
Avon Products	35–21	4.9	3.40	2.60	12.7	34.0
Bard (C. R.)	42–26	2.0	1.13	.28	11.2	14.4
Baxter Travenol	42–26	.9	2.38	.40	13.6	16.0
Becton-Dickinson	31–19	2.0	2.59	.72	11.0	14.6
Bristol-Myers	22–16	3.4	2.81	1.22	14.0	24.5
Chesebrough-Ponds	27–17	3.8	1.90	.94	10.5	20.2
Johnson & Johnson	39–26	2.1	4.49	1.70	13.7	18.6
Lilly (Eli)	32–22	3.5	3.31	1.60	13.1	22.5
Merck & Co.	32–22	3.1	3.76	1.70	13.1	27.4
Pfizer, Inc.	22–16	3.6	2.63	1.20	9.7	16.9
Revlon	22–16	2.7	3.38	1.30	12.4	19.0
Richardson-Merrell	18–12	3.5	2.59	.90	10.8	15.0
Rorer Group	22–14	3.9	1.36	.66	11.1	22.1
Schering Plough	30–20	3.8	3.24	1.24	17.4	26.4
Smithkline	17–12	1.6	3.52	1.32	11.0	23.7
Squibb Corp.	24–16	2.9	2.49	1.02	8.6	16.7
Sterling Drug	25–17	5.0	1.46	.77	9.4	18.7
Upjohn Co.	27–16	3.1	3.36	1.32	9.1	17.0
Warner-Lambert	25–16	4.2	2.42	1.20	9.1	16.4
Electrical						
Emerson Electric	26–18	3.4	2.72	1.20	12.4	21.5
General Electric	20–14	5.1	4.93	2.60	8.5	17.5
Gould, Inc.	11–7.1	4.6	3.82	1.36	8.5	13.1
Hobart Corp.	19–12	5.6	2.09	1.00	8.2	15.0
Maytag Co.	20–13	7.0	2.45	1.83	6.5	26.0
Reliance Electric	16–9.9	4.2	3.73	1.50	9.1	16.3
Thomas & Betts	25–16	2.9	2.87	1.20	12.8	21.4
Electronics						
AMP, Inc.	33–20	1.9	2.21	.60	16.0	22.3
Burroughs Corp.	33–20	1.9	5.43	1.40	12.4	14.5
Digital Equipment	35–19	.0	3.36	Nil	17.4	17.4
General Signal	18–10	3.2	2.52	1.00	10.1	13.8
Hewlett-Packard	40–24	.4	4.58	.60	15.4	17.2
IBM	28–20	4.5	18.49	11.52	10.0	20.4
Motorola	27–16	2.2	3.62	1.00	9.6	12.6
Perkin-Elmer	36–20	1.7	1.58	.40	10.3	13.0
RCA Corp.	19–12	5.2	3.32	1.40	7.6	15.5
Raytheon Co.	14–8.2	2.6	3.97	1.20	13.9	16.8
Schlumberger, Ltd.	25–16	1.3	4.89	1.10	18.5	23.6
Texas Instruments	35–21	2.1	5.26	1.68	11.5	15.4
Financial						
Bank of New York	8–6.5	7.1	5.43	2.32	7.8	13.8
BankAmerica	14–9.5	4.2	2.84	.94	9.6	15.5
CIT Financial	12–8.3	7.0	4.00	2.40	5.8	12.5
Citicorp	16–10	5.0	3.17	1.16	9.2	14.5
First Charter	12–7.1	5.0	3.37	.80	13.0	13.5
Manufacturers Hanover	11–7.6	6.0	5.11	2.08	7.5	13.4
Morgan (J. P.)	15–10	4.9	5.60	2.20	7.8	13.6
National Detroit	7.6–5.6	5.4	5.01	1.68	7.9	12.1
Northwest Bancorp	13–8.7	4.2	3.14	1.04	8.4	13.6
Texas Commerce	14–9.8	3.1	4.08	1.22	9.9	15.0
Foods						
Archer-Daniels-Midland	14–7.5	1.2	1.66	.20	12.9	15.2
Beatrice Foods	17–11	4.3	2.47	1.08	10.2	18.0

Table 10–5. (Continued)

Company	P/E Ratio 1968–1977	Cash Dividend Yield	Earnings per Share (Last 12 Months)	Dividends per Share (Indicated)	Earned Growth Rate 1968–1977	Profit Rate 1968–1977
CPC International	12–9.2	5.4	5.62	2.70	7.1	15.8
Campbell Soup	16–12	4.8	3.53	1.60	6.7	13.9
Central Soya	12–7.9	4.6	1.66	.70	7.9	12.8
Consolidated Foods	17–11	5.9	3.04	1.50	6.2	13.2
General Foods	15–11	5.2	3.40	1.64	7.1	15.5
General Mills	19–13	3.3	2.58	1.00	10.5	16.9
Heinz (H. J.)	14–9.4	4.1	4.25	1.60	8.8	13.3
Kellogg Co.	17–13	5.2	1.82	1.20	10.0	25.2
Kraft, Inc.	13–9.6	5.5	5.84	2.60	7.0	13.7
Quaker Oats	18–11	4.2	2.82	1.04	8.5	14.0
Ralston Purina	18–13	3.1	1.41	.50	11.3	17.3
Standard Brands	17–12	5.0	2.47	1.36	7.6	15.6
Machinery and equipment						
Baker International	18–11	1.6	2.30	.44	19.0	23.1
Black & Decker	34–22	3.3	1.41	.60	9.1	15.6
Briggs & Stratton	16–11	4.6	2.53	1.26	10.8	22.8
Bucyrus-Erie	16–8.4	4.2	2.64	.80	9.2	15.8
Clark Equipment	13–8.4	5.4	4.70	1.80	8.4	14.9
Combustion Engineering	17–9.7	4.5	4.31	1.80	8.3	14.1
Cooper Industries	13–6.3	2.6	5.29	1.44	13.3	19.1
Deere & Co.	11–6.7	4.4	4.30	1.40	10.2	15.1
Dover Corp.	13–8.9	2.7	4.26	1.20	16.2	21.6
Dresser Industries	13–7.9	2.0	5.02	.88	16.6	23.7
Ingersoll-Rand	16–10	5.4	5.59	3.00	8.4	16.0
Joy Mfg.	16–9	5.0	2.84	1.64	8.2	13.4
Smith International	15–8	2.3	4.45	.92	17.3	20.5
Xerox Corp.	34–22	3.8	5.22	2.00	16.0	21.7
Metal producers						
Cleveland-Cliffs	13–8.4	3.8	4.32	2.20	8.4	12.9
St. Joe Minerals	11–6.9	5.3	2.73	1.30	12.5	20.6
Metal Products						
Continental Group	11–8.2	7.4	4.16	2.20	6.7	13.1
Crown Cork	12–8.4	.0	3.59	Nil	16.0	16.0
Emhart Corp.	10–5.9	5.4	5.52	2.00	8.2	14.0
Harsco Corp.	7.8–5.5	5.4	4.50	1.60	9.9	15.9
Hoover Universal	12–6.8	5.3	3.26	1.12	12.3	21.3
Signode Corp.	15–10	3.5	4.38	1.32	10.3	15.3
Timken Co.	9.9–7.2	6.0	6.92	3.00	6.8	12.4
Oil, gas, and coal						
Ashland Oil	10–6.4	6.6	4.87	2.00	12.9	21.4
Continental Oil	11–7	5.3	2.95	1.40	9.4	14.7
Exxon Corp.	10–7.8	7.3	5.49	3.20	7.8	15.5
Helmerich Payne	14–7.6	.9	3.74	.36	15.5	17.0
Kerr-McGee	22–14	2.9	4.31	1.25	11.5	15.2
Louisiana Land	21–12	5.4	2.54	1.20	16.0	32.5
Mobil Corp.	9.3–6.2	6.8	9.70	4.20	7.8	13.3
Phillips Petroleum	15–9	3.7	3.65	1.20	7.6	13.2
Pittston Co.	13–7.5	5.2	.99	1.20	19.5	26.1
Quaker State	22–13	5.9	1.38	.88	11.1	19.6
Standard Oil (Cal.)	9.4–6.4	6.5	5.96	2.60	7.6	13.1
Standard Oil (Ind.)	11–7.8	5.8	6.95	2.80	8.8	14.2
Texaco, Inc.	10–7.3	8.3	3.23	2.00	7.0	13.8
Union Oil (Cal.)	9.8–6.4	5.0	7.87	2.40	10.4	15.3
Paper						
International Paper	15–9.8	5.0	5.17	2.00	6.8	12.9
Kimberly-Clark	13–8.7	5.8	5.81	2.60	7.0	12.4
Union Camp	15–9.2	4.7	4.69	2.00	11.2	17.7
Printing and Publishing						
Donnelley (R. R.)	17–12	3.1	2.71	.88	8.4	12.4
Dun & Bradstreet	24–17	4.2	2.20	1.40	8.6	22.3
Gannett Company	25–15	3.3	2.70	1.40	10.9	16.1
McGraw-Hill	21–12	4.4	2.24	1.00	7.2	14.7
Time, Inc.	16–9.2	3.7	4.73	1.50	7.3	16.0
Times-Mirror	16–11	3.5	2.23	1.80	11.6	13.3
Recreation						
CBS, Inc.	15–9.8	4.6	6.56	2.40	14.0	24.3
Disney (Walt)	39–19	.8	2.74	.32	10.7	11.5
Eastman Kodak	33–21	4.2	4.28	2.22	9.9	19.6
Howard Johnson	22–10	3.0	1.41	.40	10.4	13.1
Retailers						
Carter Hawley	17–11	5.8	2.41	1.00	9.0	15.1

Table 10–5. (Continued)

Company	P/E Ratio 1968–1977	Cash Dividend Yield	Earnings per Share (Last 12 Months)	Dividends per Share (Indicated)	Earned Growth Rate 1968–1977	Profit Rate 1968–1977
Eckerd (Jack)	26–14	2.4	2.19	.64	17.1	21.4
Federated Dept.	19–12	4.3	4.08	1.60	8.3	14.4
K-Mart	30–18	2.9	2.37	.72	14.1	17.4
Longs Drugs	32–19	2.5	1.93	.64	19.5	24.5
Lucky Stores	16–10	5.3	1.48	.82	12.8	25.6
Macy (R. H.)	12–7.5	4.0	5.99	1.65	8.5	12.5
Melville Corp.	18–9.9	3.9	3.01	1.16	18.0	27.3
Penney (J. C.)	24–16	4.8	4.57	1.76	9.0	14.9
Petrolane	13–7.2	3.1	3.64	.90	19.4	24.8
Revco (D. S.)	22–12	2.2	2.04	.52	16.0	19.7
Rite Aid	31–12	1.9	2.02	.42	15.4	18.0
Safeway Stores	12–8.9	5.4	4.03	2.20	8.0	14.7
Sears, Roebuck	24–17	5.5	2.62	1.27	7.3	13.1
Southland Corp.	19–11	2.6	2.51	.72	11.9	14.6
Standard Brands Paint	31–18	1.8	2.10	.56	16.1	20.3
Winn-Dixie	16–11	4.3	3.57	1.68	14.1	21.8
Textiles						
Collins & Aikman	16–10	6.1	1.89	.72	8.6	14.2
Tobacco						
American Brands	9.8–7.4	6.9	6.43	3.50	6.6	13.9
Reynolds Industries	10–7.5	6.1	8.83	3.50	10.5	19.0
U.S. Tobacco	14–9.2	4.6	2.90	1.60	10.2	20.6
Transporation						
Consolidated Freight	12–6.8	4.2	4.49	1.10	14.9	21.0
Delta Airlines	16–9.7	1.8	6.12	.80	14.4	17.4
Emery Air Freight	38–22	3.9	1.27	.92	16.6	39.3
McLean Trucking	12–6.9	3.3	2.48	.58	17.3	21.3
Transway International	13–8.4	6.0	3.35	1.60	6.8	16.5
Utilities						
American Nat. Resources	10–7.4	7.2	5.92	3.00	6.4	13.9
AT&T	12–9.5	7.7	7.30	4.60	3.8	10.8
Arkansas-Louisiana Gas	11–7.8	6.1	4.05	2.00	7.7	16.2
Central & Southwest	14–10	8.2	2.16	1.34	5.0	14.9
Central Louisiana Electric	13–9.3	5.9	2.71	1.52	7.1	16.8
Central Telephone	14–9.5	6.9	2.85	1.68	7.1	16.3
Cleveland Electric	11–8.7	9.0	2.54	1.84	4.4	14.5
Columbia Gas	11–8	8.4	3.89	2.34	4.9	12.2
Enserch Corp	12–8.4	6.0	2.96	1.36	7.5	15.5
Florida P&L	13–9.1	7.6	3.95	2.08	6.8	12.7
Florida Power	14–9.1	8.2	4.49	2.48	6.0	13.4
Houston Industries	14–10	7.0	4.38	2.12	7.8	14.5
Houston Natural Gas	15–8.8	4.0	3.27	1.00	18.3	24.2
NICOR, Inc	11–8.1	8.5	3.80	2.40	5.7	15.5
Northern Indiana P.S.	13–9.5	8.2	1.87	1.50	5.4	14.2
Northern Natural Gas	9.1–6.6	6.2	6.62	2.40	9.9	16.9
Oklahoma G&E	15–11	8.4	2.09	1.54	3.9	14.6
Oklahoma Natural Gas	9.8–7.7	7.0	3.70	1.60	8.7	17.7
Panhandle Eastern	11–7.1	5.9	6.09	2.60	5.6	18.2
Peoples Gas	9.1–6.7	8.1	4.92	2.80	6.9	14.8
P.S. Indiana	13–9.6	8.1	3.16	2.16	4.6	14.6
Rochester Telephone	15–10	8.3	2.29	1.44	6.1	12.0
Southern Natural Resources	11–7.6	2.8	4.68	1.05	13.1	18.7
Southern Union	13–8	6.9	3.19	1.68	7.0	14.5
SW Public Service	12–9.5	8.4	1.70	1.20	5.4	18.5
Tampa Electric	15–11	6.9	2.19	1.32	5.9	13.5
Texas Eastern	14–8.5	5.1	5.27	2.10	8.3	15.6
Texas Gas Trans.	11–7.4	5.8	5.44	2.64	8.0	14.5
Texas Oil & Gas	18–9.9	1.2	3.71	.36	23.4	24.5
Texas Utilities	15–12	7.5	2.41	1.52	6.3	14.2
Tucson G&E	11–8.2	8.0	2.02	1.32	6.1	13.9
Miscellaneous						
ARA Services	26–17	3.5	4.24	1.45	9.3	12.9
Anchor Hocking	12–7.2	5.4	4.67	1.60	8.7	13.7
Automatic Data	41–23	1.7	1.76	.52	18.9	21.0
Engelhard Industries	14–7.7	5.5	3.76	1.20	17.5	23.6
Genuine Parts	25–16	3.0	2.45	1.10	12.0	19.4
Grainger (W. W.)	23–13	2.4	2.41	.76	16.6	20.7
Rollins, Inc.	25–14	3.3	1.89	.60	21.2	25.9
400 Standard & Poor's	15–12	4.8	11.65	5.07	7.3	13.5
Dow Jones Industrials	13–10	5.8	89.23	47.30	6.0	11.6
Dow Jones Utilities	11–8.4	8.3	13.92	8.72	4.6	12.1

WHEN TO BUY

When you buy any stock, there are two important considerations: value and timing. Value is determined by fundamental analysis; timing can be improved by technical analysis.

Fundamentalists are concerned with the basics: the corporation's financial strength, record of growth and profitability, and investment acceptance. They use those data to project the future price of the stock. They buy stocks when they believe the stocks to be undervalued and sell the stocks when they become fully priced. They are slow to trade; they are patient; and they hold for the long term. Eventually, they make money, but as Lord Keynes noted, "In the long run, we'll all be dead."

Technical analysts concentrate on what *is* rather than what *should be*. They believe that (1) the stock market is rooted 15% in economics and 85% in psychology, (2) the action of the stock, not the corporation, is the key factor, (3) Wall Street follows the leaders—major institutional investors such as investment companies, insurance firms, and pension funds, which account for nearly two-thirds of all NYSE trading. When the big boys start to buy, regardless of the reason, the price of the stock will go up; when they sell, no matter how excellent a company may be as to fundamental worth, the price of its stock will go down.

TECHNICAL INDICATORS

The technical analyst relies on trends. He knows that a trend in motion can be assumed to remain intact until there is a clear reversal. As long as the trend is up, even though there may be minor dips, the price of the stock will continue to rise. It's the opposite on the downside. The technician buys *up* stocks in *up* groups in *up* markets. He sells, or sells short, in the reverse situation.

There are scores of technical indicators, but the most widely and easily used can be found on the daily financial pages. They are most effective when confirmed by a consensus of several indicators. Most practitioners include charts.

Technical analysis is not as complex as outlined by some Wall Streeters (usually those who make money by selling charts and counsel). Here are some examples of what you can look for:

Most Active Stocks

The most active stocks are the volume leaders, the most popular stocks on one trading day. Skip the big companies, such as AT&T, Exxon, and General Motors. They have so many shares that their names appear frequently.

In a bull market, concentrate on groups and shares of smaller companies. The occurrence of the same names several times within a week or two indicates that major investors are buying; and since those institutions act as a herd, follow the leaders. If you're investing, the stocks they are purchasing could be a good buy. If you're trading, they could lead you to quick profits of 20% or more.

On April 13, 1978, the airline/transport stocks were popular: Lockheed,

Boeing, TWA, and UAL (see Table 10–6). If the activity continues, it is probably a buy signal in a bull market. But if the prices of the leaders are falling in a bear market, it's time to consider selling or selling short. *Always look for further confirmation from charts of the industry and the individual company.*

Highs and Lows

The list of highs and lows, which reports activity a few days later, can be equally useful. (See Table 10–7.) Again, it's that trend that counts. In April 1978 there was unusual interest, on the upside, in secondary stocks (Jantzen, Phillips, Van Heusen, and Scott's), in machinery manufacturers (Dover, Eltra, and Gleason Works), and, possibly, in financial equities (Credit Financial and Financial, Santa Barbara). On the downside, the attention was focused on utilities (Illinois Power and Portland GE). In both cases, confirmation of the moves could signal a breakout. Forget about the preferreds, because their prices move with the cost of money.

Again, check other indicators and then look at the charts. Once a stock starts to move, that trend is likely to continue.

THE IMPORTANCE OF CHARTS

Charts form the basis for the final decision to buy or sell. They report what actually happened in the marketplace. They do not lie, but their interpretation can be difficult. Yet if you stick to simple trend lines for timing your security transactions, you will be right 80% of the time.

Two typical charts of Johnson & Johnson are shown in Figures 2 and 3. Figure 2 covers a 12-year span; Figure 3 reports market action from March 1976 through November 1977. Charts are also available on a daily, weekly, and monthly basis.

The long-term chart, Figure 2, shows that J&J moved up strongly from 1966

Table 10–6. Most active stocks, Thursday, April 13, 1978.

	Open	High	Low	Close	Change	Volume
Cutler Ham	41¼	45½	41¼	44¾	+3¾	721,400
Digital Eq	39⅝	39⅞	38⅝	38⅞	−1	350,300
ArchDan M	13⅞	14⅝	13¾	14⅝	+ ¾	291,000
FedNat Mtg	15	15¼	15	15⅛	+ ¼	271,700
Citicorp	20⅜	20⅞	20⅜	20⅞	+ ½	250,400
Lockheed	18½	19⅞	18½	19¾	+1⅛	245,000
Marsh Field	23	26¼	22⅞	25	+2¼	227,500
Boeing	36	37⅜	35⅞	36¾	+ ¾	213,900
Cont Data	25¾	27¼	25¾	27⅛	+1⅜	210,700
Southern Co	17	17	16¾	17	+ ⅛	209,300
Exxon	45½	45⅝	45	45⅛	− ¼	205,800
ArizPub Svc	20⅜	20½	20¼	20¼	− ⅛	185,400
TransW Air	15⅜	15⅞	15⅜	15¾	+ ⅝	176,700
UAL Inc	22⅜	23	22⅜	22⅝	+ ⅛	172,000
Vornado Inc	11¾	11⅞	11⅛	11¾	+ ⅛	171,000

Table 10–7. New highs and lows, Tuesday, April 18, 1978.

NEW HIGHS—39

Airco Inc	Dover Cp	IowaBeef	Scottys Inc
Allied Pd	Eltra Cp	Jantzen Inc	ScuddDVst
Arkans Best	Filtrol	JohnsnCn	Shapell Ind
Autom Ind	FinlSanta B	Koppers pf	SnapOn Tool
Best Prod	Fleming Co	LevFd Cap	Sterchi Bro
Brown Grp	FooteConB	M-A-COM	US Shoe
Camp Tagg	Gemini Cap	vjNoCentRy	VFCorp
Carlisle	Gleasn Wks	NwstStlW	Wachovia pf
Caro FrgtC	Heileman	PhilVanH	Woods Cp
Credit Fin	Hillenbrnd	viPittFW pf	

NEW LOWS—27

BkTr 4.22pf	GaPw 2.52pf	LongIL pfK	PortGE pf
Borden	GaPw 7.72pf	Mesta Mach	PSEG 5.28pf
CnPw 2.43pf	Ill Power	OhEd 8.20pf	PSEG 7.52pf
Coopr TR pf	IllPw 8.24pf	OhEd 8.64pf	TrnGPL 8.64pf
DetE 2.28pr	Itel 1.44pf	Pennzl pfB	UnEl 4pf
DukeP pfG	JerC 13.50pf	PhEl 8.75pf	WnUn dep pf
Duq 4.20 pfG	LITCO	PortGen El	

to 1972–1973, then dropped in the bear market, and in early 1977 started to rise again. The short-term chart provides more details and reveals that the stock plateaued until November, when the uptrend took over.

J&J is a quality company. At 74, its stock was selling at 19 times current earnings. That compares with a ten-year multiple between a high of 39 and a low of 26. By fundamental standards, J&J was a bargain, but was it time to buy?

The trend line can help you find the answer. To plot it on the chart, use a ruler and sharp pencil to draw a straight line connecting the last two or three *low* points. In Figure 2, they are 63, 65, 67; in Figure 3 they are 70 and 71½. The line establishes the base and becomes the support level for buying an upmoving stock and selling a downtrending one.

On both charts, the trend is starting to be favorable. By projecting the trend lines, you can guesstimate the possible gain to over 80. That small profit might be OK for a trader but is not enough for an investor, who should look for a 20% profit. That sets the target price at about 95, the price from which the 1976 decline began.

The key to the wise use of any trend line is the overall market. The time to buy is when you locate an *up* stock in an *up* group in an *up* market. At 74, an aggressive investor might buy because of the high quality of the stock but the conservative would wait for confirmation of the trend and an up market. The real profits will come with the middle of a move, not the first few points. When the trend continues and you can draw a trend line to 85 or 90, it's probably time to buy *if* the general market is favorable. (By mid-July, J&J was over 83.)

The trend line is a terrific signal. As long as it is up, the light is green; when there's a confirmed downswing, such as occurred in March 1977, the light turns

Figure 2. Johnson & Johnson stock over 12 years.

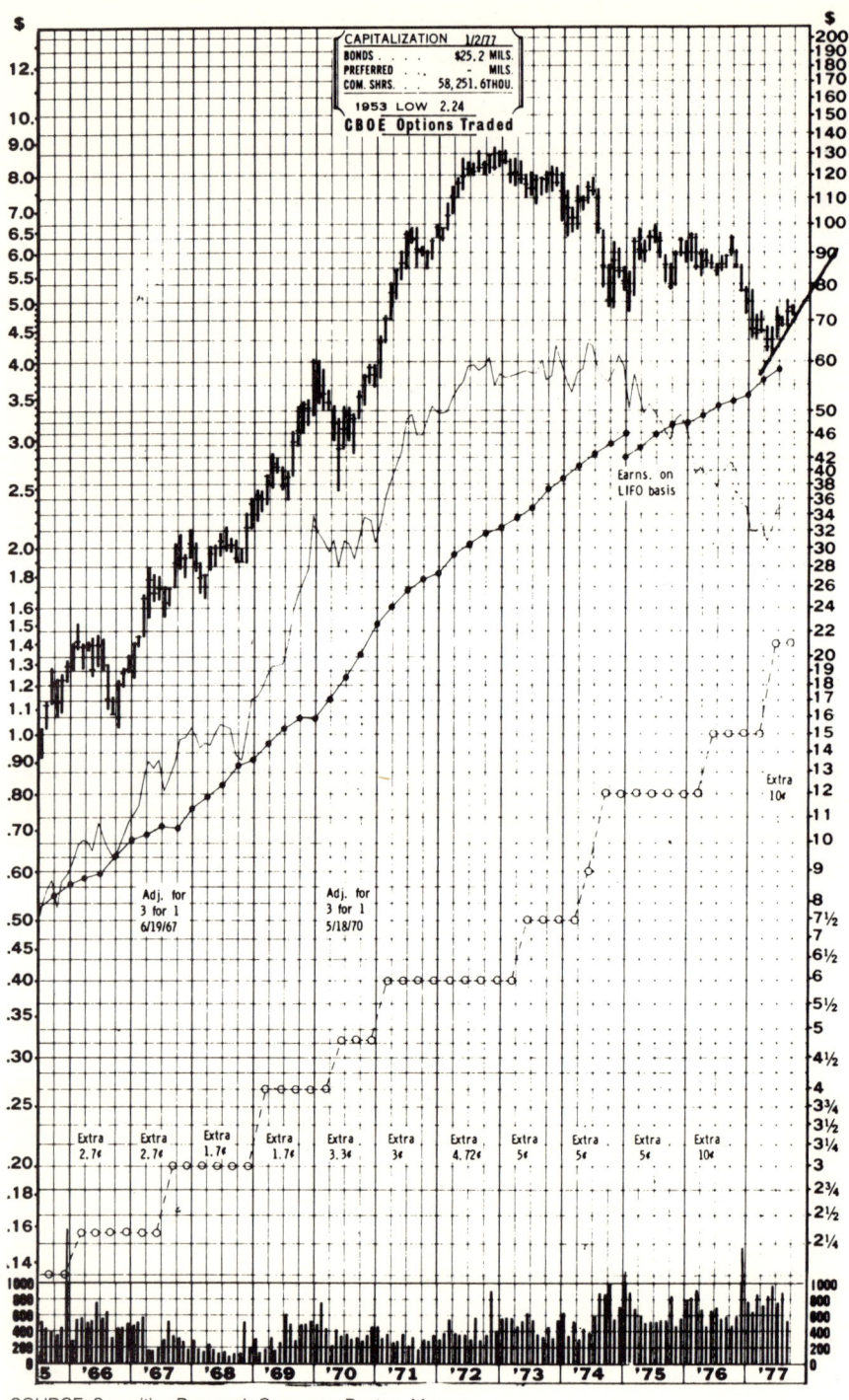

SOURCE: Securities Research Company, Boston, Mass.

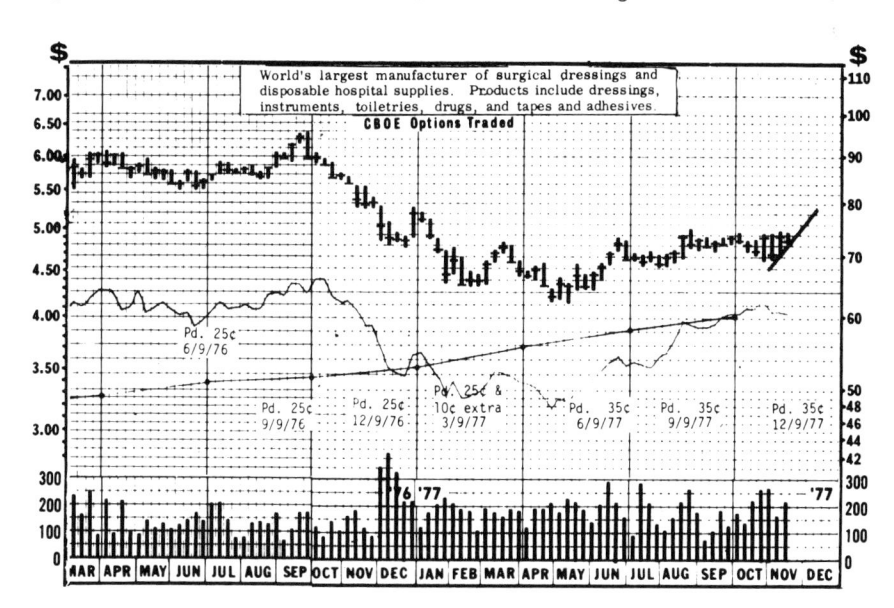

Figure 3. Johnson & Johnson stock, March 1976 through November 1977.

SOURCE: Securities Research Company, Boston, Mass.

amber, signaling caution. When it reverses, as it did in early 1977, it's red and time to get ready to sell.

Stocks tend to repeat patterns, so take another look at the long-term chart in Figure 2. It shows that J&J moves in fairly long swings: almost continually up in the early 1970s, within a narrow range in 1972–1973, then a short, sharp dip, and recently the start of an upmove.

Charts can also be used to check resistance levels: when the upmove may slow. With J&J, that would be about 80, the point from which the last major decline started. Investors who bought there will start selling when the stock rises enough to permit them to break even. The extra supply will push the price down for a while. If the stock starts up again, the next resistance level will be in the mid-90s, and so on. Once you have decided to buy any stock, check the chart and wait until the trend is favorable. You do not achieve gains when a stock holds within a narrow range. And, as we'll see, charts can be used to determine when to sell.

USING PRICE/EARNINGS RATIOS

Fundamental analysis is useful in discovering the value of a quality stock. Value is relative; it is measured by the ratio of the future price to the current price. One of the handiest value yardsticks is the price/earnings (P/E) ratio: the per share earnings divided by the market price. The figure can be found in the daily financial reports under the fifth column of both NYSE- and AMEX-traded securities. It can be the base for projections of future stock value. The P/E ratio of J&J, when the stock was at 74 with annual earnings of $3.88 per share, was at the low end of the 1967–1976 range of 43–19.

To project the future value, the fundamentalist estimates future earnings and multiplies by a reasonable P/E ratio. Over the past decade, J&J has boosted profits by an average of 18% a year. But since the 1976 gain was only 11%, let's be conservative and assume a 12% annual profit rise. Now make these projections:

	Per Share	Price If the P/E Ratio Is		
Year	Earnings	19	21	24
1	$3.88	74	81½	93
2	4.34	82½	91	104
3	4.86	92	102	116½

Thus, in 24 to 36 months the total gains with J&J may run between 28% (24% appreciation plus two annual dividends of 2.0%) and 63% (57% appreciation plus 6% dividends).

There's no guarantee that such gains will be achieved, but with any sort of a bull market they are logical target prices. Such projections can be made only with quality stocks. They will not work with shares of companies that are cyclical, erratic, or unseasoned.

BUYING RULES

Buy quality stocks when:

1. *The economic and stock market prospects are favorable.* It seldom matters how many winners you do *not* buy. What hurts is the number of losers you *do* buy.

2. *The stock is undervalued by historical standards.* It is selling at a P/E ratio that is below its 10-year range at a time when corporate prospects are bright.

3. *A stock is becoming popular.* That is indicated by more investors starting to buy, as indicated by the higher volume shown on the financial pages or at the bottom of the chart.

4. *The chart action indicates a confirmed uptrend.*

5. *There are logical prospects of worthwhile gains* as the result of a price rise due to higher corporate earnings and a stronger, upmoving market.

WHEN TO SELL

Very few people, professionals or amateurs, are *good* sellers. They sell either too soon, before maximum gains have been attained, or too late, after the stock has suffered a substantial loss.

If you miss a good buy, there's always another opportunity. If you fail to sell wisely, you probably will lose money and may deplete your capital. Worthwhile investment returns are as much the result of minimum losses as of maximum gains. You must learn to accept a quick, small loss when your projections do not work out.

The timing of selling is important at two points:

1. *When you have a profit.* It is never easy to sell stocks when they are high-priced and popular. Most people want to squeeze out a few more points. When a stock reaches a target price, get ready to sell. When it soars to an unrealistic high, get out. As Baron de Rothschild, one of the most successful traders of all time, said when asked the secret of his success, "By always selling a bit too soon."

2. *Before you have a big loss.* The loss point is signaled by charts. When the price of the stock breaks down through the trend line, be cautious. When the decline is confirmed, sell.

A trader would sell when the penetration of a volatile stock is 5%; of a stable one, 8%. With a $50 stock, that's 2½ and 4 points, respectively. A conservative investor should consider selling when there is a 10% drop, but with a strong stock he might wait until the loss, from the high or cost, is 15%. Of course, with long-term holdings of quality stocks, you can hang on and wait for the eventual recovery. But that is not the wisest use of your savings. See Figure 4 for the details of making up losses.

RULES FOR SELLING

For effective portfolio management, sell when:

1. *You have a profit and better gains are likely with another stock.* In June 1974, Melville Corp. was a bargain at 9. It was selling at five times earnings, and profits were rising. In September 1976, the stock reached its target price of 26. Prospects for a further rise were poor. It was time to sell and put the proceeds in a stock with greater potential. (For the record, the stock dropped 20% before it started up again.)

Figure 4. What it takes to make up losses.

PORTFOLIO RECOVERY PERCENTAGES

PORTFOLIO DECLINES	11%	18%	25%	33%	43%	54%	65%	82%	100%
10%									
15%									
20%									
25%									
30%									
35%									
40%									
45%									
50%									

This graph illustrates the importance of conserving your assets when the market is in a decline. For example, if your total assets decline 25% in a falling market, they must then appreciate 33% just to break even.

SOURCE: Stolper & Co., Inc., San Diego, Cal.

2. *The original reasons for purchase no longer hold.* You bought because (a) your study showed that the company was sound and had good prospects for profitable growth; (b) you believed something good would happen (a stock split, a big contract, an acquisition, or a new product); or (c) the chart showed an uptrend with heavy volume.

If the stock did not fulfill your hopes within a reasonable period, you were wrong. Sell unless there is a strong market and your optimism still seems justified.

3. *The stock, or industry, becomes unpopular.* Once Wall Street sours, it can take months, even years, for a recovery. Regardless of how favorable the fundamentals, do not try to buck the trend.

4. *Corporate earnings drop for two consecutive quarters.* The company is not fulfilling your projections. Do not hang on its hopes.

5. *The dividend income falls short of your needs.* If you bought the stock to get an 8% yield and its price rises so that the return is only 5%, sell and buy another security which will give you that 8% return on your current investment. The idea of calculating yields on your cost may be comforting, but it's not the best use of your money.

EXAMPLE: You buy 100 shares of Toonerville Trolley at 40 ($4,000) when the dividend is $3.20 per share ($320 annual income). The price of TT goes to 64 ($6,400), but the dividend stays the same. Your return is only 5%. That is the time to sell, take your profit, and reinvest for a better return.

Even after taxes and commissions for selling and buying, you'll have about $5,700 to buy 100 shares of Dogpatch Utilities at 57. Since it is paying $4.50 per share dividend, you'll receive $450 a year, almost an 8% yield.

6. *The company announces plans to issue convertible securities.* Potentially, that puts more shares on the market and will dilute corporate earnings. Usually, CVs are issued when the price of the stock is at a high level. The odds are 2:1 that the stock price will drop in the next few months.

7. *The price of a stock runs up on news that the company is to be taken over.* Proposals do not always end in marriage. Of 56 stocks that moved up on news of a proposed merger, 71% fell 25% or more in the next nine months.

8. *A stock moves up very rapidly in a short period of time.* Of 55 NYSE-listed stocks that achieved a 50% gain in less than one year, 39 fell 25% or more in the next six months.

In broad terms, those selling rules apply to all types of securities. Knowing when and how to sell is one of the most important skills in successful financial planning.

EXTRA INCOME FROM OPTIONS

If you want to be almost sure of annual income of 15% or more, learn how to write options. The goal requires modest capital, strict discipline, and a knowledgeable broker. It's an excellent strategy for conservative investors, especially retirees who want a check every month.

Options are a cross between stocks and commodities. They offer certain, limited income to investors and high leverage to speculators. The most popular options are calls: the right to buy a specified number of shares (usually 100) of a specified common stock at a specified (striking) price before a specified expiration date. Calls on some 200 NYSE-listed common stocks and one AMEX stock are traded on five exchanges.

For stocks selling under $50 per share, the prices of calls are quoted at intervals of five points: 25,30,35, and so on; for those trading at over $50 per share, at ten-point differentials: 70, 80, and 90; for those over $100 a share, at twenty-point jumps. Expiration dates are set every three months on the Saturday after the third Friday of the stated month: January, April, July, and October; February, May, August, and November; March, June, September, and December. Prices are quoted for three of the four expiration months.

The cost of the option is called a premium. Its value varies with the duration of the contract, the type of stock, corporate prospects, and the tenor of the stock market. Premiums run as high as 15% of the value of a volatile stock with an expiration date seven months hence to as low as 3% for a call on a stable stock with a striking date of less than a month. All option income is taxed as short-term gains.

There are also puts: the right to sell a stock at a specified price. Since only a small number of puts have been listed for trading, let's concentrate on calls.

Making Extra Money with Calls

For conservative financial planning, writing (selling) calls on stocks you own can be a profitable investment strategy. You accept a sure, limited profit rather than a potentially greater gain. When you write a call, you start with an immediate profit and, because most calls are not exercised, a good chance of retaining the stock. In effect, the premium can be considered an extra dividend.

For easy figuring, here are quotations on calls for Master Products (MP). It's December; the stock is selling at 46; and dividends are 60¢ quarterly.

Option	Price	January	April	July
MP	40	7	8	No quote
MP	45	2	3	4
MP	50	½	1½	2

There are many ways to use calls, but to build a long-term portfolio and enhance current income, the best approach is to write calls "out-of-the-money": at a striking price above your cost. In the winter, you buy 100 shares of MP for 46 ($4,600) and write a July 50 call for 2 ($200). (For lower commission costs, try to work with 300 shares or more.) If the stock stays below 50 by July, you pocket $320: $200 premium plus $120 in dividends. Your return is 7% for eight months, an annual rate of 10.5%, and you still own the stock and can write new calls in August. If the stock moves over 50 and the call is exercised, your profit will be greater: $320 from the premium and dividends plus $400 appreciation, or $720. That's a 15.7% immediate yield or an annualized rate of return of 23.5%.

You are protected on the downside: 46 cost minus the 2-point premium, or a price of 44. Below that figure, you will suffer an out-of-pocket loss, but there's protection there, too. When the value of the stock falls, the premium will keep pace and you can buy back your call at, say, ¾. That will reduce your premium income to 1¼ ($125), but now you can write a new call, say, October 50 at 1½ when the price of the stock bounces back. Over several years, with a quality stock, it's possible to end up with a profit even though the price of the stock declines.

Note that these are gross profits and do not include transaction costs. On the average, commissions and fees will reduce returns about 10%, depending on the number of calls and the prices of the stock and options.

Rules for Writing Options

Work on a programmed basis. Have a minimum of $45,000 so you can develop a monthly program—roughly, a stock investment of $5,000 for each of the nine months of quoted calls. That will enable you to count on regular premium income, double up when unusual opportunities arise, or wait for a month or two.

Set a target rate of return. If you want 15% annual return, look for 6- to 9-month contracts with premiums of over 10%. You won't find worthwhile sales every month, so you must shoot for higher premiums. The dividends should more than offset the commissions.

Concentrate on quality stocks, those which you would like to own. Speculative issues can be too volatile, and although their premiums may be high, you can end up with stocks which have declined sharply in price over the period of the option. Quality stocks are more predictable.

Own the stock before you sell a call. When you become an expert, you can buy the stock immediately after you write the option. Before then, don't try to outsmart the professionals.

Look for uptrending stocks. If the stocks rise in price rapidly, they may be called before expiration date, so you can reinvest the proceeds of the sale. A successful call writer should be glad to have someone else make money too.

Write far-out calls, those with expiration dates eight to nine months hence, at the outset. The longer the option period, the greater the percent of premium. The time span will give you a chance to get a feel of how the options market operates.

Watch your timing. It's best to sell a call when the stock has risen to a price which you think is too high. The premium will be greater and if the stock drops back, as it probably will, you can buy back the call and write a new one.

EXAMPLE: Dr. Steinberg buys 300 shares of Johns-Manville at 30½ and waits. In August, he sells three February calls, at the striking price of 35, for 1⅝ for a net return of $451.51. By November the stock is down, so the calls are trading at ⅜. He buys them back at a net cost of $125.13 for a short-term profit of $326.38.

A few months later, he sells three November calls, also at 35, for 1⅛ for $295.93. In July, he buys them back at ⅜, again for a profit of $170.80.

Even though the price of JM is just about at its cost, Dr. Steinberg has pocketed over $1,200 from premiums and dividends and still owns the stock. That's an 11.4% return, which can be upped by writing new calls.

Play games first. Before you start a call-writing program, set up a paper schedule and make dry runs for a couple of months. Work with five stocks and write calls, in theory, at different striking prices at different expiration dates. Each week, check the prices to see how you fared. Be sure to include the hypothetical dividends. For the ex dividend date, the day on which owners of the stock are eligible for the payout, check Standard & Poor's *Stock Guide*.

The highest premiums will come when the striking price is below the quotation of the stock. In the example, when the stock is at 46, the premiums for the 40 call are 7 and 8. There'll be good premiums when the strike price is close to the market price. In the example, at 45, the premiums are 2, 3, and 4 for the three expiration dates.

The lowest premiums will be when the call is "out-of-the-money"—at 50, with premiums of ½, 1½, and 2 respectively. If the stock gets to 50 by the strike date, you'll have a triple profit: from the premium, the dividends, and the four-point rise from 46 to 50. Such returns may be greater than you would have by writing the shorter calls, but only if the stock moves up.

Keep a separate bookkeeping system. Options are a special breed. A special options-only account will make it easier to fill out your tax return.

Forget about taxes. It takes 12 months to qualify profits for the lower capital gains tax, and no listed options run more than 9 months. But you can still get the lower tax rate on profits on stocks when held for more than one year.

For more specific information, read a book about options or attend a lecture held by your broker. There are scores of ways to use options to boost your income and, if you are a swinger, to speculate. But, I can assure you, a successful options program requires close supervision.

BEATING INFLATION WITH DIVIDEND-BOOSTING STOCKS

One of the greatest advantages of investments in common stocks is that stocks, when properly selected, can beat inflation. By buying shares of quality corporations which are likely to increase their dividends at an average annual rate of 10%, even investors in the 50% tax bracket can stay even with 5% inflation. Those with lower tax rates can come out ahead, thanks to the benefits of compounding. Over 20 years, an initial yield of 4.62%, paid recently by Deere & Co., will grow to a return on original cost of 56.82%. After adjusting for inflation, the income will be almost 14% on investment.

In Table 10–8 is a list of stocks which meet those inflation-fighting standards. The stocks have current yields of about 4% or more, and over the 1968–1977 decade they increased their payouts at an average annual rate of at least 10%.

Table 10–8. Beating inflation with dividend-boosting stocks.

Stock	Recent Price	Current Dividend	Current Yield	Yield on Current Cost 5 Years	Yield on Current Cost 10 Years	Yield on Current Cost 20 Years	Yield on Current Cost Adjusted for Inflation* 5 Years	Yield on Current Cost Adjusted for Inflation* 10 Years	Yield on Current Cost Adjusted for Inflation* 20 Years
Avon Products	45⅜	$2.20	4.85%	7.10%	11.22%	25.50%	5.69%	7.58%	11.66%
Coca-Cola	39½	1.54	3.90	6.15	9.37	20.23	4.94	6.33	9.22
Deere & Co.	26	1.20	4.62	8.27	13.10	30.46	6.65	8.88	13.92
Kellogg Co.	23⅜	1.10	4.71	6.12	9.63	21.90	4.92	6.50	10.01
Melville Corp.	25⅞	.96	3.71	6.38	11.98	35.29	5.10	8.08	16.12
No. Natural Gas	39	2.40	6.15	10.97	18.56	46.82	8.82	12.54	21.36
Okla. Natural	32½	2.00	6.15	12.55	21.08	52.49	10.06	14.20	23.96
Quaker Oats	22½	1.04	4.62	9.96	11.87	24.89	6.40	8.04	11.38
Standard Oil (Ind.)	47¾	2.60	5.45	7.85	12.15	26.87	6.30	8.21	12.25
U.S. Tobacco	29¼	1.50	4.79	7.28	12.10	29.71	5.85	8.17	12.31

SOURCE: Wright Investors' Service, Bridgeport, Conn.
*Inflation at rate of 4.5%, 1978–1982; 4% thereafter.

That means that in a relatively short time, including a severe recession, their dividends doubled!

The adjusted returns are based on an inflation rate of 4.5% for the next five years and 4% thereafter. Those projections may seem modest in view of the persistent 6% inflation of the mid 1970s, but they represent the consensus of leading economists. If inflation does stay high, or rise, your net return will be less, but it will still be much more than that from most fixed-income holdings. Over the years, the values of quality stocks increase.

High long-term returns from such stocks are not guaranteed, but they are logical because all those corporations have long and fairly consistent records of strong, profitable growth. Even if the companies falter now and then, you will still come out ahead as long as they retain their quality rating. A shrewd money manager would sell before the dividends fail to come up to expectations.

Yield on cost is not a perfect measure of return. It ignores the time value of money and the question of yield on replacement cost or market value. Yet, on a comparative basis, the criterion is sound for long-term investing and financial planning. Investors who reinvest their dividends will, even after paying taxes, be able to retire with similarly attractive returns on original cost.

Over 16% Return on Cost

Melville Corporation is a good example of what you can hope for. The company is a major manufacturer and retailer of shoes and apparel. It deals in basic, always needed products, so it has every prospect of continuing its growth and profitability. When its stock was selling at 25⅞ and the dividend was 96¢ per share, the current yield was 3.71%. Based on a continuation of the average annual increase of 13% of the past decade, the dividend, as a return on present cost, will be 6.38% in five years, 11.98% in ten years, and a whopping 35.29% in twenty years. Even with adjustments for inflation, the 1998 yield, on cost, will be 16.12%. That is $417.11 on the $2,587.50 investment in 100 shares today.

In addition, you are almost sure of appreciation with such quality stocks. There will be interim fluctuations in prices; but as long as the dividends keep rising, the value of the shares will go up, too. The steady increase in payouts will attract more investors, and over the years their buying will boost the stock's value.

There will be periods when, if you need the money quickly, you may have to sell at a loss. But those periods will be rare, and over the next two decades the rewards will be far greater than such risks. It is conceivable that, by 1998, the common stock of Melville will be selling at many times its current quotation.

Take the prospects for Oklahoma Natural Gas. The present $2 per share dividend, with an average annual increase of 10%, will grow to $14.54 by 1998. If the payout is only 50% (low for utilities) and the price/earnings ratio is a modest multiple of 10, the price of the stock will be almost 300, or 10 times its current quotation. Sounds impossible? Well, so does the fact that, just to stay even with inflation, your income will have to double (or more) every 12 years!

Background for Projections

At the time the selections in Table 10–8 were made, in the spring of 1978, there were extra advantages:

1. Most quality stocks were selling at bargain prices, well below their historic values. Such rewarding projections were not possible in the boom years when so many growth stocks were priced at unjustifiably high levels.

2. Until recently, growth stocks provided small returns of 1% to 2%. Now that more corporations are raising their dividends, yields are becoming more attractive.

3. Corporate balance sheets are sounder and capital structures less leveraged than in the early 1970s. With greater cash flow, financially strong, quality firms can finance expansion easily and still raise their payouts.

4. The corporations listed have proven records of high profitability. They are prudent investments which are suitable for fiduciary portfolios and will therefore continue to attract major investors.

5. The listed stocks are the types which will become more popular with the passage of the proposed legislation to eliminate double taxation of dividends.

6. There are few investment risks. As long as the listed companies keep moving ahead, there will be minimal declines in the prices of their stocks. Your money will be safe and the returns rewarding.

That does not mean that you should always hold every stock. Even the best of corporations run into trouble now and then. But generally speaking, the stocks listed are those you can put in a trust or retirement fund and forget until you are ready to withdraw funds for after-work years.

Finding Candidates

Your broker can help you select stocks like those listed in Table 10–8. If you prefer to do it yourself, look for stocks of quality corporations (rated A− or higher by Standard & Poor's) that have boosted their dividends by an average of at least 10% a year over a decade and are continuing to report strong growth and profitability. You will get fair returns today and excellent yields in the future, and you will have a better than average chance for worthwhile appreciation. With investments like those, plus a little common sense in timing buying or selling, everyone can beat inflation!

U.S. GOVERNMENT OBLIGATIONS

At some time, U.S. government bills, bonds, or notes can be useful in financial planning, but generally they are suitable only when you: (1) have temporarily unemployed funds, (2) place safety above all, (3) don't know what else to do with your money, and (4) are experienced enough to speculate on margin.

The interest and capital gains of all U.S. government debt obligations are taxable so, in the selection and sale of those securities, use the guidelines suggested for corporate bonds. There is, however, one important difference: *you do not have to worry about credit ratings.*

The major types of federal debt securities are listed in Table 10–9 and described below.

Treasury bills. Ninety days to one year; minimum purchase of $10,000 face value. The bills are sold on a discount basis that reflects interest paid to maturity. That is, a one-year 6% bill costs $9,400; twelve months later, it can be redeemed for $10,000 for a 6.7% return. T-bills are the equivalent of cash, have a ready market, and can be rolled over into new issues. They are issued in bearer form (no name and address), so they should be kept in a safe place. *Excellent for short-term holdings.*

Treasury notes. One- to five-year maturities, semiannual interest, active market, and competitive yields. Available in $1,000 units. *Can't be beat for safety, modest income, and money needed in a few years.*

Treasury bonds. Medium-term (5 to 10 years) and long-term (up to 30 years) available in units of $1,000 to $10,000 face value in both registered and bearer form. Interest, at moderate to good rates, is paid semiannually. There's an active market, and there are daily quotes in the financial press. *Safe and sure with maturities to fit every financial planning schedule.*

Federal agency bonds and notes. Available in units of $1,000, $5,000, and $10,000 with interest rates slightly higher than those of straight federal debt. They are often hard to buy and sell in odd lots, but you're sure of all payments. *Fine for income and, when they are acquired at discounts, they appreciate to redemption price.*

Government National Mortgage Association (Ginnie Mae) pass-throughs. Securities backed by a pool of FHA and VA mortgages on residences. They are available for $25,000 or, with a sales load, in $1,000 units representing shares in a "mutual" fund. They pay over 8% by passing through the interest and amortization in monthly checks. Since most home mortgages are repaid or refinanced in an average of 12 years, total income will decline after that date. Payments are made on the twenty-third of each month. *Excellent for retirees or for those who do not need the income and can take advantage of automatic reinvestment to gain the benefits of compounding with Ginnie Mae funds.*

Table 10–9. U.S. government debt securities.

Issue	Maturity	Minimum
U.S. Treasury		
Bills	3 months (91 days)	$ 10,000
Bills	6 months (182 days)	10,000
Bills	1 year (360 days)	10,000
Notes	1979–1980	1,000
Notes	1981–1983	1,000
Notes	1984–1986	1,000
Federal Agency		
Banks for Cooperatives	1979	5,000
Banks for Cooperatives	1982	5,000
Fed. Inter. Credit Banks	1979–1980	5,000
Fed. Inter. Credit Banks	1981–1989	5,000
Fed. Nat. Mortgage Association	1979–1980	10,000
Fed. Nat. Mortgage Association	1981–1983	10,000
Fed. Nat. Mortgage Association	1984–1989	10,000
Fed. Nat. Mortgage Association	1996–2001	10,000
Farmers Home Administration notes	1982–1993	25,000
Farmers Home Administration notes	1981–1992	100,000
GNMA certificates	1981–1992	5,000
Export-Import Bank	1979–1983	5,000
U.S. Postal Service	1981	10,000
Int. Bank for Reconstruction	1979–1980	1,000
Int. Bank for Reconstruction	1980–1982	1,000
Int. Bank for Reconstruction	1983–1988	1,000
Small Business Administration	1985–1988	10,000
Penn-Central (guaranteed)	1980–1986	10,000
Wash. Metro Area Transit	2012–2014	5,000

SOURCE: Adapted from David M. Darst, *The Complete Bond Book* (New York, McGraw-Hill, 1975).

Note: U.S. Treasury bills and notes can be purchased from banks, brokers, or, initially, direct from Federal Reserve banks. Federal agency issues can be purchased from banks or brokers.

U.S. savings bonds. Series E and H bonds can no longer be used to postpone tax payments on interest until redemption. No interest is paid on E bonds bought over 40 years ago. There's one 10-year extension for H bonds purchased after May 1959.

The new series EE bonds sell for $25 and can be redeemed for $50 in 11 years and 9 months. The average interest rate is a puny 6%, but no tax need be paid until maturity. Series HH bonds, in denominations from $500 to $10,000, have 10-year maturities, with interest averaging 6% paid semiannually, and are immediately taxable. *Buy these only if you are very patriotic or are "requested" to do so by your boss.*

U.S. retirements bonds. Sold in $50, $100, and $500 denominations. Designed for individual retirement account investments, they pay 6% compounded semiannually. Cannot be sold, discounted, transferred, or pledged as collateral, and early redemption is subject to a 10% penalty. *For those who place safety above income.*

Generally speaking, financial planning should include government securities only for income or for temporary funds. There are times when there can be profits from appreciation and the use of leverage. Aggressive investors with large-denomination bonds can speculate by borrowing up to 90% of face value to buy bonds when they look for a lower interest rate. That will drop the value of the bonds to provide a quick profit. The interest on such bonds, when the bonds are acquired at a substantial discount, can offset most of the cost of a bank loan. *But that is only for the wealthy, wise, and daring.*

INVESTMENT COMPANIES: CONVENIENCE AND DIVERSIFICATION

Investment companies are commonly called "mutual funds," although that term really describes only open-end funds (those whose shares are bought and sold at net asset value). They provide more convenience than performance. They are suitable for beginning investors, for people who don't have the time or desire to handle their own portfolios, and for those, such as retirees, who want special services. By and large, their investment performance has not been outstanding unless the investor was smart enough to take advantage of the opportunity to switch funds in line with the market: from growth to income when the market dropped and interest rates rose and back to growth when the market rallied.

Investment companies sell shares and pool the receipts to buy stocks, bonds, bills, notes, and convertibles to meet specific investment objectives. There are some 800 different, publicly traded investment companies plus thousands of common trust funds run by banks and insurance companies. They range from ultraconservative to highly speculative.

Whenever you entrust your savings to someone else, it costs you money for sales commissions, management, and reports. Those expenses come off the top, so even when you buy no-loads (without sales commissions), your returns will be less than you could attain with the same types of investment. A management fee of three-quarters of 1% doesn't sound like much, but it's $750 on a $100,000 portfolio. That's 15% of a $5,000 annual rate of return.

For most people, no-loads are best. If you prefer to have your broker handle all details, the average 8.5% "load" will reduce the amount of your savings that is invested: only $915 of every $1,000 purchase goes to work. To offset the cost, a load fund must get a 10% higher return for ten years to match the net proceeds of a no-load fund.

For the performances of investment companies in up and down markets, see Table 10–10. The biggest pluses for investment companies are:

• *Diversification.* You have partial ownership of 50 or 100 or more securities for the same dollars you might invest in five or ten holdings. That lessens the risk, but it also limits profits because the biggest gains usually come from two or three winners.

• *Convenience.* Most money management firms control several funds with different investment goals. They permit shareholders to switch, for little or no cost, from growth to income in a down market and vice versa in a bull market.

Table 10–10. Some fund ratings in up and down markets from *Forbes* magazine.

Performance Rating in Markets Up	Down	Fund Name	Last 12 Months	10-Year Average Annual Growth	Last 12 Months Dividends	Total Assets (in Millions)
Stock Funds (Load)						
A+	A	Charter Fund	21.4%	7.3%	1.1%	$ 15.5
B	B	Comstock Fund	15.2	1.4	3.1	95.5
A*	A*	Fidelity Destiny (from 7/70)	20.9	—	2.6	92.2
B	A	Founders-Special	12.4	5.6	1.8	15.0
B	B	Pioneer Fund	3.6	3.1	3.7	476.4
B	B	Plitrend Fund	25.5	1.9	2.1	12.3
B	B	Vance Sanders Common Stock	16.0	3.4	2.0	43.2
Stock Funds (No Load)						
A*	B*	Acorn Fund (from 2/70)	10.9	—	1.7	43.4
A	B	Contrafund	0.8	2.5	2.8	46.4
A*	B*	Dreyfus 3rd Century (from 3/72)	15.4	—	1.3	25.8
A*	A*	Evergreen Fund (from 10/71)	41.2	—	1.2	90.0
B*	B*	Hamilton Income (from 12/70)	−2.1	—	5.4	49.9
B	A*	Janus Fund (from 2/70)	13.1	—	1.2	20.7
B	A	Mutual Shares	16.7	7.5	1.8	45.0
B	B	Naess & Thomas Special	14.7	1.8	1.9	11.4
A*	A*	Sequoia Fund (from 7/70)	31.8	—	1.6	44.9
B	A	20th Century Income	46.0	5.0	1.3	2.8
B	B	Windsor Fund	5.2	2.8	4.3	574.8
Stock Funds (Closed End)						
B*	A*	Assets Investors (from 1/69)	32.2	—	0.3	6.1
A+	A	Japan Fund	40.6	20.1	1.0	200.7
Funds for Investing Abroad (Load)						
A	A+	Templeton Growth Fund	24.9	17.7	0.8	170.5
Balanced Funds (Load)						
A*	C*	Income Fund/America (from 2/71)	−4.9	—	6.4	163.7
A+	C	Kemper Total Return	4.1	1.3	5.4	42.1
B	C	Union Income	−4.2	0.7	7.3	56.8
Balanced Funds (No Load)						
A+	F	Louis Sayles Mutual	−1.6	−1.4	4.7	96.7
A+	F	Stein Roe Balanced	−2.9	−1.7	4.0	108.3
		Standard & Poor's 500 Stocks	−4.9	−1.3	5.3	

SOURCE: *Forbes* magazine, August 21, 1978.

Note: The ratings are based on performance in each of three rising markets and three falling markets. To get a high score, a fund must show superior performance in all three up or down periods. In up markets, the top 12.5% of all funds are initially awarded an A+, the next 12.5% get A, the next 25% get B, and so on. In down markets, the ratings range from A to F, with an occasional A+ for outstanding performance. The up markets were 5/26/70 to 1/11/73, 10/3/74 to 9/21/76, and 3/6/78 to 6/30/78. The down markets were 11/29/68 to 5/26/70, 1/11/73 to 10/3/74, and 9/21/76 to 3/6/78. Capital gains distributions, but not income dividends, were reinvested. No allowance for sales charges.
*Does not cover full 10-year period.

• *No decisions.* The professional managers do the research, determine the strategy, and order the purchases or sales.

• *Accurate records.* Periodically, the fund will send you a complete record of your account. That helps you with tax filing and enables you to reduce taxes by matching sales against purchases for lowest gains or highest losses.

Other benefits, which apply to specific situations, include:

• Automatic reinvestment of all income and appreciation so that your savings compound for greater total returns.

• Regular checks monthly or quarterly. That is handy for older relatives or retirees who need steady income.

• Life insurance at low cost available in two forms: (1) Term life for contract plans when you agree to invest a specified sum over a period of time. It guarantees that your survivors will receive the full amount of your investment commitment. (2) Family protection, typically five-year renewable term life insurance up to $50,000 (with the privilege of insuring your spouse to half that amount). It is usually available without a physical exam, so it is excellent for people who have difficulty in obtaining regular coverage.

• Profit insurance, which can be bought in connection with certain load funds. A small premium guarantees that you will get back your full investment if all income is reinvested in additional shares of the fund for at least 10 years. Its best use is to lock in profits; you rewrite the policy to keep pace with the rising value of shares.

EXAMPLE: In April Mr. DeVoe buys 10,000 shares of Dempster Fund at $5 each. The investment is $50,000, but with the 8% load only $46,000 is working. He buys profit insurance for a premium of 6% ($3,000 spread over 10 years).

By September, the bull market pushes the price of each unit to $6, so DeVoe cancels the old policy and buys a new one on the current investment value of $60,000. The cost is small because there's credit for the original premium. And so on. No matter how low the market gets at the end of the contract, DeVoe is sure of getting $60,000.

Special Investment Companies

In general, you should choose funds to meet specific financial goals: income, growth, balance, or whatever. But there are times when you may want to consider special funds.

Closed-end funds. Unlike open-end funds, which have a constant flow of money in and out as investors buy and sell shares at current net asset value, closed-end funds have fixed capitalizations. Their shares are traded like regular stocks, so their prices reflect supply and demand. They are usually available at discounts of 15% to 20% from the value of the underlying holdings. Apparently, investors feel that their money will be locked in and, to take advantage of new opportunities, management will have to sell good stocks.

Closed-end funds offer these advantages: (1) You are buying quality stocks below their current market value. (2) The dividends are paid on the full dollar's worth of the assets; thus, at a 20% discount, an 8% dividend becomes 10%. (3) With automatic reinvestment of income, you buy new shares at bargain prices.

The big question is whether the shares will still be selling at discounts when you want to cash in. Generally, closed-end funds are most worthwhile when you expect the market to rise and want above-average income. For the performance of some closed-end funds see Table 10-11.

Dual funds. Dual funds are a variation of closed-end funds. They offer two separate investment vehicles: *capital shares* and *income shares*. You can buy one or both. All money paid in, for both types of shares, is placed in a single pool. All capital growth is credited to holders of capital shares. All income, from dividends and interest, is paid to holders of income shares. Thus every shareholder has $2 serving his investment goal for every $1 invested, and more than that when he buys at a discount.

The income shares are like preferred stocks in that they have a stated, minimum, cumulative dividend: 5% to 7.5% on the offering price. Recently, income shares traded below net asset value, so the returns were higher.

Dual funds have a limited life; for presently available funds, it is from 1979 to 1985. At that time, all income shares will be paid off at a price guaranteed in the prospectus or swapped, on a dollar-for-dollar basis, for capital shares. That can be an assured gain; for income shares of Scudder Duo Vest, recently at 7⅜, to $9.15 in 1982.

The prices of capital shares move in line with the values of the underlying stocks. The payoff also comes at maturity, when the redemption price will reflect the appreciation of both types of shares and, hopefully, will eliminate the current 20% discount. The risk is that, at termination, there will be insufficient assets left after payment of income shares. But you would still own shares in a standard mutual fund.

Income shares are excellent for fixed returns. Capital shares are best for investors who do not want current income and are willing to wait for appreciation. For the performance of some dual-purpose funds see Table 10-12.

Other special funds. There are scores of other special funds. For investors there are funds which make tax-free payments from principal and leave the balance, plus income and appreciation, for long-term investments. Private debt

Table 10-11. Some closed-end funds.

Fund	Recent Price	Net Asset Value	Discount	Dividend	Yield
Adams Express	12¼	$14.35	−14.6%	$1.15	9.4%
Carriers & General	12½	14.75	−15.3	1.00	8.0
General American	10⅛	12.79	−20.8	1.22	12.1
Tri-Continental	20⅛	23.25	−13.4	2.18	10.8
U.S. & Foreign	16	20.57	−22.0	1.32	8.2

Table 10–12. Some dual-purpose funds.

Fund	Capital Shares Price	Capital Shares Net Assets per Share	Capital Shares Difference	Income Shares Price	Income Shares Dividend	Income Shares Yield
American Dual	8¼	$ 8.91	−7.4%	14⅜	.84	5.8%
Gemini	20¼	26.78	−24.4	15¾	1.20	7.6
Income & Capital	6½	8.26	−21.3	10¾	.94	9.1
Leverage	13¼	17.07	−22.4	13⅝	.75	5.5
Scudder Duo Vest	7⅜	9.34	−21.0	9¼	.71	7.7

funds, usually sponsored by financially oriented firms such as insurance companies, invest public money, often in joint ventures with their own funds, in mortgages. Sometimes there are sweeteners such as warrants or rights to common stock. The returns are high and, eventually, some of the equity holdings will pay off too. For the performance of some private debt funds see Table 10–13.

For speculators there are commodities, hedge, and letter stock funds. Commodities funds have high costs but offer potentially dazzling returns if the fund manager is either smart or lucky. Hedge funds use leverage, sell short, and engage in arbitrage. Letter stock funds purchase unissued stock at 25% to 50% below market value. They must hold the shares for a fairly long period, during which, hopefully, the company will prosper so that the shares can be offered publicly at a substantial profit.

Consider using some of the conservative funds in your financial planning, but take a chance with the speculative ones only when you have extra money which you can afford to lose. Such funds are mentioned here as a warning, not as a recommendation.

Money market (liquid asset) funds invest in Treasury bills and notes, bank certificates of deposit, and commercial paper. They offer rates that are competitive with interest and special privileges such as prompt reinvestment of income, the right to shift money to another fund under the same management, and check writing to take advantage of the float.

These funds are terrific when interest rates are 10% and higher, but in recent years their benefits may be largely a matter of convenience and quick profits. Interest is paid daily, and you can add to or withdraw from your money at any time, even by a phone call.

Table 10–13. Some private debt funds.

Issuer	Recent Price	Dividend	Yield
American General	30	$1.80	6.0%
Fort Dearborn	15	1.24	8.3
Mass. Mutual Income	14⅝	1.21	8.3
Vestaur Securities	14½	1.31	9.0

Money market funds are excellent parking places for idle cash. If you want to gain a few extra dollars and have the fun of a trick technique, you can arrange for check-writing privileges. If you deal with a fund that is many miles from your home, you will get daily interest for the 7 to 14 days it takes for your check to clear.

EXAMPLE: Dr. Emrich, in Miami, puts spare cash in Money Management Fund in Pittsburgh. He pays his $1,000 monthly rent with a special MMF check. Since the check takes 10 days to clear, he earns 7.5% daily compounded interest. If he does that every month, the interest will amount to about $25 a year. That's really financial planning!

The various types of investments are compared in Table 10-14.

SAVINGS PLANS

Savings plans are such an important part of financial planning that some repetition is warranted. Savings, or thrift, plans permit the employee to contribute a fixed percent of salary, usually to a maximum of 10%, to be matched by the corporation. Thus you have $2 working for every $1 you save. Your contribution is taxable, but the interest income on the total savings is tax-free until withdrawn. The plan is usually part of the corporate retirement program. You have a choice of investing in company stock, in a diversified stock fund, or in corporate bonds and fixed-income holdings.

"When you have a choice," says Tom A. Dowse, vice president of Bank of America, "put a substantial portion in fixed-income holdings. Over the years, investments in corporate stock can lock in too much capital in one basket." Maybe he's right about most plans, but much depends on the quality and growth of the company. Each situation should be judged on the basis of your overall assets, your goals, and your ability to shift assets from one fund to another to meet changing conditions.

The one major caveat is this: Do *not* use matched money to speculate in the hope of higher returns or the theoretical benefits of tax-exempt securities. The money represents savings for retirement, and it should be invested carefully, wisely, and fully. Even if the funds do not perform too well, the matching money will assure high total returns. The tax savings may look tempting but, over the years, they will not be enough to offset the magic of compounding.

EXAMPLE: A 45-year-old executive diverts $200 a month from a savings plan to buy municipal bonds. He figures that the 5.5% tax-free yield is equal to about 10% taxable income: higher than the 8.5% return from the thrift plan. But that extra 3% yield can make a tremendous difference when compounded, and that $200 can become $400 with the matching funds.

Here's what could happen: At age 65, he takes out $125,000 from the thrift plan, pays $15,000 in federal income taxes, and has $110,000 left. By contrast, a well-managed municipal bond fund would grow to about $87,000. That's $23,000 less, all because of the lower yield and slower compounding.

Table 10–14. Comparison of various types of investments.

Degree of Effort Required for Management Decision	Security or Savings	Reward: Approximate Yield, %	Variability— Standard Deviation, %	Ownership Risks — Market	Ownership Risks — Business or Credit	Creditorship Risks — Interest or Money Rate	Creditorship Risks — Purchasing Power or Inflation
	Security						
H	Speculative common stock	15	12	H	H	L	L
H	Speculative mutual funds	12	10	H	H	L	L
H	Growth common stock	10	8	H	H	L	L
M	High-quality common stock (blue chip)	8	6	M	M	L	L
M	Investment mutual funds	8	6	M	M	L	M
M	Income common stock	7	2	M–L	M–L	M	M
M	Balanced mutual funds	7	3	M–L	M–L	M	M
M	Convertible preferred stock	7	3	M–H	M–H	L	L
M	Convertible bonds	8	3	M–H	M–H	H	H
L	Corporate bonds, AAA	7	2	L	L	M	M
L	Corporate bonds, below BAA	8	2	M	M	H	M
L	Municipal bonds, tax-free	5	2	L	L	H	H
L	Government bonds	7	2	L	L	H	H
L	Short-term government bonds	6	2	L	L	L	H
	Savings						
L	Variable annuity	7	1	L	L	L	M
L	Credit Union	6	1	L	L	L	M
L	Savings and loan associations	6	½	L	L	L	H
O	Life insurance savings	4	1	L	L	L	H
O	Mutual savings banks	5	1	L	L	L	H
O	Commercial banks	4	½	L	L	L	H
L	Swiss bank account	0	0	L	L	L	H
O	Cash box	0	0	L	L	L	H
O	Mattress, drawer, desk	0	0	L	L	L	H

SOURCE: Stolper & Co., Inc., San Diego, Cal.

H = high; M = moderate; L = low; 0 = zero.

INVESTMENT CLUBS

A pleasant and often profitable way to invest some of your funds is by membership in an investment club. You pool your money with others, so the total sum becomes substantial. And, of course, the experience should help you become more familiar with investment terms and processes.

Most investment clubs meet monthly, with each member contributing $25 to $250 each time. Meetings are devoted to listening to research reports, discussing potential purchases or sales, and making decisions by majority vote. For information, accounting forms, and a monthly publication, write to National Association of Investment Clubs (NAIC), Box 220, Royal Oak, MI 48068.

According to NAIC, there are three rules for investment club success:

1. *Dollar cost averaging:* investing each month's contributions at once regardless of market conditions. In a bull market the money will buy stocks whose values go up; in a fluctuating market the steady buying process lowers the average cost; in a bear market the money picks up bargains. According to some studies, that is better theory than practice. Still, the principle is sound when it is applied to stocks whose prices swing widely. Your dollars buy more shares at low points.

2. *Reinvestment of all dividends and profits:* to gain the snowballing effect of compound interest.

3. *Investing for the long pull:* looking ahead and buying stocks with a capacity to double in value in a few years.

Here are some investment club checkpoints:

Common tie. The group should have a fraternal, church, business, or community connection. Be cautious about trying to blend age with youth, wealth with modest savings, or experienced investors with amateurs.

Similar investment goals. If some members want to speculate and others prefer long-term holdings, split the funds into, say, 25% for risky trading and 75% for blue chips. Whatever you do, set a policy and stick to it.

Limited membership. A club should have a minimum of 10 people and a maximum of 25. Experience indicates that 15 is the most effective number.

Active participation. Make certain that everyone not only attends and is actively involved but also makes regular contributions.

Education. Although the goal is to make money, even a moderately successful club will be worthwhile if members learn about risks and rewards, Wall Street terminology, sources of information, how to judge securities, how to keep records, and so on.

Most brokerage firms will provide speakers; excellent films can be obtained from the New York Stock Exchange and American Stock Exchange; and, when the club is established, invitations can be extended to treasurers of local corporations and professional money managers.

No self-promotion. The club should not be a means of self-promotion by a registered representative. In fact, be cautious about including any broker. Members tend to rely too heavily on anyone they consider a "professional," so they fail to develop their own initiatives and decision-making powers.

Formal procedures. An investment club is a legal entity as well as a business. There must be officers, minutes, and reports, so there should be guidelines (or rules) as to investment philosophy, responsibility for records, allocation of costs, and so on.

Devil's advocate. The club needs a member or members who will question the research and pick flaws in the recommendations. Unanimous consent is seldom effective in investing.

Friendly, easy withdrawal. If some member should need his funds, move from the area, or prefer to make his own judgments, he should be able to withdraw his funds without trouble.

Use one broker. A small account is not profitable, so you will have to choose someone who is willing to look to the future or, more likely, is already serving one or more club members.

Formal organization. Investment clubs are much more than a way to spend a social evening. Several states have specific regulations, and every club must meet IRS requirements. For federal tax purposes, investment clubs are treated as partnerships, so members must include taxable income on their personal returns. There must be an identification number for the club, and the annual report must provide information on stock transactions, dividend disbursements, and items entitled to special tax treatment (dividends from qualifying domestic corporations, capital gains and losses).

For details of operation and accounting, write NAIC for its *Investment Club Manual* and IRS for Publication 550, *Tax Information on Investment Income and Expenses.*

TEACHING YOUR SPOUSE ABOUT INVESTMENTS

Teaching your spouse about investment is easy and can be fun.* But unless you are extremely knowledgeable and patient, do not try to be the schoolmaster. All your spouse needs to learn is enough to judge the quality of the advice from other people: banker, broker, or investment counselor. A little knowledge and a lot of common sense can separate fact from fiction, of which there will be plenty because widows are a prime target for so-called counselors.

First, have her read basic books (see the Bibliography), attend lectures of local brokerage firms, colleges, or adult education schools, and learn how to read the financial pages. Then help her to set up her own account with a gift, her own savings, or an inheritance.

If she proves successful, keep adding funds each year. Many a wife has done a better job of managing the household budget, or the funds of a club, than her husband has done in managing the family savings. Let her work directly with your broker to make her own selections and sales. It's OK to keep an eye on the monthly statements, but let her make her own mistakes and score her own triumphs.

---

*Although women control the majority of wealth in this country, the fact is that most investments are handled by the husband, not the wife.

If you do make suggestions, concentrate on explanations of the rewards and risks, just as you should do with your own portfolio, and caution her about taxes. If she takes a profit at year end, it could throw you into a higher tax bracket. Alternatively, her losses might be valuable in cutting your payments. Once in a while, it could be advantageous to file separate tax returns.

RULES FOR SUCCESSFUL INVESTING

As with all phases of financial planning, there are basic rules for investing. No matter how wise, experienced, or successful you may feel you have become, review the following commandments at least once a year. After you have sustained a substantial loss, check them to find out where and when you went wrong.

It may be true that rules are meant to be broken, but the stock market is a battleground where the amateur competes with shrewd, tough-minded professionals. The rules are digested from the experience of several successful money managers. They not only can help you survive in Wall Street but, better yet, show you how to make your money work more profitably toward your goals.

Maintain a cash reserve in interest-bearing bank deposits, government securities, or cash insurance values. It should be sufficient to cover living expenses for three months.

Investigate before you invest. Get the facts. Do not act on tips or rumor. Subscribe to one factual advisory service, and read at least one daily and one weekly financial publication. When you have questions, get a report from your broker's research department. Then make your own decisions.

Investigate after you invest. There is no such thing as a permanent stock investment to be locked away in a strong box—if you want to maximize your returns. Modern business is so competitive and is subject to such powerful political and economic pressures that even the best companies falter now and then.

Watch the financial changes and stay with stocks only when there are logical, fact-backed reasons to anticipate continued growth and profitablility. Even then, watch the charts to spot unfavorable trends.

Invest for total returns, income plus appreciation. The rewards are greater and the taxes lower than if you buy only for income. Total returns are the one sure way to stay ahead of inflation.

Invest only in healthy industries, ones in which the leading companies earn at least 10% on stockholders' equity, have recently increased earnings, or have well-founded prospects for higher profits.

Invest only in quality stocks, those of financially strong, growing, profitable corporations whose shares are held by 15 or more institutional investors.

Diversify your investments but not too much. In a small portfolio, have no more than five stocks and add to those holdings until you double your original investment. Beyond that, add one new stock for each $5,000, preferably $10,000. For a $100,000 portfolio, set a limit of ten stocks and add new ones for each new $20,000 investment.

Do not become married to any security. "Give loyalty to your family and friends, but don't waste it on a scrap of paper."

Buy only when you can anticipate a substantial price rise. "Substantial" means at least 25% in the relatively near future. With high-dividend stocks, the rise can be as little as 15%: 3 points for a stock selling at 20.

Buy into an uptrend. Look for *up* stocks in *up* groups in *up* markets. That will give you the advantage of momentum and popularity and lessen the possibilities of losses.

Review any stock when its P/E ratio goes above its average annual high multiple for the last ten years. That is not the last word, but it's a good indication that the stock may be moving into dangerously overpriced territory.

Sell when you can no longer anticipate a further price rise. That will occur when (1) the stock is fully valued, (2) the prospects for the company or the market are poor, (3) the chart signals a downtrend.

Sell when you make a mistake—when the stock or market does not perform as anticipated. The first loss is the smallest. If your stock drops 10%, check with your broker. If the decline continues, sell unless you feel certain that the situation is temporary and will be overcome by corporate action or prospects. Today's low can be tomorrow's high.

Watch the tax selling date, 12 months after the period when the stock started to move up. That is when many buyers, eager to take advantage of the lower long-term capital gains tax rate, will sell. The extra supply will almost always cause a temporary setback.

Never take any action which you do not understand. If you are uneasy about the action of a stock or the recommendation of an adviser, use your common sense. More often than not, you'll be right. Besides, you will feel more comfortable if you make your own decision.

MIXING YOUR PORTFOLIO

How you mix your portfolio depends on your income, resources, goals, sleep-well point, and the trend of the stock market. A conservative should be comfortable with the breakdowns in Table 10–15. A more aggressive investor would lessen debt and raise equity holdings. Table 10–16 shows how much $200,000 will be worth after 20 years in various combinations of stocks and

Table 10–15. Suggested portfolio mix.

Age Bracket	Bonds Corporate	Bonds Government	CVs*	Tax-Exempts	Common Stocks
30–39	20%	20%	30%	—	30%
40–49	25	25	20	10%	20
50–59	30	20	10	20	20
60 up	40	20	20	—	20

*Convertible securities.

Table 10–16. What $200,000 will be worth at the end of 20 years in various combinations of stocks and bonds.

	Return		
	7%	10%	12%
100% bonds	$772,000		
75% bonds	579,000	$ 579,000	$ 579,000
25% stocks	193,000	336,000	482,000
	$772,000	$ 915,000	$1,061,000
50% bonds	386,000	386,000	386,000
50% stocks	386,000	672,000	964,000
	$772,000	$1,058,000	$1,350,000
25% bonds	193,000	193,000	193,000
75% stocks	579,000	1,080,000	1.446,000
	$772,000	$1,273,000	$1,639,000

SOURCE: Stolper & Co., Inc., San Diego, Cal.
Assumptions: 1. The 7% interest can be obtained with high-grade bonds for the next 20 years.
2. Funds will be immediately reinvested at the same rate.
3. No further contributions.
4. Since the plan is tax-deferred, this in a sense provides for inflation.

bonds. The table supports what has been stressed: that bonds are dead investments in that they will never be worth more than their original par value. A 20-year bond issued at $1,000 will be worth only $1,000 at maturity. All gains will be the result of compounding of the interest. The maximum rate of return is always the coupon rate, here 7%.

Common stocks are live investments. They can provide regular income and, when of quality companies, have the ability to appreciate in value. Their returns are not limited; they can be 10% or 12%. The 75% invested in stocks ($150,000) will grow to $1,080,000 at 10% and to $1,446,000 at 12%. That is not difficult when dividends are reinvested and corporate profits keep rising.

SUMMARY

Successful investing is a long, slow, boring process. It requires wise selection, plenty of patience, and confidence that value will out. If you buy quality stocks when they are undervalued, you will always win in the long run. In the interim, however, it can be mighty nerve-wracking to watch the prices of your holdings plummet because of a bear market, panic selling by big investors, or temporary and usually unjustified fears.

The most profitable course is to sell quickly when the stock price dips sharply. If you do prefer to hold on, do so only as long as the corporation continues to boost revenues and earnings. Eventually, ever-rising profits will be reflected in higher stock valuations. In Wall Street, fortunes are built from the bottom up, and usually only after years of waiting. There's no shortcut to investment profits, whether you make the decisions yourself or delegate the responsibility to someone else. *Always invest in quality when the value is low and the prospects are bright.*

GLOSSARY

These definitions refer specifically to the stock market, but with variations many of them may apply to other types of investments such as real estate, retirement plans, and insurance.

American Stock Exchange (AMEX). An auction market for the sale and purchase of securities of corporations with fewer shareholders and smaller capitalizations than companies listed on the NYSE have.

annual report. The formal financial statement issued by a corporation each year.

assets. What a company owns or is owed. See *current assets* and *fixed assets*.

asset value. The market value of all securities and cash on hand. The asset value of stocks is usually expressed on a per share basis.

balance sheet. A condensed financial statement showing the type and amount of corporate assets, liabilities, and capital.

bear market. A declining stock market.

blue chip. The stock of a major corporation known for its ability to make money and pay dividends.

bond. An interest-bearing certificate of indebtedness by a corporation or government body that is often secured by a mortgage or lien.

book value. An accounting term to show the net worth (assets minus liabilities) of a corporation with respect to common stockholders. To obtain book value on a per share basis, divide the net assets of the corporation by the number of shares of common stock outstanding.

broker. An agent who handles orders to buy and sell securities, commodities, or other property. Also called account executive, customer's man, and registered representative.

brokerage firm. An organization that deals in securities, usually a member of the NYSE and/or other stock exchanges.

call. An option to buy a certain number of shares, usually 100, at a specific price within a specified period of time.

call protection. A provision of long-term bonds and preferred stocks that permits redemption before maturity date. Usually the call is at a price higher than par and cannot be exercised for at least five years after issue.

capital gain. Profit from the sale of a capital asset, such as a security or real estate. If acquisition is less than 12 months past, the profit is short-term and is taxed as regular income. If acquisition is more than 12 months past, the profit is subject to a lower tax rate.

capital loss. The opposite of capital gain: a loss from the sale of a capital asset. All capital losses are tax deductible to some degree.

closed-end fund. An investment company with a limited number of shares that are traded on a stock exchange. Prices reflect supply and demand and are usually below net asset value of the underlying securities.

collateral. Securities or other property pledged by a borrower to assure repayment of a loan.

commercial paper. A short-term negotiable security of a corporate borrower.

commission. The fee paid to a broker for the execution of a sale or purchase of securities.

common stock. A security which represents ownership in a corporation. Holders assume greater risks than do owners of bonds or preferred stocks, but they may gain greater rewards from dividends and appreciation in the market value of the stock.

compound interest. Interest earned on principal and accrued interest income.

convertible. A bond, debenture, or preferred stock that may be exchanged for common stock or another security, usually of the same company.

current assets. Cash, investments, accounts receivable, materials, and inventories that a company owns or is owed.

current ratio. Current assets divided by current liabilities. Usually a safe minimum for investment is a 2:1 ratio, but that depends on the type of business.

custodian. A bank, broker, or trust agency that holds an investor's securities for safekeeping.

debenture. A bond or promissory note backed by the general credit of a corporation rather than any specific property.

depreciation. The decrease in the value of property caused by wear and tear, decay, or decline in price. It is charged against earnings, usually over the estimated useful life of the building, machinery, or whatever.

discount. The amount deducted from the regular or par value of a preferred stock or bond or from the net asset value of a closed-end fund.

discretionary account. An investment portfolio for which an investment adviser or broker has the authority to buy and sell securities without consulting the owner or client.

dividend. A payment in cash, or stock, to shareholders according to the number of shares held. Owners of preferred shares are usually paid a fixed sum; the dividend of a common stock varies with the fortunes of the company.

dual fund. A type of investment company that offers both capital and income shares. All money paid in is placed in a single pool. Holders of capital shares receive all appreciation; income share owners get all dividends and interest. The investor can buy one or both types.

earned growth rate (EGR). The annual rate by which a company's equity capital is increased by net earnings after payment of dividends. To determine EGR, start with the per share earnings, subtract the dividend payment, and divide the remainder by the book value per share at the beginning of the year.

equity. Ownership in a company by a holder of common or preferred stock.

face value. The value of a bond shown on the face of the certificate. Generally, it is the amount to be paid at maturity.

fiduciary. A person or institution holding a position of trust, usually one that has to do with investments and finances.

fixed assets. The land, buildings, machinery, and equipment owned by, or owed to, a corporation.

fixed-income security. A bond, debenture, or preferred stock on which a set rate of interest is paid. Also applicable to savings certificates and Treasury bills, notes, and so on.

front-end load. The commission charged by an investment company for purchase of shares. Usually it is 8.5% to 9% for stock funds and 3.5% to 4.5% for bond funds. The deduction means you have less money working for your investment objective.

fundamental research. The analysis of industries and corporations based on such factors as sales, assets, earnings, profitability, growth, and management.

gross national product. The total value of all goods and services produced in the country during a specified period.

growth stock. Shares of a company with a record of rapid growth in earnings, usually an annual average of 10% or more.

income statement. The part of a corporation's annual report that shows sales, expenses, operating profit, gross earnings, taxes, and net income.

index. A measure or average of prices of stocks traded on an exchange or of securities of a group or industry.

institutional investor. An organization that invests its own assets and money held in trust for others: a corporate pension plan, investment company, insurance firm, university endowment fund, foundation, or bank. Institutional investors account for nearly two-thirds of all transactions on the NYSE.

interest. The payment, to a lender, for the use of money; the money paid to bondholders by a corporation.

investment company. An organization that sells shares to the public and invests the proceeds in securities. The objectives determine the types of investments: bonds for income, stocks for growth, and so on with a growing number of variations.

investment counsel. A person, or organization, who, or which, advises on investments and may render investment management services.

investor. A person whose primary concern is the use of money to make more money through interest, dividends, and capital appreciation. Safety of principal is the most important consideration.

leverage. The use of existing assets, such as securities, as collateral for loans to buy securities. Also, the corporate use of nonequity capital, such as borrowed money, to increase the returns on equity.

liabilities. All claims against the company: accounts payable, wages and salaries due, declared but unpaid dividends, accrued taxes, bank loans, and long-term debt.

liquidity. The ability to convert assets into cash quickly.

listed security. A corporate stock or bond issue traded on a stock exchange.

load. The commission, or sales charge, for the purchase of shares of an open-end investment company, bond fund, or insurance policy.

locked in. The feeling some investors have when they are reluctant to sell a security because of the heavy taxes on their profits.

margin. A loan to an investor by a broker with securities purchased with the loan as collateral. The Federal Reserve Board sets margin limits, recently at 50%.

market price. The last reported price at which a security sold.

money market fund. An investment company that invests in short-term, liquid assets such as Treasury bills, federal notes, certificates of deposit, commercial paper, and banker's acceptances.

municipal bond. A debt issued by a state, county, city, town, village, or public authority. The interest is exempt from federal income taxes and, in general, from state and local income taxes within the state of issue. Puerto Rico bonds are exempt from federal and all state income taxes.

mutual fund. The term properly applied only to open-end investment companies but usually used to describe all investment companies.

net asset value. The net worth, based on closing market prices, of all securities owned by an investment company divided by the number of fund shares outstanding.

net change. The difference in the value of a security between closing price today and that of the day before. The figure +¾ means that the price of a share rose by 75¢.

New York Stock Exchange (NYSE). The major auction market for the purchase and sale of common stocks and corporate bonds. All corporations listed are major companies with established leadership, strong finances, and broad public ownership.

no-load fund. An investment company that does not make a sales charge for the purchase of its shares.

open-end fund. An investment company that continually issues shares as it receives new capital or that stands ready to redeem shares at net asset value.

option. The right to buy (call) or sell (put) a fixed amount of a given stock, usually 100 shares, at a set price within a set period of time. The purchaser hopes the value of the stock will rise; the seller is willing to accept a sure, limited profit.

over-the-counter (OTC) market. The auction market for the purchase and sale of securities not listed on the stock exchange.

paper profit. The unrealized profit on a security or other property.

point. A change of $1 per share of stock, a change of $10 in the price of a bond (which is quoted as a percent of each $1,000 face value), one unit of change in market average, or 1% of a mortgage loan.

portfolio. All securities held by a person or institution for investment or speculation. Usually, it contains a mixture of stocks, bonds, and real estate.

preferred stock. A stock with a claim to dividends on corporate earnings before dividends are paid to common shareholders. Dividends are usually at a fixed rate.

premium. The amount by which a bond or preferred stock sells above par value. Also, money paid by the buyer, or received by the seller, of an option.

profit rate (PR). The percent of profit earned on money invested by holders of common stock. A PR is determined by dividing earnings per share by the per share book value at the beginning of the year.

prudent man rule. An investment standard for securities; the securities purchased should be those which a prudent person of discretion and intelligence seeking a reasonable income and preservation of capital would purchase.

put. An option to sell a certain number of shares, usually 100, for a specified price within a specified period.

quality. The characteristics of a security as determined by corporate financial strength, profitability, growth, consistency, and the reliability of profits and growth, price stability, and future prospects.

rally. A brisk rise, after a decline, in the price level of a stock market or a security.

real estate investment trust (REIT). An organization, similar to an investment company, that concentrates its holdings in real estate loans, mortgages, and real estate–related securities.

registered representative (RR). A full-time employee of a brokerage firm who has met requirements of the NYSE and SEC. Also known as account executive and customer's broker.

reward/risk ratio. The possible gain versus the possible loss. If an investor thinks that a security now at 20 can either rise to 30 or fall to 15, the R/R ratio is 10 up, 5 down, or 2:1.

rollover. A transaction used to postpone taxes. For example, a retirement fund payout is not subject to taxation if the money is reinvested, in an individual retirement account, within 60 days. A rollover is similarly used with stocks and commodities to push the tax payment date from one year to the next.

round lot. A standard unit of trading or a multiple of that standard. On most securities, it's 100 shares of stock and $1,000 face value of bonds.

savings bond. A debt of the U.S. government available in two series: EE for small denominations and HH in $500 to $10,000 units.
savings certificate. Evidence of a long-term savings account in a bank or savings and loan association. It pays a fixed rate of interest, and earnings are compounded to increase the stated yield.
Securities and Exchange Commission (SEC). The federal agency that regulates securities, stock exchanges, brokerage firms, investment companies, and investment advisers.
security. A certificate that gives the owner a share in a publicly owned corporation or that certifies a loan to a corporation or government body.
security analyst. An individual who makes judgments on the value of securities.
sinking fund. Money regularly set aside by a government agency or corporation to redeem its debt.
speculate. To risk money in hopes of making money from market fluctuations. Safety of principal is not important.
split. A division of corporate shares. A two-for-one split for a company with 1 million shares results in 2 million shares. Each stockholder receives an additional number of shares equal to his previous holding.
stock dividend. A dividend paid in securities rather than in cash.
stock market. Any auction market, but usually the NYSE.
stock price. The value of one share of common stock: the result of a buyer's acceptance of a seller's offer.
stop order. An order, to a broker, to buy or sell at a designated price. Often used to limit a loss or protect a profit.
striking price. The price of a share of stock at which an option is exercised.
tax shelter. An investment vehicle in which certain expenses can be offset against regular income or in which taxes on income normally subject to tax are deferred.
technical analysis. A study of the market and of stocks based on supply and demand. Price movements, volume, trends, and patterns are charted to assess future market movement. A technical analysis reports *what is* and not *what should be*.
thin market. A market in which there are comparatively few bids to buy or offers to sell.
timing. Deciding the most appropriate time to buy or sell, a valuable tool in enhancing profits and cutting losses. Its use relies on technical analysis, but it may also involve fundamental considerations.
Treasury bills. Debt obligations of the U.S. government that mature in three, six, or nine months or one year. They can be purchased in minimum units of $10,000.
Treasury note. A debt obligation of the U.S. Treasury that matures in one to five years.
unlisted security. A security not listed or traded on a stock exchange and usually available in the over-the-counter market.
value. The ratio of tomorrow's price to today's price. It suggests the price at which the security will sell in the future on the basis of current and prospective earnings, dividends, and corporate equity capital. Investment success is buying a security when it is undervalued and selling it when it becomes fully priced.
volume. The number of shares traded in a market or specific security during a given period.

warrant. A certificate giving the holder the right to purchase stock at a stipulated price and usually within a set time period. Frequently, a warrant is offered with debt securities as an inducement to buyers who want to hold an equity position in the corporation. Warrants sell on hope, not value.

yield. The interest or dividend paid on a security expressed as a percent of the security's price. It can be actual, coupon, or current. *Actual yield* is the rate of return based on net purchase price. It will be higher than the coupon yield if the security is bought below par and lower if purchased above par. *Coupon yield* is the rate stated on the face of the bond. *Current yield* is the rate of return on the market price of the security. It is calculated by dividing the dollars of the payment by the current quotation. *Yield to maturity* (YTM) is the rate of return on a bond held to maturity. It includes appreciation, if any, from the current market price.

11 Special Investments and Speculations: Handle with Care

There are scores of special investments you should know about even if you do not use them. Some, like commodities and mortgage futures, can be supplements to, or substitutes for, securities and real estate, but unless you are experienced and have ample resources, they are usually too speculative to become integral parts of financial planning. They require more capital, more expertise, and more time than most executives and professionals have.

Other special "investments," such as art, antiques, diamonds, and race horses, are better for fun and personal satisfaction than for profit. It's true that, in recent years, the values of many such holdings have increased rapidly, but with a few exceptions the investments are illiquid, do not provide income, and involve heavy costs for buying and selling. They should be considered as adjuncts to lifestyle and not as investments to enhance your net worth.

Here's a summary of some of the special "opportunities":

COMMODITIES

The dismal stock market of the mid-1970s made many people turn to commodities trading, because that is one of the few areas in which an individual with small capital can strike it rich. He can also lose money—fast.

To most people, commodities are a speculation, not an investment. Two out of every three transactions end in losses. The trick is to keep the losses low and score big with a few profitable selections. Yet, with wise planning, expert assistance, and strict discipline, trading in commodities can double or triple your money and build your estate quickly. Luck helps too.

Commodities trading is different from investing in stocks. When you buy a common stock, you own part of a corporation and share in its profits, if any. If you pick a profitable company, the price of its stock will eventually move up and you will be able to sell at a gain. In commodities there is no equity. You buy on hope. Once the futures contract has expired, there's no tomorrow. If your trade turned out badly, you must take a partial-to-full loss.

Commodities futures are traded, on independent exchanges, in wheat, corn, soybeans, cotton, orange juice, metals, currency, and so on. Prices are quoted daily in the financial press. The futures are part of a system of hedging: removing or reducing the risk of one commitment by taking an offsetting position with another, usually with a different delivery (maturity) date.

EXAMPLE: Farmer Frank plants what he hopes will be a 10,000-bushel soybean crop. He wants to be sure that he will receive a minimum price when the crop is harvested. In the spring, he sells two futures contracts of 5,000 bushels each for December delivery at $5.30 per bushel. If the market price, in December, is $5.00, Frank loses 30¢ per bushel in the cash market but makes up the loss by buying back his futures contracts for 30¢ less than he received. The opposite happens when the December price rises to, say, $5.60 per bushel. He makes 30¢ per bushel in the cash market and loses as much on his contracts. Either way, farmer Frank is assured of that $5.30 per bushel.

At the same time, Famous Foods, which sells its products throughout the year, wants a predetermined cost for its soybean purchases. The purchasing agent buys futures in the appropriate forward month. If the price rises, he pays more in the cash market but profits when he sells the futures contracts. Or vice versa.

In both cases, there must be someone to take the opposite side of the transaction. That's the role of the speculator. He assumes the risk because he thinks he can buy or sell the contracts at a profit before the delivery date. Not so long ago, January soybeans moved from about $5.10 to $6.90 a bushel in less than six weeks. For some speculators, that was very profitable because the $1.80 move was worth $9,000 per contract on a small margin of $2,000. The big plus for commodities trading is that low margin: cash requirements of 5% to 10% that vary with the commodity and the broker's standards. Commissions are small; they average $35 per round trip.

If you are tough-minded, emotionally stable, and have money to risk, do your own trading. For most people, however, the best course is to work with an expert directly or through purchases of shares in commodities funds, which are the latest sales gimmick for Wall Street brokers. The professionals use time-tested techniques and computers to catch trends, limit losses, and let their profits run.

In managing commodities funds for his clients, Richard D. Donchian, a specialist with Shearson Hayden Stone, uses 5- and 20-day moving averages (MAs) compiled over 14 years. Under his system, losses are always limited because positions must be closed out at definite points when the price of the commodity fulfills certain preset requirements of the MA. Because profits are not limited, the system automatically captures as gain a large slice of the middle of the rise or fall when there is a long, sustained move. Donchian's plan requires substantial capital: $70,000 to trade in 26 commodities or $40,000 for a mix of 18 commodities and money-related instruments such as Treasury bills.

With such diversification, the losses of a few positions are more than offset by the gains in other positions. In the boom years of 1973, 1974, and 1975, a hypothetical portfolio, after commission expenses, showed returns of +299%, +305%, and +54%, respectively. But in 1977 there was a 3% loss.

The trading and handling costs will startle even the sophisticated stock trader. Even though the commissions run about $35 each, one commodity fund, in one 90-day period, reported adjusted brokerage fees of $200,385 on assets of $7.2 million, *plus* 20% of net profits, *plus* a payment equal to 1% of the net monthly equity (subject to downward adjustments when net monthly commissions are over 3.2% of the fund's net assets), *plus* the interest on the cash reserves. At one point, the "cost" items totaled as much as 40% of the overall investment.

Don't turn the page too fast. With their usual ingenuity, Wall Street brokers are developing ways to let everyone trade in commodities: commodities funds. The funds are similar to mutual funds in that individuals can buy shares in a professionally managed portfolio. Currently, the minimum "investment" is $5,000: five shares of $1,000 each. Units are available through Paine Webber Jackson & Curtis now, and Dean Witter Reynolds, Inc. and Shearson Hayden Stone are awaiting SEC approval for their versions. Before you pawn the family jewels to make that big killing, read the prospectus carefully and review every item with your registered respresentative. Like many Wall Street packages, these new funds may be a better deal for your broker than for your savings.

Still, if you have extra money and are willing to recognize the risks, go ahead. You will be buying diversification and professional management working under a system that will miss some of the sensational rallies but should also avoid the devastating losses which are the bane of individual commodities traders who do not have adequate capital to take a number of positions. But do not add the money to your net worth until it's in the bank!

Commodities Options

Commodities options are for super-swingers only. They are calls or puts on commodities futures. The glib come-on is that you cannot lose more than the cost of the option and you can make a bundle fast. That is true if you are smart and shrewd, you watch price shifts, and you have a skilled broker. Unfortunately, this type of trading has attracted fast-buck operators who have either absconded with customer funds or gone bankrupt. At best, commodities options are outright speculations; at worst, they are swindles.

Precious Metals

The hottest off-beat "investment" recently has been gold. With inflation and lack of confidence in the dollar, the value of the metal has soared. Recently, it went above $250 an ounce—an almost unthought-of price a decade ago.

To the optimists, that is only the beginning. Goldbug James Dines says, "If you're young, buy and hold gold and gold stocks and you're sure to be rich. If you're older, the wealthy ones will be your children and grandchildren." He forecasts that the price will go to $400 an ounce. Pessimists argue that "Gold is a close second to Las Vegas" and point out that, from 1933 to 1977, the average annual rate of increase in value was only about 3.5% compounded.

One thing is sure: gold and gold stocks should *not* be viewed by normal standards of security analysis. Their prices have little to do with corporate profits and growth. Instead, they reflect world psychology, international politics, and the economic policies of major nations. If you do "invest" in gold, you have three choices:

1. *Companies listed on major stock exchanges:* Homestake Mining, Campbell Red Lake, Dome Mines, and so on. Those companies are major producers of

gold and other metals. They have impressive growth and profit records; their shares are widely traded; and their stock quotations move with the world price of gold. Profits may not be spectacular, but as long as the price of the precious metal keeps rising, you'll make money. Or lose, when metal values decline.

2. *Kaffirs*. These are stocks of South African gold producers. Shares are available on the American Stock Exchange and over the counter as American Depository Receipts (ADRs). ADRs are certificates, issued by American banks, that represent deposits of shares of foreign corporations abroad.

Earnings have been limited by rising costs and the South African law that requires mines to take the lowest average economic grade of ore and not concentrate on rich veins.

Kaffirs move as a group. Their prices are quoted weekly in *Barron's*—individually for the most widely traded stocks and as a group in the foreign stock summary. Per share prices are modest; dividends are good to high; and gains or losses always reflect the price of gold.

3. *Holding companies*. You can invest in ASA Limited, a closed-end investment company with 77% of its assets in South African mining shares; Anglo-American Corporation, the largest mine-financing firm; or Anglo-American Gold Investment Company, with holdings in a score of gold mines. When you do, you're buying the equivalent of shares in a mutual fund.

Gold Futures

Gold futures are traded on the Winnipeg Commodity Exchange. Each contract represents one 400-ounce bar of .995 pure gold. You must keep a minimum margin of $4,000 and be patient, because exchange rules limit the daily move to $2 an ounce. It's an inexpensive way to speculate.

Gold Coins

If you buy gold coins, do so as a collector, not as an investor. Values depend on the price of gold and the worth of the coins to collectors. That, in turn, is based on the rarity and condition of the individual pieces.

Traders seldom make money because of the high entry and exit costs. The same goes, double, for gold bars. By law, the gold must be weighed before each transaction and, for safety, must be stored in a depository. Those costs eat up most of the profits.

Krugerrands

Krugerrands are South African one-ounce gold coins. Because of coinage and distribution costs, they sell at 5% to 8% premiums above the price of gold. Sales taxes can add another 6% or so. Here again the price move has to be substantial to yield a worthwhile gain. There's no income; for most people, the reward is the joy of possession. That is not exactly a sound reason for such coins to be included in any financial plan.

Speculators can make money with gold if they are willing to trade: buying at dips and selling after rises. The technique can be used with the metal, with gold stocks, and with gold coins. By using charts and other technical indicators, speculators buy at the start of an uptrend and hold until there is a confirmed reversal. During the months (seldom more than a year), they trade frequently. It's a tricky business, but at certain times and for limited periods it can be very profitable.

There are people who consider themselves "gold investors." They hold the metal, in some form, for years. Since they receive no income, the profits must be substantial to offset costs and the magic of compounding. According to one knowledgeable broker, "The majority of these individuals have lost faith in the American economic system and are looking for a haven for their savings." That's not my idea of a good recommendation for gold as part of a long-term financial plan. In my view, gold is still a speculation and not an investment. But there's nothing wrong with speculating if you can afford to lose and understand the risks.

MONEY-RELATED FUTURES CONTRACTS

One of the fastest growing areas of futures trading involves money instruments: mortgage futures, government bonds and bills futures, and international currency. All those are traded on established exchanges. Again the futures are designed for hedging. Bankers, institutions, manufacturers, importers, and exporters want to be sure of the future cost of their goods and services. For speculators, the lures are the small margins and the opportunities for quick profits. Be very, very cautious. You're an amateur playing in a professional league.

Here are some of the widely used instruments.

Mortgage Futures

The basic unit is a $100,000 Government National Mortgage Association (Ginnie Mae) certificate representing a portfolio of FHA and VA mortgages. Each carries a stated interest rate, typically 8%, and is priced at about 100. Futures are bought and sold by bankers, builders, big investors, and mortgage lenders as a hedge against changes in the cost of money. They lock in their profits by buying in the cash market and selling in the futures market, or vice versa.

With a margin of $1,500 to $3,000, speculators can control a $100,000 unit and hope to double their money with a shift as small as one-half of 1% in the interest rate.

Treasury Bond Futures

Treasury bond futures also are $100,000 units, this time of U.S. government bonds maturing in 15 years or more. The contracts are designed as hedges against shifts in long-term interest rates, but they have become a popular vehicle for tax postponement.

Because not all Treasury bonds in the package mature beyond the time limit and not all carry 8% coupons, premiums and discounts vary. To give you an idea of how trading works, here are some details.

The bond futures are quoted in one thirty-second of a point ($31.25 per contract). The daily permissible price move, below or above the previous close, is 24 thirty-seconds, or $750 per contract. The basic margin, for each $100,000 contract, is $1,250 cash (more if the value declines). On spreads (the simultaneous purchase and sale of contracts in the same or different securities), the margins vary with the policy of the brokerage firm, but they are still comparatively small.

The investor protects his position against adverse market factors—lower bond prices due to higher interest rates and the opposite—by buying contracts with one maturity and selling those with another—just like Farmer Frank and his soybeans. There are scores of match-ups, because the spreads can involve contracts for government funds, Treasury bills, and Ginnie Maes. Speculators take opposite positions.

Bond futures are also used by wealthy individuals who want to roll over or postpone taxes, preferably until after they are dead. By the use of spreads covering two tax years, it is possible to create paper losses for the current taxable period and offset them with gains the following year. At that time, the spreader, if still solvent, starts over again. The broker gets richer and Uncle Sam poorer.

EXAMPLE: In midsummer, year I, Mr. Warbucks notes that prices of bond futures are rising, so he sells a December contract short and, simultaneously, buys a March, year II, contract. If all goes well, he will be able to take a loss on the short December position on his tax return filed April 15. The loss will be offset by the gain on the March contract. Now he has some eight months to set up another rollover to avoid taxes on the March, year II, income.

For individuals, this is a highly sophisticated technique. Success requires substantial capital, considerable knowledge, constant attention, a shrewd tax adviser, and a little luck.

Treasury Bill Futures

Treasury bill futures are for short-term hedging, because T-bills are loans for one year or less. They are used to protect positions against changes in short-term money rates. Again, they are for professionals and can be tricky because of their limited-life maturities.

Currency Futures

Currency futures are hedges (and speculations) in foreign currency traded on the International Monetary Market (IMM) of the Chicago Mercantile Exchange. The primary users are corporations dealing in goods and services around the world. They want to minimize their monetary risk exposure.

For small margins of 1.5% to 4.2%, roughly $1,500 to $2,500, you can control large sums of money: $100,000 Canadian, 500,000 Deutsche marks, 25 million Japanese yen, and so on. The daily fluctuations of each currency futures contract are limited by IMM rules. A rise of $750 per day provides a 37.5% profit on a $2,000 investment. That's $750 less about $45 commissions and cost. If the value declines, you are faced with a wipe-out or, if you set a stop order, a loss of part of your security deposit. If you sell short, it's the other way around.

None of these money-related futures contracts should be part of basic financial planning. They should be considered speculations, not investments.

DIAMONDS AS MAN'S BEST FRIEND?

Diamonds have been rewarding in recent years. Since 1967, their annual average appreciation has been 30% on paper and a lot less in real life. The negatives are that all gems are illiquid, cannot be used for show, and are expensive to buy and sell—a round-trip commission is at least 10% plus cost. Diamonds are better for conversation than profit.

Holdings should be limited to top-quality diamonds, which account for about 2% of the total available and sell for $5,000 to $8,000 per carat. A broker, such as Kohinoor International Ltd., a New York City broker, gathers a selection of prime stones and handles all transactions for a 5% commission, each way, plus costs.

For best results, set up a long-range program of periodic sales for income and keep reinvesting the proceeds. Generally, you'll have to hold for at least two years to assure an adequate return. But your profits, in a rising market, can be welcome. A one-carat diamond bought for $2,500 in 1972 sold recently for $7,800.

Kohinoor advises initial capital of $10,000 and a goal of $50,000 worth of stones diversified by color and cut. You need at least ten diamonds to be sure of a sale when you want money.

Another approach is to invest in certificates of a diamond investment trust. The trusts are professionally managed portfolios with shares that are sold like the shares of a mutual fund. The units are evaluated monthly, and they may be exchanged for gems, redeemed in cash or, if you can find a buyer, resold.

RACEHORSES

Probably the most exciting off-beat investments are racehorses. You need plenty of money and even more luck. Like most special "investments," the greatest rewards are personal. The most fun comes from racing; the most profits from breeding. You can buy a horse with modest potential for as little as $5,000, but you'll have to add $25,000 for board, training, and maintenance (less if you own a barn and pasture and have a willing-to-work child).

Generally, big money makes big money. One tycoon spent more than $10 million in a couple of years. In one two-year period, the horses he bought for $2 million won $1.5 million at the track and, when retired, had a book value of $8 million. Or you can be lucky. William Rudy, *New York Post* columnist, tells of one lady who bought a mare for $2,500, bred her to a free stallion who had never raced, and got a major winner. More typical, he laments, was the Du Pont heiress who paid $235,000 for a yearling that was never fit to race.

You can go it alone or join a syndicate. Purchases can be made through a dealer, at an auction, or at a "horse-in-training" sale at a track. Your costs will run from $2,500 to $25,000. Then you will need a trainer or adviser you can trust (hard to find). For professional help, contact a firm such as the Fasig-Tipton Company in Lexington, Kentucky. It works on a fee and percentage basis.

Once you own a young horse, unless you have a lot of space and facilities, you will have to arrange for boarding and training at $300 to $400 per month. At the track, boarding costs about $25 a day. If your horse becomes a winner, you'll pay 10% of winnings to both the trainer and jockey. Add blacksmith and veterinary bills and the average cost per start can run up to $1,000.

If you are lucky, you may break even from purses, but the real profit comes from breeding. That will be steady, long-term income which, in racetrack lore, "is better than an annuity." You can also pool your money in a partnership, buy a share in a syndicate (minimum, $10,000), or invest in a publicly owned breeding corporation. Typically, those companies buy in-foal mares, sell off half of the colts, and buy more pregnant mares.

Forget about significant tax losses. IRS has tough rules to make you prove you're running a business, not a hobby. To qualify for deductible business expenses, the stable must show a profit in two of every seven years. The best tax shelter comes from the lower capital gains tax on long-term profits from the sale of horses. Racing income is treated as ordinary income.

Mares can provide the best return. The horse may never race again, but foals can bring high prices. One pregnant mare, bought for $52,000, produced a foal that brought $30,000 and, in the next two years, other offspring that added an additional $64,000.

ART

Art is the most popular off-beat investment. For convenience, let's concentrate on paintings and prints, but the same criteria apply to books, antiques, jewelry, silver, and other display-for-pleasure items. The first rule, says Lawrence Saphire of New York's Blue Moon Gallery, is "Buy art and enjoy it. If it appreciates in value, consider it a bonus."

These days, that bonus is almost inevitable. In the past decade, the price of most art has risen five- to tenfold. And each year, with the poor performance of the stock market, more people become interested in collecting. That, in turn, spurs prices higher. Some items have failed to keep pace, but generally it's still a seller's market in which quality counts.

You don't have to be rich to play the game. Lithographs of works by such established artists as Thomas Hart Benton can be acquired for as little as $250 and those of some other favorites for $100 to $150. Note the word "established." Don't get the idea that you can pick up the works of an unknown artist and count on fantastic appreciation in a few years. For every great painting or sketch, there are 10,000 mediocrities.

Purchasing art is not like buying stock. You don't phone your broker and ask for 100 old prints. In the early 1970s, Wall Street learned that art and financial manipulation don't mix. Promoters, attracted by soaring art prices, envisioned broad public participation in art funds that would buy and sell paintings like commodities, solely for profit. At last report, not one of the half dozen new issues is still traded. Private, speculative syndicates also flopped. There wasn't enough good art around; the logistics proved too complex; and the experts disagreed as to selections. Art funds have been successful in Europe where there's a long tradition of nonsecurities investments, but their shares are expensive and hard to sell.

Whatever you do, get expert help. Many dealers will welcome outside capital to enable them to move up their price range. For the name of a reputable one in your area, check Art Dealers Association, 575 Madison Avenue, New York, NY 10022.

You can work with a dealer directly or through a syndicate. Saphire likes to have $50,000 to buy at his discretion. After deducting basic costs, such as insurance, he splits profits on a 50–50 basis. Once a purchase is made, he insists on a legal form that makes the painting security for the investment.

Syndicate participations run from $5,000 to $20,000 and usually involve 15 to 20 people. "They must be my friends—knowledgeable people who know art," insists Saphire. Other dealers, especially from outside New York, are likely to be more tolerant. "A pool of $100,000 is enough to buy a good painting by a well-known European artist. For some Americans, the cost is less." says Saphire. "I buy only when I have good reason to believe the work can be sold within one year at a 50% profit. That would mean almost a 25% gain for investors."

If your funds, and confidence, are limited, look for original graphics and multiples: limited editions by artists who sign, number, and supervise the production of 25 to 250 copies of their work.

The size of an edition influences values. A print from a large run may command $150 to $300; one from a run of less than 100 may go for $1,100 to $2,500.

The scarcity of works of a first-rate artist automatically sets a base value, but an artist's fame does not guarantee that every work is worthwhile. Here's advice from Saphire:

Deal only with reputable galleries and dealers who know where, what, and when to buy or sell. Select rather than accumulate. You are buying both esthetic and capital appreciation. Look for underrated painters. Many artists are accepted by one generation, dismissed by the next. Wait for what you want. You will make the most money when a painting is bought at the right place.

Insure all art treasures and update their values annually so that you will have proof of their worth when required. Get a certificate of authentication showing the history: former owners, places exhibited, and so on. Don't buy on impulse. Go to an auction with a predetermined financial limit. It's too easy to catch "auction fever" and go overboard. Be careful about acquiring anything less than ten years old. Fads and cocktail-party enthusiasm can be bad news for the unsophisticated.

Never compromise on quality. Buy works of established artists. You can speculate later, when you know the risks. Think not only of the amount of money but of how the painting will look on the wall. Buy only what you like.

Investment values can change suddenly. If the print is lovely, it can always be hung in your home or office.

Shopping by Mail

If you're too busy to attend an auction, you can shop by mail. Major galleries sell catalogs of upcoming exhibits. At the back of the booklet, you'll find a range of expected prices: $3,000 to $5,000 for a Grant Wood print, for example. You bid $3,800. If that is above the reserve price (the minimum the seller will accept), the assistant auctioneer will act for you. If the formal bids stop at $3,600, you will get the art at about $3,700. The exact spread is set by the auctioneer and varies from $25 for low-priced items to $200 for more expensive objects.

Watch the Taxes

As a general rule, IRS sets low valuations for all types of art. That is fine for estate purposes, but it can cause problems when charitable gift deductions are involved. In determining estate taxes, IRS will accept 25% of the aggregate of the highest hypothetical retail price less the amount of the sales commission, which can be 25% or more. For charitable gifts, IRS rules that the value must be reduced by the amount that would be ordinary income or short-term capital gains if the property had been sold at what would have been considered a fair market price.

If the art has been held over one year, a full deduction can be taken if it is donated to an institution whose focus is art. But the value is reduced by 50% of the potential long-term capital gains if the recipient is not directly connected to art. In other words, if you become wealthy enough to benefit by a tax deduction from a gift of art, make sure that you name a qualified institution. And, of course, the evaluation, to suit IRS, must be made by a reputable authority, preferably one recommended by The Appraisers Association of America, 541 Lexington Avenue, New York, NY 10022.

A handy guide to help you get started in collecting is *Buying Art on a Budget*, by Joanna Eagle. Collecting art can be fun. Investing in art can be profitable. But to make a success of both, you must love art first and consider the monetary benefits second.

We've devoted considerable space to special investments and speculations not because we recommend them, but so you will understand the risks as well as the rewards. Special investments usually require expertise and almost always are more enjoyable than profitable. They can be a long-term hedge against inflation, but basically they are speculations. They should be considered in financial planning only for extra savings and for the joy of possession, not as a major means of building your estate.

12 How to Use Life Insurance in Financial Planning

Life insurance is one of the most useful tools of financial planning, but not all forms assure the best use of your money. The type, amount, and provisions of every policy should be carefully considered before purchase and reviewed periodically after purchase in relation to your overall program.

The major purpose, and greatest value, of life insurance is to provide family protection: to bridge the gap between the assets you now have and those which will be needed by your survivors after you die. But in varying forms, life insurance is sold for many other purposes: forced savings, assured retirement income, to make gifts, to avoid or minimize taxes, to provide extra employee benefits, and so on. In many cases, those policies are an expensive way to achieve such non-death-protection goals.

Perhaps the easiest way to understand life insurance is to go back to basics. A group of people join together and pay money into a common pool managed by an insurance company. The insurer invests the savings, guarantees their safety and some minimum returns, and agrees to pay stipulated death benefits to the heirs of each participant. Contributions by participants are based on age and life expectancy. Since the risks of early death are shared with others, the costs of policies are based on averages determined by historical data. When you pay premiums, you are betting that you will outlive the average American of your age and sex. You have a 70% chance of winning. The latest calculation of how long most people can expect to live is given in Table 12–1.

Table 12–1. How long can you expect to live?

| Present Age | Life Expectancy, According to Actuarial Tables ||
	Male	Female
30	71.7	78.5
40	72.6	79.0
50	74.1	80.1
60	76.8	81.8
65	78.7	83.0
70	80.9	84.4

SOURCE: U.S. Department of Health, Education, and Welfare.

Note: Recent statistics indicate that these projections are on the low side.

The insurance company makes money to pay claims in several ways: (1) by basing death assumptions on actuarial tables that do not fully reflect the lengthening life span, (2) by charging commissions and fees which are deducted from your savings, (3) by benefiting from the proceeds of lapsed policies (25% of policies issued by the Equitable Life Assurance Society, the third largest U.S. insurance company, lapsed within one year of issue and another 10% the second year), (4) by investing premiums at a high yield and paying interest and dividends at a lower rate.

For financial planning, the greatest attraction of life insurance is security. You know that (1) at your death your heirs will receive the face value of the policy less any loans taken out against cash values and (2) the policy will remain in force as long as the premiums are paid and even longer when there's a provision for an automatic premium loan from the accumulated cash value.

The best time to buy life insurance is when you are young and healthy. The costs are low, and the premiums stay fixed for a predetermined time or as long as you live. A young family with limited net worth should own the maximum amount that can be paid for without undue hardship: directly through personal savings or indirectly through company or association group plans. Such protection creates an instant estate at the death of the breadwinner.

Adequate coverage costs less than most people think. For as little as $349 a year (less than $1 per day), a 25-year-old man can assure his family of $100,000 death benefits with a five-year, renewable-convertible term insurance policy! Straight life costs more, but it can be a protection against inflation because, with its fixed premiums, later-in-life payments will be in depreciated dollars. (But, of course, the fixed face value of the policy will mean less purchasing power for the heirs.)

TWO MAIN CHOICES

You have two broad choices when you buy death protection: term life and straight life. Term life is like a fire insurance policy; it protects for a limited period of time at a low rate. At expiration, it's worthless, although it can usually be renewed at a higher annual cost.

Straight life, also called ordinary or whole life, includes a forced savings account in ever-increasing cash values which can be used as collateral for loans. The face value remains the same, but the insurance company dollars diminish as your savings increase. After 20 years, about one-third of the protection represents your contributions plus accumulated dividends. In the example in Table 12–2 the $25,000 whole life will grow to a death value of $31,200 but the payout will include only $15,700 of the insurance company money.

Since the premiums of term life are lower than those of comparable straight life, the difference can be used for your own, more rewarding, investments. As Table 12–2 shows, even at a 5% return, that difference will boost total death proceeds, after 20 years, to $38,100, which is $6,900 more than the proceeds of the straight life policy. That's a gross return, because you will have to pay

Table 12–2A. Whole life insurance: $25,000 policy taken out at age 35 with dividends left to accumulate at 5% annually.

Policy Year	While Alive, Whole Life Policyholder Has Cash Value and Accumulated Dividends*	At Death, Survivors Will Receive	
		Actual Insurance Protection	Death Benefits and Accumulated Dividends*
1	$ 75	$24,975	$25,050
5	2,150	23,300	25,450
10	5,800	20,700	26,500
15	10,100	18,300	28,400
20	15,500	15,700	31,200

Table 12–2B. Term insurance: $25,000 five-year renewable policy taken out at age 35 with premium difference invested at 5% annually.

While Alive, Term Policyholder Has		At Death, Survivors Will Receive Death Benefits and Invested Premium Difference
Invested Premium Difference	Actual Insurance Protection	
$ 475	$25,000	$25,475
2,600	25,000	27,600
5,700	25,000	30,700
9,200	25,000	34,200
13,100	25,000	38,100

SOURCE: Steven Glenn, C.L.U., Miami, Fla.

*Dividend illustrations are based on the 1978 dividend scale (and interest rate on accumulations). They are not guarantees or estimates of the future.

taxes on the income and realized capital gains of your invested money. Before you buy any more life insurance, get quotations on both types of coverage and project the benefits with your desk calculator.

Straight life does force savings, so for most people the best solution is a combination. If you do concentrate on term coverage, keep in mind the advantages of using the premium savings for other rewarding investments: (1) *for safety,* income-producing securities similar to those which would be purchased by the insurance company, and (2) *for growth,* quality stocks and real estate the total returns from which will help you build your net worth.

Here's another way to look at the two types (see also Table 12–3):

• Straight life premiums remain fixed. Dividends can buy additional coverage, reduce premiums, or be taken in cash to boost your income. You are entrusting your money to an insurance company, paying substantial commissions to the agent and management fees to the company, and getting a guaranteed interest return of about 3%. In recent years, however, the dividend yield has been higher, generally over 6%. You must decide whether you want to accept those costs or invest more profitably on your own.

Table 12–3A. What $1,000 worth of insurance costs.

Type of Policy	Annual Premium When Purchased at Age		
	25	35	45
5-year renewable-convertible term (premium for first 5 years)	$ 3.49	$ 4.45	$ 9.10
10-year renewable-convertible term (premium for first 10 years)	3.65	5.05	10.20
Level-premium term to age 65	7.30	10.60	15.99
Ordinary life	12.64	18.09	27.58
20-payment life	21.48	27.83	36.59
20-year endowment	41.27	42.14	45.54

Table 12–3B. What $1,000 in annual premiums buys.

Type of Policy	Death Benefits When Purchased at Age		
	25	35	45
5-year renewable-convertible term (premium for first 5 years)	$300,000	$220,000	$110,000
10-year renewable-convertible term (premium for first 10 years)	300,000	200,000	100,000
Level-premium term to age 65	130,000	100,000	60,000
Ordinary life	80,000	55,000	40,000
20-payment life	50,000	40,000	30,000
20-year endowment	25,000	25,000	20,000

SOURCE: Adapted from *The Unique Manual* (Cincinnati, Ohio: The National Underwriters Company, 1978).

- Term premiums rise sharply as you grow older. The spread from the cost of straight life narrows, and at age 65 the premiums are about the same.

For most people, a combination is the best solution but, at all times with all types of insurance, the total death benefits should be the key. *Buy protection first.* The other benefits are secondary—and expensive.

HOW POLICIES WORK

The path of progress of straight life is shown by the example of a $10,000 policy on a 25-year-old man paying an annual premium of $167.40 detailed in Table 12–4. Note how slowly the cash value grows and how the dividends, when automatically used to buy additional coverage, boost the death benefit.

A more rewarding, more economical step would be the "fifth dividend option" that is available from several major companies. It permits the use of dividends to buy one-year term at *net* rates: no commissions or fees. The extra term protection is convertible to whole life without evidence of insurability, and the

Table 12-4. How straight life policies work: $10,000 policy.

End of Year	Guaranteed Cash Value	Annual Dividend	Total Paid-up Additions	Cash Value Additions	Death Benefit with Additions
1	$ 0	$ 6	$ 16	$ 6	$10,016
2	70	12	49	18	10,049
3	200	18	98	36	10,098
4	350	24	162	61	10,162
5	490	30	244	94	10,244
6	640	36	340	134	10,340
8	950	49	581	239	10,581
10	1,270	62	882	379	10,832
12	1,550	72	1,234	554	11,234
15	2,000	82	1,818	869	11,818
17	2,310	94	2,264	1,128	12,264
20	2.790	105	2,992	1,583	12,992

SOURCE: Steven Glenn, C.L.U., Miami, Fla.

Note: The interest-adjusted cost is $3.53 per $1,000 of insurance if surrendered at the end of 10 years; $2.61 if surrendered at the end of 20 years.

total benefits are greater. At the end of 5 years, they are $10,278 versus $10,244 for the straight life reinvestment; at the end of 10 years, $12,119 versus $10,882; at the end of 15 years, $13,726 versus $11,818, and at the end of 20 years, $15,573 versus $12,992.

There is one big plus for straight life: the privilege of borrowing against the cash values. Generally, this is not a good idea, because it can decrease the death benefit, but there are exceptions:

1. If you have old policies which permit loans at 6% interest. You can make money by investing the proceeds at higher yields: in bonds or stocks paying 8% or more. And you can deduct the cost of the interest from your federal tax return.

2. If you need extra money to start a business, buy a house, or pay for unexpected expenses. Cash values in insurance policies are a ready, liquid reserve.

The best term insurance choice is a policy with a guaranteed renewal clause, which permits you to buy a new policy without a physical exam. And if you are older, consider adding convertibility: the right to shift to whole life at any time. Some companies limit the privilege to ages below 65 or 70. The premiums are higher, but the conversion is still worthwhile because, in that age range, you can buy straight life, with its cash value buildup, for the same dollars.

Here's a safety tip: With any policy consider paying extra for a waiver of premium, a guarantee that, if you should become disabled, the premiums will be paid by the company and thus keep the policy in force.

With disability policies, compare the definitions. *Your are disabled if you cannot perform:*

1. "Any occupation for remuneration or profit." Avoid this because you may still be able to shuffle papers or talk on a telephone.
2. "Any occupation you have become fitted for due to education, training, and experience." Be cautious. Insurance payments may stop if a physician becomes a teacher even if the salary is much lower than previous income.
3. "Your occupation for 24 to 72 months." Prefer this because this is what your policy should protect: your inability to work as a dentist, physician, architect, or whatever.

Since the costs are comparable, make certain that you are buying the protection you want. By changing the deductible and the period of coverage, you can find a policy which will fit your pocketbook. This is another area in which it pays to shop.

HOW MUCH INSURANCE?

There's no easy answer to the "how much" question because so many other items must be considered: goals, net worth, future expenses, income, and family needs. As a rule of thumb, insurance experts urge life policies whose proceeds will total four to five times annual salary. A better, statistically based approach is summarized in Table 12–5. In the table, the amount of needed insurance is based on the age of the survivor/beneficiary. There are a wife and two children. The goal is to replace 75% or 60% of your current after-tax income.

To use the table, multiply the factor under 75% or 60% by your present gross earnings. The result is the approximate amount of life insurance you will need. For example, with $30,000 income and a wife age 25, for 75% of earnings, you will need 7.5 × $30,000 = $225,000; for 60% of earnings, you will need 5 × $30,000 = $150,000. When your spouse is 35, it's 8 × $30,000 = $240,000 and 6 × $30,000 = $180,000. If either, or both, of the figures are between the listed data, use an average.

EXAMPLE: A 45-year-old man who is making $65,000 wants to be sure that his family will have 75% of his earnings. To find the income replacement, he multiplies the $65,000 by 7.5 to get $487,500. At the 60% level, the projected need will be $357,500. The formula assumes that the proceeds are invested at

Table 12–5. Determining the amount of life insurance you will need to replace 75% or 60% of your gross earnings.

Present Gross Earnings	25 Years 75%	25 Years 60%	35 Years 75%	35 Years 60%	45 Years 75%	45 Years 60%	55 Years 75%	55 Years 60%
$23,500	6.5	4.5	8.0	5.5	8.5	6.5	7.5	5.5
30,000	7.5	5.0	8.0	6.0	8.5	6.5	7.0	5.5
40,000	7.5	5.0	8.0	6.0	8.0	6.0	7.0	5.5
65,000	7.5	5.5	7.5	6.0	7.5	6.0	6.5	5.0

SOURCE: First National City Bank, New York.

5% and that the survivors gradually convert the principal to family use so that, at the widow's actuarial death, everything will be gone.

Table 12–5 does not take into account any income from savings, investments, and Social Security, so don't be alarmed if your total insurance—group and personal—is somewhat less. The other sources of income can be your security blanket. Besides, realistically, the need for income will lessen when the children are on their own. And, of course, the widow can go back to work or may remarry. Projections are a frame of reference, not a set-in-concrete necessity.

A more accurate approach, keyed to your own needs, is to follow the same steps used in overall financial planning: total your assets and determine the cash needed at death—what your heirs will need for what and for how long. The most convenient format is the worksheet of your insurance agent. Analyses prepared by Steven Glenn, C.L.U., an instructor and top producer for Connecticut Mutual in Miami, Florida, are presented in Worksheets 14 and 15. The examples also show the importance of differing financial goals and lifestyles:

Mr. Able (A) and Mr. Baker (B) are close to the same age: 36 and 30. Both have children ages 9 and 6, and both earn about $36,000 a year. Mr. A, an educator, has greater savings, primarily for education, including the opportunity for graduate study. He is very concerned about college for his children and he does not want his widow to have to work.

The analysis shows that Mr. A needs $349,053 to meet his objectives. To bridge the substantial gap between his current assets and future needs, Glenn recommends term insurance of $226,053. The cost will be $40 a month now and will rise over the years. He also anticipates that there will be revisions at review time when changes occur: more income, an inheritance, a new job, the oldest child out of school, and so on. Says Glenn, "Every insurance program should be flexible and be revised periodically."

Mr. Baker, who will inherit his father's business, is less interested in advanced education for his children. He is willing to settle for a minimal $1,000 a month after-death income, and he assumes that both his widow and children can go to work.

Much against the counsel of Glenn, who, unlike many life insurance agents, recognizes that the primary role of life insurance is family protection, Mr. B insists on buying straight life. "Yet," sighs Glenn, "he could have done so much more. At the same cost, he could have bought term enough to assure full family protection."

Glenn's analysis shows that Mr. B's total insurance needs will be $202,192. Since he already has $57,000 protection, the new coverage should be $145,192. But Mr. B cannot afford the $2,500 annual premium for whole life, so he settles for $30,000 at a monthly cost of $28.95. If he dies prematurely, his family will be short $116,000. Concerning that and related problems, Glenn says:

I usually suggest term first, but I point out that term should never be used when there is a permanent need for insurance to provide estate protection or business continuation. The value of life insurance is its unique ability to assure protection. Its low cost makes

Worksheet 14
Analysis of Life Insurance Needs

Name: MR. ABLE   Ages: Husband, 36; Wife, 36; Child, 9; Child, 6

	Cash for Family		Income for Family				
	Final Expenses Emergency Fund	Mortgage Cancellation	For 9 Years Until Oldest Child Is 18 (per Month)	For 3 Years Until Youngest Child Is 18 (per Month)	Educational Fund	For 12 Years Until Wife Is 60 (per Month)	Life Income from Wife's Age 60 (per Month)
Objectives	$5,000	$50,000	$ 1,800	$ 1,800	$40,000	$ 1,800	$ 1,800
Assumed Benefits							
Social Security	255		845*	724*			345
Pension benefits							
Cash assets	4,745	7,255					
Income assets							
Unmet objectives			955	1,076	40,000	1,800	1,455
Needed to complete objectives: $349,053			80,455	21,090	40,000	92,892	71,871
Present life insurance: $123,000			80,255				
Need to complete objectives: $226,053			200	21,090	40,000	92,892	71,871
Unfilled objectives			955	1,076	40,000	1,800	1,455

SOURCE: Steven Glenn, C.L.U., Miami, Fla.

*$362 per month will be paid to each child from 18 to 22, if in an accredited school and unmarried, provided total family benefits are not over $845 per month.

200 YOUR MONEY & YOUR LIFE

Worksheet 15
Analysis of Life Insurance Needs

Name: MR. BAKER Ages: Husband: 30; Wife: 28; Child: 9; Child: 6

	Cash for Family		Income for Family			
	Final Expenses Emergency Fund	Mortgage Cancellation	For 9 Years Until Oldest Child Is 18 (per Month)	For 3 Years Until Youngest Child Is 18 (per Month)	Educational Fund	For 12 Years Until Wife Is 60 (per Month)	Life Income from Wife's Age 60 (per Month)
Objectives	$10,000	$31,000	$1,000	$1,000	$40,000	$1,000	$1,000
Assumed benefits							
Social Security	255		977*	837*			398
Pension benefits							
Cash assets							
Income assets							
Unmet objectives	9,745	31,000	23	163	40,000	1,000	602
Need to complete objectives: $202,592	9,745	31,000	2,014	3,527	40,000	85,936	30,370
Present life insurance: $57,000	9,745	31,000	2,014	3,527	10,714		
Need to complete objectives: $145,592					29,286	85,936	30,370
Unfilled objectives					29,286	1,000	602

SOURCE: Steven Glenn, C.L.U., Miami, Fla.

*$418 per month will be paid to each child from age 18 to 22, if in an accredited school and unmarried, provided total family benefits are not over $977 per month.

it possible to use the extra money—the difference between the low premium of term and the relatively high payments for whole life—for more rewarding investments.

The insurance company guarantees only about 3% return; and while recent dividends have been higher, they have not equaled the 8% of bonds or the higher returns possible with real estate. In my own case, I own $200,000 term and 15 acres of land which, I believe, will double in value in the next few years.

The easiest way to explain the value of term insurance is by the diagram [Figure 5] which I used with these analyses. It shows the comparative costs of both types starting at age 30. Until age 65, the term is cheaper, but it costs more every five years or so. The crossover comes at this age and creates a new ball game. You may be worth more and your needs will probably be less, unless you have an estate tax problem. Depending on the circumstances, you can then decide whether to convert to whole life, at lower cost and rising cash value, or drop some of your protection.

Figure 5. Costs of straight life and term insurance.

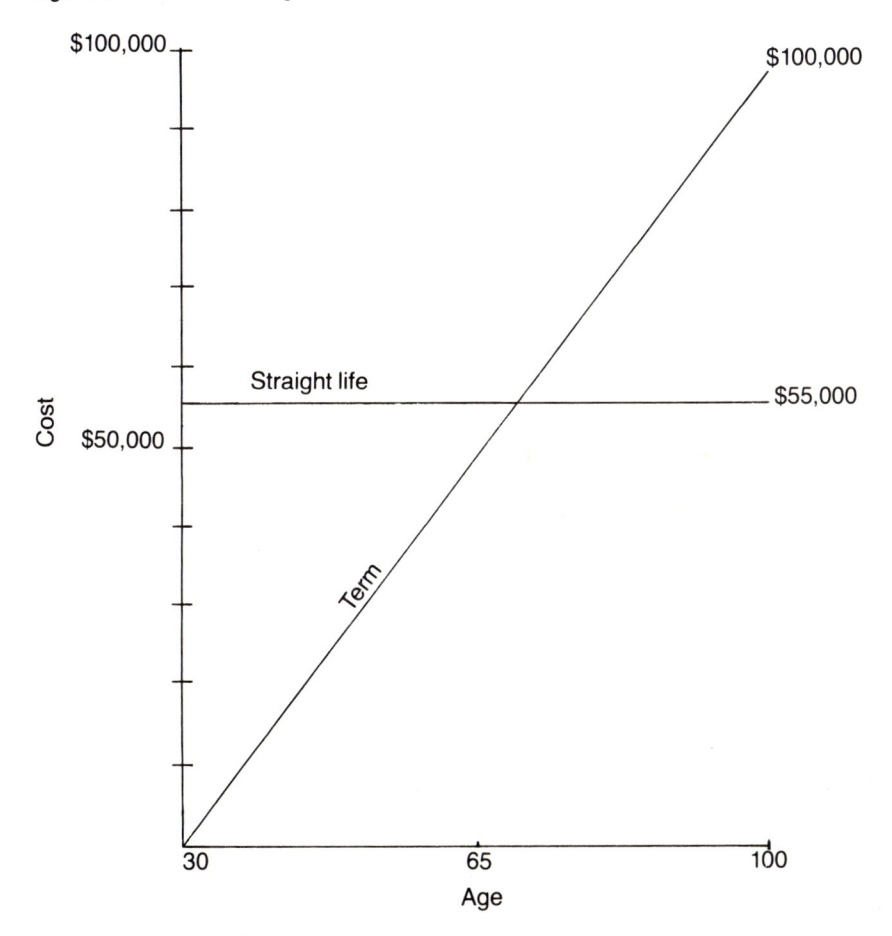

SOURCE: Steven Glenn, C.L.U., Miami, Fla.

Your insurance agent has tables for quick reference. To calculate the needed protection, they discount the future to find the current value. For Mr. A multiply the $1,800-per-month income by 144 months (the 12 years before both children will become adults). Then double that to take into account the 144 months until the wife reaches age 60, when she is eligible for Social Security. Discounted by 6% to take inflation into account, and less the Social Security benefits until both children are 18, the total dollars needed now are almost $350,000. But Mr. A already has $123,000 coverage, so that is subtracted to get the recommended $226,053 protection.

SOCIAL SECURITY BENEFITS

On Worksheets 14 and 15 is a very important set of figures: the extra income from Social Security benefits to survivors. They include a $255 death benefit (which may be eliminated), large aids to minor children (under age 18 and 22 when full-time students), and a modest pension when the widow reaches age 60. The younger you and your children are, the greater the benefits and the less the need for individually achieved income protection after death.

The calculations are complex, but broadly speaking the payments for the widow and children are based on the total of the two highest years of the breadwinner's earnings. In 1978 that was $29,400, which represented the maximum limit of $14,100 income in 1976 and $15,300 in 1977.

With Mr. A, the monthly check will be $845 for the next 9 years when both children are minors and $724 for the next three years until the youngest child becomes a legal adult. If the children fulfill their father's hopes of college, the checks will keep coming until age 22.

Social Security benefits are more important as death benefits than for financial planning. They provide welcome income that will probably increase to meet inflation. They are an excellent example of how society meets economic and social needs.

INSURANCE VARIATIONS AND COMBINATIONS

There are scores of variations and combinations of both term and straight life insurance. Most of them are sales packages designed to attract savings and serve specific consumer wants more than need. Some are blends of term and straight life; others offer a fixed premium and decreasing coverage; still others involve borrowing against cash values. For executives or professionals, there are plans whereby the employer chips in. You name it and the insurance industry has it.

To give you an idea of the possible choices, here are a few of the most widely used special policies. Their details vary with the insurer, but they follow similar patterns:

Decreasing Term

The face value of the original decreasing term policy is high and declines over the years. The premium remains the same. Such a policy is an excellent temporary protective tool. For example, if you have a 25-year $50,000 mortgage on your new home, you buy a policy whose face value declines annually at a rate parallel with the amount of the loan paid off. As another example, to be sure there are sufficient funds for tuition when your son is ready for college, buy five-year renewable and convertible term, annual renewable term, or, if there may be graduate education costs, ten-year decreasing term.

Minimum Deposit Insurance (MDI)

MDI is usually sold as a painless way to finance your life insurance. You borrow against the cash value to pay premiums. If the actual premium is $270 and the dividend averages $150, you borrow $120 from the accumulated cash value.

But there are disadvantages: (1) It takes a long time, 10 to 15 years, for the difference between term and MDI to benefit the policyholder. (2) Interest charges become part of the carrying costs and are tax deductible only when you pay cash for four of the first seven premiums. Thus the entry fee for a 25-year-old could be as much as $8,000 on a $100,000 policy. (3) You must get high returns on investing the money you would have paid in premiums. Table 12–6 shows how MDI works. Savings do increase with the policyholder's tax bracket, but the more you borrow, the less will be the proceeds for your beneficiaries at your death. And don't let the salesman kid you, MDI is an expensive way to buy protection.

Still, if you are willing to use the leverage of borrowing, MDI can be a tool for providing family protection and funds for business investment. In most cases, MDI becomes feasible for those over age 50 because it takes about 15 years for the cost of the term insurance to become higher than the dividend payout. Then the loan becomes greater than the cash value so that the cash outlay begins to outpace the deductible interest.

To see if MDI would be worthwhile for you, study Worksheet 16. Table 12–7 provides a shortcut to find how much you will pay for money borrowed to pay premiums on your MDI policy. Once you know the interest cost, find the number of years to retirement and multiply the annual premium by the factor in the table.

Table 12–6. How MDI works for younger buyers.

| Tax Bracket | At 6% Yield on Alternative Investments || At 9% Yield on Alternative Investments ||
	Years Until Savings Begin	Savings at 65	Years Until Savings Begin	Savings at 65
		Age 35		
35%	14	$11,417	17	$ 9,798
45	11	17,826	13	18,282
		Age 45		
35%	11	$ 5,545	13	$ 4,299
45	9	8,908	10	8,429

SOURCE: Professor Stuart Schwarzschild, Georgia State University, based on low-cost term and MDI policies of Provident Mutual Life Insurance Co.

Worksheet 16
Determining If MDI Is Worthwhile

Age 50, $100,000 Straight Life (New England Mutual), 42% Tax Bracket

1. Present value of policy	$26,474
2. Annual premium	2,280
3. Premiums to pay at age 65: 15 years × $2,280	34,200
4. Total interest to retirement: $2,280 × 9.7 (see Table 12–7)	22,116
5. Tax savings on interest: $22,116 × 42%	9,289
6. After-tax interest cost to retirement: $22,116 minus $9,289	12,827
7. Cash value at retirement*	54,738
8. Net cash position at retirement: $54,738 minus total of lines 3 and 6	7,711
9. Value of invested premiums: $2,280 × growth factor of 26.9 (see Table 12–7)	61,332
10. Total return: $7,711 plus $61,332	69,043
11. Cash advantage of MDI: $69,043 minus $54,738	14,305

SOURCE: C. Colburn Hardy, *Funk & Wagnalls Guide to Personal Money Management* (New York: Funk & Wagnalls, 1976).

*Plus any dividends not used for the purchase of one-year term and terminal dividends. Based on the after-tax rate of 7% for 15 years.

Split-Dollar Insurance (SDI)

If you work for a corporation that believes in extra benefits for its executives, SDI can provide a lot of coverage for a small cost. It's the result of splitting the premium payments between the company and the employee and using the dividends to reduce premiums. Unlike all-inclusive pension and profit-sharing plans, SDI can be set up on a selective basis.

The corporation pays the portion of each annual premium that represents the increase in cash value. The favored executive is responsible for the balance of the yearly cost, a sum that is large at the outset but decreases rapidly. There are

Table 12–7. Guide to interest costs and investment growth.

Annual Rate	Factor When Number of Years to Retirement Is			
	10	15	20	25
Interest				
5%	3.2	7.7	14.7	25.1
6	4.0	9.7	19.0	33.2
Growth of investment				
6%	14.0	24.7	39.0	58.2
7	14.8	26.9	43.9	67.7
8	15.6	29.3	49.4	79.0

SOURCE: C. Colburn Hardy, *Funk & Wagnalls Guide to Personal Money Management* (New York, Funk & Wagnalls, 1976).

two beneficiaries: the corporation, which gets the cash value of the policy, and the widow or children of the employee, who receive the remainder.

EXAMPLE: To reward a 36-year-old executive, company X arranges for a $100,000 SDI policy. In year 1, the employer pays $225, the cash value, and the executive comes up with $1,940, probably borrowed from the company. In year 2, the corporation pays $1,825 and the executive $275. From year 5, company X pays the entire premium of $1,905. (See Table 12–8.) If the insured employee dies, the company receives the cash value of the insurance: $225 in year 1 and rising to $37,000 in year 20. The employee's heirs get the balance: $99,775 down to $63,000, and less if the husband borrowed for the first payment.

SDI is a relatively inexpensive way to retain and reward key employees. The young executive has more insurance than he could otherwise afford; the company accepts a small added business expense and is sure of getting back all of its contributions whether the employee lives, dies, quits, or retires. For the recipient, SDI is not quite as rewarding as it may appear to be: the recipient must pay regular income taxes on an amount equal to the cost of one-year term insurance at his current age. Still, compared with the death benefit, that will be a small sum.

IRS Section 79

A group life insurance program that enables the employer to deduct life insurance premiums as a business expense is permitted under IRS section 79. It is best suited for employees with high salaries. When the group is from one to nine, the opportunity must be extended to all employees. When over ten employees are involved, the employer may establish or superimpose a plan based on any one criterion or a combination of criteria: age, marital status, period of employment, position, income bracket, and so on.

The company pays the full premium, but a portion may be passed on to the

Table 12–8. Split-dollar plan: $100,000 ordinary life; annual premium $2,350.

Year	Dividend	Net Premium (Annual Premium Less Dividend)	Cash Value	Increase in Cash Value (Employer Pays)	Net Premium Less Employer's Contribution (Employee Pays)	Employee's Death Benefit
1	$ 185	$ 2,165	$ 225	$ 225	$1,940	$99,775
2	250	2,100	2,050	1,825	275	97,950
3	315	2,035	3,900	1,850	185	96,100
4	385	1,965	5,775	1,875	90	94,225
5	445	1,905	7,680	1,905	0	92,320
11–20*	12,600	36,200	37,000	33,300	2,490	63,000

SOURCE: Adapted from data furnished by Edwin K. Chapin, C.L.U., New York, and material published in *Business Monthly*, © 1978 United Media International, Inc., 306 Dartmouth Street, Boston, Mass. All rights reserved.

*The sum of the 30-year dividends minus the net premiums for the first 20 years.

individual. The employee gets a tax break, because he is charged only for the additional compensation and pays tax, at rates set by the Uniform Premium Table, on the economic benefit of one-year term insurance in excess of $50,000. As explained by Glenn O. "Pete" Smith, a Fort Lauderdale insurance counselor representing PRO Services, Inc.:

This is an excellent approach for participants in small professional corporations and a good bargaining point for an executive taking a new job with a large company.

Under 79, you can choose between a number of combinations of term and whole life insurance:

1. For death benefits and savings: a mix of term and straight life.
2. For deferred payments: an annuity when you start retirement.
3. For extra old-age income: a deferred compensation agreement with the corporation which pays the premium and deducts the term insurance cost. The corporation owns, and is beneficiary of, the permanent portion (nondeductible). Thus, the cash value is a corporate asset and, subject to certain restrictions, comes back to the company tax-free. At retirement, the employee receives income for a specified number of years. The term policy is owned and paid for, by the heirs of the insured.

IRS section 79 should be reviewed with an insurance and tax counselor before use and periodically thereafter. Congress may make changes in the tax provisions. There will, however, probably be a grandfather clause to protect current arrangements, and even with higher taxes the special insurance may be worthwhile.

Adjustable Life (AL) or Life Cycle Insurance

The latest package created by major insurance companies is called adjustable life or life cycle insurance. The advertising theme is: "You'll never need to buy another policy." AL provides a choice of either term, with limited cash value, or participating straight life, with ever-higher cash values. The unique feature is that you can adjust the term according to your protection needs and available savings. Adjustable life insurance is:

1. *Convenient*. Because there is only one policy, there's only one notification for a new address or change of beneficiary and only one insurance company to pay.

2. *Flexible*. You can raise or lower the total coverage and the amount of the annual premium; you can lengthen or shorten the period of protection and the premium payment time.

The flexibility is ideal for financial planning. When you're young and short of money, you buy more term; when your income increases, you switch to straight life with higher premiums and much greater cash values. The changes can be made at specific anniversary dates without canceling or adding policies. If you run into unexpected expenses, you can reduce the premium for that year with a corresponding drop in the length of the current protection period, say from ten to five years. If you get a bonus, you can increase the premium payment and broaden your coverage and shorten the payment period.

EXAMPLE: A physician starts practice at age 30, marries at 34, fathers twins at age 36, and is financially secure by age 40. Similar changes can be made to age 75. For the details see Table 12–9.

The minimum term policy of AL is for ten years. Technically, at the lowest premium, term insurance does not build cash value, but to keep the premium level, the company must set an early years rate that is higher than the cost of a similar term policy based entirely on the buyer's mortality rate. To a limited degree, then, the term policy does build cash value. The straight life policy continues to accrete cash value. An added advantage is that no medical exam is necessary to obtain the lesser of $20,000 or 20% more insurance, which is a sort of cost-of-living increase.

Generally, AL is more expensive than straight life. Bankers Life of Des Moines, Iowa, offers a straight life $100,000 policy on a 25-year-old man with a base premium of $1,653, subject to reduction by dividends. The same protection by an AL policy to age 81 would cost $1,750.

Split Life Insurance (SLI)

Split life insurance is a package deal that provides an annuity for the insured and death protection for the family through term life. For every $1 you put up for the annuity, you can buy $100 of renewable term. The premium for the annuity remains the same, and the premium for the term policy rises with age.

EXAMPLE: At age 40, Bill Brach spends $2,500 to buy an SLI annuity that will pay him $500 a month at age 65. Then he spends an extra $245 to buy a $100,000 annual renewable term policy payable to his wife. He keeps paying premiums, but when the term gets too expensive, he drops part of that coverage. Thus he plans for his future and also protects his family.

The combination is convenient and sounds attractive, but there are disadvan-

Table 12–9. Adjustable life insurance.

Age	Situation	Face Value and Type of Policy	Annual Premium
30	Limited cash	$50,000, ten-year term	$ 258.12
32	Income up, most debts paid, can afford more	$50,000 straight life with level payments	878.75
34	Marries; needs added protection	$75,000 straight life with level payments	1,344.52
36	Wife has twins; more income but not enough for all straight life	$125,000 term to age 72 with level premiums	1,644.52
40	Ample income; building retirement plan; adds protection and switches to straight life	$135,000 straight life with level premiums	2,699.67

SOURCE: Adapted from *Physician's Management*, August 1978; based on data from Bankers Life of Des Moines, Iowa.

tages and there can be tax problems. Compared with regular annuities, SLI has small cash value. Also, at death, taxes must be paid at ordinary income rates on the excess of the death benefits (cash value) of the annuity over the net premiums paid. At the end of 10 years, for example, premium payments may total $25,000. At death the benefit will be $36,790, so the $11,790 difference is taxable.

On the other hand, the total death benefit of $125,000 ($136,790 minus $11,790) will be greater than the proceeds of more costly $100,000 ordinary life. When properly structured, the proceeds of the term insurance can be tax-free. That is possible when Mr. Brach owns the annuity and Mrs. Brach owns the term policy. The tax liability can be tricky, so be sure your agent gets a further OK from the insurance company home office.

SLI is an intriguing concept, and it can be useful in some situations; but not all the insurance is being used for family protection. If you opt for straight life coverage, consider adding SLI for added protection and your own retirement. But it should be a supplement to your financial planning.

Variable Life Insurance (VLI)

Historically, the face value of straight life insurance remains fixed. Unless you live a long time and reinvest all dividends, your heirs will never get more than the stated amount of the policy. Recently, in efforts to offset inflation, some companies have started to offer variable life insurance: all or part of the premiums is invested in common stocks rather than mortgages and bonds. The goal is a higher total return from income plus appreciation. If the money manager does well, the death benefits will be greater, but even in a deep bear market it will never be less than the face value.

In theory, that is a wise way to offset inflation. If the market value of the underlying securities rises at a net annual rate of 7%, the face value of the policy will double in a little over 10 years. In practice, there are drawbacks with VLI:

1. *High premiums.* The premiums are 10% to 20% higher than those of comparable straight life and much higher than for term. For $100,000 coverage for a 45-year-old man the annual cost for VLI is $2,900. For straight life it is $2,300, and for 20-year term it is $1,200.

2. *High costs.* Under a VLI contract, the yield must be close to 4%: a 3% a year base plus about three-quarters of 1% for administration and mortality expenses. In the first ten years, the value of the investment portfolio must therefore go up 10% to achieve a 1% higher death benefit.

3. *Risky borrowing.* Since any loan will be based on cash value, it's possible that, in a deep bear market, assets would be so depleted that the borrower would have to come up with added collateral. And since every loan reduces the amount of invested funds, chances of appreciation will be less. For example, when you borrow $7,500 of a $10,000 cash value, only $2,500 will be working for income and appreciation.

4. *Taxes.* There are still questions about who gets taxed, but they will become

a factor only if the company's investments are rewarding. Income or capital gains levies on the increase in the policy's cash value are not likely, but your beneficiaries may have to pay something on the difference between the policy's face value and the actual death benefit if the stock market continues to rise.

With VLI in a declining stock market you cannot win but you won't lose. In an uptrending market the rewards can be attractive. If all the VLI assets were to yield 8%, the $30,747 face value of VLI, at a cost of $1,000 annually for a 40-year-old male, would grow to $36,642 in five years and to $71,196 at age 65. A comparable straight life policy would remain static with a constant face value of $49,500. The realistic returns of VLI will probably be somewhere in between, because not all assets will be invested in common stocks.

In your financial planning, write these words at the top of your worksheet: "Life insurance is best for protection." But do not overlook special policies. They can be convenient, can save time, can force savings, and can help you reach several secondary goals simultaneously. But unless costs are shared with your employer, special life insurance policies are expensive and do not always represent the best use of savings.

SHOPPING FOR INSURANCE

Costs of life insurance are difficult to compare. The initial low price of one policy may be offset by future benefits of another policy, and vice versa. In a large measure, the differences are sales tools: combinations developed to attract new customers and hold old ones. Generally, the greater the convenience and the larger the number of options, the higher the cost. It's the old story of paying someone else to do what you can do yourself. Still, insurance leaders are trying to provide some national yardsticks.

The traditional basis for comparison of whole life insurance policies is net cost:

- For a nonparticipating (without dividends) policy, net cost is the sum of all premiums over a set number of years.
- For a participating (dividend-paying) policy, net cost is the sum of all premiums minus dividends minus cash value at the end of the time period of coverage.

Net cost is simple, but it's neither complete nor accurate. It ignores the importance of time and interest. Thus policy A, with an annual premium that starts at $400 and decreases to $200, has the same net cost as policy B, which has a premium that starts at $200 a year and increases to $400. Yet policy B is a better value because the extra money, not spent in the early years, could have been earning income.

In recent years, many state insurance commissioners and trade associations have been pushing the idea of interest-adjusted cost (IAC) to calculate the average annual cost of protection. The interest is factored in and compounded. Thus 4% interest (standard in the insurance industry) is added to the first year's premium, then the second year's premium is added to the total and 4% interest is added to the new sum, and so on. Comparisons are usually made for a 20-year period by means of a constant factor.

Consumers Union (CU) agrees with the IAC concept as applicable when the policy is cashed in while the insured is living. But CU feels that there should be a different measure if you die while the policy is in force. Then your heirs get the full death benefits, so the cash value becomes irrelevant. CU adds a net payment computation which starts with the total premiums (adjusted for interest) and deducts the dividends (also adjusted for interest).

So far, because of the many variables such as conversion benefits and cost when held to maturity, the yardsticks are not universally applicable. They do, however, provide a basis for comparisons. For ratings and costs, send for *Guide to Life Insurance,* Consumers Union of the United States, Inc., 256 Washington Street, Mount Vernon, NY 10550, or write for a free *Consumers Shopping Guide for Life Insurance,* State of New York Insurance Department, Albany, NY 12224.

To give you an idea of what you will receive, see Tables 12–10 to 12–12 for data on typical policies issued at ages 35 and 50. Table 12–10 is for term insurance; Table 12–11 is for $10,000 whole life nonparticipating; Table 12–12 is for $10,000 whole life participating. All three tables give 20-year average gross premiums and the interest-adjusted cost for 10 and 20 years to male insureds. (*Note:* The data are for reference only, since many policies have variations. See your life insurance agent for complete, up-to-date details.) Cost alone should not be the deciding factor in choosing life insurance, but your

Table 12–10. Male $25,000 five-year renewable and convertible nonparticipating term insurance.

Company	20-Year Average Gross Premium	First-Year Premiums	Interest-Adjusted Index 10-Year Payment/Cost	Interest-Adjusted Index 20-Year Payment/Cost
		Age 35		
Aetna Life	$ 7.48	($4.29)	$ 4.86	$ 6.73
Connecticut General	8.07	(5.11)	5.60	7.37
Equitable (Iowa)	7.98	(4.94)	5.45	7.25
Paul Revere Life	7.35	(4.14)	4.84	6.62
State Farm	7.57	(4.85)	5.06	6.85
Travelers	7.75	(4.54)	5.16	7.01
		Age 50		
Aetna Life	20.32	(12.12)	14.94	18.87
Connecticut General	26.08	(12.56)	14.96	22.90
Equitable (Iowa)	25.39	(12.63)	15.16	22.49
Paul Revere Life	25.35	(11.69)	14.08	22.12
State Farm	20.40	(13.88)	16.90	19.38
Travelers	25.35	(12.38)	15.10	22.48

SOURCE: *Consumers Shopping Guide for Life Insurance,* State of New York Insurance Department, 1977.

Table 12–11. Male $10,000 nonparticipating whole life insurance.

Company	20-Year Average Gross Premium	Interest-Adjusted Index: 10-Year Payment	Interest-Adjusted Index: 10-Year Cost	Interest-Adjusted Index: 20-Year Payment	Interest-Adjusted Index: 20-Year Cost
		Age 35			
Aetna Life	$18.05	$18.05	$ 9.12	$18.05	$ 9.38
Allstate Life	17.71	17.71	7.49	17.71	8.84
Connecticut General	18.40	18.40	8.63	18.40	8.55
Firemen's Fund	19.20	19.20	10.11	19.20	10.07
Hartford Life	19.47	19.47	9.63	19.47	9.82
State Farm	18.79	18.79	7.53	18.79	8.89
Travelers	17.20	17.20	8.72	17.20	9.02
		Age 50			
Aetna Life	33.21	33.21	18.22	33.21	20.26
Allstate Life	32.11	32.11	15.91	32.11	19.26
Connecticut General	33.30	33.30	17.63	33.30	19.47
Firemen's Fund	34.49	34.49	19.27	34.49	21.27
Hartford Life	34.63	34.63	18.73	34.63	21.04
State Farm	34.63	34.63	17.25	34.63	20.73
Travelers	35.52	32.52	17.83	32.52	20.22

SOURCE: *Consumers Shopping Guide for Life Insurance,* State of New York Insurance Department, 1977.

Note: The payment index indicates the average annual cost measured over the first 10 or 20 years if you intend to continue paying premiums; the cost index indicates the cost if you cash in the policy at the end of 10 to 20 years. Actual costs depend on dividends paid.

agent should be able to offer logical explanations of the costs and benefits of the policies he's selling. As with investments, it's more important to feel comfortable than to save a few dollars.

RELY ON YOUR INSURANCE AGENT

A good insurance agent is important to financial planning. He or she can help you with accurate information for projections, show you how to get the most protection for your dollar, provide counsel, arrange loans, answer questions, and, at your death, hasten payments and guide your heirs. There are two handy checkpoints: an agent who is a chartered life underwriter (C.L.U.), and a company that is licensed to do business in New York, New Jersey, and Pennsylvania, where state authorities set high standards of financial security and conduct.

CONSIDER TOTAL FAMILY INSURANCE NEEDS

Since financial planning involves everyone in the family, there can be other questions regarding life insurance.

Should there be wife insurance? Yes, as long as your wife is a wage earner or there are young children. If your wife is adding to family income, judge her insurance needs as part of your overall income and budget planning. Group insurance, at her job, is a welcome, no-cost-to-you benefit. Personal insurance

Table 12–12. Male $10,000 participating whole life insurance.

Company	20-year Average Gross Premium	Interest-Adjusted Index: 10-Year Payment	Interest-Adjusted Index: 10-Year Cost	Interest-Adjusted Index: 20-Year Payment	Interest-Adjusted Index: 20-Year Cost
		Age 35			
Aetna Life	$24.45	$22.75	$11.32	$19.25	$ 8.17
Connecticut General	22.04	20.08	6.91	18.30	7.59
Connecticut Mutual	17.99	16.44	6.00	15.44	6.34
Equitable Life	22.99	19.44	7.86	17.28	7.01
Home Life	23.12	19.36	7.01	16.19	5.24
John Hancock	24.71	22.24	9.22	19.20	7.87
Massachusetts Mutual	22.92	19.31	6.53	17.14	6.33
Northwestern Mutual	22.95	18.70	5.68	16.22	5.51
Prudential	23.60	19.44	8.04	17.60	6.85
		Age 50			
Aetna Life	41.35	37.14	19.50	31.17	16.23
Connecticut General	39.38	34.07	14.69	31.33	16.76
Connecticut Mutual	32.62	29.56	12.77	27.62	14.34
Equitable Life	40.06	34.30	16.13	31.06	16.33
Home Life	39.67	32.92	14.22	27.13	12.21
John Hancock	42.07	37.19	17.35	32.29	16.43
Massachusetts Mutual	39.66	32.89	13.76	29.53	14.71
Northwestern Mutual	39.75	31.98	12.52	28.28	13.59
Prudential	42.51	33.97	16.58	29.36	14.47

SOURCE: *Consumers Shopping Guide for Life Insurance*, State of New York Insurance Department, 1977.

Note: The payment index indicates the average annual cost measured over the first 10 or 20 years if you intend to continue paying premiums; the cost index indicates the cost if you cash in the policy at the end of 10 to 20 years. Actual costs depend on dividends paid.

can be a handy way to assure replacement of her financial contributions and, if she is so inclined, a way to build the family's net worth and estate.

If the mother dies when there are young children, there will be extra costs for a housekeeper and, probably, private school. Guesstimate those expenses and buy an insurance policy large enough to provide the extra money needed: at least $5,000 a year until the children are in their late teens.

In both situations, buy term insurance unless one of you feels the need for the forced savings or comfort of ever-rising cash values of whole life.

Should there be child insurance? The best arguments for life insurance for children will come from the agent: low cost, saving for college, and guaranteed insurability. The facts are not so persuasive. At death, there will no loss of income, which supplies the primary purpose of life insurance.

Still, the costs of coverage are low because the premium rate is locked in. For a $10,000 straight life policy on a 4-year-old child, the annual premium is $74, the same amount needed to buy $4,000 extra protection for 35-year-old Dad.

Nor do future premiums rise rapidly. For a $10,000 nonparticipating (no dividends) policy, the premium payments are as follows:

Age of Purchase	Annual Premium	Premium Payments through Age 65	If Money, Paid to 65, Is Invested at 5¼%
16	$102.20	$5,110	$24,413
20	115.40	5,308	22.036
24	130.90	5,498	19,884

Granted that future premiums will be paid with depreciated dollars, insurance still doesn't work out profitably as a savings program. Most of the extra interest earned on the early-age premiums goes to the insurance company. The argument that, because of a future health impairment, the child will not be able to get life insurance later, also is weak. According to the Institute of Life Insurance, 92% of the people who apply for insurance are accepted at regular rates.

There are, however, alternatives which may fit better into a financial plan:

Family Plan

The family plan is a package with whole life for the breadwinner and small term policies for the spouse and children. For $124 a year, a 30-year-old man, with a 25-year-old wife, can buy:

- For the husband, $5,000 in dividend-paying straight life.
- For the wife, $5,000 term decreasing at $150 per year to $1,250 at age 50 and expiring at age 65 with the privilege of conversion to straight life.
- For each child under 25, $1,000 term convertible to straight life up to a value of $5,000.

Guaranteed Insurability Riders

Guaranteed insurability riders on straight life policies of children allow the purchase of additional insurance at stipulated ages or on occasions such as marriage or birth of a child. At a typical cost of $4.50 a year, you can add a rider to a $5,000 policy on a 15-year-old boy to give the boy the right to buy up to $5,000 of cash value insurance at ages 22, 26, 30, 35, and 40. If he exercises all options, he can have $30,000. But there's no guarantee of the same premium rate.

This may be a handy way to start a youngster with life insurance, but it should not be part of your own financial planning.

WHICH POLICIES TO DROP

For most of your life, financial planning will concentrate on growth: on adding to your savings and assets. Later in life, usually toward retirement, the time comes when the wisest course is to start divesting and thus reduce living costs. The gap bridged by life insurance has narrowed or disappeared because of increased wealth (from income, investments, or inheritance) or decreased expenses (no more college bills or mortgage).

When you make your annual review of net worth and budget projections, spend an extra hour in calculating future family need while you live and if you die. Then factor in inflation and a reserve fund for buying something you or your spouse have always wanted to own. Finally, determine the value of surplus assets with a potential for income.

As a rule of thumb, figure $1,000 annual income for every $10,000. That represents the cost and benefits of a lifetime annuity at age 65. (An experienced investor can get almost the same return and still have capital at his death.) Be realistic and assume that you and your spouse will live beyond actuarial ages of limited-period annuities. But do not be too pessimistic and pile up too much wealth. You can't take it with you. Finally, when you and your family no longer need large financial protection, start reducing your insurances or take paid-up coverage for a lesser amount—unless, of course, you want to leave a large sum to your children or a charity.

If you have term insurance, you'll have to make a decision at age 65 anyway. At that time, term costs become comparable with those of straight life. If you have regular life policies the premiums of which must continue to be paid (although probably at a lower level because of the use of dividends), consider cash value and the age of the policy.

Cash Value

In most cases the cash value will still be substantially less than the face value. If you take the cash now, you have to calculate whether you can invest the money so profitably for the years you expect to live that you will come out ahead. If, for example, you have a $5,000 face value policy with a cash value of $3,000, you must (1) be confident that you can invest that $3,000 to earn $2,500 in the next six years and (2) recognize that you will lose if you die in that period.

Age of Policy

If you own two policies taken out at different ages that are equal in face value, drop or cash in the newer one. If you own two policies taken out at about the same age, one with a mutual and one with a stock company, cash in the stock policy if it's over ten years old, the mutual one if it's under ten years old.

When It Pays to Switch

What with inflation, expensive old policies, versatile, inexpensive new ones, and your own financial needs, there will come a time to consider switching straight life policies which have accumulated high cash values. As a general rule, switching is not profitable. You will have to pay commissions on the new purchases and, although the face value of the new policy will be the same as that of the old one, the cash value will be less for several years. Before you let your insurance agent talk you into a switch, make him prove the bottom-line benefits to your financial plan.

The starting point, says Joseph Belth, professor of insurance at Indiana University, is when your present policy has a retention rate that is 10% greater than that of the new policy. What he's talking about is the measurement of what the insurance company keeps for expenses and profits. The higher that is the larger the premium and the smaller the real insurance protection. Ask your agent to give you data on the policy you have and the one he's trying to sell.

Specifically, suggests Belth, buy a new policy when:

1. Your protection needs are substantially less.
2. You can invest the cash received from the old policy at high, safe returns—at least 50% above those of the old policy. That is, 8.25% when the policy dividend is 5.50%.

EXAMPLE: You're 45 and you have a $100,000 straight life policy with company A. The premium is $3,111 a year and the current cash value is $17,400. You project that you will invest the cash proceeds in bonds for an 8% return. You can:

1. Buy $83,000 straight life from company B at a yearly premium of $2,238. The $1,392 interest from the bonds will reduce that to a net of $846 for total savings of 2,265.
2. Buy $83,000 renewable term for a $1,440 annual premium, which is almost offset by the bond interest. You will still have full protection; but you can no longer count on the ever-higher cash value buildup, which is one of the major attractions of whole life.

In both cases, the switch will be worthwhile only if the investments are safe and sure and the money will not be needed in a hurry. If you have to withdraw funds when interest rates are high (and bond prices are lower), you may have to take a loss. For more details, see Table 12–13.

A slightly different approach to switching life insurance policies, recommended by Consumers Union, is shown in Worksheet 17. Ask your agent to help you fill it out. If the new policy comes out ahead on any count, consider switching. If it's better on all counts, get the new policy.

WHEN AND HOW TO BUY ANNUITIES

If your life insurance agent is typical, he will try to sell you an annuity as part of your financial planning, especially when you are older or have substantial

Table 12–13. Factors involved in switching life insurance policies.

	Company A			Company B		
Age at Purchase	Annual Premium	Cost per $1,000	Cash Value	Annual Premium	Cost per $1,000	Cash Value
35	$2,182	$21.75	—	$1,181	$18.03	—
40	2,552	25.44	$ 7,700*	2,201	21.93	$ 5,200*
45	3,111	31.03	17,400*	2,705	26.97	14,300
50	3,858	38.50	27,100*	3,314	33.06	24,100
55	4,838	48.30	37,200*	4,136	41.28	34,400

SOURCE: *Personal Finance Letter*, December 11, 1975.

*Cash value buildup is based on a policy taken out at age 35. The amount of cash value refers to buildup reached when policyholder is at age on left.

Worksheet 17
Determining Whether to Switch Life Insurance Policies

		Amount
1.	Face value of present (old) policy	_____
2.	Current cash value of old policy	_____
3.	New insurance needed if old policy is cashed in (1 minus 2)	_____
4.	Annual interest if cash value of old policy is invested at 6% a year	_____
5.	Annual premium of old policy	_____
6.	Annual premium of new policy	_____
7.	Net payment on new policy (6 minus 4)	_____
8.	Premium savings (5 minus 7)	_____
9.	Cash values of policies at age 65: Old policy if continued	_____
	New policy—current cash value of old policy (2) minus future cash value of new policy	_____
10.	Dividends: Old	_____
	New	_____

SOURCE: Consumers Union, Mount Vernon, N.Y.

extra cash. An annuity should be considered an investment, not life insurance. The primary purpose of an annuity is to provide after-work income as long as you and your spouse live. An annuity is a kind of personal retirement program. It can be purchased in one lump sum or by periodic savings. Its income accumulates tax-free until withdrawal, usually at age 65. At that time, the returned capital is tax-free and the balance is taxable as ordinary income.

When you buy any kind of annuity, you turn your savings over to a life insurance company which applies one investment approach for the life of the agreement: fixed income (primarily through bonds), growth (via a variable portfolio), or balance (a combination of bonds and stocks). The rate of accumulation depends on the returns from the investments. Currently, it runs from 7% to 8%. If the returns are higher, you will have a larger retirement income; if they are lower, you'll get less but never less than the agreed-in-advance sum.

Deferred Annuities

Deferred annuities are lump-sum payment contracts that can be bought from most insurance companies by almost any adult. At age 65, the payout starts.

EXAMPLE: Mr. Allis, age 55, inherits $20,000, with which he buys a single-payment deferred annuity. Starting at age 65, he will receive a monthly income of about $165.60 (the exact amount depends on the issuing company). If he wants to have the payment continue as long as his 53-year-old wife lives, the monthly check will be less.

As with any annuity, Mr. Allis is betting that he will outlive the actuarially projected age of 78 and his wife hers of 81. If both die soon after retirement, he loses. But if both die before 65, their heirs will receive the death benefit representing the purchase price plus accumulated income and appreciation.

The interest rate is guaranteed for five years (in New York State, one year). Some companies sell deferred annuities with no load, but most charge a sales commission of from 5% to 8.5%. So you may have only 91.5% of every dollar working for you.

Added advantages are that you can borrow against your savings or take out up to 6% of your original investment each year, at, of course, the cost of lower net income over the years.

How Much Income a $10,000 Annuity Buys

Table 12-14 shows the monthly income that a man and woman, both age 65, can buy from major insurance companies for a single $10,000 payment under two types of annuity plans. These are not deferred annuities; the payment starts at once and continues until the single annuitant dies. There are no death benefits for the survivor.

Ask your insurance agent to describe other annuity plans. Life and ten years certain, for example, guarantees a lifetime income; but if the annuitant dies before the end of ten years, the beneficiary receives the same monthly income for the remainder of the decade span. Other types of annuities are for longer periods of time but pay less per month.

Savings Annuity

A savings annuity wraps a tax shelter around savings certificates issued by a thrift institution. Usually it requires a minimum investment of $30,000. The tax

Table 12-14. How much income a $10,000 annuity buys.

	Nonqualified				Qualified*			
	Lifetime		Life and 10 Years		Lifetime		Life and 10 Years	
Company	Male	Female	Male	Female	Male	Female	Male	Female
Aetna Life	$84.68	$74.07	$78.03	$71.30	$87.30	$76.36	$80.44	$73.51
Connecticut General	81.31	72.17	74.87	69.24	82.97	73.64	76.40	70.65
Connecticut Mutual	84.70	76.96	79.34	74.48	89.37	81.33	83.81	78.74
Equitable Life	89.39	78.27	82.81	75.86	94.19	82.47	87.26	79.94
John Hancock	85.55	75.93	79.80	73.35	88.93	79.00	82.97	76.32
Metropolitan	86.77	77.44	80.97	75.42	92.28	82.69	86.09	80.50
Occidental	82.68	73.60	77.25	71.16	84.97	75.65	79.40	73.14
Pennsylvania Mutual	87.22	78.20	80.75	75.17	96.04	85.46	87.22	81.14
Prudential	84.93	77.06	80.55	74.07	96.52	86.59	89.49	83.28
Travelers	86.03	74.45	80.78	72.67	87.91	76.33	82.57	74.45

SOURCE: Based on data from A. M. Best Co., Oldwick, N.J.
Note: Many figures exclude state premium tax, and some have variations in terms.
*Sold to participants in tax-benefited retirement plans: group pensions, Keogh plans, IRAs, and tax-sheltered annuities.

savings are substantial. On a straight six-year certificate paying 7.75%, the return to an individual in the 40% tax bracket would be an effective 4.65%. There would be no tax on a savings annuity, so the full income would compound. The insurance company takes title to the certificate, but you can retain control and decide what you want to do with the money at maturity. Warning: IRS is debating whether to continue approval.

Investment Annuity

Again IRS has some questions about the taxation of the policy, but an investment annuity may be worthwhile for a wealthy individual. Keystone Provident Life Insurance Company has a policy that lets you manage your own investments. You can:

1. Make your own investment decisions and never be locked into any one financial approach. That is, you can switch from bonds to stocks in a strong market or vice versa when stock values fall.
2. Borrow against your assets.
3. Liquidate in units of $5,000 as long as you keep a minimum balance of $5,000.
4. Accumulate income tax-free until withdrawal.

Since Keystone receives no income from your investments, there are fees: an initial $75 to defray setup costs, a nominal bank custodial charge, and an annual premium. The premium decreases with the size of your contract: three-quarters of 1% of the first $50,000; one-half of 1% thereafter. The benefits come with compounding. On a $50,000 investment yielding 7¾% annually with quarterly compounding, an executive in the 50% tax bracket will have assets of $256,290 in 25 years. Without the tax-deferred benefit, the total would be $131,120. If the executive wants extra death protection, he can put in $100,000. Immediately, he will get $177,000 in life insurance coverage. Since the money, under this policy, compounds at 6¾%, the savings will grow to $250,000 at age 65. At withdrawal, taxes will be paid on the $150,000 growth, not the original $100,000.

Insured Annuity

The insured annuity is typical of many special packages. Concept 4, sponsored by Federal Life Insurance (Mutual) and distributed by Wellington Management Company, has a fixed account that guarantees rates of return: 7.5% for the first year, 6% for the next four years, and 4% thereafter. There's an extra "dividend" if earned income is sufficient.

There's also a variable account consisting of shares in one or two of six Vanguard Group funds. You can pick the goal you want: growth, growth and income, balance, or whatever. The original principal is insured against loss if you die before age 65 or until the money is used to buy an annuity. If you invest $50,000 in shares of growth fund and die a few years later when a bear market has reduced the value of the shares to $45,000, your beneficiaries will get the full $50,000—for a small extra premium.

Concept 4 also provides tax savings when you borrow against the collateral of the fixed account. For example, an executive in the 50% tax bracket who invests $102,000 can allocate $52,000 to the fixed account and use the balance to buy mutual fund shares. He can then borrow $50,000 from the fixed account at 6% simple interest.

Meantime, he receives guaranteed interest: 7.5% on the $2,000 free balance ($150), 4% on the borrowed $50,000 ($2,000), plus income and appreciation on the $50,000 now invested in fund shares. Hopefully, that will be a 10% total return as reported by some growth funds in recent years. In the 50% tax bracket, the loan cost nets to $1,500, so the executive "earns" $650 on his $50,000 borrowed money. And there's always a 100% tax shelter until the funds are withdrawn or used to buy an annuity. The loan must, of course, be repaid.

In your financial planning, review options such as these special packages, but always view them as investments, not life insurance. Their value depends on that basic time and money equation, and it should be carefully projected so that you are sure you're making a worthwhile commitment, not just buying a conversation piece.

PROTECTION

Life insurance is such a broad, diversified field that it's impossible to cover all the options and offerings. There are many ways in which you can use life insurance in your financial planning. Before you make any decision, however, review the alternatives with your agent and write, at the top of your planning program, *Life insurance is for protection*. When you use it for any other reason, such as retirement, savings, tax avoidance, or investments, you will be paying for convenience rather than protection.

Combining Life Insurance and Investments

Table 12–15 will give you an idea of how life insurance and investments can be combined. It shows both the guaranteed and the possible returns of such blending. Note that the insurance proceeds are sure, whereas stocks present risks along with the promise of higher rewards.

GLOSSARY

adjustable life. An insurance policy which can be added to or subtracted from, changed between whole life and term, and lengthened or shortened in protection so that one policy can provide insurance over the years.

annuity. A contract that provides income for a specified period of time, usually with payment starting at retirement.

decreasing term. A contract the face value of which declines while the premiums remain the same.

deferred annuity. An annuity the payments on which begin at some future date. Taxes on income and appreciation are deferred until withdrawal.

IRS section 79. A group life insurance plan that permits the employer to deduct the premium as a business expense. It can be used as a fringe benefit for selected employees.

Table 12–15. Combined insurance and investment income from $1,200 per year for 35 years from age 30.

Nature of Income	Guaranteed Results*				Possible Results		
	Whole Life	Term + Savings at 5% Yield	Term + Stocks at 9% Return	Whole Life	Term + Savings at 5% Yield	Term + Stocks at 9% Return
Cash at 65	$35,000—cash value of policy	$23,000 in savings; no insurance	0	$76,000—cash value and dividends	$62,000 in savings; no insurance	$127,000—investments + dividends + gains
Estate if insured dies at age 30½	$60,000 death benefit	$60,660—death benefit + bank deposit	$60,000 death benefit	$60,000 death benefit	$60,675—death benefit + deposit + interest	$60,690—death benefit + investment + dividends + gain
Estate if insured dies at age 64½	$60,000 death benefit	$63,000—death benefit + savings	$60,000 death benefit	$120,000—death benefit + added insurance bought with dividends	$122,000—death benefit + savings + interest	$187,000—death benefit + investment + dividends + gains
Estate if insured dies at age 65½ without new insurance	$35,000—cash value of policy	$23,000—savings; no insurance	0	$76,000—cash value + dividends	$62,000—deposits + interest	$127,000—investments + dividends + gains

SOURCE: Adapted from information from Edwin K. Chapin, C.L.U., New York, and Wright Investors' Service, Bridgeport, Conn.

*Actually, there's no guarantee that stocks will yield 9%, but they have done so over a 35-year period. With quality stocks, the return is almost guaranteed.

split-dollar insurance (SDI). A policy the premium of which is split between employer and employee. The corporation pays the portion of the premium representing the increase in annual cash value, and the employee pays the balance.

split-life insurance (SLI). A package term life policy that provides an annuity for the insured and death protection for the family.

straight life. A policy that provides a predetermined sum at the death of the insured. Cash values are built up by the payment of premiums larger than needed for protection alone. Also called *ordinary* and *whole life*.

term life. A policy that provides protection for a limited period of time. There are no accumulations of cash value. The policy can be renewed or converted to straight life, normally to age 65.

waiver of premium. A means of relinquishing a regular insurance premium payment. A premium is usually waived when the insured is disabled if the policyholder has paid an extra fee.

years-certain annuity. An annuity that guarantees payment for a set number of years even if the annuitant dies.

13 Don't Go Overboard to Save Taxes

GLOSSARY

Usually, a glossary is listed at the end of a chapter, but the subject of taxes may raise some questions of definition that must be answered earlier. Here's a summary of the terms that are most significant to tax filers.

capital gain. The profit from the sale or exchange of a capital asset—generally all the property you own and use for personal purposes, pleasure, or investment: home, furnishings, car, stocks, bonds, collections, real estate. Gains on property held for less than one year are short-term and are taxed as regular income. Profits on property held for more than 12 months are long-term and are subject to lower taxes.

capital loss. Loss from the sale or exchange of a capital asset. All capital losses are tax-deductible to some degree.

dividend. Payment, in cash or stock, to shareholders; usually taxable at the highest rate.

earned income. Wages, salaries, tips, and other employee compensation subject to deductions for Social Security taxes. Fully taxable. Does not include welfare, disability, and Social Security benefits.

income averaging. IRS-approved methods of computing tax payments on income received over a period of time.

interest. Payment to a lender for the use of money. A bank pays interest on savings accounts; a corporation on its bonds. Taxable at maximum rate except interest from municipal bonds.

joint return. A tax return filed on income of both husband and wife. In most cases, the tax will be less than if the individuals filed separately.

tax bracket. The tax rate, expressed in percentages, that is used to compute tax payments. For the federal levy, a single taxpayer pays no tax until his income is over $3,300, since there is a personal exemption of $1,000 and a standard deduction of $2,300 ($100 more if there are dividends). Then the tax rate is 14%. A more affluent married couple, with no dependents and adjusted income (after exemptions and deductions) of $43,200, would pay $12,140 plus 48% of income up to $47,200, when the rate rises to 50%. The maximum levy is 70%.

tax-exempt income. Interest on debt issued by a state, county, city, town, village, or public authority which is free from federal income taxes and, in general, from state and local income levies within the state of issue. There is one exception: income from Puerto Rican bonds is always tax-free.

tax preference. Items to which a minimum tax applies. Concerns only wealthy taxpayers.

unearned income. Interest from thrift accounts, bonds, notes, mortgages, dividends, rents, royalties, pensions, annuities, profits from the sale of property, fees, and gifts—generally, but not always, income not subject to deductions for Social Security taxes.

To understand and, possibly, to file, your own income tax returns, read a book or guide, attend lectures at adult school, visit the local IRS office, or consult a professional tax adviser. The regulations are getting more complex all the time even though the form looks easier.

Everybody likes to save taxes. It makes you feel good to know that you have money that does not have to be shared with the government and you have a cost savings and higher earnings. But tax savings alone should never be the sole factor in any financial investment or estate planning decision. A tax shelter should be a sound business venture and unless tax savings, in the sale of property, are more than 20%, they are seldom worthwhile except for those in the highest tax brackets.

Unfortunately, many people become so anxious to beat Uncle Sam that they fail to look at the whole picture and tend to forget the obvious: that taxes are what you pay for the services in modern society and, in many cases, are levied only when there's a profit. In almost every financial transaction, we all have silent partners: federal, state, and local governments. In their rush to minimize tax payments, thousands of otherwise intelligent men and women:

- Refuse to sell when they have a substantial gain.
- Wait until death so that their estate gets their investments at current value and their heirs can use these higher prices as a base for future taxes. (Recent legislation has changed this somewhat and, in many cases, set the evaluation of inherited property as of December 31, 1976, but that is now awaiting further clarification by Congress.)
- Let assets decline in value rather than pay a tax.
- Give away property and the tax burden with it.
- Seek tax shelters that will enable them to use tax deductions against current income and fail to consider that this may be only postponing the inevitable levy.

Once in a while, one of these strategies will make sense but, even then, usually only for the wealthy. *For most people, taxes should be a secondary factor in any phase of financial planning.*

TAX LAWS

Before getting into details of tax savings, let's summarize the present tax law as set by the revolutionary 1976 Tax Reform Act and modified in 1978. The major provisions are set forth below.

1. Extend the holding period for long-term capital gains to 12 months. Profits realized in a shorter period are subject to regular income taxes.

2. Reduce the amount of long-term capital gains subject to tax to 40% and eliminate the other 60% from tax preference items (as of November 1978).

3. Permit short-term losses to be credited against regular income: $1 for every $2 loss, to a maximum of $3,000 with carryover of excess to future years.

4. Set a one-time exemption, up to $100,000, for profits on the sale of a home

when the seller is age 55 or older and has lived in the house for three of the past five years.

5. Limit deductions on rental of vacation home, boat, or motor home. If you use any of these for more than two weeks a year or more than 10% of the days rented out, you can deduct, for maintenance, depreciation, and utilities, no more than the rental income plus such customary tax-saving items as property taxes and mortgage interest. In other words, the former benefits of renting your vacation spot are pretty much eliminated.

6. Tighten the rules for home office expenses so that deductions are allowed only if the room is used regularly as an office, is the principal place of your business or profession or, if you work for someone else, is used for your employer's, not your, convenience.

7. Make significant changes in estate and gift tax computations (see Chapter 15).

8. Provide new standards and rules for deductions for moving expenses, day care, alimony payments, and child support.

9. Raise the tax on preference items to 15% from 10%: to the greater of $10,000 or half the regular income tax liability. Preference items include accelerated depreciation on property, intangible drilling costs of oil and gas wells, depletion allowances, and stock options.

10. Beginning with years after 1978, establish a new form of alternative minimum tax which takes effect only when that tax is higher than the regular income tax plus the 15% minimum tax. This will hit few taxpayers but here's how it works, according to Research Institute of America:

To compute the alternative minimum tax, add, to your regular taxable income, the untaxed (60%) portion of long-term capital gains plus excess itemized deductions (preference items). After a specific exemption of $20,000, the income is taxed as follows: 10% of the first $40,000; 20% of the next $40,000; 25% on any excess.

EXAMPLE: Bob Barton has taxable income of $90,000, including $40,000 of a long-term capital gain of $100,000. He has no 15% minimum tax or excess itemized deductions. The first step is to add the $60,000 of the untaxed long-term capital gain to the $90,000 taxable income, for a total of $150,000. Then subtract the $20,000 exemption, leaving $130,000. Finally, compute the tax:

10% of $40,000	$ 4,000
20% of $40,000	8,000
25% of $50,000	12,500
Total	$24,500

Bob can ignore this because it is less than the tax he has to pay anyway: about $37,000.

Both the 1976 and 1978 Tax Reform Acts are complex laws whose interpretations are still being clarified, so consult your tax adviser before you take any actions involving the sale, transfer, or gift of sizable property. Wise counsel can save you a lot of money.

CALCULATING THE TRUE WORTH OF TAX SAVINGS

Now that you know the ground rules, let's see why taxes should seldom be the determining factor in the sale of property.

On gains, when the stock or real estate is held for 12 months or more, the taxable portion is only 40% of the profit. For most people, the maximum levy is 50%, so the effective tax is 20% or less. In the 36% tax bracket, that means you pay 14.4% and keep 85.6% of the profits.

Says investment adviser John Winthrop Wright: "For most investors, it does not pay to sell a stock for a tax loss unless the savings are greater than 20% of the market value." Keep that in mind when your broker urges you to take year-end tax losses. Such a policy may be foolish and costly. As with so many things on Wall Street, few people bother to do their arithmetic. Of course, property of any kind should be sold when the prospects are so poor that there is almost no chance that it will increase in price enough to recover the loss.

On paper, the attraction of a tax loss is that it can be used against taxable gains in other securities, but you cannot avoid the tax forever. When the new stock which you buy with the proceeds of the tax-loss sale is eventually sold, you will have to pay a tax on the entire gain because you have already used up the tax-loss offset.

To consider a tax-loss sale, you should have (1) a stock or property in which there is a substantial loss and (2) another stock (property) in which you hope to make a *real* profit. (Remember: Uncle Sam "owns" 20% of any gain. That is, if you buy a stock at 5 and it rises to 10, the gross profit of $5 is reduced because 40% ($2) of that gain is taxed; in the 50% bracket the levy is $1 so the net profit is $4.

Here's how to make your calculations: You bought 100 shares of a stock at $60 per share. It is now at 50, so you have a paper loss of $1,000 and can take advantage of the costs of commissions on both sides of the transaction.

Buy:		
	Original investment: 100 at $60	$6,000
	Brokerage costs (rounded out)	100
	Total cost	$6,100
Sell:		
	100 shares at $50	$5,000
	Brokerage costs (rounded out)	90
	Proceeds	$4,910
	Capital loss: $6,100 minus $4,910	$1,090
	Tax benefit at 25%	$272.50

This represents a 14.3% loss on the total investment and a tax benefit on base cost of 3.6% and on proceeds of 4.4%. That's not much. If the stock went to below 50, the sale might be justified in terms of the tax benefit. The real key is the stock itself. If it has prospects of moving up 3 points soon, you'll do better to hold off, because the rise will offset the tax benefits and save commissions. But that decision should be based on the value of the security, not the tax savings.

Note that if you had followed the counsel in Chapter 10, you would have sold at 54 or at the outside at 51, taken the loss, and put your money to work in a promising situation. These are the points of a 10% and 15% decline which should signal trouble ahead.

To put the question in other terms: since the maximum tax-loss benefit to most people will be 20%, a 20% loss means a net tax savings of 4%. Commissions on the round trip will be about 3%, so the real benefit is about 1% of the value of the securities involved. And even that is only a postponement of inevitable taxes.

That 20% figure can also be used to avoid selling too soon and to decide when to switch for more income. If you sell too soon, to avoid taxes, you will have less money to invest and your new holdings will have to rise to greater heights.

EXAMPLE: Dorothy Jones bought 100 shares of Aspen Electronics at 50. They are now selling at 100, so she has a $5,000 gross profit in 14 months. In the 40% tax bracket, she will pay 16%, or $800 in taxes. After deducting commissions, she will have about $9,100 to reinvest. Thus, the new holdings will have to pick up $900 to break even. It may be a lot easier for Aspen to rise another 9 points than for the new choice to perform as well or better. Of course, if the stock is overvalued at 100, you should sell and look for new, underpriced opportunities. But that's an investment, not a tax, decision.

$$SY = \frac{HY}{1 - TBP}$$

where SY = switch yield (on new securities)
HY = hold yield (on present securities)
TBP = tax bite percentage

Bill Jones bought Aspen Electronics at 20. At 100, the annual per share dividend is $4, or a 4% return. He's nearing retirement so wants more income. On the $80 per share profit, his tax is 20%, or $16, if he is in the 50% bracket (less for most people). To justify a switch for income only, he should buy a stock under this formula:

$$SY = \frac{4}{1 - .16} = \frac{4}{84} = 4.8\%$$

Bill should look for new opportunities that yield at least 6%.

LONG-TERM TAX TACTICS

In financial planning, it's always important to keep looking ahead: to project what you will have and what you will need five or ten years from now. At one of those points, you will have to make a decision as to the use of your assets. Usually it will be based on the need for more income, but when substantial assets are involved, the trigger may be tax savings.

There are several types of arrangements which can postpone or minimize taxes by transferring ownership of property directly through sales or indirectly through a trust agreement. They are long-term commitments which are difficult to change, so they should be entered into only after careful consideration and detailed discussion with an experienced lawyer.

Installment Sale

An installment sale can be worked out directly or through a trust. It's most useful when a normal sale would incur heavy federal taxes and possibly state taxes also. A *direct* installment sale works like this: Mr. Beane, who is ready to retire, wants more income. He has stock worth $250,000, which he bought, many years ago, for $25,000. If he sold outright, he would have to pay a tax of about $73,000. His holding is still a growth stock, so the dividends are a skimpy $1,399 a year.

He sells his shares to his son for $250,000 under a long-term, 19½-year, note at 5% interest to be paid off at $1,666 per month: 14 times the current return. On his $20,000 annual income, Mr. Beane, Sr. would pay regular taxes on only $18,718, because $1,282 a year would represent a return of capital. Mr. Beane, Jr. would deduct the interest on the sale contract and, after he sold the shares, pay taxes on the income received from the reinvestment of the proceeds. The total payments to Beane, Sr. would be $389,961: $250,000 for the stock plus $139,961 interest. For report purposes, these are the calculations:

Sales price	$389,961
Less: 5% interest	139,961
Adjusted sales price	250,000
Less: cost basis	25,000
Capital gains on installment basis	$225,000

Since there is a 10-to-1 relation between the sales price of $250,000 and the cost price of $25,000, 10% of the monthly installment payment would be tax-free, to Beane, Sr., as a return of capital. He would pay taxes, at the long-term capital gains rate, on 90% of the monthly check.

Interest	$ 598.12
Long-term capital gain	961.54
Tax-free return of capital	106.84
Total monthly payment	$1,666.50

To provide the income needed for the monthly payment to his father, Beane, Jr. sells the stock and reinvests the $250,000 (less commissions) in shares of one or more no-load mutual funds. He arranges for a monthly check of $1,666.50. Since the net investment is reduced by commissions from the sale of the stock, the fund return must be about 8.5%. That may require an invasion of principal, small if Beane, Jr. pays his taxes on the income from other resources, greater if he uses the fund returns. In about 20 years, the son will own the shares free and clear and can then decide whether to continue holding them or to shift to other investments.

A variation of the plan would start with a larger return of capital and a smaller interest payment; thus most of the Beane, Sr. income would be a nontaxable return of capital. There are strict requirements for such an installment sale, so, again, consult an experienced attorney and make sure that the terms of the agreement meet all IRS regulations.

An *indirect* installment sale, as explained in Chapter 15, starts with an irrevocable trust. That lets the assets pass to Beane, Jr. tax-free. The trust buys the property or securities and, with an independent trustee, tailors the payout schedule to fit Beane, Sr.'s financial needs. There can be variations. For example, if Beane, Sr. planned to work another ten years, there could be no payments until retirement. The trust would have to pay taxes on its income, but the taxes would probably be at a lower rate than he would pay. Alternatively, the payout could be spread out for a fixed period of time but not more than Beane, Sr.'s actual life span. By keeping down the total return, the maximum tax for the father would be 20% if he were in the 50% tax bracket.

OTHER TAX-SAVING ARRANGEMENTS

There are other, less risky, less exotic ways to save taxes on both a short- and long-term basis. One of the best is a partnership which involves members of the same family who, presumably, trust each other and have common interests. The structure allows the transfer of income to a family member who is in a low tax bracket. That reduces the tax bite while you live and at your death. Except for your personal partnership interest, the property transferred will not be included in your estate.

The form and operation of partnerships are subject to IRS scrutiny, so consider such an agreement only when the assets are large enough to justify a knowledgeable attorney and when you are willing, and able, to spend time in management.

When you establish a family partnership, the original property is considered a gift with taxes to be paid on any sum above $3,000 a year ($6,000 when the spouse chips in).

General partnership. Here the key consideration is control. IRS insists that (1) all participants be informed and involved, at regular meetings, through formal minutes, (2) after distributions, proportionate to each partner's interest, are made, the recipient must act on his or her own, and (3) the managing partner must be adequately compensated.

Limited partnership. Here the managing partner (which can be you) is the boss. He can act as he sees fit but must accept full liability. The other participants have nothing to say, but their liability is limited to their financial contribution.

Other variations of in-family arrangements include trusts and gifts, which are explained elsewhere. But there's one tactic which can be used as soon as your children are old enough to work. It's simple: let them file their own tax return. Under current law (always subject to congressional revision), each child can earn $3,300 a year without owing a penny to Uncle Sam. It figures this way: (1) a personal exemption of $1,000; (2) a standard deduction of $2,300. If the youngster fills out a W-4 form, otherwise known as an Employee's Withholding Allowance Certificate, no tax will be withheld and the child gets more take-home pay.

If you are a professional or small businessman, put your child on the payroll when eligible. Reasonable wages are tax deductible and, because it's a small, home business, there are no withholdings for taxes, Social Security, or unemployment compensation. But this money cannot be used to pay expenses for which you are legally liable: medical and dental bills, education, and so on.

TAX-DEFERRED SAVINGS PLAN

The No. 1 tax-deferred plan involving savings is a pension or retirement program. As explained in Chapter 8, this permits tax deductions for contributions and tax-free accumulation of income and appreciation until withdrawal. A first cousin is the deferred annuity: money is set aside by lump sum or contractual agreement, and there are no taxes until the payout, usually at retirement time. These can be used to save taxes on business contracts.

EXAMPLE: Jim Watson, age 45, sells his successful practice for a net of $100,000 and a ten-year employment contract. He buys a deferred annuity paying 7¾%. By the time Jim is 55, the policy compounds to $201,135. Jim quits his job and arranges to draw $10,000 a year tax-free as a return of capital.

In the next decade, the annuity grows to $264,974. Now Jim has a choice: to take about $26,000 a year to pay income taxes or split the money by taking $13,768 a year (also taxable) and leaving the rest of the money at interest. If he lives to age 80, his heirs can count on a $351,675 inheritance. It's the magic of compounding.

When you choose a deferred annuity, shop around. Sales charges can run from 5.5% to 20%; management fees and mortality expenses cost 1% to 2% a year. The costs may seem small, but they are deducted throughout accumulation and payment period, so they reduce investment income. And look for a cost-of-living increase. If you live long, it will be worthwhile.

Before committing yourself to any type of annuity, get full details from the insurance agent. The sales pitch on how much money you'll "save" may be intriguing, but there can be future liabilities. Part, or all, of the annuity payment will be taxed as ordinary income.

INCOME AVERAGING

Income averaging is useful when you are moving into a higher tax bracket or have had an unusually profitable year. Your tax is based on average income over the past five years. The income in the averaging year must be more than 120% of the income over the average base period.

EXAMPLE: In his first year of practice, after four years of part-time work while completing his education and training, dentist Dan Henry has an adjusted taxable income (AJI) of $30,000. For the four preceding years, his AJIs were $9,000, $9,000, $6,000, and $4,000. To get his average base income, Dan:

1. Adds the four preceding year incomes plus the zero bracket amount for each year. For 1973–1977, the zero bracket amount was $2,200:

    $11,200 + $11,200 + $8,200 + $6,200 = $36,800

2. Divides by 4 to get $9,200 average base income: $\frac{\$36,800}{4} = \$9,200$.
3. Multiplies (2) by 120% to get $11,040: $9,200 × 1.20 = $11,040.
4. Subtracts (3) from his last year's AJI of $30,000 to get $18,960 as his averageable income: $30,000 − $11,040 = $18,960.
5. Pays federal income tax on the $18,960, not the $30,000 income.

Income averaging can be used only when the averageable income, for the year of use, is over $3,000. The taxpayer cannot take advantage of such other benefits as optional tax tables or maximum tax on personal service taxable income. Nor can he include premature or excessive distributions from self-employed retirement plans. As a rule of thumb, the annual rise in income will have to be at least $5,000 to justify income averaging, but a lot depends on previous years' earnings.

Similar savings are possible with ten-year income averaging, which applies to lump-sum distributions from a qualified retirement plan. Because the payouts involve corporate and personal contributions and income and appreciation of fund assets, the tax calculations can be very tricky. Before you make a decision on how your savings are to be withdrawn, consult your company's industrial relations department and then double check with your own tax adviser.

TAX PLANNING

For convenience, most people delay tax-related decisions until year end. That is when it's easy to add gains and subtract losses to get a total picture. Yet it is usually wiser, and more productive, to review the tax aspects of your financial planning every few months. Do that by keeping running records of all investment transactions. Pay particular attention to the 12 months time span for more favorable tax treatment. The surveillance will enable you to decide when and whether there are advantages to short-term profits or losses. Holding another couple of weeks could pay off.

Still, even with advance planning, there can be opportunities for tax savings at year end. Basically, they involve shifting the tax liability to the future. You don't have to use such sophisticated tactics as a rollover with silver futures.

If you are in a higher tax bracket as the result of a raise or big gains:
- Apply insurance dividends to premium payments or use the cash to buy shares of a tax-free bond fund. Both remove taxable income.
- Make additional charitable gifts or pay your pledge early. Send in a check for next year's United Way donation or give appreciated securities to your college alumni fund—for example, stock for which you paid $2,000 that is now worth $4,000. Now you can deduct $4,000 from taxable income.
- Boost contributions to your pension and/or profit-sharing plan. The vol-

untary allocations can be withdrawn at any time without penalty. Meantime, the earnings will accumulate tax-free.
- Buy investments that will mature next year: six- to nine-month Treasury bills. The income will be taxable next year, when you may be in a lower tax bracket. But watch out if you expect to be paying more taxes next year.
- Give your spouse some dividend-paying stocks to take advantage of the $100 per person dividend exclusion.
- Try to arrange for your raise to start in January.
- Investigate the possibility of getting your raise or bonus in some form of tax-free benefit such as a medical reimbursement plan for dental bills.

If you expect to be in a higher tax bracket next year:
- Sell high-income-yielding securities and buy low-dividend growth stocks or discount bonds. The capital gains will be subject to a lower tax rate.
- Switch some assets such as bonds or savings accounts into tax-free municipal bonds. But be sure that you are in a high enough tax bracket to really benefit.

Up to this point, the discussion has centered on tactics: using available means to accomplish a specific, immediate end. Now let's broaden our sights and talk about taxes in terms of strategy.

SHORT-TERM TAX STRATEGY

For wealthy individuals in high tax brackets, a favorite ploy is to use a rollover. The rollover occurs when a loss is taken this year to offset current gains and new gains are taken next year in a way which will turn short-term gains into long-term, lower-taxed profits. (See Chapter 11.) Here's a widely used variation:

Frank Farley has a short-term gain from real estate, so he sets up a silver straddle by simultaneously buying silver futures for delivery this year and selling a similar contract short for delivery next year. The loss taken on one side of the hedge is matched against the real estate gain and thus reduces this year's taxes. Early next year, Mr. Farley closes out the other side of the hedge and records a long-term gain which is roughly equal to the eliminated short-term gain.

That was a standard technique for many years, but recently IRS won a court case when it protested on the ground that (1) the rollover was not part of a closed and completed transaction because the taxpayer kept a balanced position while creating his loss and (2) the investor lacked an expectation of a profit and therefore should not be allowed a deduction on the loss side.

Don't give up, yet! A wise lawyer or tax adviser may still be able to come up with legal ways to achieve similar tax savings. That's what you pay them for.

LONG-TERM TAX STRATEGY: TAX-EXEMPT BONDS

When you reach a high tax bracket and have extra savings (those not eligible for retirement plans or other tax-deferred programs), take a long, hard look at tax-exempt securities. Such securities are also called minicipals; they are bonds issued by states, local governments, and certain public authorities. Their interest is exempt from federal income taxes and usually also from state and local taxes in the state in which the bonds were issued. Nor does the interest have to be reported.

Tax-exempt bonds are one of the most valuable tools of financial planning: no tricks, no gimmicks, just no income taxes. But they should be used judiciously and as part of a long-range program. In most cases, they should be considered tax-free savings accounts.

Generally speaking, municipal bonds are not worthwhile for people in the 25% tax bracket, of minimal benefit for people in the 36% tax bracket, and really wise holdings only for people who pay at a high total tax rate: federal plus state plus local levies. As a rule of thumb, tax-exempt securities should provide returns equal to a taxable 10% or more.

The basic types of tax-exempt debt are the following:

General obligation bonds backed by the full taxing power of the issuer. The payment of interest and redemption is a primary obligation, so general obligation bonds usually have the highest ratings and the lowest yields. That is not true if the municipality continues to operate at a deficit (New York City) or has huge unfunded pension obligations (Philadelphia).

Insured bonds, which are general obligations of smaller municipalities whose payments of interest and principal are insured by private firms. The protection boosts the bond ratings, so you get extra safety with good-to-high yields.

Limited tax bonds backed by the full faith and credit, but not the full taxing power, of the issuing body. The issue might be secured by the receipts of a particular tax or facility. Limited tax bonds are not widely used, but they may be of local interest.

Revenue bonds based on income from projects built, operated, or maintained by local governments and authorities: toll highways, bridges, waterworks, sewers, and so on. The quality of revenue bonds varies with the financial success of the underlying enterprise. Enterprises range from the top-quality New Jersey Turnpike to the low-rated, financially troubled West Virginia Turnpike. Variations include (1) bonds issued by local housing authorities under contracts with federal agencies which, in effect, provide a guarantee of payment, and (2) utility debt floated by government-owned utilities—Colorado's Platte River Power Authority or New York State Power Authority.

Special assessment bonds, which are usually small, almost neighborhood issues secured by special levies on taxpayers benefiting from such improvements as new streets or sewers. Their investment values are limited.

Industrial development bonds, which result from efforts to attract industry. Many states and some local governments issue industrial development bonds to finance the construction of plants, buildings, and facilities which are then leased to private corporations. The bonds are paid by the rents or revenues of the project. Some of the bonds have double protection: the credit of the issuer (which may be doubtful) and that of the user (which may be a well-known company such as Alabama Power, Exxon, or General Motors). Thus the bonds can be quality debt suitable for long-term holdings.

Environmental control revenue bonds, which represent a newer version of double-guaranteed debt. Coconino County, Arizona, may be totally unfamiliar to you, but its bonds, issued by a public authority to finance a power plant, are guaranteed by A-rated Tucson Gas & Electric Co.

Hospital bonds available from single institutions but, more frequently, issued through state or regional hospital building authorities. They are not as liquid as most debt issues, but they carry high coupons, have long call protection, and, because of federal restrictions on competition and hospital bill payment agreements, can be safe, long-term investments. But they are *very* illiquid.

How Tax-Exempts Are Issued and Sold

Most municipal bonds are offered in serial form; specific amounts mature annually over the life of the issue. The yields vary with the maturity date; those which become due in a few years pay a lower rate of interest than those due in 15 or 20 years. People want a premium when they wait for their money.

Tax-exempt bonds usually are issued in denominations of $5,000 and $10,000, but their prices are always quoted in units of $1,000: at 98, the cost is $980, or 98% of the face value. Interest is paid semiannually by means of attached coupons. The investor clips the August 15 coupon and gives it to his bank for collection and does the same thing on February 15.

A handy item for the investor who wants his money at a future date is a revenue bond where the interest rate is related to the maturity date—for example, North Carolina Municipal Power Agency Catawba Electric Revenue Bonds, Series 1978: 5.20% for redemption in 1986; 5.60% for 1990; 6.05% for 1995; 6.45% for 2000; and 6⅞% for 2020.

Taxable Versus Tax-Exempt Yields

Now let's see how municipal bonds can be useful in financial planning. The investment attraction, of course, is the freedom from taxes. For an individual in the 50% tax bracket, a 5% tax-exempt yield is equivalent to a 10% return from a taxable corporate bond, and more than that if there are also state and local levies. The higher your tax bracket the greater the benefits. If you substitute sufficient tax-exempt income for currently taxable income, you may move down to a lower tax rate.

The specific percent advantages are shown in Table 13–1. In making your calculations, use your *effective* tax rate, not the one which is shown for your gross-income bracket. In most cases, that will be the tax rate finally used after all deductions, credits, and adjustments. It can be much lower than the percent figure in the table.

Handy calculation. To determine the equivalent after-tax yield of tax-free bonds, divide the reciprocal of your current tax bracket into the yield of the

Table 13–1. Tax-exempt vs. taxable income (000 omitted).

If Your Taxable Income Is*		Your Federal Income Tax Bracket***Is	To Equal These Tax Free Rates						
Married (Joint Return)**	Single		5.75%	6.00%	6.25%	6.50%	6.75%	7.00%	7.25%
			You Would Have to Earn This Much from a Taxable Investment						
$ 16–20	$14–16	28%	7.99%	8.33%	8.68%	9.03%	9.37%	9.72%	10.07%
20–24		31	8.33	8.70	9.06	9.42	9.78	10.14	10.51
		32	8.46	8.82	9.19	9.56	9.93	10.29	10.66
24–28	16–18	34	8.71	9.09	9.47	9.85	10.23	10.61	10.98
	18–20	36	8.98	9.37	9.77	10.16	10.55	10.94	11.33
	20–22	38	9.27	9.68	10.08	10.48	10.89	11.29	11.69
28–32		39	9.43	9.84	10.25	10.66	11.07	11.48	11.89
	22–26	40	9.58	10.00	10.42	10.83	11.25	11.67	12.08
32–36		42	9.91	10.34	10.78	11.21	11.64	12.07	12.50
36–40	26–32	45	10.45	10.91	11.36	11.82	12.27	12.73	13.18
40–44		48	11.06	11.54	12.02	12.50	12.98	13.46	13.94
44–52	32–38	50	11.50	12.00	12.50	13.00	13.50	14.00	14.50
52–64		53	12.23	12.77	13.30	13.83	14.36	14.89	15.43
64–76	38–44	55	12.78	13.33	13.89	14.44	15.00	15.56	16.11
76–88		58	13.69	14.29	14.88	15.48	16.07	16.67	17.26
88–100	44–50	60	14.38	15.00	15.63	16.25	16.87	17.50	18.13
100–200	50–60	62	15.13	15.79	16.45	17.11	17.76	18.42	19.08
Over 200	Over 100	70	19.17	20.00	20.83	21.67	22.50	23.33	24.17

SOURCE: Lebenthal & Co., Inc., New York.
*Net taxable income, after exemptions and deductions, from all sources, "personal service" and otherwise.
**Assumes that all income, including investment income, is earned by one spouse.
***Your personal tax bracket is the rate at which the next dollar of taxable income you earn would be taxed under present law. All computations, including approximation of combined tax brackets, are rounded off on the side of conservatism.

bond. In the 42% tax bracket, the reciprocal is 58%. So if the bond pays 6%, divide by .58 to get the equivalent taxable yield of 10.34%.

If you want to plan ahead, with 6% inflation and assuming commensurate salary increases, you'll move into a higher tax bracket about every three years under current tax laws. After-tax yield on the bond will rise half a percentage point or so with each bracket jump until you hit the 70% maximum tax.

You'll reach the 50% bracket in about three years and 55% in eight or nine years. At that time, your after-tax yield on the investment will be 13.3%.

How to Choose Tax-Exempts

In selecting municipal bonds:

1. *Be sure that the tax benefits are worthwhile.* As Table 13–1 shows, an investor in the 42% tax bracket who buys a tax-exempt bond with a 6% yield will be getting the equivalent of a taxable, fixed-income return of 10.34%. With inflation at 6%, the real net will be 4.34%. But if that 10.34% is one-third from dividends (taxable at 42%, so 3.45% × 42% = 1.45%) and two-thirds from appreciation (taxable at 42% so 6.90% × 21% = 1.45%), total taxes will be 2.90%. That leaves 7.44%, which, after 6% inflation, nets to 1.44%. To put it another way, if a substantial portion of the comparable taxable return represents capital gains, the stock or real estate will be a better hedge against the loss of purchasing power.

2. *Check ratings.* As is true of corporate bonds, all major tax-exempt issues are related by financial services. Few bonds below Baa (Moody's) can be regarded as investments. But they can be good speculations.

3. *Calculate state and local tax exemptions.* Many states extend the tax-exempt benefits to income on bonds issued by governments and authorities in that state. If you have a choice between comparable bonds, it's usually wise to choose local ones over those from out of state.

In New York City, a couple making as little as $30,000 a year might pay total federal, state, and local taxes at a 50% rate. Thus a tax-free municipal bond of the city would be a valuable tax-saving tool.

Here's a helpful hint: Puerto Rico bonds are fully exempt from federal and state income taxes. Most are rated A, are readily marketable, and pay 7% or more. But that high return reflects investor concern about the financial stability of the commonwealth.

4. *Select by maturity date.* Try to buy bonds which will mature about the time you will need money, as when Junior starts college in 1987 or when you plan to start retirement in 1999.

5. *Look for discount bonds,* those selling below par. You get a competitive yield and ultimate capital gains. For example, with a 4% coupon, a municipal due in ten years might be selling at 70 ($700) for a 5.7% return. When it's redeemed at $1,000, there will be $300 appreciation—roughly $30 per year.

EXAMPLE: John Costley, in the 50% tax bracket, has $50,000 to invest as the result of selling his house. He wants to have the money available when he retires in ten years, so he looks at bonds which mature at that time.

If he buys $50,000 of 5.5% municipals at par, he will have a tax-free return of $2,750 a year, or $27,500 at the end of the decade for total assets of $77,500.

With the same $50,000 he can buy a package of discounted municipals with a par value of $70,000 and a coupon rate averaging 3.5%. He will receive less income—$2,450 per year for a total of $24,500—but at maturity the bonds will be worth $70,000. After paying a 20% tax on the capital gains ($4,000), he'll net $20,500, which plus the $70,000 par value means a total of $90,500, or $13,000 more than if he had bought bonds at par.

Drawbacks to Tax-Exempts

Tax savings are always welcome, but do not forget that there are negatives. Tax-exempts are just another type of bond which, at this time, happen to have special features. One of these days Congress might remove the tax exemption, but you would probably be protected by a grandfather clause which would safeguard the benefits of outstanding issues. In considering the use of municipal bonds in your financial planning, remember these drawbacks:

1. *Fixed income.* The interest will be the same for the life of the debt; there is minimal chance for appreciation; and there is maximum probability of real-value loss due to inflation. Over its 20- to 30-year life, the typical tax-exempt bond will lose almost all of its original purchasing power.

2. *Prices that are not guaranteed.* The value of any debt issues moves with the changes in interest rates: up when the cost of money declines (rarely in recent years) and down when it rises. You can never be sure of getting back your full investment if you have to sell before maturity.

3. *Poor marketability.* Most municipals are sold to large investors; so when an individual deals in lots of ten or fewer, he must pay more when he buys and receive less when he sells. The spread between bid and asked prices can be as much as 5 points ($50 per $1,000 bond).

4. *Nondeductible interest.* If you borrow money to buy tax-exempts, you cannot deduct the interest charges on your income tax return.

Tax-Exempt Bond Funds

If you're undecided about which bonds to select or have limited funds, ask your broker about tax-exempt bond funds. There are two types:

Unit trusts buy a package of about 30 different long-term issues and sell shares, usually at $1,000 each. Interest is passed through to shareholders as requested: monthly, quarterly, or semiannually. The professional managers make no changes in the portfolio until a bond is called or defaults. Your rate of return remains the same, typically from 5.5% to 7.0% depending on the time of offering.

But there can be extra costs and problems:

1. A sales commission of up to 4.5%, so not all your savings go to work.
2. A redemption price, if you need your money early, of as much as 2.5% below the net asset value of the bonds.

3. A limited life of about 20 years because when, as the result of calls or maturities, the principal is reduced to 40% of the issuing value, the sponsor may have the right to terminate the trust, sell the bonds, and distribute the proceeds.
4. Lower than cost value at an early sale. Shares of series E Nuveen tax-exempt bond issue offered at $10,000 in September 1972 were quoted at $7,000 four years later.

Managed funds are managed portfolios; the bonds are bought and sold in anticipation of shifts in interest rates. Shares are available for $1,000 (100 units at $10 each). According to the sales literature, "They open the tax-exempt bond field, previously available only to the wealthy, to the common man."

Tax-exempt bond funds first became available in 1977. They were a hot product for Wall Street until their glamor faded with rising interest rates and, in many cases, inept management. Still, for long-term holdings, they have merit for some people. The shares are sold no-load or with commissions up to 8.5%. Yields flucuate from as low as 5% to as high as 8% depending on the money market and the quality of the underlying securities.

Both types of tax-exempt bond funds have definite advantages over direct purchases: diversification, comparatively small investment, so-called professional management, convenience, opportunity to shift to other mutual funds under the same sponsor, and protection against loss or theft: you get a certificate, and the bonds are held in custody by a bank.

But the most important financial planning benefit is the automatic reinvestment of interest to buy additional shares. Reinvestment assures you of the benefits of compounding, so your savings grow faster than if the payouts were taken in cash. That is one of the few ways in which fixed income holdings can offset the erosion of inflation. And, of course, there are no taxes to be paid on the interest and only the lower capital gains levy on appreciation.

TAX DEDUCTIONS

One area in which it does pay to heed taxes is in the deductions for the cost of services, fees, and aids related to your investments. You can take off your federal income tax:

Commissions and fees paid for the purchase and sale of property. Suppose, for example, you buy 100 shares of United Enterprises at 20 and sell them at 19¼. Your gross loss is $75, but your tax deduction is $169.52: the $75 loss plus commissions of $45.14 for buying and $43.99 for selling plus a New York State tax of $3.75 and fees of $1.64.

The cost of investment and real estate books and advisory publications.

The subscription or newsstand price of financial, investment, or real estate newspapers and magazines.

Investment counsel fees.

Fees for preparing tax returns.

Interest on margin accounts and loans.

State and local transfer taxes.

Cost of safe deposit box when used to store securities and deeds.
Custodian and trustee fees.
Accounting and auditing expenses for keeping records of investments.
On short sales, dividends paid to buyers and premiums for borrowed stock.

You *cannot* deduct:

Legal fees for negotiating the sale or purchase of property.
Expenses incurred in production of tax-exempt income.
Interest on loans secured by tax-exempt securities.

How Long to Keep Your Records

Complete, detailed, accurate records are essential for tax returns if only because of the possibility of a tax audit. At the end of each month, when you pay bills, file in a separate folder all receipts, statements, invoices, and so on of items which qualify for tax deductions. Check each one to be certain that it contains full information of the financial books purchased, the names of those entertained for business purposes, and the gifts made to charities or college. Next month, add the canceled checks. Five minutes spent now can save you five hours in the future.

Each year check the oldest files and eliminate those which you are *sure* are no longer needed. Here are some guidelines as to how long to keep your records:

Accounting	*Retain for*
Accounts paid (invoices)	3–5 years
Appointment book	1–3 years
Bank statements	3–5 years
Securities transactions	3 years after sales
Deposit books and slips	3–5 years
Insurance	
Accident reports and settlements	6 years
Disability and sick benefits	6 years
Insurance records and payments	6 years
Tax Information	
W-4 forms	2 years
Tax returns	4 years
Retirement and pension plan records	Permanent
Medical Records	
Child	To age 26
Adult	10–15 years
X-rays (unless updated)	5–8 years
Deceased	5 years

14 Tax Shelters: Best for the Wealthy, Good for the Wise

Tax shelters, such as oil and gas deals, cattle raising and feeding programs, orange groves, vineyards, and equipment leasing, are usually more intriguing than profitable. For most people, they are better conversation pieces than investments. But when you work with reputable people, have adequate financial resources, shrewd counsel, and plenty of patience, properly selected tax shelters can build capital, act as a hedge against inflation, and defer taxes on income.

In my experience, 90% of the people who invest in tax shelters do not understand what they are getting into. They have an idea that they are buying something that will keep them from ever paying taxes. Obviously, IRS would not permit that, and Congress is constantly closing loopholes.

Tax shelters are a means of deferring, not avoiding, taxes. An individual invests money in the hope that the money he retains by delaying his tax payment can be invested elsewhere to produce revenue enough to cover the tax payment when it finally comes due. The best tax shelter is always a sound business proposition the potential rewards of which are greater than the sure risks. Unless you are very wealthy, the tax benefits should apply to sheltered income, not to outside earnings.

The tax deductions come from interest on the loan which represents part or all of the investment, from depreciation, from certain operating expenses, and from investment credits. They can be credited against the investor's income, so they have maximum impact for people in high tax brackets. Successful tax shelters can provide almost continuous tax benefits; unsuccessful ones give the investor only a couple of years grace on his tax bill. Usually, the investor ends up with a loss and a bigger IRS bill.

PARTICIPATION IN TAX SHELTERS

These days, thanks to the energy shortage, oil and gas ventures are the most popular type of tax shelter. Their format, tax savings income, and capital gains (or losses) are typical, so let's use them as examples of what to look for and guard against. Later, we'll look into other areas of opportunity and, for real estate, refer back to Chapter 9.

Broadly speaking, there are three ways to join an oil and gas tax shelter:

1. As a limited partner in a large, publicly registered program.
2. As a limited partner in a private project.
3. As a joint venture participant with unlimited liability in a private deal.

Nowadays, there are few small programs sponsored by independent oil men with one or two drilling rigs. Public registration requires an enormous amount of paperwork for the SEC and authorities in states where the partnership is to be sold. A public offering with more than 100 participants requires the manager to have a net worth of the lesser of $250,000 or 15% of the total money raised.

The best bet is to deal with specialists like ENI Corporation, headquartered in Seattle, or Omni-Exploration, Inc. of Radnor, Pennsylvania. Both sponsor public funds that invest with established independent oil and gas companies and also serve as consultants. With millions of dollars in capital, they can obtain diversification, flexibility, lower administration and sales costs, and the benefits of their own skill and experience in analysis. Units are offered at from $5,000 to $15,000 each.

Under Omni programs, the investor must get back 120% of his money before the manager earns a right to production. Then this revenue is shared: 75% to the investor and 25% to the general partner. The sharing of costs and revenues varies, but as a rule of thumb, the general partner should not receive more than 15% of his capital contribution if he participates in the original income and 20% if his compensation is deferred until after payout.

TAX ASPECTS

Drilling programs sponsored by ENI generally seek to generate tax write-offs of about 90% of invested capital during the first three or four calendar years and have most "deductions" in the first year. The initial tax advantages are related to intangible drilling costs (money spent for labor, fuel, preparation, shipping, repairs, and so on). For a simplified, hypothetical example of the after-tax benefits of a drilling program based on an estimated write-off of 90% of invested capital see Table 14–1.

The tax factors are complex, so consult an experienced tax adviser. You can deduct losses of unsuccessful wells; but if the well proves out, the intangible drilling costs become an item of tax preference. The costs are then subject to a special tax of 15% with an exemption of $10,000 or half the regular tax, whichever is higher. Still, for those in high tax brackets, that $10,000, which is, in effect, a tax-free deduction, is nothing to be sneezed at. Table 14–1 shows what happens. In addition, a significant portion of the cash flow may be tax-free

Table 14–1. Tax benefits from drilling program.

	Tax Bracket		
	50%	60%	70%
Investment	$30,000	$30,000	$30,000
Write-off (from income of well or earnings)	27,000	27,000	27,000
Tax savings at 50% tax rate	13,500	16,200	18,900
After-tax investment	16,500	13,800	11,100
Percent of investment at risk	55	46	37

because of the percentage depletion allowance. Under current tax regulations, 22% of gross oil and gas income (not to exceed 50% of net) can be nontaxable for certain investors. The distributions to the investor are net royalties above all operating and management expenses. Depending on the individual tax status, as much as 25% of cash flow can be depletion or tax-free income.

The following checkpoints, from D. Bruce Trainor of Omni-Exploration and Victor D. Aldaheff, chairman of ENI Corporation, apply to oil and gas drilling but are wise with all tax shelters:

1. At least 85% of the investment should be devoted to drilling-related activities. The more money spent to seek oil and gas, the better the chances for success.

2. The general partner should not benefit at the expense of limited partners. One of the main reasons for the poor repute of smaller oil and gas deals has been the ability of the general partner to profit no matter what happens. He's in Oklahoma and you're in Oshkosh, so there's almost no way you can check operations. As far as possible, all potential conflicts of interest should be disclosed in the prospectus.

3. Sharing should be on a program payout basis. The first 15% to 20% of "profits" can go to the general partner, but then 50% of the next distribution should go to the investors.

4. Assessments should be spelled out in detail. Preferably, the extra funds should be limited. If the well is successful, most investors won't hesitate to put up more money. The question—and often manipulation—comes when the well does not pan out as soon or as well as expected.

5. All investors should be able to get out of the deal without undue penalties. Terms should be described in detail in the prospectus, but be realistic. You cannot expect to get back your full investment in the early years, and you will probably have to settle for a sale at a hefty discount.

Exit ability is important if you plan to donate all or part of your shares to charity or to another member of your family. Not everyone wants to stay in the oil business.

6. Read the prospectus. Too many people are so anxious to avoid taxes that they hear the story they want, not the truth. In the well-publicized Home-Stake Production Company scandal, the prospectus stated that there was a conflict of interest in ownership of land adjacent to the oil drilling area and that the promoters had a history of legal controversy.

7. Make sure that it's a good business proposition, not just a tax dodge. That means that, without tax benefits, there should be a 15% net return, cash flow in 12 to 18 months, the probability of getting all your money back in four to five years, and an overall doubling of your money within a ten-year period.

8. Check the sponsor's record and reputation. In the past, most oil and gas tax shelters were packaged by small, regional brokerage firms, but these days, major financial organizations are becoming sponsors. Just because the lead firm is well known in Wall Street is not a guarantee of success, but at least management recognizes its corporate responsibilities.

Talk to someone who has been involved in previous deals with the same people. If you are making a substantial investment, retain an independent specialist who is not part of the offering.

9. Have adequate resources. With any type of tax shelter, never invest money you will need—ever. Think ahead five or ten years. There is always the risk of unexpected hazards: a dry hole, a blow-out, or price or tax changes. The only thing limited about a partnership of this type is that, when properly structured, you cannot lose more money than you put in.

10. Invest in three programs. That will spread your risks; and although you may have a call for extra money, the odds are good that, over a period of time, the call will be against paper gains and the overall results will be worthwhile in income and appreciation as well as tax benefits.

CATTLE AS TAX SHELTERS

When you get to the 50% tax bracket, have extra money, and want to have some fun and also impress your golfing companions, take a look at cattle feeding and cattle breeding programs. Each provides tax-deferred rather than tax-sheltered income. With rollovers, you can delay payment of taxes on your gains and use your losses to offset previous or future profits.

Cattle Feeding

These days, most cattle are prepared for market in large commercial feedlots. The process requires huge capital, which is often raised by investment companies such as Oppenheimer Industries of Kansas City. The specialists sell limited partnerships for $5,000 or $10,000 each. The leverage is high: zero to 10% down payment on immature animals with the balance from a purchase money mortgage. If the market is strong and the operation well run, you can make money. But the deal can be disastrous if, as in 1974, beef prices plummet. The feed lot operator can go bankrupt, and you'll end up with plenty of losses. Here's how a cattle feeding program is supposed to operate:

The syndicate buys feeder cattle weighing 200 to 800 pounds, fattens them for 90 days, and sells them when they reach market weight of 900 to 1,150 pounds, hopefully at a profit. In the meantime the investor deducts from reported income the interest on the loan (in the year incurred), sales commissions, and costs of feeding, caring for, and marketing the animals. On a $10,000 investment, a lucky investor in the 50% tax bracket can write off about $4,500 and still hope for a normal profit. The real trick is to postpone taxes by rolling over from one deal to the next: buying this year and selling the next. The proceeds are then reinvested in more feed and livestock.

Generally, a partnership has a life span of seven years. At the end, the syndicate is dissolved and the investors are supposed to get back their money plus cash equal to a 10% annual rate of return plus 75% of the remaining profits.

Cattle Breeding

A cattle-breeding program is best for investors seeking long-term capital gains. Garrett Cole, vice president of Oppenheimer Industries, explains that breeding cattle are maintained specifically for the production of calves. The investor has a choice of herds: *commercial cattle,* which are safe and modestly profitable, and *registered cattle,* which are more expensive and more glamorous but are highly speculative because they have no public market.

All cattle born to the herd start with zero value. Profits are treated as capital gains, which are almost always long term because the cattle owner is entitled to use a cash basis for his accounting. Here again, the tax benefits are large and immediate: the original purchase qualifies for accelerated (150%) depreciation, special bonus depreciation, and a 10% investment credit. Add the interest on a 95% loan and the costs of feeding, and operations and total deductions can run up to 200% of cash outlay. That's a good deal for the wealthy.

Caveats

Since you will probably be miles away from the feedlot or range, be sure to deal only with an established, reputable firm, preferably one which puts up some of its own money. Read the prospectus line by line and recognize that not all your money will be working, because sales commissions are high (up to 10%) and management fees will run 5% or more.

Be wary of promises or predictions of big profits. The honest operator will not set specific returns, but he will set target goals of 4% to 6% over a three-year period. When the tax benefits are added, cattle feeding or breeding can be a rewarding proposition for those in high tax brackets. And as Cole notes, "You'll have a lot more fun than investing in municipal bonds."

EQUIPMENT LEASING

The equipment-leasing type of tax shelter covers everything from a Boeing 747 to an IBM computer to freight cars. The best deals are those which involve big-ticket items, equipment that is too expensive for most companies to buy. The lessee is willing to let someone else have the tax benefits of loan interest, rapid depreciation, and investment tax credit. Leasing avoids the need for cash or an onerous loan commitment and eliminates problems of obsolescence.

Equipment leasing usually involves large sums, so it is handled by groups of investors with a minimum participation of $10,000. Since the collateral is readily salable, purchase loans represent a high percent of the equipment value and extend for a comparatively long period of time, up to ten years. This is one tax shelter that lets you see what you own and know who will be paying the rent. The best deals combine tax benefits with profits on the sale of the property at the end of the lease.

Computer Leasing

Mr. Loman earns $100,000 a year, and so he is in the highest tax bracket. He borrows to purchase a share in the ownership of a big IBM computer which is rented to a local manufacturer by a well-known equipment leasing firm. He has triple security: the machine and two reputable organizations.

The total deal involves $500,000 and $50,000 is taken off the top by the promoter, accountant, and lawyer. The deal is so structured that: (1) Mr. L pays nothing for the tax shelter because the income from the lease pays off the principal of the loan and (2) for every $1 he puts up, Mr. L is able to show a $3 loss from depreciation and interest.

At the end of four years when the depreciation tails off, Mr. L and his associates expect to sell the computer at a small profit. Even if that does not happen, Mr. L has deferred his big taxes for four years. The biggest risk is that the computer will be made obsolete before the full benefits are attained.

Renting Boxcars

A new-to-the-public variation of equipment leasing involves boxcars. The cars are rented to capital-short railroads. Traditionally, the deals have been handled by banks and finance companies, but alert promoters, like Railcar, Inc. of Atlanta, Georgia, package units which are sold through regional brokerage firms.

The acquisition and management costs are high but, say the promoters, the investor should get a 20% return. Each car costs about $30,000 depending on age, type, and condition. Each day the leased car is in service, loaded or not, a railroad somewhere pays a base rate of $10.39 plus a per diem incentive fee of $11.55 plus 5.1¢ per mile for an anticipated average use of 50 miles per day. In the first five years, the total projected return is $24.49 daily.

Railcar, Inc. gets a fee of $1,000 per car plus insurance costs and, over the years, charges 12% of revenues for maintenance and administration. The investor pays 20% cash and borrows, usually from a local bank, the balance on a ten-year loan.

As a rule of thumb, 60% utilization of the boxcar is necessary to cover principal and interest. At 85% use, the gross income is about $7,600 a year. Tax deductions are allowed for depreciation, management fees, interest on the loan, and a one-time 10% investment credit. If you deal with a reputable firm and are in a high tax bracket, boxcar leasing can be a profitable holding as a business venture and as a tax shelter as long as rail volume is heavy.

WATCH OUT FOR EARLY TERMINATIONS

As noted in the discussion of oil and gas deals, tax shelters are easy to get into but difficult to get out with your shirt, especially when the termination is earlier than anticipated. Even a supposedly safe real estate deal can be perilous when used solely as a tax shelter. To point out the ever-present tax liabilities, here's an example cited by Ayco Corp., a financial planning organization:

Under a limited partnership, ten men each paid $10,000 cash and took, in toto, a $900,000 nonrecourse mortgage to buy a $1 million building. The project was set up for annual depreciation of $40,000 and for the interest, but not the reduction of the principal, to be paid by the partnership.

After seven years, one partner sold his interest at the price he paid: $10,000 cash and $90,000 representing his share of the mortgage. The withdrawal was expensive because he owed taxes on his $28,000 long-term capital gain that resulted from the reduction of his $100,000 base by his $4,000 yearly share of the depreciation to $72,000. He was in a high tax bracket, so he had to pay at a 30% rate ($8,400). He ended with $1,600 out of the $10,000 cash. That wasn't as bad as it appeared to be, because the depreciation saved him $16,800 in ordinary income taxes. In effect, he turned $28,000 of ordinary income into a $28,000 long-term capital gain.

To show the variety of tax-saving techniques which are available with tax shelters, here are alternatives suggested by a tax-wise attorney. The partner could have reduced his tax by giving his interest to his son. He would thereby have reduced his long-term capital gain by $10,000 to $18,000 and saved $3,000 in taxes. As for accounting, what happens is this: Before the gift, the taxpayer's balance sheet showed a $72,000 asset representing his share less depreciation plus his $90,000 share of the mortgage. The gift increases the donor's net worth by $18,000, the difference between the liability and the assets he has disposed of. The $18,000 becomes a long-term capital gain.

Better yet, he could have eliminated the tax by a gift to charity. Although the gift creates an $18,000 gain, the market value of the gift ($100,000 less the $90,000 mortgage) produces a $10,000 charitable gift deduction. In the 60% tax bracket, that is a $6,000 tax savings which offsets the $6,000 in taxes payable on the $18,000 long-term capital gain.

The investor does lose the $1,600 which would have been his after-tax proceeds from the sale. But if he had given the sum to charity, he would still be ahead of the game, because he gets credit for a $10,000 gift which cost only $1,600.

Now you see why it is so essential to consult a tax expert, project all possible contingencies, and determine tax consequences if you have to get out of a tax shelter early.

BE CAREFUL; BE SKEPTICAL

Just because you do well with a couple of tax shelters, do not become cocky and reach too far. Most unusual tax shelters are promotions devised by tax lawyers to take advantage of what they believe to be loopholes in the law. It may take a little time, but all of them will be subject to IRS investigation and, probably, ban.

The master recording deal is typical of what to avoid. Under that tax shelter, Mr. Barnes, who is paying a 70% tax on some of his income, buys a master record for an inflated price and then licenses a record producer to manufacture copies and to pay royalties on the sales. Mr. B puts down 10% cash and takes out a large nonrecourse loan (no personal liability) for the remainder of the purchase price. He then claims big tax deductions on the entire purchase. Or, at least, he did until recently. IRS threw out some of these recording deals until the "investor" could show that he expected the venture to be profitable and that the payment was a fair price for the master recording. As Barnum said, "There's one born every minute." And the richer and more selfish they are, the harder, and faster, they fall.

Tax savings, avoidance, and postponement can be important, but they are usually worthwhile only for people in very high income brackets. They should be considered only when the real dollar benefits are at least 20% of the value of the property involved. Tax shelters are tricky, and except for real estate, they should be used only when they are sound business investments and involve extra money which you can afford to lose. Like it or not, everyone who makes money has a partner in Uncle Sam. If you treat that partner fairly, there'll be no trouble and hopefully there will be profits. But if you try to be cute and take advantage of every loophole, you will win only if you have a competent adviser and are lucky. Never (well, hardly ever) make any decision on the basis of tax savings alone.

For an idea of how tax shelters compare, see Table 14–2.

Table 14–2. How tax shelters stack up.

Type	Tax Benefits	Cash Flow	Appreciation Potential	Risk
Real Estate				
New multifamily	High	Good	Good	Moderate to high
Old multifamily	Moderate	Moderate	Moderate	Low
Commercial	Moderate	Moderate	Moderate	Low
Raw land	Low	Low	Good	High
Government housing	Very high	Low	Very low	Moderate
Agriculture	High	Moderate to low	Good	High
Oil and Gas				
Exploratory drilling	High	Good but speculative		Moderate to high
Developed drilling	High	Moderate		Moderate
Income program	Low	Moderate to high		Moderate
Cattle				
Feeding	High; short-term deferral		Good but speculative	High
Breeding	High; longer-term deferral	Low	Speculative	High
Ranching	High	Low	Speculative	High

15 Using Trusts for Financial Planning

Trusts can be an important tool of financial planning when you are in a fairly high tax bracket (at least 30%) and have assets you can set aside, substantial inherited or accumulated property, or special family needs such as dependent parents or college costs. Broadly speaking, they are more valuable in estate planning than in financial management, but as we'll see, there are times when a trust can be used effectively to further living goals. Usually, a trust is set up many years before its full impact is felt. That's why it is so important to go slow and carefully consider possible future changes: death, divorce, separation, illness, financial gains or losses, and so on. In establishing any type of trust, today's optimism must be weighed against tomorrow's possible pessimism.

A trust is a written legal document whereby assets are turned over to someone else to hold and manage for the benefit of a third party. In varying forms, trusts can be used to avoid or postpone taxes, shift ownership of property temporarily or permanently to someone else, preserve the privacy of an individual's estate, keep assets out of the hands of creditors, and assure that your wishes with regard to your estate will be carried out, possibly while you live and certainly after you die.

Trusts go back to the Middle Ages, when they were created to disguise the actual ownership of property in order to circumvent laws or feudal obligations. They provided that the benefits of the property could flow to the creator of the trust while the legal ownership was held by a trustee: the individual, and later the organization, responsible for the management and administration of the assets assigned under the agreement. Modern trusts are vastly more complicated, but their basic concepts are much the same: they assign property and responsibility to someone else under spelled-out conditions.

Some trusts can be established by filling out a printed form, but it is always wise to have such a document prepared by an experienced, knowledgeable lawyer. The lawyer can word the agreement to meet legal requirements and state exactly what the trustee can and cannot do. It's usually best to provide for considerable flexibility and permit the trustee to exercise judgment within the framework of your wishes. Laws can be revised and circumstances can change over the 10, 20, or 30 years of the life of the trust.

There are no legal limits to size. A trust can have assets as little as $1,000 or as huge as $100 million. Because of the expense of preparation and maintenance, there are, of course, practical limits. But the real measure of a worthwhile trust is not cost or assets; it is purpose. That's why I am reluctant to cite too many examples. The trust which suits your brother with a wealthy wife may be foolish for you if your spouse has her own, and struggling, business.

CHARACTERISTICS OF A TRUST

For the average individual or family, the most important benefits of a trust are the ability to:

1. Minimize income and death taxes.
2. Assure that your wishes with regard to your assets will be carried out—occasionally while you live and certainly after you die.
3. Provide a flexible means of administration and accommodation to changes unforeseen at the time the trust was entered into.
4. Avoid the necessity of probate.
5. Eliminate the need for guardianship for your children.
6. Keep some assets out of the hands of creditors.
7. Assure privacy of the assets and distribution of your estate.
8. Permit the retention of professional assistance.

Here are examples of trusts which can be used in financial planning. But let me repeat that under no circumstances should you set up a trust without competent legal counsel. What may appear beneficial today can cause severe problems in the future. Trusts are not a panacea. They can be useful, but they can also be dangerous to your own and your family's well-being when things do not work out as anticipated.

CATEGORIES OF TRUSTS

All trusts can be categorized by origin—testamentary or living—and by type—revocable or irrevocable. The groupings are not exclusive; both testamentary and living trusts can be revocable or irrevocable, and both revocable and irrevocable trusts can be set up by will or while you are living. Each variation has its own use as shown by the following examples. Once you know your objectives and available assets, consult your attorney as to which type or form—if any—will be most effective.

A *testamentary trust* is set up by will and does not become operative until after the death of the creator. In the will, the individual directs the establishment of a trust and may specify what property goes into the trust.

A *living trust,* known in legal parlance as *inter vivos,* can be started anytime and takes effect immediately. Both a testamentary trust and a living trust provide that the assigned assets will be administered by a trustee who will manage the properties and will make distributions to certain individuals or organizations as specified.

A *revocable trust* is just what the title states. It can be terminated at any time.

An *irrevocable trust* is an agreement which cannot be canceled until the death of the creator. The person who sets it up loses the right to terminate the trust. He or she cannot receive any income, use the assets for a loan, or in any way exercise control of the assets. Once the trust is established, the grantor is out of the picture.

Testamentary Trusts

Testamentary trusts are excellent for keeping a family together after the death of the grantor. They provide income for living expenses of the beneficiaries; they can keep and maintain the home for the surviving spouse and children as long as needed; and they can, for example, permit the trustee to sell the house and invest the proceeds.

The widest use of testamentary trusts is to help avoid future estate tax levies against the property (see Chapter 16.). A testamentary trust permits the estate to be passed on to the heirs of the deceased. Each time there's a transfer, there's an estate tax. Part of the levies can be avoided by giving the children only life estates, that is, the right to the use of the income or assets under the trustee's direction as long as the children live. At a child's death, there will be no estate tax because he owns nothing.

There's no advantage to the grantor, but there's no tax for one future generation as long as the total transfer per child does not exceed $250,000.

EXAMPLE: Mr. Jones owns land under a building. It is worth $250,000, and it is rented for $25,000 a year. In his will, he creates a trust with the property as the major asset. The bank, as trustee, is instructed to pay the income to his son, Jones, Jr., and, on Junior's death, to Jones III. There will be no estate tax if the property, at Junior's death, is valued at less than $250,000. The trust provides income and avoids taxes. But unless the trust is properly drawn and gives the trustee considerable discretion, the property cannot be sold if its income or worth declines. Jones III might end up with a not-too-worthwhile inheritance.

The creator of any testamentary trust either must have a crystal ball or be willing to assign full authority to the trustee—something which many older people are reluctant to do. This summary shows how such trusts can be valuable in financial planning even though the major benefit comes with the estate.

Living Trusts

Generally, living trusts are the most valuable type for financial planning. They can be created at any time; and when they are revocable, they can be terminated just as quickly. The assets of a revocable trust remain your property even though their administration is turned over to someone else. The advantages are the following:

1. You can keep adding to the trust assets as long as you live. That makes it possible to start with a modest allocation and add money or assets when you feel flush. Taxwise, you will do better if the savings are sheltered in a personal retirement plan or deferred annuity, but the contributions may be locked or, if withdrawn, be subject to penalties.

2. You can make withdrawals if you suffer financial reverses.

3. Tax savings in the money placed in a revocable trust are not subject to a gift tax, because the creator does not have absolute control over the trust management. To avoid estate taxes which might have to be paid by the beneficiary, the trust agreement must state that the beneficiary, usually your spouse, will

receive all income for life and that the principal will pass to another beneficiary, probably a son or daughter, at her death.

4. At death, the trust assets do not become part of your estate, so there will be lower administration costs and possibly lower estate taxes also.

That's why a revocable trust is often used with out-of-state property. Otherwise, there could be jurisdiction problems.

EXAMPLE: Mr. Munn, who owns a home in Michigan, is transferred to Texas. He plans to retire back home, so he puts title to the Michigan property in a revocable trust. If he should die before he returns, the trust, not Mr. Munn, will remain the owner and the trustee can make the decision whether to hold or sell.

A secondary benefit is that the assets in the trust can be distributed immediately after your death. That assures adequate funds to your heirs while the will is being settled.

5. You can change trustees, because you maintain control of the trust assets. A revocable trust will enable you to test a bank's management ability.

EXAMPLE: Bill Wilkins, a widower, has accumulated $400,000. He plans to leave everything to his young children, but he wants to be sure that, at his death, the professional trustee will invest wisely and provide the personal empathy which he feels his youngsters will need. He establishes a revocable trust and names the bank as trustee.

Three years later, Bill decides that the bank cannot do the job: its investment performance has been poor, and the officers are too aloof to enthuse the children. He revokes the trust and makes other plans.

The danger is that, until he protects his property in some other manner, the assets will be included in his estate if he dies soon after the cancellation.

6. You can prepare for the future by setting up a "dry" trust with no assets. A dry trust is a legal entity which will be ready to accept property in the future. The annual bank charge will be a nonrefundable $100 or so. That's not much for keeping you—and your spouse—happy.

Irrevocable Trusts

As noted, an irrevocable agreement puts all trust assets out of your control. At death the property will not become part of the estate; but under the unified estate and gift tax provisions of the latest tax law, the original assets are considered a gift. In effect, they are brought back into the taxable estate and, for tax computation purposes, valued at their worth at the time of the establishment of the trust. The best bet with an irrevocable trust is to use property that is likely to grow in value over the years. The beneficiaries will receive the assets at a low valuation and thus be liable for a smaller tax bill.

EXAMPLE: Gene Gray, age 65, owns 1,000 shares of a small company in which he has great confidence. The current value of the stock is $10,000. He puts the stock, together with some income-producing assets, in an irrevocable trust. When Gene dies, at age 70, the stock is worth $50,000. For tax purposes, however, it is valued at $10,000—if Gene's lawyer did his job properly.

Short-Term Trusts

Short-term trusts are usually living trusts set up primarily to avoid taxes by transferring income from persons in high tax brackets to persons whose tax rate is much lower. In theory, they are advantageous; in practice, they are suitable for only a limited number of situations. By law, a short-term trust has a minimum life of ten years or the lifetime of the individual for whose benefit the trust will operate. As long as the property is in trust, all income goes to the beneficiary. The following are situations in which short-term trusts can be useful:

For aged parent. Mr. Macwithey is in the 40% tax bracket and, each year, contributes $3,200 to the support of his 80-year-old mother. He has to earn $5,000 to provide this sum. He has $40,000 in 8% bonds, which yield $3,200 annually. He uses the bonds to set up a short-term trust for his mother (but not a Clifford trust if his contribution fulfills legal obligations of support). Now Mrs. Macwithey has the income she needs and Mr. Macwithey pays less taxes because his reportable income is lower. At the end of the trust—at her death or ten years—he will get the bonds back.

For college fund (also explained in Chapter 7 but worth repeating because of its value in financial planning). David Winston has an eight-year-old daughter who, he expects, will start college in ten years. He places a $15,000 inheritance in a short-term trust with his daughter as beneficiary. He arranges for the money to be invested in shares of a unit-trust bond fund yielding 8% a year. With prompt reinvestment of the interest, the trust value will compound to almost $35,000 by the time the girl is ready for college. In the unlikely event that there will be income taxes, they will be small enough for David to handle from his earnings.

For minor children. Lawyer Louis has four children, all under 12 years of age. His net income, before exemptions, is $37,000, of which $3,000 represents interest on $60,000 worth of government bonds. He pays a tax of $8,870, so he nets $28,130. He can save taxes by setting up four separate trusts in each of which he deposits $15,000 in bonds. Now each youngster gets $750 income on which no taxes are due and Louis saves about $1,875 a year in taxes. Even if the youngsters begin to earn money on their own, the tax levy, when the income reaches a taxable level, will be only 14%.

Despite the apparent benefits, use short-term trusts cautiously because:

1. You lose control of your property and cannot get it back until the trust is terminated.
2. You are giving, to someone else, income which you may need in the future.
3. You tie up assets which may be needed for financial emergencies.

If you decide a short-term trust is worthwhile, *do* set aside only property which does not require special handling: rental real estate or stock representing controlling interest in a corporation. *Don't* be carried away by the idea of tax avoidance. Ten years can be a long time, and during it many things can happen to you and to the people whom you are trying to help.

What it comes down to is wise financial planning: *Never place tax benefits above personal or family needs.*

SPECIAL TYPES OF TRUSTS

With their usual ingenuity and ability to take advantage of legislative provisions, or lack of them, lawyers have devised scores of different types of trusts. Here are some which may be useful in financial planning:

Totten Trust

A Totten trust is a bank account established by one person in trust for another, without formal agreement. It is a tentative trust; it is revocable at will until the depositor dies or completes the gift. There's no cost.

The trust can be set up for your spouse with yourself as trustee or by a parent for a child or grandchild—again with the donor as trustee. As creator of the trust, the donor has the right to dip into the account whenever he needs money.

When the donor dies, an adult beneficiary can get the money as easily as if it were in a bank account; but when the beneficiary is a minor, there can be problems. When the account involves less than $1,000, the money can be paid only to the minor's parent, parents, or guardian. Above that amount, the parent or guardian must post bond and make a full report to the court.

Some estate lawyers feel that Totten trusts are not wise when the beneficiaries are quite young and the deposit is small. They prefer to eliminate the need to appoint a guardian for the property by a bequest, in the will, authorizing payment of a specified sum to a custodian named by the donor under the Uniform Gifts to Minors Act.

Insurance Trust

An insurance trust is an irrevocable living trust. You transfer the ownership of life insurance policies to the trust, which becomes the beneficiary. Then you name your spouse and/or children as beneficiaries of the trust. At your death, the proceeds go to your heirs without probate and without estate taxes. To avoid possible problems, it's a good idea to add a clause that, in case of separation or divorce, the spouse's interest in trust assets passes to another beneficiary. Don't be bashful about including such a provision. Even the best of marriages can falter.

Insurance trusts are most helpful to protect a sizable estate. As the husband grows older and wealthier, he can plan ahead by assigning ownership of life insurance policies to his spouse. That can be tax-free when the cash value of the transferred property is below $3,000 a year—roughly the worth of a $10,000 straight life policy after 15 years of premium payments. But when the widow dies, as stressed in other chapters, there will be no marital deduction on her estate, so taxes could be substantial. By setting up an insurance trust, the husband can assure that his widow will have income and, if needed, some of the principal and that, at her death, the assets of the trust will go directly to the children.

Caution: In a few states, when the insurance is paid to the trust under will, the proceeds may be treated as if they had been paid to the estate and thus are taxable. Your attorney knows how to solve that problem.

Insurance trusts can also be helpful in protecting heirs.

EXAMPLE: Mr. Homeyer has a spendthrift wife. Since life insurance represents a substantial portion of his estate, he has two choices:

1. To arrange that the death proceeds of his insurance be paid out in installments. That inflexible arrangement will limit his widow's expenditures, but it may work hardships in case of genuine need. There will be minimal growth of assets, because the earnings of the cash residue will be small.

2. To create an insurance trust and empower the trustee to pay, to Mrs. Homeyer, all income and as much principal as is required to assure her well-being. The arrangement also makes possible greater growth of the assets when wisely invested.

An insurance trust is not quite as simple as it sounds. There must be provision for payment of the premiums until the policy is paid up. The dividends can reduce the annual outlay, but the trust must have other income-producing assets or some provision for annual additions. Here again, you need a lawyer to avoid trouble with the IRS. To assure that the yearly contributions qualify as "gifts of present interest" (nontaxable up to $3,000 annually), the trust agreement must permit the beneficiary or beneficiaries to withdraw any new money. Otherwise, the IRS may rule that the premium payment money is a "gift of future interest" and therefore is taxable.

It seldom makes sense to include term insurance in an insurance trust because there's no cash value. When straight life policies are used, the provisions of gifts apply: a maximum of $3,000 a year to a lifetime maximum of $30,000. But when high-value policies are involved, the gift tax will probably be lower than the ultimate estate tax.

Sprinkling Trust

A sprinkling trust is useful only for estate planning. It permits the trustee to use discretion in the allocation of income and principal according to the needs of the beneficiaries.

EXAMPLE: Mr. Dyer has three children, all in their early twenties. He creates a sprinkling trust with securities that produce an income of $10,000 a year. At his death, the trustee can vary distribution. In one year, for example, the trustee can boost the payout to the daughter in medical school and make modest payments to the other children. In the next year, he can allocate the major share to the son, who has just had an expensive operation. A more detailed example of the use of a sprinkling trust which provides $10,000 a year to benefit three adult children whose needs change annually is given in Table 15–1.

The toughest decision with a sprinkling trust concerns the termination date.

Table 15–1. Sprinkling trust: $10,000 annual income.

Year	Needs of Sally, Age 21, Student	Jim, Age 22, Working	Vera, Age 18, Student
1	$6,000 for medical college	$2,000	$2,000 for tuition aid
2	$3,000 for medical college; has part-time job	$5,000 for operation	$2,000 for tuition aid
3	$3,000 for medical college—still working	$3,000 for training course	$4,000 for college year abroad
4	$2,000 to supplement internship income	$5,000 for marriage and new home	$3,000 for tuition aid

Note: Following year 4, as prescribed by the trust agreement, the assets are to be distributed equally among the children.

Since the termination may not occur for many years after the trust is established, it's difficult to project future needs or non-needs. If you set the dissolution time too early, one child may still be a minor and need a guardian if both you and your wife die. If you set the date too late, say when the youngest child reaches age 25, the older children must wait a long time.

Consider the termination date carefully in relation to the available resources and the children's probable interests and money-making ability.

Pourover Trust

A pourover trust is a special type of trust which must be created before a will is drawn. It's handy and flexible, and it is a sort of catch-all into which estate assets can be "poured" after death. It assures confidentiality and permits assets to be distributed before the will is probated. It can be an excellent shelter for proceeds of pension and profit-sharing plans and insurance policies.

EXAMPLES: Ten years ago, Mr. Hart created a trust for his son, and now he's revising his will to leave even more to Junior. He does not have to establish a new trust; he can specify, in his revised will, that the additional assets will be "poured over" into the old trust. No fuss, no bother, no taxes.

• Dr. Fleck has a $360,000 estate, of which $200,000 is life insurance. His will leaves everything to his wife and, if she dies first, in trust for the children. If the children are named as contingent beneficiaries and they are still young, there will have to be a legal guardian after both parents die. A pourover trust eliminates that need and reduces the red tape, expenses, and limitations on the use of assets which are an integral part of a trust-less estate.

• Schoolteacher Keehner, retired to Florida, owns the family farm in Maine. Her estate will go to her nieces and one nephew. A pourover trust solves the complex, and costly, problems of dispersed ownership and also avoids the necessity for probate in both states.

Residence Trust

A residence trust can be either revocable or irrevocable, and it can be used with the old homestead and thus avoid what can, for many people, be an emotionally difficult decision. The trust holds title to the house; and when there are other assets to produce income, it permits the survivor to live rent-free for life. The trustee must be in full control to avoid taxes.

If the trust is revocable, the home will become part of the taxable estate. If it's irrevocable, there can be alterations or termination. The best bet is to set up the trust so that the survivor has use of the house for life and the children take over at her or his death. Be sure to give the trustee broad powers. If the property becomes burdensome, it would be best to sell and buy a smaller house.

Check state laws, some of which limit disposition of property by will and may mandate that the home go to the surviving spouse at once.

Alimony Trust

An alimony trust is similar to a living trust; usually, it is irrevocable. In the negotiations at the divorce, it can be set up to provide income enough to satisfy the alimony to the wife and support for the children. Upon the death or remarriage of the wife, the trust income will continue to support the children to age 21. If there are no children, the trust principal reverts to the grantor.

The alimony trust is a good example of the value of trusts. It guarantees steady payments for the wife and children, since the trust will be professionally managed, and it eliminates the possibility of the husband having to share future increases in wealth with his former wife. On the other hand, it's an expensive procedure for the man because a trust large enough to throw off such support income can force the set-aside of a large portion of the trust creator's assets.

The taxes can be complex. The alimony portion is taxed to the wife; the income used for child support is taxed to the husband; and undistributed income is taxed to the trust. If the trust is irrevocable and the husband has no control over it or opportunity to get it back, the principal is excluded from his gross estate at death. But if he can retrieve assets on any terms, IRS may insist that they be added to his estate.

Installment Sale Trust

An installment sale trust is a tax avoidance plan similar to an installment sale (Chapter 13). An irrevocable trust buys appreciated property and pays for it, with interest of at least 5% a year, over a predetermined period of time. The payment span should be limited because, if the trust creator dies before the note is satisfied, the entire amount of the property will be taxed in his estate. If the trustee has power to sell the assets, the trust must pay a tax on any capital gains between the original value and the sale price.

Family Equity Trust

The family equity trust is a 100% rip-off which has been ruled illegal by IRS and the courts. According to the glib salesman (who charges a "modest" $1,000 fee for drawing the agreement), all family income transferred to the trust is sheltered from federal income taxes. You charge living expenses to the trust and never pay a nickel to Uncle Sam.

Well, it's surprising how fast a family equity peddler leaves town after the deal is completed! There is, however, some balm if you have been suckered into such a deal: the fee paid to the salesman can be taken as a deduction for investment and tax advice!

Charitable Trusts

Charitable trusts are discussed in Chapter 16. They involve gifts to eleemosynary institutions, so they enable you to "give while you live," reduce current income taxes, lower estate taxes, and, in some cases, receive income from the property given away.

Broadly, the gifts can be made:

1. Through a trust of your creation, such as a family foundation, which will make a gift or gifts to recognized charities to create a memorial for the donor, loved ones, or a family member, to establish a scholarship fund, and so on.

Once established, a charitable trust must be maintained and file voluminous reports. It is worthwhile only when there are, or will be, substantial assets.

2. To a trust set up by the recipient such as a hospital or college. The institution pools the gift with other assets in a common trust fund. The donor receives a prorated share of the fund's income as long as he or she lives. At death, the property goes to the institution. In effect, you are loaning assets and receiving income as an annuity.

Bank Trusts

Bank trusts are handy vehicles for widows' estates, for professional management of savings, and for tax savings when the trusts are irrevocable and do not permit the donor to benefit in any way. They are living trusts, and in recent years they can be started with as little as $1,000. Here are two typical situations:

1. New York's Chemical Bank's Chem Vest provides investment advice to small investors for a fee which is the greater of $250 or one-fourth of 1% of the value of the assets. The client can (1) leave securities in street name (a designated broker) and trade through that stock exchange firm, (2) hold the securities, registered in his name, in a lockbox, or (3) have the bank place the securities in a custody account for a fee of about $250 a year. In theory, the lower execution costs, which are possible because of bulk buying and selling by the bank, will offset the custodial cost. In practice, that would probably require ten trades of 100 shares of a $60 stock in a year to cost less than the discount broker's fees.

2. Schroder Trust Co. of New York, which normally refuses to accept personal trusts smaller than $250,000, will establish a living trust with assets as little as $1,000 when the trust document is prepared by the client's lawyer.

Schroder handles all accounting and arranges for the trust account to be with a savings and loan association or securities firm. The fee is one-fourth of 1% of the trust assets with a minimum of $190, so the trust should total $76,000. That's lower than the statutory trust fees which, in New York State, start at $7 per $1,000 for assets up to $300,000. For that minimum $76,000, the legal fees would total $532 a year.

The customer can direct investment of trust assets into (1) high-yield certificates of deposit issued by the participating S&L or (2) shares of First Index Investment Trust, a no-load fund sponsored by the Vanguard Group, whose holdings are indexed according to Standard & Poor's 500 Stock Price Index.

Other banks have special trust funds that make investments for different investment goals: income, growth, or a balance. The income is reinvested without taxes until withdrawal. At that time, you or your beneficiary will have to pay taxes, which can be reduced by installment payouts (see Chapter 13).

Bank trusts are more convenient than profitable. They can be worthwhile if you do not want to be bothered with money management, plan to move from your home state, or are willing to settle for mediocre returns: about 6% for stock portfolios and up to 8% for fixed-income holdings.

No matter what the type of trust, be ready to use only assets which you do not need now and do not anticipate needing in the future. Tax benefits are welcome, but they should be weighed against future financial requirements. By and large, trusts are useful in financial planning only when you have accumulated substantial wealth and have a strong base of sure, adequate resources. That go-slow approach is essential to living trusts and important with testamentary trusts.

Always, always consult your attorney and do your homework! Trusts can be useful, but they are not a panacea.

GLOSSARY

beneficiary: The one who receives benefits from a trust.
charitable remainder trust: A form of a trust whereby the donor, while living, gives away all or part of his or her assets to a charitable organization. The donor receives income as long as he or she lives.
charitable trust: A trust whose purpose is to aid IRS-qualified charities and so is eligible for special tax treatment.
Clifford trust: A short-term trust that must continue for ten years and one day or to the death of the beneficiary, if earlier. Income goes to a beneficiary; principal reverts to the donor at termination. Cannot be used for legal support.
corpus: The assets of the trust. Also called *principal* or *res*.
executor: The person or institution who carries out the terms of a will.
fiduciary: A general term describing anyone entrusted with the handling of other people's assets.

grantor: The person who creates a trust by putting assets into it. Also known as *creator*, *settlor*, or *testator*.

inter vivos: A trust established while the grantor is living.

irrevocable trust: A trust that the grantor cannot dissolve. The opposite of a revocable trust.

life insurance trust: A trust that involves a gift or series of gifts of life insurance.

living trust: See *inter vivos*.

pourover trust: A trust to which other assets can be added. It allows assets to be distributed before the will is probated.

probate: The process of proving a will's validity. Often used to describe the administration of an estate.

remainderman: The person who receives assets of a trust when the trust terminates.

reversionary trust: A trust under which the principal returns to the grantor after a specific period. See *Clifford trust*.

revocable trust: A trust that the grantor can dissolve or change.

short-term trust: See *Clifford trust*.

sprinkling trust: A trust whereby the trustee has discretion to distribute principal and income according to the needs of the beneficiaries.

testamentary trust: A trust created by will. The opposite of *inter vivos*.

Totten trust: A bank account established by one person in trust for another without formal trust agreement.

trustee: The person, often a bank, which has legal ownership of a trust's assets and manages the assets for the beneficiaries.

16 Estate Planning to Reduce Taxes and Protect Property

Too many executives and professionals judge success by the size of their incomes. That's logical. On the average, a financially successful individual will earn over $2 million in his or her career.

But income alone cannot protect your loved ones after you're gone. That's the role of estate planning, which in this guide can be described as "the thoughtful arrangement of one's affairs and the disposition of one's estate: the assets and liabilities left by a person at death."* For more information, read the books listed in the Bibliography.

The basic steps in estate planning are not difficult if you have organized your life and finances properly, but you will need technical assistance from your lawyer and, when wealthy enough, other specialists. Your goal should be to arrange your affairs, primarily through a will, so that your beneficiaries can retain a greater share of your estate by minimizing taxes and providing for proper failure management of your assets.

Estate planning is such a broad and generally complex subject and involves so many legal details that this guide will summarize only a few of the important steps to take, suggest questions to ask, and outline examples of what can be accomplished. Estate planning is supplementary to financial planning.

WHERE AND HOW TO START

Estate planning should start with broad objectives and then narrow to specific projects and terms. It should be sufficiently flexible to be expanded, contracted, and revised. Just as with your financial plan, *start* estate planning as soon as you have accumulated any type of property—a car, securities, real estate, or a home—*revise* your program when you get married or when there are new federal or state laws, and *review* your program frequently, especially when there are major changes in your life or livelihood—children, divorce, death in the family, illness, dependent relatives, a new position, or a move to another state.

The first and most important step is to prepare a will (Chapter 17). The provisions should reflect your net worth and, of course, how you wish to pass on your property. In the early years, you will probably want to leave everything to your family, but later, when you have accumulated substantial assets, you will be in a position to take a broader view and use part of your wealth for other

---
*Richard S. Ziegler and Patrick F. Flaherty, *Estate Planning for Everyone* (New York: Funk & Wagnalls, 1978).

purposes. As one of my Yale classmates points out when he asks for alumni fund contributions:

Plan your estate to protect your family, to leave a modest sum to your children and then give, now or later, the balance for future generations to have the same privileged education you had. Most of us made it on our own. So can our children. They are better educated, smarter, and more competent than we were at the same age. And many of them are already making more money than we ever did. Your money can do much more as a charitable gift than as an inheritance.

Keep that counsel in mind in all your estate planning.

Once you have protected your family, you should be concerned with the wisest use of your assets. In a sense, what you do with your property is an extension of your philosophy and lifestyle. All too often, successful men and women become so concerned with accumulating wealth that they forget that, although money can seldom buy happiness in life, it can do so after you die.

To my mind, one of the saddest endings of a successful life is the passing on of a substantial estate in a manner alien to the character, concern, and wishes of the deceased: to an already well-to-do relative, to a fifth cousin whom the deceased never met, or, worse yet, to taxing authorities—all because of failure to plan the estate properly.

DISTRIBUTION OF AN ESTATE

Broadly speaking, there are not likely to be complications with an estate of less than $250,000. When there's a will, the distribution will be clear, the settlement costs modest, and the taxes nil if the survivor is the spouse and small if everything goes to the children. With larger estates, especially those of corporate executives and professionals, there can be problems and mistakes:

1. Corporate executives and professionals tend to live up to the last dollar (and more) of their incomes because their want lists expand at the same rate as their incomes. When they die, they leave a shell which may be resplendent on the outside but is almost empty within; they have little or no savings because they have neglected financial and estate planning. It's the old story: if you spend it today, you won't have much tomorrow. That may be OK for a bachelor, but it can be tragic for a family.

2. Executives and professionals become so immersed in their careers that they neglect to plan their estates and fail to make changes to meet new family needs and obey revised tax laws.

Once you have accumulated even modest wealth, it may no longer be wise to leave everything to your spouse and for her or him to pass everything on to the children. Once the youngsters are grown, it's a new ballgame and, at any age, without proper estate planning, most of your wealth may go for taxes. Under the latest tax laws, the levy on the estate of the first to die may be small, but when the survivor dies, Uncle Sam and state authorities can take away much of the residue.

Death can come suddenly, and the will which was ideal when your net worth was $110,000 will be almost useless when the assets are $500,000.

3. Willingness to turn all estate planning over to someone else. Time and again, the busy executive becomes so engrossed in accumulating wealth that he or she neglects to monitor investments to make sure that the returns are adequate and that the estate is so set up that there will be maximum income for heirs. Advisers should never be given carte blanche.

As a conscientious attorney will tell you, there's nothing sadder than to have hard-earned wealth decimated by unsupervised investments, unnecessary taxes, and once-wise, now-foolish policies and decisions. The primary purpose of all estate planning should be to preserve capital by making prudent investments for income first and appreciation second, not the other way around as so many glib counselors do when their decisions are not checked or vetoed.

4. Concentration on short-term success and neglect of long-term objectives. Money in the checking account is essential, but it is seldom enough for unexpected needs while you live and almost never sufficient after you die.

5. Failure to develop the balanced investment approach that is important in financial planning and essential in estate planning. The imbalance most dangerous to your heirs occurs with company stocks, especially when the stocks were purchased with borrowed money. While you live, you are in a position to make protective moves if the value of the stock declines. Such changes are difficult, if not impossible, after your death. Your widow may have to sell at a heavy loss.

6. Failure to plan realistically for your own retirement or your family's future if you die before you quit work. Too many people assume that the corporate annuity is the only answer and accept it without proper examination. In most cases, a pension plan is valuable, but it should never be the only source of after-work, after-death income.

7. Procrastination in converting real estate to a more liquid asset. Property will add to the total value of your estate; but unless the land and buildings produce income, taxes can drain away most of your heirs' income. As you grow older, develop a schedule to sell the most distant and least desirable holdings.

STEPS YOU CAN TAKE

The selection of an executor—the individual or institution responsible for administering your estate after your death—is outlined earlier. But you must provide something to be administered and arrange for sufficient liquid assets to cover:

1. Death expenses (funeral costs, debts, and administration). As a rule of thumb, they will total 7½% of the estate: $30,000 on a $400,000 estate. Taxes can be paid later, but plan for them too. Each time you review your will and estate plan, ask your lawyer for an estimate of death taxes and make certain there will be cash, insurance, or securities available for those certain expenses.

2. Living costs for your family for at least six months. Projections of those expenses after your paycheck stops should be made periodically: after you're married, when a child is born, and later when the children become independent. Always work on the basis of your current income and net worth and not on hopes of an inheritance, no matter how probable it may be.

If you're now spending more than you make, there'll be trouble, but on the average the widow will need at least 60% of your present income. If she is able to work, make that a plus. And do not assume that she will remarry. Only a small percentage of widows do. To find the liquid assets your estate will need, use Worksheet 18.

At the beginning, the major savings will be in the elimination of payments for Social Security, insurance, and income taxes. Later, the widow will have some choice on what she wants to eliminate. Once the estate is settled and she has a clear idea of available assets and probable income, she can decide whether she can afford to stay in the old home, belong to the same clubs, and continue the former lifestyle. It may be a blow to your pride to accept the fact that she

Worksheet 18
Liquid Assets Your Estate Will Need

Family Expenses (2 Years)*	Amount
Mortgage payments	_____
Property taxes	_____
Home insurance	_____
Home repairs and maintenance	_____
Heat and utilities	_____
Telephone	_____
Food	_____
Clothing	_____
Education	_____
Cars	_____
Health insurance	_____
Medical and dental care	_____
Recreation and clubs	_____
Miscellaneous	_____
Total	_____
Executor's expenses	
Cash bequests	_____
Estate taxes	_____
Fees, and so on (7½% of gross)	_____
Total	_____

*Consult your lawyer on probable taxes.

may not have enough money to do those things, but she'll survive and so will the kids. Do the best you can with what you have in hand.

Note that, in Table 16–1, there's no provision for education costs for the children. Most men live long enough to pay, or provide for, those expenses. If that is not the case, modify the table accordingly. Revise the projection on the basis of what might be left in the estate after deducting costs of the last illness, estate taxes, and settlement costs. Then ask your insurance agent how long the widow can expect to live according to actuarial tables. Add a few years if she comes from a long-lived family.

Next, arrange to set aside a portion of the insurance proceeds for a nest egg: as an annuity or, if preplanned, a trust in which income and principal can be used. It should not be touched until other resources have been exhausted. And before you become too pessimistic, mentally set aside Social Security benefits as a reserve fund. They can be substantial when there are minor children and helpful when the widow reaches age 62.

THE IMPACT OF THE 1976 TAX REFORM ACT

If you have not changed your will or updated your financial plan in the past several years, call your lawyer *immediately*. Delay can be expensive, because the 1976 congressional action made almost revolutionary changes in estate taxes. Generally, they are advantageous for modest estates (those under $400,000) of the *first* to die, but they can be costly when the same amount is left by the surviving spouse.

Broadly speaking, the changes important to estate planning were:

1. Raising the marital deduction (the exemption when one spouse dies) to the greater of $250,000 or one-half of the adjusted gross estate of the deceased. On a $300,000 estate, the $250,000 cut the taxable value to $50,000.

2. Replacing the old exemptions—$30,000 in gifts in a lifetime and $60,000

Table 16–1. What a widow will need.

Item	Present Average Expenses	Widow's Expenses
Housing and utilities	$ 8,000	$ 7,000
Food and clothing	5,000	4,000
Telephone*	600	750
Insurance, Social Security, profit sharing	4,500	400
Car	3,300	1,800
Health care	1,100	500
Recreation and vacation	5,000	4,000
Income taxes	6,000	2,000
Charity	2,000	1,000
Savings	2,500	500
Miscellaneous	2,000	2,050
	$40,000	$24,000

*Statistics show that widows use the telephone more frequently.

for an estate—by a new unified tax credit that will rise from $38,000 in 1979 to $47,000 in 1981. That works out to equivalent exemptions of from $147,333 to $175,625, so that, normally, there's no estate tax if the gross estate (before allowable deductions) is less than the unified tax credit.

3. Establishing new bases for evaluating property: for marketable securities, the value as of December 31, 1976; for many other assets, the original cost in relation to the period of ownership, especially after the end of 1976. (*Note:* This is still not definite, so consult your lawyer.)

Tax-Saving Steps

Proper estate planning can minimize, if not eliminate, all or most estate taxes by the use of trusts and transfer of ownership by gift or sale. If your marriage is secure, the estate plan should seek to have the husband and wife own about the same dollar assets (cash, securities, insurance, and property). If your family relationship is shaky, the best solution will probably be some sort of trust.

Such decisions can be difficult and complex, so they should be developed and discussed with the aid of a competent attorney. Insofar as possible, be slow to make the original allocation, stay flexible, and try to stay in a position to modify, even reverse, your actions if justified later. It's *your* money.

Details of Tax Act Provisions

The marital deduction is clear: the surviving spouse is entitled to deduct up to $250,000 from the estate of the deceased. *But that benefit is* not *available at the death of the survivor*. In addition, there's that unified tax credit as follows (from the 1976 Tax Reform Act):

Year of Death	Unified Tax Credit	Taxable Estate (Before Tax Is Due)
1979	$38,000	$147,333
1980	42,500	161,562
1981 and on	47,000	175,625

The unified tax credit is a lifetime credit which applies against the estate tax. If taxable gifts are made over the years and some of the unified credit is used, only the remainder, if any, is available. You are still allowed to make gifts, to any one person, without tax, to an annual maximum of $3,000 ($6,000 with spouse). Above that limit, you must pay a gift tax. Gifts made, and gift taxes paid, within three years of death are automatically included in the donor's gross estate.

Now let's see the tremendous difference, in taxes, between a planned and unplanned estate. To repeat, the big problem is the estate of the second to die. That's why trusts can be so valuable.

EXAMPLE: In 1981 (when full benefits of the law apply), Dr. Brown and Dr. Smith die. Each leaves a gross estate of $500,000. Dr. Brown wills everything to his wife, and under the marital deduction the first $250,000 is tax-free. The remaining $250,000 qualifies for the unified tax credit, which, after expenses, cuts the federal estate tax due to $23,800.

Mrs. Brown receives about $476,200. When she dies, a few years later, the net estate will be subject to taxes of $100,708, so the children end up with only $375,492.

Dr. Smith takes a planned approach and divides his estate. He gives half to his widow now and places the balance in trust for her while she lives and for the children at her death. At Dr. Smith's death, the estate tax is $23,800, the same as that paid by Dr. Brown. The real savings come at the death of Mrs. Smith. Then the tax is levied only on the money which the widow receives directly—another $23,800 for a total payment to Uncle Sam of $47,600. That is about 38% of the $124,508 paid by the Brown family. As the result of careful planning and a few dollars for legal fees, the Smith children receive $452,000! (See Table 16–2.)

In real life, of course, there will be other factors, but the savings of a properly planned estate will be similar. Lack of planning can be very expensive.

Evaluating Property

The changes in the method of evaluating estate property can be very important when assets are long-held. Previously, property was valued either at the date of death or six months thereafter, regardless of the original cost. Thus there was no tax on appreciation; there was only a tax on the final value. That's why many older people held on to their assets until death. Now, there are two sets of rules:

1. Marketable securities, such as stocks and bonds, among the deceased person's assets are valued as of December 31, 1976, regardless of cost. The data for most publicly owned companies are available in printed reports. Thus, if Grandpa bought a stock at an adjusted price of $2 per share in 1940 and held it until his death in 1978 when the stock was trading at $100 per share, the tax base would be the stock price as of the end of 1976, at, say, $80. The income tax would be paid on the $20 per share capital gains when the heirs sold.

Table 16–2. Unplanned vs. planned estate: with $47,000 credit (starting in 1981).

	Adjusted Gross Estate		
	$300,000	$400,000	$500,000
Unplanned estate (Dr. Brown)			
Taxes, estate 1	$ 0	$ 0	$ 23,800
Taxes, estate 2	40,800	74,800	100,708
	$40,800	$74,800	$124,508
Planned estate (Dr. Smith)			
Taxes, estate 1	$ 0	$ 7,800	$ 23,800
Taxes, estate 2	$ 0	$ 7,800	$ 23,800
	$ 0	$15,600	$ 47,600

SOURCE: Based on Internal Revenue Service tables.

Note: These are generalized figures and do not take into account other deductions, credits, and so on. Now you see why it is essential to consult a competent tax attorney.

2. The tax calculation for nonmarketable property such as real estate, antiques, and jewelry starts with the original cost. The tax is paid on the time the assets were held after December 31, 1976 in relation to the total period of ownership.

EXAMPLE: Marcia Sills bought a piece of land on December 31, 1966 for $10,000. It was passed to her heirs on December 31, 1976 and was finally sold on December 31, 1986 for $30,000 for a capital gain of $20,000. The time span of ownership of the land was 20 years, so the gain is assumed to have taken place evenly at the rate of $1,000 a year. Because the post-1976 period was ten years, half the total time of ownership, the tax base is 50% of the capital gains or $10,000.

In 1978, Congress suspended the application of this carryover basis and may abandon it entirely. Currently, this is a confused area. The big problem, of course, is the determination of the cost of the property. Too often, the only person who knows the original cost is gone and the evaluation depends on old records, if any still exist. If the deceased did not leave receipts, deeds, checks, appraisals, or other validation, the burden of proof is on the heirs. Regardless of what Congress does, it's wise to develop and keep accurate records *forever*. One helpful source of information: the appraisal made for insurance coverage.

OTHER TYPES OF ESTATE PLANNING

Every estate is different from every other one. The laws of states vary; federal rules are subject to revision; and individuals operate under different circumstances. Yet in almost every situation, wise estate planning can pay off, especially when trusts are used. (For more information, see Chapter 15.) Here are two quite distinct but generally typical examples of solutions to estate planning problems: (1) independent businessman (IB) and (2) business executive (BE). The outlines are broad, and they should not be considered definitive. To repeat: *always see your lawyer first.*

Independent Businessman (IB)

As a small entrepreneur, Mr. IB has struggled to build his business and is just beginning to get things rolling. He has been too strapped for cash to buy more than a modest amount of term life insurance ($100,000). His home is heavily mortgaged, and most of his assets are in his business. An accurate valuation of this company is important to his heirs but is difficult to determine (see Worksheet 19).

The book value (assets minus liabilities) does not reflect the corporation's true worth, so consideration must be given to the earning power of the business. When an enterprise involves modest risk (one that is likely to continue after the death of the proprietor), one way to get a fair estate planning figure is to capitalize the earnings: to multiply Mr. IB's salary by a factor of between 5 and 10.

To be conservative, divide the total value in half and hope that the ultimate sale price will be greater because the business can be sold either in the open market or under a buy-sell agreement with other employees, usually with the aid of a life insurance program.

Worksheet 19
Estate Planning: Independent Businessman

Annual income: $35,000   Wife and two children.   Total assets: $402,500.

Assets

Life insurance		$100,000
Home (joint tenancy)		
Market value	$ 90,000	
Less mortgage	50,000	
		40,000
Business		
Book value	$200,000	
Capitalized earnings ($35,000 × 5)	175,000	
	$375,000	
Divided in half		187,500
Retirement fund		25,000
Cash (own name)		5,000
Investments: stocks, bonds, mutual fund		30,000
Personal effects		15,000
Total		**$402,500**

At this point, the total estate may not be large enough to justify two trusts. For purposes of illustration, however, let's make these assumptions: (1) the value of the business will grow and (2) Mrs. IB has a will of her own which leaves everything to her husband if she dies first and to the children if she is the survivor.

At Mr. IB's death, $60,000, representing the home, cash, and personal effects, will go directly to his widow.

To trust A: $242,500 consisting of the business ($187,500), retirement fund ($25,000), and investments ($30,000). Provisions:

1. All income to wife.
2. Principal to be available to wife when needed.
3. At wife's death, assets to trust B.

To trust B: life insurance of $100,000. Provisions:

1. All income to wife.
2. Permission to invade principal after wife has used all of trust A and needs money to pay for education of the children and/or to maintain herself.
3. At wife's death, the trust will continue for the benefit of the children until the youngest child is 21, when the assets will be divided between the two children.

There will be no federal estate taxes as long as either Mr. or Mrs. IB lives, and probably none after their deaths—unless the values of the trust assets swell.

Business Executive (BE)

Mr. BE has an annual income of $83,000: $75,000 salary and $8,000 from investments. His total assets are $600,000, primarily $300,000 in corporate and personal insurance and $115,000 in investments. His wife has outside income of $15,000 from investments, and his grown-up daughter is a successful career woman. Thus the after-death income needs of Mrs. BE and her daughter are much lower than those of the IB's, even though Mrs. BE lives on a higher scale. The disposition of Mr. BE's estate can vary but, again for illustration, let's assume two trusts. (See Worksheet 20.)

At Mr. BE's death, his widow will receive $130,000 directly: the home ($60,000), the cottage ($25,000), cash ($10,000), personal effects ($15,000), and stamp collection ($20,000). She will have ample funds to spend: $10,000 cash, $20,000 or more from the sale of the collection and some personal effects, and much more if she sells either or both of the houses.

Mr. BE is not sure that his wife will be able to handle a lot of money, so he sets up two trusts to be managed by a local bank. Basically, the provisions are similar to those of the trusts of Mr. IB: income to the widow, principal to be used if needed to maintain her customary style of living (and the courts have interpreted that liberally), and, at her death, residue to trust B.

The assets of trust A will total $170,000: retirement fund of $55,000 and

Worksheet 20
Estate Planning: Business Executive

Annual income of $83,000: $75,000 salary; $8,000 investments.
Total assets: $600,000:
Wife with investment income of $15,000. Grown, independent daughter.

Assets

Life insurance		$300,000
Home (joint tenancy)		
Market value	$100,000	
Less mortgage	40,000	
		60,000
Vacation dwelling (joint tenancy)		25,000
Cash		10,000
Retirement fund		55,000
Personal effects		15,000
Collections: stamps		20,000
Investments (own name)		
Savings certificates	$ 15,000	
Mutual fund shares	20,000	
Stocks and bonds	55,000	
Real estate	25,000	
		115,000
Total		**$600,000**

investments of $115,000. Trust B will hold the $300,000 life insurance with provisions that the assets will go to the BE daughter at the death of her mother.

To repeat: the tax problems start with the death of the survivor. It would be feasible to use only one trust for the insurance; the $300,000 total of the other assets would not be taxed at Mr. BE's death because of the marital deduction and unified tax credit. But if Mrs. BE dies soon after her husband, there will be heavy taxes unless there are provisions for charitable gifts. Even with the two trusts, the final properties left to the BE daughter, unless severely depleted, will be subject to federal and, probably, state levies.

Note in both examples: (1) There are no provisions for expenses of administration of the estate, debts, and expenses of last illness and funeral. Those expenses would be taken from trust B. (2) There could be a number of variations. The BE retirement fund could be allocated to trust B, and part of the investments could be left directly to charity or given to the daughter.

As in all phases of financial planning: *Define your objectives; inventory your assets; and consult your advisers*—here, your lawyer.

QUESTIONS TO ASK IN REVIEWING YOUR ESTATE PLAN

Here are some typical questions to ask yourself, and then your attorney, when you make an annual review of your estate plan. They are designed to make sure that all provisions of your will and plan are up to date and that there will be an easy, inexpensive settlement for our heirs.

1. Executor
    Individual
       Availability?
       Interest?
       Ability: too old? Ill?
    Institution
       Same or better personnel?
       Convenience?
2. Guardian
    Individual
       Moved?
       Divorced? Separated?
       Died?
       Interested?
       Competent?
    Institution
       Still the best choice?
3. Property
    Have you:
       Added new assets? In the same state? Out of state? In community property state?
       Changed cash position materially?
       Changed investment position?

Is all the property—home, real estate, investments, retirement fund—set up so that assets can be quickly available to heirs?
4. Insurance
    Increased? Decreased?
    Beneficiaries updated?
5. Retirement Plan
    Increased? Decreased?
    Provisions changed?
6. Inheritance
    Have you or your spouse inherited a sizable sum?
7. Gifts
    Can you afford to make gifts:
        To children?
        To spouse?
        To college or charity?
    Should the gifts be without strings, or should they be set up to provide income while you and spouse live?
    What form of gift is most tax-advantageous?
8. Will
    Deletions:
        The names of deceased or divorced heirs?
        References to property which has been sold?
    Additions:
        The name of a new grandchild?
        Description of new property: boat or vacation cottage?

Finally, ask your lawyer for information on changes which should be made because of new tax laws or regulations. Delay can be costly and annoying to your loved ones.

TO GIVE OR NOT TO GIVE

In getting-ahead years, most people make charitable contributions as part of their personal philosophy, in discharge of their community responsibility, in response to social or business pressure. A liberal giver might allocate 10% of *gross* income to church, college, United Way, social service agencies, and philanthropic foundation. Most people, however, are not so dedicated to helping their fellows and feel that a very fair share is 10% of *net* income. Either way, the tax benefits are important because gifts to IRS-qualified charities or institutions are tax deductible in the year they are made. Every donated dollar provides savings as well as satisfaction.

All contributions should be budgeted annually against family-determined priorities, and unless there are severe stringencies, payments should be made according to plan: $X per week to church or synagogue (with double-amount checks when you miss a service); $Y every month to the United Way if you're not under a payroll deduction plan, and on-paper set-asides for the fireman's ball and the save-something campaign.

Just as in all areas of financial planning, contributions should be reviewed periodically. That applies to the donee as well as the amount. If your daughter is a Girl Scout, raise your gift if only to help her less affluent friends. And when your son goes away to school, reduce local allocations and start new ones. Always relate gifts to your ability to pay, and do not try to "beat" your neighbors. Charity is important, but it's only one of your budget commitments.

Try to set up a five-year plan for all major donations. That will enable you to be a "good grad" at college reunions and your spouse to have her name on a plaque in the new wing of the hospital. One pledge of $5,000, to be paid over a few years, is more impressive, and usually more helpful to the recipient, than $6,000 given sporadically.

To avoid family arguments on priorities for "big gifts," let your spouse make the first choice and you the next, both within a set time frame and included in the budget. You may have to struggle to meet the first payment of a substantial gift, but checks for charity will soon be almost as routine as those for utilities, and will be a lot more satisfying.

TAX BENEFITS ON FAMILY GIFTS

Now let's examine the tax facts which apply to gifts made within a family. There is no formula that can be used to indicate if and when gifts should be made to your spouse, children, or grandchildren. Usually the opportunities arise later in life after college bills have been paid. When savings begin to accumulate, review the tax consequences of gifts with your attorney and/or tax adviser. A combination of the annual exclusion, specific exemptions, and gift-splitting election allows a potential donor to transfer a great deal of property to family members and thus escape the federal estate tax.

EXAMPLE: A husband and wife can give $60,000 to each of their children and children-in-law: $3,000 by each donor, to a lifetime maximum of $30,000 to each recipient. Since the income or appreciation from the gift after its transfer to your donee will escape gift and estate taxes, it's a good idea to start gifts early. Even if you should die within three years after making a gift, so that the date-of-death value of the property counts as part of your taxable estate, the income during the three-year period will not be included.

Present value of money. When you make an outright gift, you lose the use of the property for the rest of your life. You forfeit two sources of income: that of the property and that of the gift tax. On a $100,000 gift, the federal levy would be $15,525. To determine the economic loss, compound that tax at, say, 6% for ten years, to get $27,000. That would have been the result if the tax money had been invested rather than paid to Uncle Sam.

Income position. There are two aspects of income position. (1) From *the donor* aspect, the higher the tax bracket the greater the current savings on the income that would be received if the property were retained. (2) From *the donee* aspect, the lower the tax bracket the greater the tax savings with income-producing assets. Thus the choice could be between grandfather in the 50% tax bracket and grandson, who would pay 14% on income above exemptions and deductions.

Fresh-start basis. A gift is taxed on its worth at the time of the transfer. Property in an estate is taxed on its value as of December 31, 1976. When assets have a low original cost, it may be advantageous for beneficiaries to use the higher estate tax base.

State inheritance taxes. In New York, the inheritance taxes run from 2% to 21%.

OTHER TYPES OF CHARITABLE GIFTS

When you are older and still need income, consider gifts under life income contracts and trusts. The donor gets an immediate tax deduction at the current value of the property and can count on income as long as he or she lives.

EXAMPLE: Mrs. Clark, age 70, plans a $10,000 bequest to St. Mary's Hospital. She owns 400 shares of ABC, which is selling at $25 per share but paying only $160 in dividends. Since she bought the stock at 5 many years ago, a sale would require a substantial capital gains tax payment.

She can have her wish and income too by transferring the stock to the hospital's pooled income fund (PIF). The PIF pays 7%, or $700 a year. The gift does not become available to the hospital until after Mrs. Clark dies.

Alternatively, her son Ted, who has just made a substantial profit on a stock sale, gives $20,000 in cash to the hospital to establish a memorial for his mother. The money is added to the PIF, and Ted gets $1,400 a year income. On the basis of his age and the PIF's past rate of earnings, IRS values the gift at $16,238 ($20,000 less a tax benefit of $3,762). Since Ted's effective investment is $16,238, the income represents a real annual return of 8.6%.

The tax break would be greater if Ted gave the appreciated securities. When 100 shares of stock rise in value from 110 to 200, a sale would mean a capital gains tax of about 20% ($1,800). By transferring the stock to PIF, the cost would be $14,438 ($20,000 minus $3,762 of realized income tax savings of the gift minus $1,800 in avoided capital gains taxes).

There are also trusts which pay an annuity for the life of the donor. The most popular types are:

Charitable Trust

The charitable trust is a separate, individual variation of PIF. It provides for a fixed percentage of assets as income to the donor and ownership of the assets by the institution. The income is variable because the market value of the property may fluctuate. The percent can be 5% or higher, but it cannot be changed after the trust is established. The higher the percent of payout the greater the annual income but the smaller the charitable deduction.

Charitable Remainder Annuity Trust

The charitable remainder annuity trust is like the charitable trust except that the income is a fixed sum rather than a percent of assets. Again the minimum payment is 5% of the market value of the property on the day the agreement is signed. The income can be higher and the charitable deduction lower.

Any gift-income arrangement must be carefully checked by a competent tax-estate lawyer. Generally, the IRS regulations are as described, but there are exceptions, special rulings, and possibly changes by Congress.

AIDS TO ESTATE PLANNING

With the base of a sound financial plan, estate planning will be easy, but there are extra, easy-to-care-for considerations which are summarized in the following questions and decisions for life insurance policies. Use the same dig-into-details approach to all of your major assets: home, investments, retirement plan, and so on. Searching examinations can be irritating chores, but they will make it easier, and less expensive, for your heirs—as you may have learned from handling your parent's estate.

1. Are ages on policies correct and validated with proof?
2. Should beneficiaries be changed because of a new marriage, birth, divorce, and so on?
3. Are the settlement options automatic or optional?
4. Will the proceeds be protected from creditors?
5. Are the proceeds to beneficiaries judgment-proof?
6. Will the proceeds qualify for the marital deduction at death?
7. Is the automatic loan lapse-proof?
8. Is there a waiver of premium if you are disabled?
9. Do you need a rider for accidental death benefits?
10. Can you save money by paying premiums annually or in advance?
11. Should you use dividends on participating policies to buy additional insurance?
12. What about loans against cash value? Should they be refinanced? Will they be payable from proceeds of the policy or will the residual estate be liable?
13. If the policy owner is other than the insured and not the beneficiary, will there be a gift tax and how will it be paid?
14. Are simultaneous death and short survivorship provided for?
15. Can you save money by changing ownership of the policy?
16. Can you save money, or build greater flexibility for your estate, by changing beneficiaries?

Finally, it's important to choose a payout for the proceeds of your life insurance. Refer to Chapter 12 and then make your decision with the aid of your attorney and, once you have reached tentative conclusions, in consultation with your heirs. If your loved ones do not understand the options—and why you chose them—there could be future trouble through mistakes or misunderstanding. Broadly speaking, you have these choices with life insurance policies:

Lump-sum payout. In a lump-sum payout arrangement your beneficiaries will get a check for the face value of the policy less any outstanding loans. That is most appropriate if your widow and/or children know how to manage money and will be able to invest wisely to meet their personal needs of income or growth. It can be dangerous for the inexperienced and devastating for spendthrifts.

Interest option. An interest option provides for leaving the proceeds of the policy with the insurance company, which pays interest, usually quarterly, to the beneficiary. The guaranteed rate is about 3½%, but in recent years the payment has been over 6%—close to that paid by thrift institutions. That is safe but not as rewarding as investing in quality bonds or high-dividend-paying common stocks. You can spell out the method of payment, but the beneficiary has the right to make a change, usually within 60 days after the death of the insured.

Fixed-period option. A fixed-period option is similar to an annuity; the proceeds, both interest and principal, are paid out in equal monthly installments over a set period of time, say, 10 to 15 years depending on the age and needs of the beneficiary. That is an excellent security blanket, but the interest rates are not likely to be as high as can be obtained from payout securities such as Ginnie Maes (Chapter 10).

Fixed-amount option. Under a fixed-amount option a specified amount is paid until the proceeds are exhausted. That is safe and sure, but again the return is after the insurance company takes a cut for administration.

Life income option. The life income option is a straight annuity; the money is paid as long as the recipient lives. There are many variations, but usually the arrangements can be made so that any unpaid balance, at the death of the beneficiary, is paid to heirs. That may sound appealing, but the interest rate is low and, with inflation, the value of the fixed dollars is less every year.

In all settlements, except the interest-only option, the first $1,000 of interest is deductible from income.

I realize that this chapter does not provide all the answers, but as stated earlier, estate planning is so complex and can involve so many factors, especially when large assets are involved, that you should always consult an experienced attorney and look for assistance outside this guide.

One final caution. A financial plan is not a substitute for an estate plan. While you live, you can control most of your expenses and investments, but once you are gone, the law, and lawyers, take over. If you really love your family, one of the most meaningful actions to take is to prepare, affirm, and maintain an estate plan for yourself, your spouse, and your children. What you do *now* will determine what they can do—or not do—in the future.

17 The Importance of a Will

If you and your spouse do not have wills, call a lawyer now—at once. The lack of a will can destroy the best financial planning. In fact, no financial plan can be considered complete unless and until there are valid wills for all adults in your family: husband, wife, parents, adult children (over age 18 in most states), and blood relatives. Yet seven out of ten people fail to have wills, and an estimated one-third of those last testaments are out of date!

A will is a legally executed written instrument by which an individual makes disposition of his or her estate to take effect after death. Every estate, regardless of size, must be settled by law. That means the property will be distributed and there will be expenses: for the funeral, court decisions, administration, and probably taxes. If you prepare a will, those assets will be allocated as you desire. If you die without a will ("intestate") or your will is proved invalid, the distributions will be determined by the impersonal operation of state statutes with no regard to your wishes or the needs of your heirs. In some states, for example, the law requires that the distribution be one-third to one-half to the surviving spouse and the balance to the children, regardless of their ages or financial circumstances. A wealthy son who hasn't seen his father for years will get as much as his poor sister who stayed home to nurse her mother.

Practically speaking, everyone has a will: his own or the state-prepared one. Be smart. Have your lawyer draw the papers to make sure that your financial planning will not be destroyed by negligence.

DON'T BE DECEIVED BY JOINT TENANCY

Many people think that when their properties are jointly owned, there's no need for the bother and expense of a will. They argue that the survivor will inherit everything anyway. That is partially true, but more often than not it is wrong and can be expensive and annoying to heirs. Joint tenancy has a place, but it should never be used as a substitute for a will.

Joint tenancy is just what it says: all property is owned by both husband and wife. The major advantage is that when one dies, the jointly owned assets escape probate. "Probate" is a general term used to signify the administration and distribution of property belonging to the deceased. Probate itself is a legal process which carries out the provisions of a person's will or, if there is no will, adheres to laws concerning the distribution of such property.

At death, *all*, not half but *all*, assets held jointly are presumed to have been owned entirely by the first one to die. That legal mandate can cause serious problems with taxation, title, and passage of the assets, and it can often damage, if not destroy, financial planning. In fact, you can have the fanciest will in town, but if all the property—house, cars, bank accounts, securities, and real estate—is set up in joint tenancy, the will is not worth the paper it's written on. If you leave everything in joint tenancy and simultaneously dispose of items otherwise in your will, your heirs will probably have a legal fight with tax authorities and/or relatives.

Legally, joint tenancy can be overcome only by proof that the property was paid for by the survivor entirely from her or his own money and placed in joint tenancy for convenience. The situation becomes more complex, and costly, when the joint tenant who dies did not contribute to the purchase of the property. All such assets will be taxed in her or his estate. Most lawyers feel that joint tenancy is OK for checking accounts, the home, and a few jointly used items, but they seldom recommend joint tenancy for all situations.

Other disadvantages of joint tenancy for all property are these:

1. Even with modest assets, it is difficult to put everything in joint tenancy. Without a will, the estate will be distributed under state statutes: the wealthy son will receive the same share as the crippled, impecunious daughter.

2. If debts or estate taxes have to be paid, there may be no money set aside for those obligations.

3. An executor, who will protect your heirs, can be appointed only by will or, if there is no will, by the court.

4. If both husband and wife die simultaneously, the anticipated benefits of joint tenancy can never be realized.

5. At the death of the co-owner, there are always legal requirements which can be eased or avoided by will: getting clear title to property, removing the name of the deceased from the title, and, often, getting affidavits, tax returns, consent of state tax departments, and so on.

Again, joint tenancy is convenient and does promote a feeling of greater family security than individual ownership, but it is *never* a substitute for a will. (This repetition is at the request of one of the leading estate lawyers in the state of Florida!)

THE WILL: EASY AND INEXPENSIVE

Making a will and keeping it up to date is an essential step in financial planning. Preparation is not expensive; generally, the fee is from $250 to $350. Even with large or complicated estates, the fees can be reasonable if you provide your lawyer with accurate, well-organized information and clear guidelines on how you and your spouse want the estate to be distributed. A well-drawn will can save a lot of money at settlement.

Unless your estate is complex and diverse, your regular attorney will be satisfactory. Usually, a specialist will be justified only if your assets include substantial real estate, tax shelters, or other unusual properties or investments.

Before you sit down with your lawyer, do your homework first:

1. Share your estate planning with your spouse and, when they are old enough, your children. They should be familiar with your assets and liabilities; they should be involved in the discussion of your plans for disposition; and they should understand the spirit as well as the letter of your proposed last testament.

2. Make your own funeral arrangements with a responsible adult. This may not be a pleasant subject, but it's important. Someone should know details of your wishes: type of casket, service, whether you want to be buried in a cemetery or cremated, and how much you would like spent. It will avoid misunderstandings, and probably extra expense. An emotionally distraught widow or relative may pay more attention to impressing friends than to costs. Some people prepare a written agreement with the funeral parlor.

3. Consider mortgage insurance for your home. Usually, the insurance is a term life policy the value of which decreases as the debt is paid off. At your death, there will be money enough to clear the mortgage.

4. Keep valuable papers—property deeds, mortgage agreement, insurance policies, contracts—where they can be found quickly, preferably in a safe deposit box.

5. Make certain that cash or liquid assets will be available from a separate savings account, a small joint checking account, or the proceeds of a life insurance policy which can be paid promptly through a local agent. Your heirs will need money for living expenses and, within nine months, for taxes (unless an extension is obtained from the court). Without liquid assets, something must be sold, possibly at a loss and probably at inconvenience to your heirs.

6. Keep a current list of relatives, friends, and business associates who can be helpful to your spouse and children.

7. Check the names and addresses of all beneficiaries: family, friends, charities, educational institutions, and so on.

8. Make sure there's a "delay" clause in your life insurance policies. That will eliminate the problems of simultaneous death of husband and wife. It provides that, unless the beneficiary survives by 15 days, the estate assets go to the heirs named in the will.

9. Make provisions for major expenditures such as college education. There should be ample funds—from insurance trusts or investments—for such special needs.

10. Keep records of installment sales the unpaid balance of which is covered by credit life insurance. This will automatically pay off the loan balance.

11. Decide the distribution of your estate and also that of major heirs. As noted in Chapter 16, there's a big marital deduction which benefits the first estate, but there's a heavy levy on the assets of the surviving spouse. There's no reason to pay extra taxes.

DRAWING THE WILL

Under no circumstances write your own will or use one of those handy money-saving kits. Handwritten wills are legal in fewer than half the states, and even then it's not always easy to establish their validity. One small mistake can haunt your heirs for years and may require costly litigation and time-wasting court appearances. Consult your lawyer and heed his or her counsel. As an expert in the field, the attorney knows how to carry out your wishes. You can make all the changes you wish while alive, but after your death the terms of your will must be carried out by the executor. In the will itself:

Be flexible. Instead of setting specific dollars for donations—say, $5,000 to Cousin Sue or $10,000 to Yale University—make bequests on a percentage basis: 5% to Sue, 10% to Yale, and so on. That avoids the possibility that, because of financial reverses, there may be insufficient funds to fulfill commitments. With percentages, everyone can receive something.

Be specific. Spell out what happens if a beneficiary dies before you do. Name a second or third person or institution to inherit the property in sequence. Or if the first beneficiary dies, write down whether the money should become part of his or her estate. In some states, a legacy can be passed on only to blood relatives. If you left the money to your brother, it would go to his children if he died before you. But if the bequest were to a sister-in-law who died, the money would not go to her children.

To make sure that the heirs get exactly what you want each to have, explain what you had in mind. That 100 shares of stock left to Cousin Charlie in your will made years ago may now be 300 shares because of stock splits. If you might sell the gun collection left to Nephew Stu, provide that he is to receive either the guns or the money received from their sale.

If you want to disinherit someone, say so. Otherwise, a disgruntled family member may be able to persuade a court that you had a lapse of memory and that he or she is entitled to a statutory interest in your estate. Lawyers use language such as: "After careful thought, I have determined it is better not to include a bequest to my nephew Norman."

Name executor. The executor is the individual or institution legally responsible for the management and disposition of your estate. Include an alternative choice to cover the possibility of illness, death, or inability to serve.

Think taxes. The 1976 Tax Reform Act raises the marital deduction and provides other benefits to modest estates, but there can still be state levies. If the combined net worth of your own and your spouse's estate is over $370,000, ask your lawyer about trusts. (See Chapter 15.)

Keep the will simple. Do not clutter up the important document with details. If you want to explain how you'd like personal effects to be distributed, write a letter of instructions and clip it to the will as a guide to the executor.

Be cautious about codicils—supplements that modify or change provisions.

Codicils are OK for minor revisions such as naming your son, now age 21, as trustee or executor in place of a fiduciary institution, but they can be dangerous if they are used too often. It's better to revise the will.

REVIEW YOUR WILL PERIODICALLY

A will is a living entity. It should be carefully cared for and checked every few years to make sure that the provisions conform with changing federal and state laws and your own resources and wishes. Try to schedule the review with the same attorney if you are satisfied with his or her knowledge of estate law.

Specifically, check your will when:

• *You move to another state.* When you die, the place of permanent residence determines which state's laws apply. In many cases, property owned in one state, even a bank account, will be distributed as though you had made no will unless your will is current and applicable.

• *Family circumstances change.* Obviously, great differences are made by divorce, remarriage, and new children and grandchildren. In the latter case, the best solution is to provide for equal distribution to all newcomers. Then you won't have to revise the will at each birth.

• *Financial conditions change.* If you have lost a lot of money, you may want to concentrate your bequests. If you've made a bundle, you may prefer to increase the number of beneficiaries. In both cases, keep the percentage allocations.

COMMUNITY PROPERTY

If you live in a community property state, it is doubly important to have a will if you don't want to leave all your assets to your surviving spouse. Under the laws of Arizona, California, Idaho, Louisiana, Nevada, New Mexico, Texas, and Washington, property is owned equally by husband and wife. Property and all income generated by either party during the period the two are living together is community property (CP). When one dies, his or her estate consists of one-half of the joint assets. There are exceptions:

- Assets acquired by either, before marriage or cohabitation.
- Gifts or inheritance, even during "partnership."
- Compensation received by an injured partner.

In CP states, it is essential to keep complete, accurate records. When there's any doubt, tax authorities consider everything community property. Proof is especially important in retirement states, where, generally, even property acquired in non-CP states is included. But check the local law. California has a quasi-community property law under which, unless certain legal precautions are taken, the surviving spouse or partner may claim absolute right to one-half of the estate regardless of where it was acquired.

Advice: If you live in, have lived in, or plan to live in a community property state, review your will immediately. Delay could upset your estate planning.

And to repeat once again: whether married or single, working or retired, have an up-to-date will and keep it current if you want your financial planning efforts to succeed and your estate to be properly allocated.

AFTER A DEATH

The weeks following the death of the family breadwinner are a time when haste is seldom wasteful and usually rewarding. The widow, or her representative, should take immediate steps to:

- Get 10 to 15 copies of the death certificate.
- File the will with the proper authority.
- Settle insurance policies: cashing in a small one to cover funeral expenses, recasting large ones to provide regular income directly or by rolling over into an annuity, using the rest of the proceeds to further the family's financial plan. Only rarely will the returns from an insurance policy be greater than can be obtained by investing in bonds or quality stocks. (One major exception is swapping the money for shares of a private debt fund operated by the same insurance company. If, for example, you carry life insurance with Massachusetts Mutual, your widow has the privilege of swapping the proceeds for shares of Mass. Mutual Investment Corp., an investment trust which yields about 8%.)
- Contact the local Social Security office for (1) the $255 death benefit if the widow or widower was living in the same household and (2) survivor benefits when there are unmarried children under 18 or 18 to 22 if they are full-time students or disabled.

Warning: Do not count on that money immediately. You'll be lucky to get your first check in eight months, but from then on it will arrive promptly around the first of each month as long as the widow and children are eligible.

- Check the Veterans Administration if the deceased served in the Armed Forces. Get the name, rank, serial number, branch of service, and date of discharge and then contact the local office of the VA and ask about possible benefits. Or if the deceased was a member of the American Legion or Veterans of Foreign Wars, get in touch with the post's service officer.
- Call the personnel office of the company where he or she worked. Ask about *all* benefits, such as: life insurance, unpaid salary, vacation and sick pay, health insurance, pension or savings plan, savings bonds, stock options, and bonuses.
- Check all lenders—banks, credit unions, department stores, finance companies, and credit card firms—to (1) discover whether all or part of a debt may

have been covered by credit life insurance and so will be paid off automatically and (2) give notice of the death and, when necessary, change the account to a single name.

• Advise local government authorities so that tax bills will reflect the new owner and taxpayer.

18 Choosing Your Advisers

The right advisers can make your financial planning a pleasure rather than a chore: they can help you to evaluate choices, avoid mistakes, boost financial returns directly and through tax savings, facilitate reports, and provide comfort to your spouse and assurance to yourself. But if you are like many people, the most important role of any adviser is to force you to answer, and ask, questions and take action promptly. There's nothing complex or mysterious about financial planning if you set your mind to it.

It may be wise, and often time-saving, to delegate some areas of financial planning, such as preparing tax returns and managing special investments. But until you become wealthy (when financial planning will be no longer just a personal responsibility), you must be ready to call the shots yourself.

Over a lifetime, a successful executive will have two groups of advisers:

1. Amateurs—friends and relatives plus a handful of relatively unsophisticated professionals such as a family lawyer, accountant, insurance agent, banker, and broker as quasi-investment and planning advisers. They will be valuable when you are young and on your way up. Relationships will be informal and will usually involve only small, routine payments for specific services such as drawing a will, setting up a personal retirement plan, buying life insurance, and filing tax returns.

2. Professionals—a tax specialist, investment adviser, and financial planner. They will be retained when you have made your mark, accumulated sufficient wealth to need expert assistance, or have run into trouble and find yourself unable, or unwilling, to do what's necessary to meet your goals. Some of the professionals may be called on earlier if there are crises: heavy debts, sudden wealth, or complex investments.

Now and then you may keep your original advisers, because they too will grow in knowledge and skill. But the chances are that, over the years, especially with the mobility of most executives, you will make changes. That's why it is so important to learn to make your own decisions and rely on your advisers for counsel and implementation. Such an approach will provide training for you, permit family involvement, and save money. Every time you hire someone else to do what you can do yourself, you make it harder and longer to reach your financial goals. Every commission reduces the amount of money you have for growth; every fee adds to costs.

No matter what you may be told, there's nothing complicated about the components of financial planning. You will need counsel for the proper format and reports, but if you are smart enough to acquire sufficient assets to need advisers, you can make your own decisions. Turning financial planning over to someone else will not get you off the hook. With personal retirement plans, for example, you are still legally responsible for what happens to the fiduciary funds. And in all planning, if there are errors of commission or omission, you'll be the one responsible for straightening out the mess.

THE SELECTION PROCESS

The ultimate choice of advisers should be a negative process: testing new contacts and discarding those which do not prove out. Usually, that will be a gradual process. It's difficult to stop buying insurance from classmate Ted or shift investments from a brokerage firm whose top man belongs to your country club. Try to judge advisers with the same strict standards you use in your business or profession: competence, integrity, and services. Of course, if your brother-in-law is an insurance agent and your nephew is a stockbroker, you'll probably have to compromise.

There's no right or wrong way to choose advisers, but remember that no one cares as much about your career, your family, and your money as you do. That attitude becomes more important as you accummulate wealth. Affluence will attract salesmen; and as you will learn, many professional advisers are long on promises and short on performance.

Finally, counsel is a two-way deal that requires you to set down clear objectives, provide accurate information, and make carry-outable decisions. The adviser should be just that: a source of facts, alternative suggestions, and clearly spelled out recommendations and, once decisions are made, an implementor of your wishes.

Generally, in the early years, you'll need help from a lawyer, an accountant, an insurance agent, and an investment adviser. Add a real estate agent if you own property or are involved in real estate investments.

LAWYER

A competent knowledgeable lawyer is essential. He can prepare your will, set up trusts, handle the purchase and sale of your home, advise on legal agreements, protect your interests in litigation, and, most important, *listen*. He is trained to view both sides of a controversy and to weigh pluses and minuses, as well as comment on legal implications.

In selecting an attorney, you have these general choices: a solo practitioner, a partner in a small firm, or a member of a large organization. In every case, however, you are hiring an *individual* to work for your and your family's best interests. To some extent, the choice will depend on where you live or work. In a small community, most lawyers practice alone; in a medium-size city, partnerships involve four to eight members; in metropolitan areas, a twenty-member firm is considered small. The pros and cons are obvious: greater personal service in a small office; broader skills and experience in larger firms. As a rule of thumb, look for a lawyer who has experience: at least seven years as a generalist and five years in your areas of special interest. Don't skip young attorneys, especially when they have access to older partners. They may be more up to date on new laws and regulations. And they'll work for less.

Most people choose lawyers on the basis of tradition (family retainer), propinquity (office above the bank), social relations (belongs to church or club), or public recognition (member of city council or school board). None of those criteria are discriminating standards. Nor do they necessarily relate to the individual's legal knowledge or ability to provide the services you need at the price you can afford to pay.

With a legal adviser for your financial planning, the most important consideration is *trust*. The attorney will become familiar with your finances, your goals, and your problems. He should be a good confidant and have the wisdom, maturity, and experience to question your decisions. If you are new in town, ask friends, neighbors, and business associates for recommendations. Some lawyers do advertise, but only rarely will they be the type you seek. Be skeptical of suggestions from:

1. Those whose self-interest is involved: stockbrokers, real estate and insurance agents, and bankers. They will probably suggest clients who will further their own business.
2. Judges and court clerks. These people see lawyers only in court—the one place you don't want to be.
3. Corporate executives whose contacts are primarily with members of large firms retained for legislative contacts or special knowledge.

One excellent source can be your company's house counsel. He or she can help you to eliminate unsatisfactory candidates. Once you have a list of candidates, pick three who seem most likely to help you achieve your financial goals and fit your pocketbook.

When you sit in his or her office, use a checklist of your needs. Tell the whole truth even if you have been guilty of poor judgment. Your information will be kept confidential. Knowing the full story of your net worth, income, and financial goals is the only way the lawyer can know what he is expected to do and whether he or she has the experience and time to represent you properly.

Ask questions like these:

What is the history of his or her practice and/or firm? There's no reason you should pay for on-the-job training.

Will you be dealing with him or her or with other members of the firm? The best solution may be a combination: the partner for counsel; another partner for special expertise; and a junior member or paralegal assistant for research and routine reports.

What will be the fees? Usually, charges will be of three types:

1. Time. An hourly rate ranging from $35 to $150, depending on the community, reputation, and experience of the attorney.

2. Flat rate for a specific assignment such as drawing a will, setting up a trust, or checking a contract.
3. Percentage. A predetermined portion of the amount involved in a transaction; for a trustee or executor, the fee is based on the value of the estate, trust, or investments. If the lawyer assumes additional responsibilities, such as managing property, the fee should be based on the type of work done, and not entirely on the per hour legal charges.

Before you make a final decision, ask that all operational details and fees be spelled out; be sure you know who is to do what and for how much. If you do not feel comfortable with your number 1 choice, go on to number 2, and so on, until you find someone you like and respect and whom you believe will get along with your other advisers and your family. Your selection should be a process of elimination: of canceling out individuals and firms specializing in real estate law, compensation cases, litigation, and other nonfinancial areas. Take your time and review every possibility as carefully as you analyze a proposal for a new plant or product. Over 30 years, you may be dealing with just as many dollars.

ACCOUNTANT

The same general approach can be used in finding a suitable accountant. This time, however, pay less attention to the personal relationship and more to professional competency and experience. Here are the questions to ask:

Past experience? Does the firm have other clients who are similar to you in terms of business, profession, and income level? Ask for names of several clients, and then call the references for short chats to learn their opinion of ability, service, and fees.

Areas of special expertise? Since taxes are an important part of financial planning, do firm members take refresher courses, receive specialized newsletters or journals, and belong to professional societies?

Will your tax return be processed by computer? If so, the costs should be less and there should be more time for the accountant to do the creative thinking you may need.

What about the results of appearances, for clients, before IRS? Have returns prepared by the firm been challenged frequently? If so, with what results?

Until you are well-to-do, your best bet will probably be a small firm. You will be an important client, can count on counsel from the partners, and will pay lower fees: between $50 and $100 an hour. For a long-term relationship, charges will be less.

INSURANCE AGENT

It's no longer enough to choose an insurance agent on the basis of friendship. You need someone who knows his or her business, understands your needs, resources, and goals, and is willing to work constantly to get you, and your family, the best protection for the least money. You are dealing with big dollars; over a lifetime, premiums on personal insurance can total as much as $100,000. Here are some checkpoints to help you:

Up-to-dateness. Is the agent abreast of new developments in tax and retirement laws, new types of policies, and money-saving techniques? He should attend annual seminars and lectures and have ready access to experts when your problems become complex. A good indicator is the designation as chartered life underwriter (C.L.U.). It requires two years of college-level courses, a successful record of achievement, and a relatively long qualifying period. It's no guarantee of competence, but it's a fine place to start your search.

Representation. If your agent represents more than one insurance company he can (1) get you the best deal, (2) lessen the obligation to any one firm, and (3) be able to shop around if you're turned down. Do not rule out a single-company representative, but be sure he or she is willing to go outside on occasion.

Relating needs to income. Because of the higher commissions, most agents push straight life policies, but such policies seldom provide all the answers. Find someone who starts with your needs and tailors a program to fit your income: term life when you're young, greater deductibles for disability coverage when your earnings are high, and realistic programs when you're getting ready to retire.

Costs and commissions. The days of uniform premiums are past. When policies are sizable, commissions and often terms can be negotiated. Find out how much of your money is invested for your benefit and how much goes for sales and administrative charges. Over the years, with compounding, a $50 initial savings can amount to a worthwhile benefit.

Service. The true measure of effectiveness from the agent, the firm, and the insurance companies is service. You want to be sure that claims are paid promptly and without hassles and a flood of forms. You also want to be reminded of key dates: renewals for term insurance, change of status of children, deadlines for annuities, and so on. Most important, you want someone who will fight hard for you when there are questions as to eligibility, deductibility, or whatever.

Policy planning and review. Look for someone who can explain all aspects of all policies when you buy and when there are changes in your personal or family situation. Such knowledge is especially important when insurance is a fringe benefit or involves tax savings or tax deferral. The concerned agent will try to revise existing policies before selling new ones on which commissions will be higher (and the amount of your money at work, lower).

Regardless of advertising claims, do not expect any insurance agent to be a full-scale estate planner. No matter how sincere or conscientious he or she may be, the recommendations will be built around life insurance. In many cases, life insurance may not be the best use of your savings. Finally, do not be afraid to change agents when your needs outgrow the capabilities of your original representative. The individual who is competent in Toonerville won't be much help in Los Angeles.

STOCKBROKER

Finding the right stockbroker is one of the most difficult tasks. It's easy enough to work with a friendly classmate or a jolly neighbor, but you should look for skill, experience, and judgment. This man or woman can be extremely important in successful financial planning. He or she will be dealing with your savings: the assets needed to build your estate and to reach your retirement goals. This broker, officially called a registered representative (RR), should have the competence and ability necessary to help you preserve and enhance your capital through wise suggestions of securities, mutual funds, and other types of stock-market-related holdings.

The choice of a good RR will require a thorough, painstaking search and probably several changes over the years. A satisfactory "partner" should be someone with whom you can communicate, who will listen to you, who will provide accurate, meaningful information, and who will be ever-ready to question, if not challenge, your decisions. *A good broker can help you make more money and sleep more comfortably.* Here are guidelines suggested by Richard Blackman, president of Richard Blackman & Co., Paramus, New Jersey, and author of the best-selling *Follow the Leaders*. In choosing your RR, look for someone who:

1. *Has a minimum of five years' experience.* Don't let a young broker learn his trade by experimenting on your account. Inexperience can cost you a lot of money. When you are playing to win, there is no substitute for knowledge and know-how.

2. *Earns at least $40,000 a year.* In Wall Street, do business with the winners, not the losers. That will minimize the risks of bad advice, overtrading for commissions, and pressure on you to buy new offerings sponsored by the brokerage firm. You want a broker who is interested in a long-term relationship designed to increase your capital.

3. *Is research-oriented.* The broker should have an understanding of both fundamental and technical analysis and the knowledge necessary to explain trends and charts and interpret data in a meaningful manner.

4. *Understands the "herd" instinct of institutional investors.* Specifically the RR should understand why and how they drive a big stock, like General Motors, up and down 20% in a short period. The RR should be aware of what makes institutions (who account for two-thirds of all NYSE action) tick and how to use that knowledge to help clients.

5. *Eats lunch at his or her desk.* The stock market is open 5 days a week, 6 hours a day, 30 hours a week. If your broker takes a lunch hour, you've missed 15% of a trading day. His clients will never get the full picture.

6. *Has a workable rapport with you.* There are two ways to shatter a good relationship with a RR: (a) by trying to force an opinion. If the RR has "bad feelings" or is not sure and wants to ask the firm's research department for guidance, let him do so. Respect your RR as a professional who realizes he or she cannot know everything. (b) By taking too much of the RR's time with

unimportant details or asking for information which is readily available. Plan to make your information-only calls before 9:45 A.M. and after 4 P.M. During the day, ask only about the stocks you own or are considering for purchase.

Do not be in a hurry to choose your broker. The stock market is a human institution. Take your time and find a good RR who will like to work with you, who will deserve your respect and trust, and who will be dedicated to helping you achieve your financial goals.

INVESTMENT ADVISER

Investment advisers can be divided into two types:

1. Market letters and printed advisory services. They provide information and let you make your own decisions. If you follow their advice, you are, in effect, turning your investments over to someone else.
2. Investment companies, insurance firms, brokers, money management organizations, and banks. They take complete charge of your portfolio and provide periodic reports on what has been bought and sold and on the current value of your holdings including income and appreciation.

Group 1 is best when you are starting to build your investments and want to learn about securities and stock market techniques. Market letters come in all styles and costs. Some, like Standard & Poor's *Outlook,* provide a weekly report on the market, summaries of industries, stock groups, and specific companies, updates on previous recommendations, and explanations of various types of securities, techniques, and opportunities.

Others are keyed to special objectives: growth, income, trading, technical analysis, or special areas such as options, convertibles, warrants, turnarounds, insider transactions, or special situations.

The best way to find out about market letters is by a trial subscription. The trial offers are made in ads in the financial press and, especially, in *Barron's.* For trial offers for 30 services, send $18 to Select Information Exchange, 2095 Broadway, New York, NY 10023. Checkpoints, which can also be used with group 2, include:

Audience. If the service goes to hundreds of thousands of people, its comments will be general and useful only as background. If it's directed to a small segment of investors, it's probably too expensive and too limited for your needs.

Investment philosophy. You want a money manager whose objectives match your goals: preservation of capital, growth, and income.

Clarity. Look for counsel that's easy to understand and implement. Beware of obfuscations, complex language, and generalities such as "buy on weakness"; "sell on strength." You want background information to enable you to improve your investment returns: specific buy prices, target points, and, most important, logical reasons why actions should be taken.

Areas of research. Does the commentary center on blue chips which do not require much analysis or on quality secondary issues that offer greater opportunities for profits? Are the stocks that are covered speculative or cyclical issues the gains from which are more a matter of timing than research?

Recommendations. If there are too few recommendations, you won't get a broad choice. If there are too many, you still won't know what to do. Look for model portfolios against which you can plot your strategy. Be wary of advice that is too positive. There are few certainties in the stock market. The wise writer reports probabilities and explains his conclusions.

Performance record. If the predictions and recommendations are right 60% of the time, that's a good batting average. One big success may make great ad copy, but it can be due more to luck than to skill. It's hard *not* to make money in a booming market. What you want is someone who has achieved fairly consistent results: a little higher than the averages in good times; lower, or no losses, in bear markets.

Integrity. If the individual or firm has had a brush with the law or the SEC, forget it. You cannot afford to take chances with your savings.

Extras. The extras may include services such as a summary of opinions of other advisory reports, personal consultation with the editor, or an annual portfolio review.

Here are some partly whimsical guidelines for reading market letters:

- Read for amusement, not for profit.
- Always season with the salt of skepticism.
- Do not look for facts or intelligent comparisons which are logical and sensible. They will seldom be present.
- Do the analytical comments make sense or are they just clever-sounding words and phrases?
- Does the information add to your knowledge and understanding of the stock market?
- Is the advice such that you, as a successful executive or professional, would accept it in making decisions in your own business or profession?
- Is the author a promoter or adviser?

PROFESSIONAL INVESTORS

With group 2 of investment advisers you are entrusting your savings to someone else, usually for a sizable fee. Typically, the fee for investment advisers and banks is a minimum of $500 a year against three-fourths of 1% of the first $250,000 portfolio value and one-half of 1% thereafter. With load funds, there's also a sales commission of about 8.5%. Those costs leave less money at work.

In addition to checking the integrity of the sponsor,

Concentrate on past performance of *all* recommendations for the past five and, preferably, ten years. If the organization has not been in business that long, be cautious.

A worthwhile adviser should be able to achieve average total returns of 10%, higher returns in bull markets, and only slightly lower returns in bear markets.

If anyone, without experience, can buy bonds to yield 8% to 9%, why should the paid professional not be able to do 2% better over a period of time? I know that only a few professionals have met that target, but take time to discover those winners. That added 2% annual rate of return on every $1,000 invested over 25 years compounds to an extra $16,000!

If yours is a large investment adviser, ask for annual reports of mutual funds or common trust funds under the same management. Then compare the reports with the Dow Jones Industrial Average or Standard & Poor's Stock Price Indices. Remember that a fund that starts at a market low will look good anytime.

Pay more attention to losses than gains. In bull markets, most professionals will outperform the market because of one or two big winners. The real test comes in down markets. Find out how quickly the money managers caught the downtrend and moved out of equities into fixed-income securities. A fund that drops 30% (from 100 to 70) will have to score a 42% gain (70 to 100) to break even!

Check the composition of the portfolios. If the adviser continues to hold a security when it loses 50% of its value, he's either sloppy or stupid. If he concentrates on well-known stocks, such as AT&T, Exxon, or IBM, you will be paying for services you can perform yourself. If over 25% of the holdings are in stocks traded on the AMEX or OTC, the money manager is speculating, not investing.

Watch turnover. If turnover is 50% (half the portfolio is sold each year) or higher, it's an indication that the manager either made many mistakes or is creating commissions for a friendly broker.

Be patient. After you have turned over your savings, wait a year for worthwhile gains. If the results, after six months, are poor, ask questions. If the answers are not logical, you made a mistake. Get out. Just as with stocks, the first loss with managed portfolios is almost always the least costly.

Advantages

To most investment advisers (and all mutual funds), you will have to give full discretionary power: the right to buy and sell without your OK. If you're the nervous type, do so with the understanding that you will be consulted before major changes. If you trust the organization enough to turn over your money, do not interfere. You are dealing with professionals who:

1. Have access to far more information than you can obtain. Money managers are supposed to be trained to analyze and utilize statistical data, develop comparisons, and catch trends that can be used to make better investment decisions.

2. Rely on a systematic approach to money management by means of standards and formalized procedures based on experience. Effective investing demands rules and adherence to strict standards.

3. Take a tough-minded, unemotional view of money management. They know that a stock does not care who owns it. They never fall in love with a security. They act, and react, on facts and try to buy when the stock or bond

is undervalued and has positive prospects and sell when selections fail to progress, fall out of favor, or become overpriced.

Finally, take nothing for granted. Check the reports to be sure they are accurate and complete and monitor all decisions. With growing competition and under the pressure of the ERISA prudent man rule, most professional money managers are developing higher standards if not superior performance. Hopefully, there will be fewer cases of mismanagement as shown by these case histories of bank trust departments:

• For an older, income-needing widow, the purchase of Teleprompter stock in the low 30s. The stock had never paid a dividend, and although its price did jump to 45 prior to listing on the NYSE, it fell, almost straight down, to 3½ in just over one year.

• For an elderly couple living on income from a trust fund, a substantial "investment" in shares of a bank-related real estate investment trust at 61. For two years, the dividend and capital gains distributions were liberal, but when the crash came, the stock fell to 4 with no prospects of income.

• For a Florida retiree with a trust handled in his old hometown, most of the assets were in real estate leased to prime tenants who sent their monthly checks directly to the bank. The bank was to invest the money promptly in high-income, liquid securities and use the proceeds to pay bills for its client's ailing sister. When the retiree went North, eight months later, he discovered that the bank had been keeping the rent money in a non-interest-bearing checking account. It took months of squabbling to remove the bank as trustee.

Always review the actions of every adviser periodically and, if you did not do so in the first place, get written rules and procedures.

CUSTODY ACCOUNTS

One area in which assistance beyond regular advisers can be helpful is with custody accounts. Generations ago, they were usually related to children, aged people, and the well-traveled rich. Now, in an effort to expand their services, many banks are developing special programs which provide safekeeping of securities, records of investment transactions, periodic analyses of portfolio values, and regular reports of dividends, interest, stock splits, and rights offers. The fee starts at $150 and is based on the value of the holdings.

Some banks will even buy and sell securities. For 15 securities, the fee is $150 plus $15 per transaction. Arrangements can also be made for margin loans, bill paying, and other conveniences. When you choose an institution, look for one that provides an easy-to-understand accounting report like Figure 6.

RETIREMENT PLAN MANAGERS

Similar services are available for management of a personal retirement plan by private organizations and insurance companies. PRO Services, Flourtown, Pennsylvania, and Certified Plans, Newport Beach, California, for example, handle all paperwork, track the flow of money and investments, file government reports,

Figure 6. Accounting report.

TRUST DEPARTMENT
REPORT OF TRANSACTIONS

THE REGIONAL NATIONAL BANK
1000 Maiden Lane
Anywhere, U.S. 10000

Close of business July 31, 1977
Account number 7-01-666

CURRENT ACCOUNT OF J. P. WHITE

DATE	TYPE OF TRANS.	AMOUNT OR SHARES	DESCRIPTION	RATE	MATURITY DATE	PRICE	TRANSACTION AMOUNT
6/30/77			OPENING PRINCIPAL BALANCE				$ 1,690.38
7/5/77	RD	10,000	NOTE: XYZ CREDIT CORP. 7 5 77		77	$100.00	9,960.17
7/18/77	TSFD		TRANSFERRED FROM INCOME ACCOUNT				1,236.00
7/18/77	DIST		CHECK TO ABC NATIONAL BANK FOR TRUST				3,962.45 −
7/25/77	SALE	1,000	RAPID TRANSIT COMMON			28.70	28,700.00
7/27/77	PURC	400	KELLY PHARMACEUTICALS COMMON: COST REFLECTS COMMISSION 217.16			53.00	21,417.16 −
			CLOSING PRINCIPAL BALANCE				16,206.94
6/30/77			OPENING INCOME BALANCE				1,016.17
7/5/77	INT	10,000	NOTE: XYZ CREDIT CORP. 7 5 77		77		39.83
7/5/77	DIV	1,800	WIZARD TOYS CORPORATION COMMON	10			180.00
7/18/77	TSFD		TRANSFERRED TO PRINCIPAL ACCOUNT				1,236.00 −
7/25/77	INT	50,000	PDQ CONV SUB DEB	6	94		1,500.00
			CLOSING INCOME BALANCE				1,500.00
			TOTAL PRINCIPAL & INCOME BALANCE				17,706.94

and send periodic analyses. With a bank as custodian and trustee, the professional will make all investment decisions or work with your broker. For a Keogh plan, costs run about $75 a year plus $30 for each participant plus trustee and custodial charges. PRO also arranges for life insurance and mutual fund purchases and, for a modest fee, will switch holdings into funds with different objectives. Insurance companies charge no fee because the money made from insurance premiums more than pays for the "free" services. If you can resist the sales pitch for more insurance, the services can be OK. But, again, you are paying someone else to do what most people can do themselves.

SPECIAL ADVISERS

There are scores of other special advisers for financial planning and asset management. There are even advisers on advisers. Because of their cost, such specialists should be called in only when you have substantial assets or run into financial difficulties.

The best choice is a certified financial planner (CFP), an individual approved by the College for Financial Planning. CFPs must meet standards of character and education, take a 1½- to 2-year correspondence course, pass five three-hour exams, and continue to update their knowledge.

The CFP designation is not a guarantee of competence, but at least you will be relying on a professional. In most cases, his or her role is that of a coordinator: to analyze your assets and liabilities, pick the best counsel, and, most important, keep pressuring you to act: to cut your expenses, make better use of your resources, take advantage of tax benefits, get the most value from your expenditures, save consistently, and constantly reinvest your income and capital gains.

Some CFPs, sometimes individually but usually by firms, are retained by major corporations as a fringe benefit for their executives. Their role is to help the employee reorient his or her financial plans and to suggest ways to reduce or postpone tax liabilities.

Here is an example cited by The Ayco Corporation of Albany, New York. A 40-year-old executive with a six-figure salary, whom we will call Edward Reed, made some bad investments and, ashamed to admit his mistakes, got in so deep that his worries affected his work. His employer called in an outside consultant who cut the losses, refinanced the debts, showed Mr. Reed how to take advantage of tax laws, and restructured his holdings to help him start rebuilding his estate.

One area in which such an impersonal, professional approach can be especially beneficial is when the executive has most of his assets in stock options or deferred compensation. Over the long term, those can be ruinous because of taxes on dividends and the erosion of inflation. As Ayco's executive vice president F. William Joynt explains:

In many cases, these "benefit" plans present the executive with a tax burden just at the time when he can least afford it, usually at retirement when his other investments are paying off. And if he dies before retirement, his beneficiaries may be forced to give a lion's share of their inheritance to the tax collector. The role of the professional is to point out these problems and offer suggestions to save taxes and to enhance the estate. Most executives are reluctant to make changes in any company-sponsored program even when they realize the dangers.

Advice: If you're offered such assistance, use it.

ADVISERS ON ADVISERS

Another fast-growing field is that of firms which advise on advisers. Stolper & Co., headquartered in San Diego, California, steers clients to superior money managers and also monitors those managers' performance. To give you an idea of how such a service might help you—directly or in choosing your own advisers—here are some guidelines set by Michael Stolper, president of the firm:

• Narrow your choice to firms that can provide either audited reports or at least five client references that cover a five-year period.

• Look for firms, or mutual funds, that have, each quarter for the past five years, had results comparable to those of Standard & Poor's 500 Stock Price Index. One or two poor quarters may be OK, but three can signal danger ahead.

• Compare the time lag of major portfolio shifts with those of the overall market. That will show how quickly the professional takes advantage of market swings to maximize profits, take quick losses, and/or hold for gains.

• Concentrate your search on organizations responsible for managing about $200 million. Those with less than $20 million will not have access to good research; those with over $500 million may not be able to maneuver quickly.

• Once you have signed up, review the performance every six months.

• Be patient but not foolish. If the value of your holdings drops 10%, be wary. If the fall is 15%, get out.

• Determine the investment strategy to decide whether you are comfortable with it. Typical categories are the following:

Firm A buys stocks only when it is easy to make money in the market. At the start of a confirmed bear market, 90% of assets are moved into cash or liquid assets. In a bull market, purchases are confined to issues believed to be capable of a minimum appreciation in 6 to 18 months. This money management firm sticks to smaller growth stocks of companies, with sales of $10 to $50 million a year, that would be attractive investments if privately owned.

Firm B has a rigid selling policy of quickly dumping stocks if earnings dip or stock value falls 15%. Its purchases are concentrated in industry groups that are expected to outperform the market.

Firm C buys about 12 new issues a year; it avoids cyclical industries, high-technology firms, and turnaround situations. All securities are reviewed monthly.

Firm D operates like a hedge fund: with 10% of assets, it buys put options and with 90% purchases quality securities for long-term gains.

Firm E invests only in well-known stocks. "Their managers think the typical investor will be less distressed by a 30% decline in IBM than a smaller loss in a little known corporation. They often sell securities to create the illusion of management."

Mr. Stolper's guidelines have nothing new or startling about them. They are based on a little research and a lot of common sense—as with almost everything else in financial planning. For many people who turn to financial advisers, the feeling of assurance is worth the fee. If the recommendations prove profitable, that's a bonus.

MAIL ORDER FINANCIAL PLANNING

You can even get financial counsel by mail for a modest fee. It is a computer-based service which analyzes, recommends, and updates investment portfolios and, to some degree, educates subscribers. It concentrates on a family's approach to college expenses, retirement planning, and disability protection, and it relies on answers to a questionnaire to prepare recommendations which, of necessity, must be rather standardized.

19 Executive Incentives and Perks

When you move into the middle-management level of a corporation, especially a larger one, there will probably be some sort of program for extra compensation and perquisites (perks) to provide incentives and reward outstanding performance. Those options, rights, and bonuses can be valuable in financial planning in that they represent unexpected income. In a solid, established firm, the values of the extras can be projected, but in new, smaller organizations, the extras should be regarded as "hopes" and seldom included in long-term projections. If they do prove out, great, but don't count on them. You could be caught short if you are overly optimistic.

STOCK OPTIONS

Traditionally, the favorite device for executive incentive was the stock option: the opportunity to buy corporate stock at a set price for a set period of time. If the stock was acquired below the market price and the company prospered, the rewards from the reinvested dividends and appreciation were handsome. But recent stock market doldrums and the ever-tighter legal restrictions have made stock options less widely used. Still, if the company is strong, growing, and profitable, bargain-priced shares can be an important part of financial planning.

There are problems, however. You must hold the stock for at least 6 months and, to benefit from the lower capital gains tax rate, for 12 months. A lot can happen in that year. If the price of the stock drops between purchase and sale time, you may have to pay more in taxes than your profit.

EXAMPLE: Mr. Rubinstein exercises his option to buy 1,000 shares of his company's stock at $50 when the stock is selling at $80. The tax on the $30,000 paper profit, in his 50% tax bracket, will be $15,000. That's OK if the stock price holds or rises, but that does not happen. In the next year, the market value of the stock dips to $60 per share. Now Mr. R. has only a $5,000 profit: $10,000 gain less the $5,000 tax. That's not much when he has to tie up $50,000. And if he had to pay 10% interest on borrowed money, the only benefit is the tax deduction for the interest.

The situation with stock options is more difficult when the shares are not widely traded and are classified as restricted or letter stock. By law, such shares must be held for two years before they can be sold publicly. An early sale of special shares, no matter how desperate the financial need, is subject to all sorts of problems, not least of which is taxes. There is almost sure to be a question about cost value. Even when the stock is held for the full two years, there can be trouble, especially if there are sharp changes in the stock price.

EXAMPLE: Mr. Ross, a new vice president, received an option on 15,000 shares of letter stock at $1 each. A year later, the stock had zoomed to $20, so he exercised his option for a $285,000 paper gain. The tax, about $70,000, was equal to his salary, so he had to ask IRS for a delay in payment time. Under rule 144, he could not sell the stock.

The ending was sad: by the time the restriction had expired at the end of the second year, the stock was back down to $1 per share. Mr. Ross had no profit and still owed a bundle to Uncle Sam. As a solution, he could have given the stock away to his favorite charity. That would have eliminated the necessity to pay taxes on the capital gains if the gift was made when the stock was at $20. But even that benefit was not assured. IRS might have ruled that the gift be disallowed as a subterfuge.

Advice: If you become involved with any type of stock option, consult an experienced attorney. And if the shares represent a sizable block, be ready to settle for a well-below-market price if you want your money quickly. One solution is to wait until the end of the two years and then contact a brokerage firm which specializes in hard-to-sell securities. You may get a better price, but even that will be well below the quoted value.

OTHER FORMS OF COMPENSATION

To get around the disadvantages of stock options, some companies are providing a variety of incentive plans such as:

Long-term performance bonus. This is a cash payment for meeting specific targets of earnings growth and return on investment. Even though there will be taxes to be paid, cash is always welcome—and sure.

Restricted stock plan linked to a cash payment. Under this plan executives are given stock free but can keep the shares only if they remain with the company for a preset number of years. The cash is used to pay the income tax when the restriction lapses. The plan can be a good deal but usually there are strings; for example, the cash is available only when corporate earnings grow rapidly, at 10% or more a year. That can be a tough goal in a depressed economy.

Split incentives. The split incentive plans divide the extra compensation into two classifications: (1) for a few top executives gifts of cash or stock plus a contingent stock option if the company meets certain financial goals and (2) for lower-tier managers straight stock options or a combination of cash and stock options. The incentives are usually tied to individual and corporate performance. Under the right circumstances, they can be worthwhile, but usually they are designed more to encourage people to stay with the firm than to provide opportunities for substantial extra income.

Stock appreciation rights. The special stock options called stock appreciation rights eliminate the need for option exercise for profits. The company sets up an arrangement whereby key executives are credited with the income and appreciation which they would have received if they had bought the stock. There are no actual purchases. The gains accumulate on paper and, typically, can be taken only after a certain number of years of service.

The appreciation rights eliminate the two biggest disadvantages of traditional stock options: the need for the individual to raise capital for the purchase of the stock and the risks of the marketplace.

EXAMPLE: Vice president Morison has options to buy 5,000 shares of stock at $20 each. The stock is now trading at $30 per share. To make the purchase, he would have to come up with $100,000 and be locked in for at least six months. With stock appreciation rights, however, he is credited with $50,000: the difference between the option exercise price and the market value—$100,000 and $150,000, respectively.

It's not quite that simple because (1) when a settlement is made, the gains are classified as earned income and so are subject to withholding taxes to a maximum of 50%, (2) the company receives no income from the transaction and may have to pay out cash under some circumstances, (3) the company may have to charge the payout against corporate income and set up reserves for the ultimate settlement, (4) shareholders must approve the deal—not always easy when there are income-minded relatives for the president, and (5) the employee (Mr. Morison) must meet all SEC rules regarding stock options.

Still, for the designated executive with a growing, profitable corporation, appreciation rights can be a welcome means to extra income in the future. Just be sure you understand all the terms and are convinced that the rewards are far greater than the risks. So far, most plans meet IRS regulations; but there could be changes in the future, especially if there are unusual benefits for individual executives.

Deferred compensation. The objective of deferred compensation is to postpone the tax on part of an employee's current earnings by deferring the payout of the actual dollars to a time when the individual will presumably be in a lower tax bracket, normally after retirement. The plan is well accepted; and when it is properly set up, it can be extremely helpful in long-range financial planning. It can provide a much-needed boost to net worth and after-work income.

Under the deferred compensation arrangement, the corporation holds the "bonus" and invests it for income and, when so desired, for appreciation. The employee usually has a choice: (1) to receive a specified rate of return or (2) to have the employer invest the money in "shadow" or "phantom" stock programs which use hypothetical investments as a measure of the amount to which the employee will be entitled at the end of the deferral period.

The idea is great, but the plan must be structured carefully so that IRS does not rule that an immediate tax is due on the basis that the employee has, in effect, received the money and the employer is just holding it temporarily.

In evaluating any type of special compensation, the income tax bracket of the recipient is important. Generally, there will be two taxes with a profitable option: (1) an income tax on the profit (the difference between cost and market price) which is taxable as ordinary income (for example, if stock was bought at 6 and is now selling at 11, tax is due on the $5 per share profit) and (2) a capital gains tax on the difference between the taxed figure and the sales price when the stock is sold (if the stock is sold at 22, on the $11 gain). Thus the higher the tax rate at the time of the payoff, the less desirable the postponement of such income and benefits and the more attractive the appreciation of the invested funds, because it will be taxed at the lower capital gains rate.

If you expect to be in the under-50% tax bracket when you get the extra money, deferred compensation can be a good deal. But if you anticipate that your future income will be taxed at a higher rate, consult a tax expert and let him project the various *after-tax* possibilities. Then (1) discuss the data with your boss. In a major corporation there will probably be little leeway, but in a smaller organization, it may be possible to agree upon revisions which will aid you and cost the company little or nothing more. (2) In your financial planning, use the lowest *net* figure. If you eventually get more, it will be a welcome bonus. As one compensation consultant put it:

Signing an extra compensation agreement can be an exciting event. But never rely on future income in your planning. The company can run into financial trouble; you can lose your job or fail to meet the targeted goals; and new corporate management may be in a position to change or even abrogate the agreement. It's OK to list locked-in, already-earned benefits, but never kid yourself—or your financial adviser.

For a summary of stock and bonus incentives for executives see Table 19–1.

PERKS

As you move up the executive ladder, you will be eligible for extra benefits, some as small as a free shave and haircut or meals in the executive dining room, others as monetarily significant as company-provided automobile, club memberships, and low-interest loans. Generally, the perks are tied in with a specific job, but a lot can depend on longevity and custom. The best time to discuss such extras is when you are negotiating for a new position.

One word of warning: Since some of the perks are closely related to extra compensation, they may become taxable income if Congress acts on recommendations of some of its members. Keep that possibility in mind and try to build in protection against the extra costs which could come with new legislation or government regulations. Furthermore, your company controller, mindful of possible IRS scrutiny, may charge you for personal mileage.

EXAMPLE: A 1978 brougham, supplied by the company to an executive who drives 25,000 miles a year, had total operating costs of $4,490. The controller calculated that the proportionate share for personal use of the car was $1,213. He required the executive to pay 9¢ per mile plus $63 per month, which almost wiped out the fringe benefit.

Here is a list of corporate executive perquisites:

Routine Perks
    Barber and beauty shop
    Executive dining room
    Recreation facilities
    Moving and relocation costs
    Job placement fees
    Business and professional memberships

Table 19–1. Stock and bonus incentives for executives.

Type	Description	Payoff	Taxation
Qualified	Granted at current market price until May 21, 1981, when it becomes "nonqualified."	When value of stock rises.	When held for 3 years, entire profit taxed as capital gains, but difference between option price and exercise value is tax preference item (which can push some of salary, normally taxed at no more than 50%, into high tax bracket).
Nonqualified	Can be priced below market value and, typically, available for 10 years.	When value of stock rises; if that does not happen, company can issue new options.	Reduces amount of gains treated as tax preference items because (1) at exercise, gain is taxed as personal service income (maximum 50% tax), and (2) at sale, profit (difference between exercise and sale price) is taxed as long-term capital gain.
Stock appreciation rights	Right to bonus, in stock or cash, at later date.	Depends on future value of stock.	When paid, taxed as personal service income (maximum 50% tax).
Performance plans	Stock or bonus tied to success in reaching or surpassing operating targets, usually for unit or division.	Depends on future value of stock.	At receipt, taxed as personal service income (maximum 50% tax); at sale, profit is taxed as capital gains.

SOURCE: Internal Revenue Service.

Paid attendance at business, profession, and association meetings
Tickets for local theater and sporting events
Higher Management Perks
　Company-provided automobile, boat, or plane
　Company-provided apartment
　Home entertainment allowance
　Club memberships
　Extra paid vacation
　Chauffeur
　Outside medical services for self
　Psychiatric services for self
Educational Aids
　Tuition refunds for own courses
　Scholarships for dependents
Salary and Income Benefits
　Stock bonus plan
　Stock purchase plan
　Stock option plan
　Stock appreciation plan
　Deferred salary and bonus plan
　Matching savings plan
　Matching pension plan
　Phantom stock plan
Personal Benefits
　Legal assistance
　Tax assistance
　Low-interest loans
　Longer sick pay
　Personal accident insurance
　Extra severance pay
　Extra life insurance
　Survivors' benefits
　Dental and eye care insurance
　Home health care for self
　Nursing home care for self
　Long-term disability insurance

20 Do It Yourself: Working Out Your Financial Plan

Now let's wrap it up and use the worksheets and tables in this chapter to put your financial plan into operation. (To keep this guide for future use and allow for erasures and recalculations, use a yellow pad or ledger sheets.) You can be accurate with current assets and expenditures, but the projections are only guesstimates. Over a five- or ten-year period, they will tend to balance out if you start with a reasonable plan.

Take the long view, and do not become alarmed at temporary one- or two-year aberrations. Unexpected events, such as heavy medical costs or unemployment, can raise havoc over a short period, but they should be offset by the flexibility of your plan over a longer time span.

Be realistic and set your expenditures on the high side and your income at a conservative level. If you get a big raise or make a hit in the stock market, you'll be that much ahead and can set up a reserve. But if you find you are consistently lagging behind and have no catch-up periods, revise your plan. Later, if things improve, you can raise your sights.

STEP-BY-STEP FINANCIAL PLANNING

Step 1. Use Worksheet 21 to project your income. It is based on an income increase of 8% annually from a raise in salary and/or gains from investments. The income, present and future, should be *net after taxes and Social Security*.

Step 2. Refer to Table 20–1 to estimate deductions for federal income taxes. (a) Use your adjusted income—the basis on which you file your annual federal return—after deductions, exemptions, and so on. It will be far less than gross receipts. (b) If you pay state and local income taxes, take off an additional 10%

Worksheet 21
Projecting Income (After Taxes)

	Now	5 Years Ahead	10 Years Ahead
Factor at 8%		1.46	2.16
Salary	_____	_____	_____
Other Income	_____	_____	_____
Total	_____	_____	_____

Table 20–1. Federal income taxes and rates: married, joint return.

Taxable Income	Amount of Tax	Rate on Excess
$ 11,900	$ 1,404	21%
16,000	2,265	24
20,200	3,273	28
24,600	4,505	32
29,900	6,201	37
35,200	8,162	43
45,800	12,720	49
60,000	19,678	54
85,600	33,502	59
109,400	47,544	64
162,400	81,464	68
215,400	117,504	70

SOURCE: Internal Revenue Service.

if you don't have time to get exact figures. (c) Remember that, with greater income in the years ahead, you'll be in an ever-higher tax bracket. (d) Watch for changes in tax laws. Hopefully, they will save you money, but do not count on it, especially when you reach the 50% tax bracket.

Step 3. Use Table 20–2 for deductions of Social Security taxes from gross income. Regard the money as a special savings account which will be paid out at retirement. Note how steadily the deductions are scheduled to rise. In ten years, the off-the-top take will be over $3,000 a year for the employed executive and over $4,200 for the self-employed professional. That ain't hay even though, if you and your spouse live long enough, you'll get back far more than you put in.

Step 4. With Worksheet 22 project your annual budget (Chapter 5). Here, use a summary with two parts: (a) The inflation-resistant items the annual outlays

Table 20–2. Social security deductions.

Year	Employed Tax Rate	Employed Wage Base	Employed Maximum Tax	Self-Employed Tax Rate	Self-Employed Wage Base	Self-Employed Maximum Tax
1979	6.13%	$22,900	$1,403.77	8.10%	$22,900	$1,854.90
1980	6.13	25,900	1,587.67	8.10	25,900	2,097.90
1981	6.65	29,700	1,975.05	9.30	29,700	2,762.10
1982	6.70	31,800*	2,130.60	9.35	31,800*	2,973.30
1983	6.70	33,900*	2,271.30	9.35	33,900*	3,169.65
1984	6.70	36,000*	2,412.00	9.35	36,000*	3,366.00
1985	7.05	38,100*	2,686.05	9.90	38,100*	3,771.90
1986	7.15	40,200*	2,874.30	10.00	40,200*	4,020.00
1987	7.15	42,600*	3,045.90	10.00	42,600*	4,260.00

SOURCE: Social Security Administration.
*Estimated by Social Security Administration under an automatic escalator provision linking the base to the rise in average wages.

304 YOUR MONEY & YOUR LIFE

Worksheet 22
Budget Planning

Expenditures	Now	5 Years Ahead	10 Years Ahead
Inflation-Resistant			
Mortgage	_____	_____	_____
Loans	_____	_____	_____
Insurance premiums	_____	_____	_____
Other	_____	_____	_____
Subtotal	_____	_____	_____
Inflation-Factored at 6%		1.33	1.78
Utilities and insurance*	_____	_____	_____
Maintenance and repairs	_____	_____	_____
Clothing and cleaning	_____	_____	_____
Furniture and furnishing	_____	_____	_____
Medical and dental	_____	_____	_____
Transportation	_____	_____	_____
Education and publications	_____	_____	_____
Recreation and travel	_____	_____	_____
Contributions	_____	_____	_____
Other	_____	_____	_____
Subtotal	_____	_____	_____
Total	_____	_____	_____

*If renting, include here. Add other categories if significant.

for which remain constant over the years: the mortgage, insurance premiums, and long-term loans. Adjust the loan line to reflect debt repayments and new obligations. (b) Rising-with-inflation costs which require upward adjustments. Here the projection is for a continuation of the 6% annual rate. Revisions should, of course, be made if the rate rises or decreases. Make the calculation at the first of each year at last year's inflation figure unless you are convinced that there will be a significant change soon. Remember that these are projections and do not require accurate data.

If you are renting an apartment or home, you will not have the advantage of the fixed mortgage payments, so include the outlay with the first category: utilities and home insurance.

In the Worksheet 22 projections, pay special attention to the probable costs of education and transportation: way up if you have youngsters who will be in college and want their own cars and lower when those bills are out of the way. If the tuition bills upset your budget, add a subsection to reflect a lower outlay if you plan to borrow all or part of those expenses. For example, instead of, say, $6,000 a year, assume you get a loan on which the interest and amortization will be $2,000 a year. Extend that item for more than the four years of college. And use net figures: the total expenditures minus what you expect the youngster to earn or get through a grant, scholarship, or personal loan.

For contributions, use a percent of after-tax income: from 5% to 10% depending on available funds and your own charitable policy. In a sense, the contributions will boost your base income because they are tax deductible.

Step 5. Now comes the heart of your financial planning: how you hope to utilize your assets, Worksheet 23. The projections are made on one very important assumption: that all income from interest and dividends and realized capital gains will be reinvested promptly, presumably in the same type of investment, to enjoy the benefits of compounding.

If you are conservative, most of your resources will be in savings accounts and Treasury bills. The 6% return is a working figure. You'll get a higher return with long-term savings certificates and, based on current interest rates, with T-bills. But over the longer term, you'll be lucky to average much more than 6% unless inflation gets entirely out of hand.

If you are aggressive, use the 8% factor. Compounding will raise the total returns, so you can build a margin of safety to offset possible declines in the values of the underlying securities (but not savings certificates).

And if you plan to manage your money, use the 10% factor. It can be obtained with quality common stocks, some bonds, and convertibles, and it should be the minimum for all investments in real estate or partnerships. Here again you can build in a cushion with tax benefits from depreciation, and so on. The actual dollars will vary, from individual to individual and from year to year, depending on the accounting methods used, the success of the project, and your tax bracket. Keep these notes in pencil.

Step 6. Use Worksheet 24 to get down to specifics: the amount of money you will need for special, big-ticket expenditures: college costs, aid to aged relatives, a twenty-fifth anniversary tour of Europe, and, most important, your retirement fund. The object of this projection is to get a new focus on what you will need and how long you have to acquire the necessary assets. The total should be a sum of income and appreciation and new savings.

If you start with zero and anticipate you will need $30,000 in ten years to send Junior to college, you must set aside $1,917 a year and earn 8% on that money (Table 20–3). If you have, or inherit, $13,896, you can be sure of reaching your goal with an average annual 8% return (Table 20–4). Or you can use a combination. In this example, you'll need, roughly, $3,000 a year. If you start with $1,000 and assume an 8% return, you'll have $1,080 and need to add

Worksheet 23
Projecting Working Assets

Savings and Investments	Now	5 Years Ahead	10 Years Ahead
Factor at 6% Return		1.33	1.78
Savings accounts			
Treasury bills			
Other			
Subtotal			
Factor at 8% Return		1.46	2.16
Savings certificates			
Corporate bonds			
Government bonds and notes			
Income stocks			
Mutual funds			
Other			
Subtotal			
Factor at 10% Return		1.61	2.59
Common stocks			
Convertibles			
Real estate			
Partnerships			
Other			
Subtotal			
Total			

Table 20–3. Savings needed, at various rates of return, to have $10,000 at the end of specific time period.

Rate of Return	Necessary Annual Savings over Years				
	10	15	20	25	30
6%	$716	$405	$256	$172	$119
8	639	341	202	127	82
10	570	286	159	92	55

SOURCE: C. Colburn Hardy, *Dun & Bradstreet's Guide to Your Investments* (New York, Crowell, 1978).

Worksheet 24
Computing Financial Objectives

Purpose	Available Now	Needed in Number of Years	How Much per Year*	From Income and Appreciation	From Savings
College	_____	_____	_____	_____	_____
Aid to relatives	_____	_____	_____	_____	_____
Other	_____	_____	_____	_____	_____
Retirement pension	_____	_____	_____	_____	_____
Social Security (income per year)				_____	
Total	_____	_____	_____	_____	_____

*Use this column in connection with Tables 20-3 and 20-4, which show how much is needed to obtain each $10,000.

$1,920 the first year. As the savings compound, the amount of savings can be decreased. Use your desk calculator to make projections and, if possible, arrange for the money to accumulate tax-free under a trust or uniform gift to minors.

On the retirement fund, get help from the experts: from your corporate employees benefits department, or, on a personal pension plan, your actuary. The calculations are explained in Chapter 8, but they are too complex to be generalized.

Finally, make a marginal note of anticipated Social Security payments. Social Security will be a way to bridge the income gap after age 65 and an aid in offsetting inflation. Based on present regulations, a fully covered male can hope for a monthly check of $502 at age 65 and his spouse, also at age 65, will get an additional $251. But those payments will rise with the cost of living and wages, so that, in the not-too-distant future, a couple should look for as much as $1,000 a month from Uncle Sam.

Table 20–4. Lump-sum investment needed, at various rates of return, to have $10,000 at the end of specific time period.

Rate of Return	\multicolumn{5}{c}{Necessary Lump Sum at Beginning of Years}
	10	15	20	25	30
6%	$5,584	$4,173	$3,118	$2,331	$1,741
8	4,632	3,152	2,146	1,460	994
10	3,855	2,394	1,486	923	573

SOURCE: C. Colburn Hardy, *ABCs of Investing Your Retirement Funds* (Oradell, N.J.: Medical Economics, 1978).

Step 7. Project your net worth, Worksheet 25. The worksheet relies on taking totals from other tables, getting the probable cash value of your insurance policies from your agent, and guesstimating the future net value of your home. See Chapter 6 or ask your mortgage holder.

In trying to be helpful, I started to make calculations at various rates of return, but then I realized that projection was too difficult and would not be useful across the board. That's why I suggest that you set broad objectives: for property and investments, 50% in five years and 100% in ten years; for other assets, such as your home and collections, half as much—25% in five years and 50% in ten years.

Those should be considered *absolute minimums,* because their real values will be reduced by inflation. That won't be too troublesome. At 8%, your assets will double every nine years and regular savings can provide the rest of the gain.

Some of the Worksheet 25 items, such as the cash value of life insurance, the projected value of your home, and the total of your pension plan, may be beyond your control, but their worths, barring a depression, are certain to grow over the years. And remember, there's always the possibility of higher income because of a new job, the benefits of stock options and rights, or an inheritance from your parents or Uncle Bill.

The important thing is to set targets, try to control your expenditures, increase your savings, and invest wisely to make your money work harder—all according to a clearly understood financial plan carried out with care and consistency.

No one plans to fail, but too many people fail to plan. The sad results are the same.

WHAT TO DO WHEN YOU HAVE PROBLEMS

In the traditional American manner, this guide has been optimistic and has assumed constant, almost consistent upward progress in personal income and assets. It won't be that easy, and at some time everyone will have worries, imaginary or real. The first can be destructive in that, aside from setting up

Worksheet 25
Projecting Net Worth

Net Worth*	Now	5 Years Ahead	10 Years Ahead
House (net after mortgage)			
Investments and savings			
Pension plan			
Cash value insurance			
Other			

*Targets: for total property and investments, 100% in 5 years and 200% in 10 years; for others, 50% in 5 years and 100% in 10 years.

proper safeguards, there's little most people can do about them. The second can be constructive because there are a lot of things that can be done with proper planning. Most major fears are unjustified, if only because the costs of catastrophes, such as destruction of your home by fire or storm or overwhelming medical bills, can be fully or partially offset by insurance. The insurance is, of course, an essential element in financial planning.

Yet there are some individuals who are born, or bred, worryworts. There's little this book can do to alleviate their worries (usually imaginary) beyond offering this advice:

1. When you invest, make peace of mind paramount. That means downplaying income and appreciation and putting your money where it is safe: in a savings account or bond. That may not be the wisest use for your money, but you'll lead a happier life. After all, that is what you are striving to achieve anyway.

2. When you plan, be overly conservative in your early years and save and invest to take advantage of the magic of compounding over the years. You will have to skimp in your expenditures and be willing to do without new clothing, new cars, new furnishings, and exotic vacations, but you will have more after-retirement income and your heirs will be wealthier than you ever were.

What it comes down to, of course, is that, if you are unwilling to accept risks, your ultimate rewards will be comparatively small and, with few exceptions, your financial plan will be a crutch, not a tool. Still, it's your life.

Real worries occur when your plan is not working, when your estimates of future income are too high and your projections of expenses are too low. As a result, you are unable to maintain the style of living you and your spouse want, to set aside adequate savings for the future, and in some cases to meet your current financial obligations. That is the time for action: to review and revise your financial plan. Most budget items can be controlled if you are willing to forget pride and status, spend less, recast your debts, and make better use of your assets. In most cases, the alleviation of justified worries can be constructive.

With frequent reviews of your net worth and personal budget, you should catch such problems before they become too difficult to handle. Success will require battening down the financial hatches and living *below* your income through such steps as:

1. Building your cash position by (a) reducing your expenses—selectively if possible, arbitrarily if necessary, (b) postponing planned purchases, and (c) reevaluating your goals.
2. Refinancing your fixed obligations by lengthening the pay periods on installment loans and spreading out payments to department stores, credit card companies, and so on. That will cost more in interest, but it will relieve your cash flow pressures.
3. Revising your budget to reduce variable spending to a minimum by buying less expensive meats, watching the ads for bargains, canceling magazine subscriptions, dropping club memberships, and reducing eating out, dancing lessons, and recreational items.

Do not be too hasty and upset established and generally successful routines. You are working with a long-term plan and can afford to get out of whack for a limited time. Just because the bills for Junior's dental work are double the full years' health budget is no reason to cancel all of your vacation. If you have reserves (and that's part of a sound financial plan), use them. That's what they are for. But be sure to set up a replacement program.

WHEN YOU NEED EXTRA MONEY

At some point in most every life there will come a period when there are no more reserves or even cash in the checking account. Do not panic. There are solutions.

1. *Selling non-income-producing assets which have not been used for the past five years or so.* Usually, these will be half-forgotten "heirlooms": grandma's dresser, that old painting which is too big for the living room, electric trains, dolls, and collections of stamps, coins, or records. Some of them will fetch sizable sums from dealers or, better yet, from a table display at an antique show or flea market. It won't be easy to part with them, but such once-cherished possessions are not bringing in money. After you and your spouse are gone, they will probably be sold anyway. You need cash *now*.

2. *Selling securities or real estate in which you have a substantial profit.* Ideally, they should be assets such that the potential appreciation is limited. Again you have a difficult decision, but even after paying taxes, you will be ahead of the game. However, be cautious about selling property at a loss. To do so will erode your capital at a time when you need every nickel. Of course, if you manage your investments, you should have taken the loss earlier anyway. Still, a forced sale is one way to make up your mind.

3. *Borrowing against the cash value of your whole life insurance.* The interest rates on such loans are low: 4% for National Service Life and 5% to 6% on older private policies. When you get such a loan, be realistic. Despite the best of intentions, few of those debts will ever be repaid unless you receive an inheritance or a whopping bonus. If you have such loans, your estate will be worth less because the debt will be deducted from the proceeds paid to your heirs.

4. *Borrowing against the higher value of your home by refinancing or through a second mortgage.* Not so long ago, a second loan on your house was considered the last resort of the improvident, but with rising property values, it can make sense. It's expensive; interest is at least 5% more than on the first mortgage even though some states set a maximum rate. The loan will usually be limited to 75% of your equity (the difference between the worth of the property and the balance of the first mortgage); the repayment will be rapid (five to ten years); and there will probably be a balloon at the end.

In most cases, the lender will be a mortgage company but, in smaller communities, it may be an individual. Don't be embarrassed to ask your banker for leads. Most houses have or have had a second mortgage. (For more information, see Chapter 9.)

5. *Borrowing from a bank or finance company.* If you borrow from a bank, you'll need collateral and unless your credit is good, you will have to start repayment in a month or two—before you have had time to get financially squared away.

If you borrow from a finance company, the loan can be unsecured but it will not be cheap: interest at 18% at least, and regular monthly payments. That is a last resort, and you should take it only when you cannot borrow from a relative or friend. Still, it's better than defaulting on your mortgage.

The best way to tackle any critical problem is to break it down into component parts to discover exactly what you have and what you must pay. As you examine each item, you'll discover that things are not as bad as you thought. Once you have isolated areas of major concern, deal with them one at a time. Keep your overall financial plan in mind. Hopefully, your troubles will be temporary and, in a few months, you will be back in business and moving back into your constructive budget, savings, and investments.

Appendix I
What to Do When You Lose Your Job

There will be many forces which will cause changes in or delay implementation of your financial planning, but probably the most difficult to handle will be the loss of your job. If you have set up the right kind of program, the economic problems will not be too hard to cope with, but there can be psychological difficulties for yourself and members of your family. Most of them can be lessened, if not overcome, by a planned campaign to find that new and better job. Just as with financial planning, you must set specific objectives and develop approaches that will accentuate your positives and emphasize the benefits you can bring to your new employer.

Now and then, being fired can be tragic and lead to a mental or physical collapse, drinking, family cleavage, and even divorce. But if my own and my friends' experience is typical, you will be surprised at how often losing your job can lead to a better, brighter future, get you out of a rut, and sharpen your perception, knowledge, and skills.

Time and again, what first appears to be a disaster can turn out to be a blessing. There will be some temporary discomforts, but you will discover how many opportunities are still open in your field and often in other areas which you have not had time to explore. And you will find out how helpful people can be! Keep the faith; don't panic; and look at every day as the first day of the rest of your life.

GET GOING

Unemployment is a shock to almost everyone. Even though dismissal may have been anticipated, the immediate aftermath can be filled with questions, reflections, if-onlys, and self-flagellation. None of them will help you find a new position. What's done is done.

What you should do, says Ms. Millington McCoy, partner of the New York City–based executive search firm of Bacci, Bennett & McCoy, is:

Use the high-level energy created by the crisis to develop your job-search strategy. It is time-wasting, foolish, and unproductive to look back. The hours spent in unburdening yourself to your spouse and to your friends can be better utilized to plan ahead. Unless you are unusually talented, you will need all the time and energy you can muster.

Here are guidelines suggested by Ms. McCoy for finding that new and better position. They are based on her experience in recruiting for middle- and top-management posts, but they apply to candidates for all types of executive positions.

1. *Recognize that finding the right job will take time:* at least three months and often longer, depending on (1) business conditions, (2) the market requirements for your skills, (3) your own personal limitations as to location, and (4) age. Over 50, it can be rough but not impossible.

The best time to search for a new job is when you are employed. The security provides time, eliminates monetary concerns, and makes it possible to be selective and negotiate from a position of strength. Unfortunately, most severances take place in depressed periods when there's more competition and fewer openings. But the rules still hold.

At the first inkling of potential trouble—in your industry, your company, or your division or department—tighten your financial belt, add to you savings account, and shift your investments to more liquid holdings. Your dismissal and vacation pay will cover expenses of the first month or two, but thereafter you will have to draw on reserves. Be prepared.

2. *Realize that getting a job is a numbers game:* the more contacts you make, the greater the chance for success. Do not start on a small scale and alert only a few friends, executives of competitive organizations, or just the leading executive search firms. Play the percentages. If you send out 500 résumés, you may get three replies. Do not be discouraged. It takes only one good opportunity to win!

Never be embarrassed about being out of work. Every day scores of people like you become unemployed. Mobility and personnel turnover are a part of the American free enterprise system. Most successful executives have been out of work once or twice in their careers.

Contact *every* executive search firm and, depending on your job level, *every* major employment agency in your area and in cities where there are corporations in the same general business as your former company. Although search firms are retained to fill management positions and usually do so with currently employed individuals, they welcome résumés for their inventory.

3. *Prepare two résumés:* one short and pithy, the other long and detailed. Use the first for a general mailing and the second for agencies and a handful of target companies. For guidance, check your present employer's personnel department, look at sample résumés at the library, or follow the forms in Figures 7 and 8.

Use the samples only as a guide. You are a special individual with special skills and experience which should be emphasized and tailored to the type of firm and position you hope to obtain. In your résumé, accentuate the positive by stressing accomplishments: "sales in my division, up 40% in three years," "member of reorganization committee whose recommendations saved 22% in production costs."

Be honest. Don't take undeserved credit. You never know when your statements will be checked. Use phrases like "worked with" and "member of a team." In the final analysis, you must sell your true assets.

Be objective but not bashful. You're writing a sales brochure.

4. *Use all personal contacts:* old friends, business, social, and industry acquaintances, neighbors who are executives in banks, advertising agencies, public relations firms, and other organizations which have broad contacts. Don't impose, but don't hesitate to ask for help. As Mark Twain said, "The best way to keep a friend is to ask him to do something for you."

5. *Target a dozen companies:* those for which you would like to work and those to which your skills can be useful. Learn all about them and the executives to whom you might report. Study the corporation's annual report and 10K form (available from the corporate treasurer and the Securities and Exchange Commission). Check trade publications for feature stories and news items. You want to know everything about corporate finances, sales, revenues, policies, profits, products, and, most important, problems.

6. *Find out about the officer to whom you might report:* from friends, biographies (available in *Who's Who*), trade associations, and Dun & Bradstreet's *Reference Book of Corporate Management*. Once you know his or her school, college, and previous work

Figure 7. Résumé information.

Position Wanted
Description of the specific type of job you want and your future goal. *Example:* (1) administrative assistant to president or vice president with opportunity to move into other corporate areas; (2) marketing manager of consumer products; (3) planning/development director of new products or new marketing areas.

This tells the potential employer your areas of long-term interest so he can judge your skills and experience in relation to his needs.

Summary of Experience
In concise terms, review your present and previous positions. Use key words to explain your accomplishments and responsibilities. This enables the reader to get a quick look at your qualifications so he can relate your past duties to your job objectives. Limit your summary to a few major areas so he can determine whether you can handle his job.

Example: Eighteen years of diversified experience in sales of consumer products: from in-store selling and management to wholesale administration; from salesman to sales manager of corporation with successful record of marketing and administration. In executive positions, responsible for operating within budgets, heading profit center, training personnel, liaison with manufacturing, turning store losses into profits, and, in corporation, preparing and implementing programs that boosted sales from 15% to 35%.

This is where functional résumés differ from chronological ones. Use job titles with pithy explanations of responsibilities and achievements. Here's the chance to sell yourself and to outline the problems, progress, and results. Use this type of résumé for specific positions and for specific employers. If you worked for one firm, trace the path of your progress. The format can also be used, with job titles, if you have had several positions with different firms. A chronological summary would make you appear to be a job hopper. Always use active verbs to describe your duties and accomplishments. They show movement, action, and results.

Job Title
If your background is extensive, summarize each job and achievement and provide details if necessary on a supplementary page.

Example: As sales promotion manager, developed a program for the introduction of a new product: from packaging to pricing; from marketing strategy to merchandising tactics; from test advertising to national marketing.

General Category
If your experience has been in administration, break down the areas of responsibility: administrator, sales coordinator, budget analyst, and so on. Generally, it is not wise to use both a job title and general category in the same résumé. If you must choose, pick the one with which you feel most comfortable.

Special Qualifications
List any unique background or skills, such as night school courses, languages spoken, or manufacturing background even if this was during summer vacations.

Education
List each degree received, with name of college or university, city, and state. Note honors, if any. If you do not have a degree, list extent of education, but do not include specific courses of study unless they are pertinent to a particular employer.

Publications
List any articles or other published reports, even those printed by a trade association for intraindustry projects. These tend to make you an authority.

Personal
Personal data are never necessary on a résumé. They are seldom job-related and will not get you interviews. This information belongs on the application.

Summary
Repeat, in different words, your areas of experience and interest and end with your immediate and long-term objectives.

Figure 8. Résumé format.

Résumé of Jonas C. Blake	4522 N.W. 46th Way, City, State, Zip code
Position Objective	Executive position in consumer marketing, leading to management and administrative responsibilities.
Education	Bachelor of Arts, John Jones College, Peoria, Illinois. Master of Business Administration, Peppermill College, New Orleans, Louisiana.
General Management	As product sales manager of a national consumer goods company, I was responsible for the development of one product which is now sold throughout the United States and Canada and is being introduced in seven foreign countries. This started as a supplement to an established product but, in three years, was so successful that it was spun off and set up as a profit center. Responsibilities included development of packaging, pricing, selection of wholesale and retail outlets, liaison with retail outlets, liaison with retail outlets, liaison with retail outlets, liaison with manufacturing, supervision of advertising and promotion, and, eventually, administration.
Assistant Manager	Starting as retail clerk in a single store, rose to be assistant operating manager of 24-unit drugstore chain. At various times, I was responsible for personnel, promotion, store design, and layout and purchasing of specific product lines. In addition, I worked as a troubleshooter and was able to turn three major outlets from deficits to profits.
Community Relations	In both retail and manufacturing positions, I was involved in community activities and served as a board member of local agencies and as a member of governmental study committees. I was campaign chairman of the United Way and director of the local chapter of the American Red Cross. These positions required frequent public speaking, political liaison, and legislative contacts.
Special Qualifications	Ability to analyze a situation, develop programs, and assume team leadership. Good personal relations based on mutual confidence, trust, and goodwill.

Note: The résumé should be reproduced by photo-offset, not by photocopying. The cost is less and the appearance better. Do not date your résumé; review it every three months and redo if necessary.

affiliations, try to find someone who knew him or her there and can perhaps provide an introduction.

7. *Try to meet the executive informally:* at a trade association meeting, country club, or community organization meeting. As Ms. McCoy observes:

More jobs are filled from informal contacts than by the Personnel Department. Time and again, selections are made as the result of rubbing shoulders with decision makers . . . by a good impression at a committee of the United Way or from remarks at a trade association conference. Many top executives prefer to make their own choices rather than go through the routine of corporate channels.

8. *Follow up every lead and contact:* with a phone call or note of thanks after a referral or interview. And to build for the future, send a letter to spread the good news of your new position.

SALARY AND BENEFITS

When you get to the point of negotiations, adds Ms. McCoy, *be realistic.* Larger organizations have formal salary scales, so you may not have much room for bargaining.

Most people don't understand salary ranges. They become upset if they are not offered the maximum. It's a lot better to go in at the middle level because there will be a chance for a prompt raise if you show you can handle the job. Over the long term, $1,000 or $2,000 a year won't make much difference.

Usually, discussions will be centered on the moving premium required to attract the person wanted. Most companies expect to offer an increase of at least 20% when the job is in another area. That's flexible. You won't get such a proposal if you go to Omaha from New York City, but you will when the move is reversed.

Always remember that an executive is only a commodity in the marketplace. If the demand for people or your skills is high, you will be worth more; if the market is slack or limited, you'll be lucky to start at the bottom of the pay scale for your type of work.

For broad guidelines on pay ranges, consult your executive search firm. They'll know the market and be able to advise you on realistic expectations. Usually, the only time an employer will raise the ante is when there's need for special talents. If he feels you're the right person, he can always create a new classification at a higher salary range.

Be cautious about accepting a substantial cut in income such as $30,000 when you were making $40,000. Unless there's an unusual potential, you will feel resentful, there'll be trouble at home, and the employer will be nervous and suspect that you will leave at the first better offer. There are exceptions when:

1. $30,000 is fair market value for the position.

2. The post is with a small company where the chances of quick advancement are good.

3. You honestly feel that it is the type of work you will enjoy.

Job Protection

Again I quote Ms. McCoy:

If it's a risky situation such as a small or faltering firm, ask for more money, considerable protection, and some sort of profit sharing: a bonus, stock options, and so on.

If it's a turnaround, be sure to get a fairly long commitment plus adequate severance pay because many of these do not work out.

Be wary of contracts. They can be counterproductive. The best agreement is a simple letter that states that if you are terminated for other than cause in, say, six months, you will continue to be paid for a set period.

When lawyers become involved, everything becomes more complex. Verbiage replaces trust and, if there's future trouble, there may be litigation which few individuals can afford. The way I view it, an executive job relationship is like courtship and marriage. Without mutual trust and admiration, there's likely to be a divorce.

One final warning: Be very cautious about changing careers in midlife. It's OK if you will use your same skills in a different field, say, from business to education or from government to business. But usually there will be severe pressures, mental anguish, lower income, and frustration. It's a rare individual who can handle all those and still do his job. You must be strong-minded with a deep interest in your new field and with plenty of determination to succeed. A supportive spouse helps, too.

As Ms. McCoy relates:

One of my acquaintances worked her way up to a $40,000 position with a major manufacturing company. But she had always wanted to be a lawyer. Since her husband was employed, she was able to go back to law school, where she finished with high honors. Then she joined a law firm at a competitive salary, around $20,000 a year.

She does enjoy her work but is distressed because she knows that if she had stuck to her old job, she would be making three times as much as she does now. And if she leaves the law firm, she will not be able to catch up financially for many years.

WARNINGS OF JOB TROUBLE

Even if you are not the worrying type, it pays to stay alert to possible signals that you may be out of a job. "It's a matter of being observant," says Robert Half, president of a New York personnel agency. "The employee has to act like a detective: putting seemingly trivial pieces together." His advice is to be alert when:

- Your desk stays clearer than usual. That may indicate you're getting less new work to do.
- You are asked to share a secretary, unless that is part of a department or company-wide development.
- Those in subordinate positions receive promotions.
- Other employees get special projects or choice assignments, unless you're sure it's just sharing the honors.
- An outside consultant asks your cooperation in answering detailed questions. That could be a prelude to eliminating your job or collecting data to be given to your replacement.
- You are not invited to attend out-of-the-area meetings which involve projects under your general jurisdiction.
- You are moved to a less attractive office and one of your subordinates takes over your old spot unless that is part of an overall reallocation plan.

To those suggestions Half adds these cautions:

Don't be a worry bug if there are one or two isolated signs. The slights may be exaggerated and the result of other factors entirely separate from your responsibilities. But when you are convinced that something is amiss, start looking for a job, discreetly. Then be cautious. If you misread the signs, the boss may use your job search as an excuse and you really will be dismissed.

WHY DIDN'T YOU GET THE JOB?

How you performed in an interview is, of course, the single most important factor in clinching a job. There's no way to know why you get the nod or a polite letter of thanks, but here are seven reasons why candidates fail to get high-level jobs. They are based on a study of 234 unsuccessful candidates for a corporate presidency made by Business

Careers, a New York City executive recruiting firm. The negatives may be helpful in preparing your own "final" meeting.

- Inability to "project a special competence" (even though your record of accomplishment may be excellent).
- Frequent job changes without marked advancement in salary or responsibility (not so important in early years when you may be seeking broader experience).
- Failure to "project objectivity" or appearing too emotional or too subjective.
- Verbosity and over-aggressiveness (such as lecturing the interviewer).
- Lack of success in expressing your views clearly.
- Overcriticism of former employers and executives to whom you reported.
- Poor dress or grooming.

Advice: Ask your wife or an adult child to help you rehearse. You may be embarrassed at first, but once the mock interview gets going, you may be surprised at their comments and suggestions.

APPENDIX II
The Living Costs of Moving

Time was when an executive had little choice about moving. When the boss said, "We're shifting you to Nome to beef up the Alaskan territory," he told the wife and kids, "Pack up," and set forth. No argument.

But no more. These days, most corporations are reluctant to shift personnel any distance unless they can count on strong approval by the whole family. Many a promotion and move has been delayed or canceled until the wife could finish graduate school, explore her job potential in the new area, and get a promise that the family will stay put for at least three years. Sometimes it's the woman who is asked to move and the husband who must agree.

Even after the idea has been approved at home, there still can be questions, by the employer and the employee, as to how much the new position should pay. As a rule of thumb, the moving differential, for many major corporations, is 15%. But that may not be fair to either party. A shift from Connecticut to Texas can add as much as 25% to a family's purchasing power. And a reverse promotion can have an even greater negative impact.

Figures change rapidly, but Table A–1 shows the conclusions of a survey made in 1977 by Runzheimer Affiliated Services of Rochester, Wisconsin. The data cover the costs of housing, taxation, and transportation, which make up 60% to 70% of family budgets.

The most costly areas are in a band across the northeast tier of the United States: from suburban San Francisco through Chicago to New England. As you'd expect, the South is the least expensive living area. The breakdowns in Table A–1 are for a $39,000-a-year executive with a family of four.

Table A–1. Living costs.

Area	Housing	Taxation	Transportation	Total
Westport, Conn.	$13,698	$11,748	$3,353	$28,799
Burlingame, Cal.	13,530	9,934	3,550	27,014
Minneapolis, Minn.	9,791	11,579	3,204	24,574
St. Louis, Mo.	8,021	10,328	3,071	21,420
Denver, Col.	7,799	10,215	3,102	21,116
Charlotte, N.C.	7,439	10,435	2,762	20,636
New Orleans, La.	7,163	9,804	3,261	20,228
Dallas, Tex.	7,383	9,153	3,131	19,667
Atlanta, Ga.	6,331	9,898	3,144	19,373
Jacksonville, Fla.	6,446	8,980	2,858	18,284

SOURCE: Based on U.S. government statistics.

Bibliography

Investment Reading

Amling, Frederick, *Investments*. Englewood Cliffs, N.J.: Prentice-Hall, 1978.
Barnes, Leo, and Feldman, Stephen. *Handbook of Wealth Management*. New York: McGraw-Hill, 1978.
Blackman, Richard, *Follow the Leaders*. New York: Simon and Schuster, 1978.
Christy, George A., et al., *Introduction to Investments*. New York: McGraw-Hill, 1978.
Clasing, Henry F., Jr., *The Dow Jones–Irwin Guide to Put and Call Options*. Homewood, Ill.: Dow Jones–Irwin, 1975.
Cohen, Jerome, et al., *Guide to Intelligent Investing*. Homewood, Ill.: Dow Jones–Irwin, 1977.
Crane, Burton, *The Sophisticated Investor*. New York: Simon and Schuster, 1964.
Crowell, Richard A., *Stock Market Strategy*. New York: McGraw-Hill, 1977.
Emory, Eric S., *When to Sell Stocks*. Homewood, Ill.: Dow Jones–Irwin, 1974.
Engel, Louis, *When to Buy Stocks*. New York: Bantam Books, 1971.
Farrell, M. L., et al., *Dow Jones Investors' Handbook*. Homewood, Ill.: Dow Jones–Irwin, 1974.
Fisher, Philip A., *Conservative Investors Sleep Well*. New York: Harper & Row, 1975.
Gastineau, Gary L., *The Stock Options Manual*. New York: McGraw-Hill, 1975.
Graham, Benjamin, *Intelligent Investor*. New York: Harper & Row, 1975.
———, et al., *Security Analysis*. New York: McGraw-Hill, 1972.
Granville, Joseph E., *Strategy of Daily Stock Market Timing for Maximum Profits*. Englewood Cliffs, N.J.: Prentice-Hall, 1977.
Hagin, Robert, and Mader, Chris, *The Dow Jones–Irwin Guide to Common Stocks*. Homewood, Ill.: Dow Jones–Irwin, 1976.
Hardy, C. Colburn, *Dun & Bradstreet's Guide to Your Investments*. New York: Crowell, 1978.
———, *ABCs of Investing Your Retirement Funds*. Oradell, N.J.: Medical Economics, 1978.
———, *Investor's Guide to Technical Analysis*. New York: McGraw-Hill, 1978.
Jessup, Paul F., *Competing for Stock Market Profits*. New York: Wiley, 1974.
Jiler, William, *How Charts Can Help You in the Stock Market*. New York: Trendline, 1976.
Knowlton, Winthrop, and Fuerth, John L., *Shaking the Money Tree*. New York: Harper & Row, 1972.
Levine, Sumner N. (Ed.), *Financial Analysts' Handbook*. Homewood, Ill.: Dow Jones–Irwin, 1975.
Loeb, Gerald M., *The Battle for Investment Survival*. New York: Simon and Schuster, 1965.
———, *The Battle for Stock Market Profits*. New York: Simon and Schuster, 1970.
Meltzer, Yale, *Putting Money to Work*. Englewood Cliffs, N.J.: Prentice-Hall, 1976.
Metz, Robert, *Jackpot*. New York: Simon and Schuster, 1977.

Mitchell, Samuel, *You Can Still Make Millions in the Stock Market*. Homewood, Ill.: Dow Jones–Irwin, 1975.
Noddings, Thomas C., *How the Experts Beat the Market*. Homewood, Ill.: Dow Jones–Irwin, 1976.
———, *Guide to Convertible Securities*. Homewood, Ill.: Dow Jones–Irwin, 1976.
———, and Zagore, Earl, *CBOE Options*. Homewood, Ill.: Dow Jones–Irwin, 1976.
Rukeyser, Louis, *How to Make Money in Wall Street*. New York: Doubleday, 1974.
Rukeyser, M. S., *Common Sense of Money and Investments*. New York: Simon and Schuster, 1974.
Rutberg, Sidney, *The Money Balloon*. New York: Simon and Schuster, 1975.
Sargent, David R., *Stock Market Profits and High Income for You*. New York: Simon and Schuster, 1975.
Sharpe, William F., *Investments*. Englewood Cliffs, N.J.: Prentice-Hall, 1978.
Sherwood, Hugh, *How to Invest in Bonds*. New York: McGraw-Hill, 1976.
Smith, K.V., *Essentials of Investing*. Homewood, Ill.: Dow Jones–Irwin, 1974.
Thomas, Conrad W., *Risk and Opportunity*. Homewood, Ill.: Dow Jones–Irwin, 1974.
———, *How to Sell Short and Perform Other Wondrous Feats*. Homewood, Ill.: Dow Jones–Irwin, 1976.
Train, John, *Dance of the Money Bees*. New York: Harper & Row, 1974.
U.S. News and World Report, *Stocks, Bonds, and Mutual Funds*. New York: Simon and Schuster, 1976.
Widdicus, Wilbur W., and Stitzel, Thomas E., *Personal Investing*. Homewood, Ill.: Dow Jones–Irwin, 1975.
Wuliger, Betty, *Dollars and Sense*. New York: Random House, 1976.
Zarb, Frank G., and Kerekes, Gabriel T., *The Stock Market Handbook*. Homewood, Ill.: Dow Jones–Irwin, 1976.

Real Estate

Benke, William, *All About Land Investment*. New York: McGraw-Hill, 1976.
Bjelland, Harley, *How to Sell Your House*. New York: Drake, 1975.
Case, Fred E., *Investing in Real Estate*. Englewood Cliffs, N.J.: Prentice-Hall, 1978.
Dygert, J., *Land Investment*. Englewood Cliffs, N.J.: Prentice-Hall, 1976.
Gettel, Ronald, *Real Estate Guidelines*. New York: McGraw-Hill, 1976.
Goodkind, Sanford, *Guide to Managing Real Estate*. New York: McKay, 1976.
Greenberg, Calvin, *Profit Opportunities in Real Estate Investments*. New York: McGraw-Hill, 1976.
Hall, Craig, *Real Estate Turnarounds*. Englewood Cliffs, N.J.: Prentice-Hall, 1978.
Henry, René A., *How to Profitably Buy and Sell Land*. New York: Wiley, 1976.
Maider, Chris, *Dow Jones–Irwin Guide to Real Estate Investing*. Homewood, Ill.: Dow Jones–Irwin, 1975.
Niceley, G., *How to Reap Riches from Raw Land*. Englewood Cliffs, N.J.: Prentice-Hall, 1974.
Stern, Walter, *New Investing Guide to Making Money in Real Estate*. New York: Grossett & Dunlap, 1976.
Sussex, Margie, and Stapleton, John, *Real Estate Manual*. Englewood Cliffs, N.J.: Prentice-Hall, 1976.
Temple, Douglas, *How to Make Money in Real Estate*. Chicago: Regnery, 1976.
Unger, Maurice, *How to Invest in Real Estate*. New York: McGraw-Hill, 1975.

Commodities

Angrist, Stanley W., *Sensible Speculating in Commodities*. New York: Simon and Schuster, 1975.
Gould, Bruce G., *Dow Jones–Irwin Guide to Commodities*. Homewood, Ill.: Dow Jones–Irwin, 1973.
Kroll, Stanley, *The Professional Commodity Trader*. New York: Harper & Row, 1974.
Teweles, R. J., Stone, H. L., and Harlow, C., *The Commodities Futures Game*. New York: McGraw-Hill, 1974.
Viches, Robert, *Getting Rich in Commodities, Currencies or Coins*. New Rochelle, N.Y.: Arlington, 1975.
Zieg, Kermit C., and Kaufman, Percy J., *Commodity Trading Techniques*. Larchmont, N.Y.: Investors' Intelligence, 1975.

Investment Advisory Reports

Anametrics, Inc., 299 Park Avenue, New York, NY 10017.
Babson's Reports, Wellesley Hills, MA 02181.
Commodity Research Bureau, One Liberty Plaza, New York, NY 10006.
**James Dines & Co., Inc.*, P.O. Box 22, Belvedere, CA 94920.
**Dow Theory Letters, Inc.*, P.O. Box 1759, La Jolla, CA 92038.
**Dunn & Hargitt*, P.O. Box 701, Lafayette, IN 47902.
**Granville Market Letter*, P.O. Box 58, Holly Hills, FL 32017.
Growth Stock Outlook, P.O. Box 9911, Chevy Chase, MD 20015.
John S. Herold, Inc., 35 Mason Street, Greenwich, CT 06830.
**T. J. Holt & Co., Inc.*, 277 Park Avenue, New York, NY 10017.
*Indicator Digest, 451 Grand Avenue, Palisades Park, NJ 07650.
Insider's Report, 1445 Fifth Street, Santa Monica, CA 90401.
Investors' Intelligence, 2 East Avenue, Larchmont, NY 10538.
Smart Money, 6 Deer Trail, Old Tappan, NJ 07675.
Standard & Poor's, 345 Hudson Street, New York, NY 10014.
Stock Research Corporation, 55 Liberty Street, New York, NY 10005.
**Trendex Research Corporation*, 300 Maverick Bldg., San Antonio, TX 78305.
**Trendway Advisory Service*, P.O. Box 7184, Louisville, KY 40207.
United Business Service, 210 Newbury Street, Boston, MA 02116.
Value Line Investment Survey, 5 East 44th Street, New York, NY 10017.
**Worden & Worden, Inc.*, 1915 Floranda Road, Fort Lauderdale, FL 33308.
Zweig Forecast, 747 Third Avenue, New York, NY 10017.

Job Hunting and Résumés

Butler, E. A., *How to Move In and Move Up*. New York: Macmillan, 1970.
Donaho, M., and Mader, J. L., *How to Get the Job You Want*. Englewood Cliffs, N.J.: Prentice-Hall, 1976.
Fregley, Bert, *How to Get a Job*. Palm Springs, Calif.: ETC Publications, 1974.
Irish, Richard K., *Go Hire Yourself an Employer*. New York: Doubleday, 1973.
Nutter, Carolyn, *Résumé Workbook*. Cranston, R.I.: Carroll, 1970.

---

*Emphasis on technical analysis.

Payne, Richard A., *How to Get a Better Job Quicker*. New York: New American Library, 1975.
Taylor, Phoebe, *How to Succeed in the Business of Finding a Job*. Chicago: Nelson-Hall, 1975.

Financial Publications

Barron's, 22 Cortland Street, New York, NY 10007.
Better Investing, Box 220, Royal Oak, MI 48068.
Financial Weekly, P.O. Box 26565, Richmond, VA 23261.
Financial World, 919 Third Avenue, New York, NY 10022.
Forbes, 70 Fifth Avenue, New York, NY 10011.
ML Market Letter, P.O. Box 60, Church Street Station, New York, NY 10249.
Money, 1271 Avenue of the Americas, New York, NY 10020.
The Wall Street Journal, 22 Cortland Street, New York, NY 10007.

Mutual Fund Information

Lipper Analytical Distributors, 74 Trinity Place, New York, NY 10006.
Mutual Funds Almanac, The Hirsch Organization, 6 Deer Trail, Old Tappan, NJ 07675.
Arthur Wiesenberger Services, 1 New York Plaza, NY 10004.
Vickers Associates, 48 Elm Street, Huntington, NY 11746.

Estate Planning*

Ashley, Paul P., *You and Your Will*. New York: McGraw-Hill, 1975.
Brosterman, Robert, *Complete Estate Planning Guide*. New York: New American Library, 1970.
———, *Complete Estate Planning Guide for Business and Professional Men and Women*. New York: McGraw-Hill, 1964.
Callahan, Parnell J., *Your Complete Guide to Estate Planning*. Dobbs Ferry, N.Y.: Oceana, 1971.
Clay, William C., Jr., *Dow Jones–Irwin Guide to Estate Planning*. Homewood, Ill.: Dow Jones–Irwin, 1976.
Erelicker, Morton, *Estate Planning Handbook*. Englewood Cliffs, N.J.: Prentice-Hall, 1970.
Gardner, Allen H., *Primer on Planning an Estate*. Washington, D.C.: Lerner Law, 1976.
Harris, Homer, *Family Estate Planning Guide*. Rochester, N.Y.: Lawyers' Co-operative, 1971.
Institute for Business Planning. Englewood Cliffs, N.J.: Prentice-Hall, 1976.
Kier, Jack C., *Fundamentals of Estate Planning*. Rockville Center, N.Y.: Farnsworth, 1972.
Swartz, Melvin J., *Don't Die Broke*. New York: Macmillan, 1975.
Ziegler, Richard S., and Flaherty, Patrick, *Estate Planning for Everyone*. New York: Funk & Wagnalls, 1978.

---

*Ask your lawyer for booklets covering estate planning in your state. There are a number of such publications which include data about state and local levies and requirements.

Investment Counselors

(Members of Investment Counsel Association of America, Inc., 127 East 59th Street, New York, NY 10022)

American General Capital Management, P.O. Box 3121, Houston, TX 77001
Argus Investors' Counsel, Inc., 140 Broadway, New York, NY 10005
Atlanta Capital Management Co., 230 Peachtree Street, N.W., Atlanta, GA 30303
E. W. Axe & Co., Inc., 400 Benedict Avenue, Tarrytown, NY 10591
David L. Babson & Company, Inc., One Boston Place, Boston, MA 02108
Badgley & Phelps, Inc., 1022 IBM Building, Seattle, WA 98101
Batterymarch Financial Management Corp., 60 Batterymarch Street, Boston, MA 02110
Beck, Mack & Oliver, 6 East 43rd Street, New York, NY 10017
Belden and Associates, Two Embarcadero Center, San Francisco, CA 94111
Berkley Dean & Co., Inc., 717 Fifth Avenue, New York, NY 10022
George D. Bjurman & Associates, 10100 Santa Monica Blvd., Los Angeles, CA 90067
John M. Blewer, Inc., 10 East 53rd Street, New York, NY 10022
Boberski and Company, 120 South LaSalle Street, Chicago, IL 60603
Boyd Watterson & Co., 1500 Union Commerce Bldg., Cleveland, OH 44115
Bridges Investment Counsel, Inc., 8401 West Dodge Road, Omaha, NE 68114
Brundage, Story and Rose, 90 Broad Street, New York, NY 10004
Campbell, Henderson & Co., 2661 First International Bldg., Dallas, TX 75270
Peter B. Cannell & Co., Inc., 555 Madison Avenue, New York, NY 10022
Carr Mason & Leary, Inc., 9777 Wilshire Blvd., Beverly Hills, CA 90212
Chase Investment Counsel Corp., 415 Fourth Street, N.E., Charlottesville, VA 22901
Churchill Management Corp., 9401 Wilshire Blvd., Beverly Hills, CA 90212
Clifford Associates, 523 West Sixth Street, Los Angeles, CA 90014
Cole, Ayer, McCully & Light, Inc., 1880 Century Park East, Los Angeles, CA 90067
Cole Yeager & Wood, Inc., 630 Fifth Avenue, New York, NY 10020
Cooke & Bieler, Inc., Philadelphia National Bank Bldg., Philadelphia, PA 19107
Cranbilt & Carney, Inc., 523 West Sixth Street, Los Angeles, CA 90014
Davidge & Company, 1747 Pennsylvania Avenue, N.W., Washington, DC 20006
Dodge & Cox, Inc., 1 Post Street, San Francisco, CA 94104
Eaton & Howard, Inc., 24 Federal Street, Boston, MA 02110
Lionel D. Edie & Company, Inc.,
    530 Fifth Avenue, New York, NY 10036
    445 South Figueroa Street, Los Angeles, CA 90071
    601 California Street, San Francisco, CA 94108
    229 Peachtree Street, N.E., Atlanta, GA 30303
    444 North Michigan Avenue, Chicago, IL 60611
    Philadelphia National Bank Bldg., Philadelphia, PA 19107
    2600 LTV Tower, Dallas, TX 75201
    3520 Eleven-hundred Milam Bldg., Houston, TX 77002
EMW Counselors, Inc., 277 Park Avenue, New York, NY 10017
Roger Engemann & Associates, 201 South Lake Avenue, Pasadena, CA 91101
Funds Advisory Company, 711 Polk, Houston, TX 77002
Gofen and Glossberg, One IBM Plaza, Chicago, IL 60611
Everett Harris & Co., 888 West Sixth Street, Los Angeles, CA 90017
Harris, Bretall & McEldowney, Inc., 44 Montgomery Street, San Francisco, CA 94104
Heber-Fuger-Wendin, Inc., 810 Ford Building, Detroit, MI 48226

Hotchkiss & Peckenpaugh, Inc., 208 South LaSalle Street, Chicago, IL 60604
John C. Hunt & Associates, 910 Main Street, Boise, ID 83702
Hunter, Miller & Fleming, Inc., 120 Montgomery Street, San Francisco, CA 94104
Investors Management Services, Inc., 700 East Maple Road, Birmingham, MI 48011
Johnson, Kommerstad & Denney, Inc., 201 South Lake Avenue, Pasadena, CA 91101
Dennis B. King Investment Management, 2600 El Camino Real, Palo Alto, CA 94306
Knowles & Armstrong, Inc., Pittsburgh National Bldg., Pittsburgh, PA 15222
Dale A. Lindsay, 21 West Putnam Avenue, Greenwich, CT 06830
Loomis, Sayles & Company, Inc.,
    225 Franklin Street, Boston, MA 02110
    135 South LaSalle Street, Chicago, IL 60603
    1600 Buhl Bldg., Detroit, MI 48226
    700 South Flower Street, Los Angeles, CA 90017
    788 North Jefferson Street, Milwaukee, WI 53202
    One Shell Square, New Orleans, LA 70139
    430 Park Avenue, New York, NY 10022
    1640 United Engineers Bldg., Philadelphia, PA 19103
    2 Embarcadero Center, San Francisco, CA 94111
    888 17th Street N.W., Washington, DC 20006
Mairs and Power, Inc., First National Bank Bldg., St. Paul, MN 55101
Mathers and Company, Inc., 125 South Wacker Drive, Chicago, IL 60606
McCuen & Russell, Inc., 1330 California First Bank Bldg., San Diego, CA 92101
Montag & Caldwell, Inc., 2 Piedmont Center, Atlanta, GA 30305
National Investment Services of America, Inc., P.O. Box 2143, Milwaukee, WI 53201
Neville, Rodie & Shaw, Inc., 100 Park Avenue, New York, NY 10017
Paul, Armstrong, Bender & Tindall, 9595 Wilshire Blvd., Beverly Hills, CA 90212
John H. G. Pell & Company, One Wall Street, New York, NY 10005
T. Rowe Price Associates, Inc.,
    100 East Pratt Street, Baltimore, MD 21202
    30 Rockefeller Plaza, New York, NY 10020
    1600 L Street, N.W., Washington, DC 20036
Pringle, Flinn, Elvins & Donahoe, Inc., 1001 Fourth Avenue, Seattle, WA 98154
Professional Economics Inc., 950 Boylston Street, Chestnut Hill, MA 02167
Rosenberg Capital Management, One Market Plaza, San Francisco, CA 94105
Fayez Sarofim & Co., Two Houston Center, Houston, TX 77002
Robert G. Schwarz, Inc., 615 Windermere Avenue, Interlaken, NJ 07712
Scudder, Stevens & Clark,
    345 Park Avenue, New York, NY 10022
    175 Federal Street, Boston, MA 02110
    Arvida Bldg., Boca Raton, FL 33432
    700 Investment Plaza, Cleveland, OH 44114
    540 Carew Tower, Cincinnati, OH 45202
    One Main Place, Dallas, TX 75250
    2238 Bank of the Southwest Bldg., Houston, TX 77002
    Three Girard Plaza, Philadelphia, PA 19102
    111 East Wacker Drive, Chicago, IL 60601
    373 South Hope Street, Los Angeles, CA 90017
    600 Montgomery Street, San Francisco, CA 94111
    4251 Dundas Street West, Toronto, Ontario MBX 1Y3

Securities Counsel, Inc., 408 Wildwood Avenue, Jackson, MI 49201
Standish, Ayer & Wood, Inc., One Beacon Street, Boston, MA 02108
Stein, Roe & Farnham,
    150 South Wacker Drive, Chicago, IL 60606
    1271 Avenue of the Americas, New York, NY 10020
    National City Bank Bldg., Cleveland, OH 44114
    One Financial Plaza, Fort Lauderdale, FL 33394
    IDS Center, Minneapolis, MN 55402
Stephenson & Evers, 220 Montgomery Street, San Francisco, CA 94104
TCW Asset Management Company, 800 West Sixth Street, Los Angeles, CA 90017
Templeton, Dobbrow & Vance, Inc., 476 Hudson Terrace, Englewood Cliffs, NJ 07632
Thompson, Siegel & Walmsley, Inc., P.O. Box 14569, Richmond, VA 23221
Tilden Brothers & Grannis, 134 South LaSalle Street, Chicago, IL 60603
Trainer, Wortham & Co., Inc.,
    345 Park Avenue, New York, NY 10022
    P.O. Box 2670, Santa Barbara, CA 93120
Trevor, Stewart, Burton & Jacobsen, Inc., 54 Park Avenue, New York, NY 10016
Van Strum & Towne, Inc., One Embarcadero Center, San Francisco, CA 94111
Vilas-Fisher Associates, Ltd., One World Trade Center, New York, NY 10048
Wentworth, Hauser and Violich, 2900 Crocker Plaza, San Francisco, CA 94104
Windsor Association, Inc., 1212 Two Turtle Creek Village, Dallas, TX 75219
Winrich, Kase & O'Connor, Inc., 180 South Lake Avenue, Pasadena, CA 91101

Index

accountant, choosing an, 285
adjustable life (AL) insurance, 206–207
adviser(s), 282, 293–295
  accountant as, 285
  insurance agent as, 285–286
  investment, selecting, 288–289
  lawyer as, 283–285
  professional investors as, 289–291
  retirement plan managers as, 291, 293
  stockbroker as, 287–288
Alabama Power, 233
Aldaheff, Victor D., 241
alimony trusts, 255
allowances, children's
  allocation of, 42
  scheduling, 42, 44–45
alternative minimum tax, 224
Amax, Inc., 13–14
American Depository Receipts (ADRs), 185
American Home Products, 138
American Legion, 280
American Society of Farm Managers and Rural Appraisers, 115
American Society of Real Estate Counsellors, 125
American Standard, Inc., 11
American Stock Exchange (AMEX), 153, 157, 171, 290
  South African gold stocks on, 185
AMEX, *see* American Stock Exchange
amortization
  on mortgage, 56, 162
  on real estate, 111, 113
Anglo-American Corporation, 185
Anglo-American Gold Investment Company, 185
annuity, 35, 215
  deferred, 216–217, 229
  in estate planning, 263
  insured, 218–219
  investment, 218

life insurance payout plans and, 274
money-purchase plan and, 98–99
reverse, 106
savings, 217–218
Appraiser's Association of America, The, 191
appreciation
  average total annual returns and, 136
  of dividend-boosting stocks, 160–161
  in real estate, 128–129
  rights, stock, 297–298
art, as investment, 189–191
Art Dealers Association, 190
ASA Limited, 185
assets
  coordination of, 26
  in estate planning, 259, 262, 266–269
  as gifts, in irrevocable trusts, 250
  growth of, 33–36
  income position and, 271
  in joint tenancy, 275–276
  net worth and 28, 29, 32–33
  non-income producing, selling, 310
  optimization of, 26
  in retirement, 86, 87
  taxes and, 226–228
  trusts and, 247, 248, 249, 272
  utilizing, 305
Associated Professional Consultants, 99
Association of Consulting Foresters, 114
AT&T, 76, 149, 290
  bonds of, 142
  common stock of, 6, 138
automobiles
  commutation and, 51
  improvements in, 4
  insurance on, 67
  leasing, 63–66
  in net worth calculations, 32
  operating costs of, 62–63
average total annual returns, 136
Ayco Corporation, 244, 293–294

balloon mortgage, 59, 61
bank(s)
  credit plans of, 47–48
  custody accounts in, 291
  dividend-reinvestment plans of, 76
  Federal Reserve, 106
  as investment adviser, 288–289
  managed funds, pooled, 130–131
  as trustee, 291, 293
  trusts, 256–257
Bankers Life of Des Moines, Iowa, 207
Barron's, 185, 288
Basic Educational Opportunity Grant program, 70
Beatrice Foods, 137
Belth, Joseph, 214–215
beneficiaries
  death of, 278
  in estate planning, 259–274 *passim*
  for pensions, 93, 104
  of short-term trusts, 251–252
  for trusts, 249
benefits
  calculating, in pensions, 94
  employee, 11
Benton, Thomas Hart, 189
Blackman, Richard, 287
Blue Book, 32
Blue Moon Gallery, 189
bond(s), 142–143, 164
  conventional, 141
  Federal agency, 162, 163
  Federal Reserve, 106
  funds, tax-exempt, 236–237
  Puerto Rico, 235
  U.S. retirement, 163
  U.S. savings, 163
  U.S. Treasury, 162, 163
  see also municipal bonds
book value, 143–144
Boston Edison, 140
boxcar leasing, 244
budget, personal, 39–40, 303–305
  capital spending, 38, 41
  defined, 28
  fixed expenses in, 36–37
  revision of, in problem times, 309–310
  variable expenses in, 36, 37–38

  zero-base budgeting and, 38, 41–42, 43
Bureau of Labor Statistics, U.S., 22
business executive approach to estate planning, 268–269
Business Week, 96
Buying Art on a Budget (Eagle), 191

California, aid for education in, 72
calls, *see* options
Campbell Red Lake, 184–185
capital
  appreciation, 26
  common stocks and, 138–139
  competition for, 136
  earned growth rate and, 143–144
  preservation of, 27, 261, 287
  shares, 167
  see also money
capital gains
  cattle profits as, 243
  long-term, 223
  municipal bonds and, 235, 237
  on securities, 140
  tax, 159, 296, 298–299
  on U.S. government debt securities, 162
capital spending budget, 38, 41
cash flow, 27, 64, 111, 309
  tax-free, drilling programs and, 240–241
cash position, building, 309
cattle, as tax shelter, 242–243
certified financial planner (CFP), 293–294
Certified Plans (retirement plan manager), 291
charitable remainder annuity trusts, 272–273
charitable trusts, 256, 272
charities
  contributions to, 270–271
  in estate planning, 260
  trusts for, 256, 272–273
chartered life underwriter (C.L.U.), 211, 286
charts, in stock market analysis, 150–153

INDEX

Chemical Bank, 256
Chem Vest program, 256
Chicago Mercantile Exchange, 187
Clifford trust, 251
closed-end funds, 166–167
closing costs, 59, 60
Coconino County, Arizona, 233
codicils, to wills, 278–279
CO-ED, 83
Cole, Garrett, 242–243
college, *see* education
College Board, The, 71
College for Financial Planning, 293
College Scholarship Service, 71
Columbia University, 22
commodities, 157, 168
    futures, 182–183
    options, 184
common stock, 136, 137–139
    commodities and, 182
    convertible securities and, 141
    inflation and, 159–162
community property, 279–280
commutation, costs of, 51
compensation, deferred, 298–299
compounding, 6–7
    interest-adjusted cost of life insurance and, 209–211
    of investment annuities, 218
    on municipal bonds, 237
    in retirement plan, 15–16
    of securities investments, 135, 141
    see also interest; rate of return
computer leasing, 243–244
Concept 4 (insured annuity plan), 218–219
condominiums, 51
Connecticut Mutual, 198
Consumers Shopping Guide for Life Insurance (New York State Insurance Dept.), 210
Consumers Union of the United States, Inc. (CU), 210–211, 215
conventional mortgage, 54, 55
convertible securities (CVs), 141
    conversion to, as reason for selling stock, 156
co-ops, 52

credit
    cards, 48, 49
    costs of, 47–48
    loans and, 46
    problems, 48
    tax, unified, 264–265
currency futures, 187–188
custodian accounts, *see* trust fund(s)
custody accounts, 291
CVs, *see* convertible securities

DBP, *see* defined-benefits plan
DCP, *see* defined-contributions plan
Dean Witter Reynolds, Inc., 184
death expenses, 261
death protection, *see* life insurance
debentures, *see* convertible securities
debt
    benefits of, 20–21
    convertible securities and, 141
    at death, 280–281
    funds, private, 167–168
    securities, U.S. government, 162
    service, 122
declining balance depreciation, 116, 117
Deere & Co., 159
deferred compensation plans, 298–299
defined-benefits plan (DBP), 98–99
    compared with other plans, 100
defined-contributions plan (DCP), 98–99
    compared with other plans, 100
Department of Health, Education, and Welfare, U.S., 70
Department of Labor, U.S., 105
depreciation, 115–117, 123
diamonds, as investment, 188
Dines, James, 184
diversification, of portfolio, 174–175, 183
dividend(s)
    automatic reinvestment of, 6–7
    on common stock, 137
    falling, as reason for selling stock, 156
    inflation and, 159–162
    on life insurance, 194, 195–196
    option, fifth, 195–196
    on preferred stock, 140

dividend(s) (cont.)
  premiums as, 157
  QDP II and, 140–141
divorce, 22
  alimony trust and, 255
  insurance trust and, 252
Doane Agricultural Service, 115
Dome Mines, 184–185
Donchian, Richard D., 183
"doomsday approach," to net worth calculation, 29, 32
Dow Jones Industrial Average, 136–137, 144, 290
Dowse, Tom A., 169
drilling programs, tax benefits of, 240–242
dry trusts, 250
dual funds, 167, 168
Dullea, Georgia, 22

Eagle, Joanna, 191
earned growth rate (EGR), 143–144
education
  in budget, 305
  of children about money, 44–45
  corporate aid for, 82–83
  costs of, approaches to, 68–71
  costs of, in estate planning, 263
  family's contribution to, 75–76, 77, 80–83
  financial aid for, non-government, 71–72
  government aid for, 4, 70, 72–74
  in investment clubs, 171
  about investments, of spouse, 172–173
  loans for, 68, 70, 77, 80
  short-term trusts for, 81, 251–252
educational benefit trusts, 82–83
EDUCO, 82
EGR, 143–144
Employment Retirement Income Security Act, *see* ERISA
energy, effect of, on inflation, 11
ENI Corporation, 240–242
environmental control revenue bonds, 233
Equitable Life Assurance Society, 193

equity, 51, 52
  commodities and, 182
  preferred stock and, 139
  stockholder's, 143–144
ERISA, 85, 91–92, 96, 97
  prudent man rule of, 291
  rules on investment of, 102–103
escrow accounts, 58
estate planning
  business executive approach to, 268–269
  certified financial planners and, 293–294
  charitable gifts in, 271–273
  elements requiring coverage by, 261–263
  estate distribution in, 260–261
  independent businessman approach to, 266–267
  minimizing taxes through, 259
  payout plans and, 273–274
  review of, annual, 269–270
  sprinkling trusts in, 253–259
  Tax Reform Act (1976) affecting, 263–266
  trusts in, 247
  wills in, 259–260, 275–281
Estate Planning for Everyone (Ziegler and Flaherty), 259*n*.
ex dividend date, 159
executor, 261, 269, 276, 278–279
  lawyer as, 285
expenses
  fixed, 10, 36–37
  in retirement, 86
  variable, 36, 37–38
extended repayment plan (insurance loans for education), 80
Exxon, 149, 233, 290

fair market value, 64
family
  advisers from, 282
  affected by women entering workforce, 23
  budgeting and, 42, 44–45
  college costs and, 70, 71, 73, 75–76, 77, 80–83
  equity trusts, 256

gifts made within, tax benefits of, 271–272
insurance trusts and, 252–253
investment through, by older people, 17–18
life insurance needs of, 211–213
living costs of, covered by estate planning, 261–263
trusts and, 249, 251–252
wills and, 275–276, 279
see also allowances, children's; divorce
Farmers National Co., 115
farms, as investment, 115
Fasig-Tipton Company, 189
Federal Housing Administration (FHA) mortgage, 54, 55, 60
GNMA certificates and, 162, 163, 186
prepayment and, 61
Federal Land Bank, 115
Federal Life Insurance (Mutual), 218–219
Federal Rehabilitation programs, 118
Federal Student Loan Program, 70
fees
lawyers', 284–285
mortgage, kickback, 60
Ferrara, Jack, 119
FHA mortgage, see Federal Housing Administration mortgage
fiduciary
as executor of estate, 261, 269
funds, in retirement, 102
as trustee, 105
fifth dividend option, in life insurance, 195–196
financial planning
advisers for, 282–295
automobiles in, 62–66
balancing rewards and risks in, 5, 21–22
college costs and, 68–83
compound interest, role of in, 5–7
contemporary conditions used for, 12, 23
early, importance of, 15–18, 19
executive incentives in, 296–299
inflation and, 1–2, 8–14
life insurance and, 192–221

lifestyle and, 19–27
mortgages in, 49, 53–62
net worth in, 28–37
patterns of finances and, 4
perks in, 299–301
step-by-step, 302–311
trusts in, 247–257
wills in, 259–260, 270, 275–281
see also estate planning; investment(s); real estate; retirement
First Index Investment Trust, 257
fixed-amount option, as payout plan, 274
fixed-period option, as payout plan, 274
Flaherty, Patrick F., 259*n.*
FLIP mortgages, 58
Follow the Leaders (Blackman), 287
Forbes magazine, 165
free enterprise system, inflation and, 11, 13
funeral arrangements, 277
futures
commodities, 182–184
contracts, money-related, 186–188
gold, 184–186

GAF Corporation, 141
General Motors, 149, 233, 287
general obligation bonds, 232
Giamatti, A. Bartlett, 69
gift programs, 17–18, 270
gifts, family, 271–272
gift tax, 264
"Ginnie Mae," 162, 163, 186, 274
Ginzburg, Eli, 22, 23
Glenn, Steven, 198, 201–202
glossary
on investments, 176–181
on life insurance, 219, 221
on real estate, 134
on retirement, 108–109
on taxes, 222
on trusts, 257–258
GNMA certificates, 162, 163, 186, 274
gold, 184–186
government, U.S.
aid for education from, 4, 70, 72–74
aid for timber yield increase, 114
debt securities, 162–164

government, U.S. (cont.)
  improvement of standard of living
    through, 4, 12–13
  inflation and, 10
  tax-exempt bonds from, 231–237
Government National Mortgage Association ("Ginnie Mae") certificates,
    162, 163, 186, 274
graduated payment mortgage (GPM), 58,
    59, 61
grants for education, see scholarships
graphics, 189, 190
gross national product (GNP), 13
guaranteed insurability riders, on life insurance, 213
guardian
  in estate planning, 269
  in trust planning, 252
Guide to Life Insurance (Consumers
    Union), 210

Halper, John B., 121–124
health care
  employee benefits, 11
  government programs for, 4
  in Medicare, 13
hedge funds, 168
Hertz Corporation, 63, 64
holding companies, 185
Homestake Mining, 184–185
Home-Stake Production Company, 241
hospital bonds, 233
house
  apartment, ownership of, 121–122
  closing costs of, 59, 60
  costs of, non-mortgage, 49–50
  inflation and value of, 8, 9
  as investment, 11, 51–53, 110
  mortgage and, 49, 53–62
  in net worth, 32
  refinancing, 61–62, 82, 310
  renting, vs. buying, 51–53
  residence trust and, 255
  sale of, tax exemption at, 223–224
  two-family, 119–120
  see also real estate
Hudson Institute, 13

IBM, 243
  stock of, 290, 294
incentives, 300
  split, 297
  stock options as, 296–297
income
  adjusted taxable, 229
  assured retirement, 14
  average total annual returns and, 136
  averaging, 229–230
  compounding, 5–7
  fund, pooled, 272
  mortgage and, 49, 55
  personal, 4
  position, family gifts and, 271
  projecting, 302
  in retirement, 87, 106–108
  shares, 167
  women and, 22–23
  see also income tax; salary
income tax
  alternative minimum tax and, 224
  elimination of, as saving in estate, 261
  federal, deductions from, 237–238,
    302–303
independent businessman approach to estate planning, 266–267
Indiana-Purdue University, 108
Indiana University, 214
individual retirement account, see IRA
    plan
industrial development bonds, 232–233
inflation, 1–2
  capitalism and, 13–14
  debt and, 20–21
  factor, 9, 10
  income projection and, 303–304
  life insurance and, 193, 208
  net worth and, 29, 33–34
  offsetting factors of, 10–11
  population and, 12–13
  projecting, 8–9
  real estate and, 110
  retirement and, 35, 86–87
  securities and, 138, 159–162
  taxes and, 9–10
installment sales
  direct, 227

indirect, 228
installment sale trust, 255
Institute of Life Insurance, 213
insurance, 20, 238
   agent, selection of, 285–286
   automobile, 62, 63
   disability, 4, 12, 93, 196–197
   for education costs, 75–76, 80, 82
   elimination of, as saving in estate, 262
   fiduciary liability, 105
   profit, from investment companies, 166
   self-, 66–67
   trusts, 252–253
   unemployment, 4, 11, 12
   see also life insurance; Social Security
insured bonds, 232
insured conventional mortgage, 54, 55
interest
   -adjusted cost concept, 211
   bonds and rate of, 142
   compound, 5–7, 16
   credit and, 46, 47
   on mortgages, 54, 55, 57–59
   option, as payout plan, 274
   see also compounding; rate of return
interest-adjusted cost (IAC), of life insurance, 209–211
Internal Revenue Service (IRS), 97, 98, 99
   accountant record with, 285
   alimony trusts and, 255
   annuity policies of, 218
   art valuations of, 191
   deferred compensation and, 298
   family-equity trusts and, 256
   gift income and, 273
   insurance trusts and, 253
   investment clubs and, 172
   investments and, 105
   partnerships and, 228
   perks and, 299
   racehorse regulations of, 189
   real estate and, 129
   on rollovers, policy of, 231
   rule 144 of, 297
   section 79, life insurance program of, 205–206

   tax shelters and, 239, 245
International Money Market (IMM), 187
inter vivos, see living trusts
Investing in Real Estate (Case), 112
investment(s), 173–174, 188–191
   advisers, 288–289
   annuities, 218
   for education, 76, 82
   ERISA and, 96, 102–103
   futures as, 182–188
   glossary on, 176–181
   house as, 11, 51–53
   lifestyle and, 19
   portfolio mixing in, 174–175
   in retirement plans, 98, 108
   securities as, 135–164
   stockbroker selection and, 287–288
   tax loss and, 225–226
   trustees in, 105
   see also real estate; securities
Investment Club Manual (NAIC), 172
investment clubs, 171–172
investment companies
   as advisers, 288–289
   benefits of, 164–166
   Forbes ratings of, 165
   no-load, 164
   special, 166–169
   see also mutual funds
investors, professional, 289–291
IRA plan, 97–98
   retirement income insurance policy in, 101–102
   special applications of, 103–104
irrevocable trusts, 248, 250, 255
IRS, *see* Internal Revenue Service

Johnson & Johnson, 143, 144–145, 150–153
joint tenancy, 275–276
joint ventures, in real estate
   apartment house ownership as, 121–122
   commercial property ownership as, 122–123
   guidelines for, 124–125
   land trust as, 124–126

joint ventures (cont.)
  limited partnerships as, 120–121
  subchapter S corporation as, 124
  syndicates as, 123–124
Joynt, F. William, 293–294
junior preferred stock, 140

kaffirs, 185
Kahn, Herman, 13
Keogh plan, 97–98
  compared with other plans, 100
  increase in, 104–105
  investment and, 102–103
  professional corporation plan and, 99, 101
  retirement plan managers and, 293
Keynes, John Maynard, 149
Keystone Provident Life Insurance Company, 218
Kohinoor International Ltd., 188
Krugerrands, 185–186

land trust, 124
Lavely, Joseph A., 108
lawyer, choice of, 283–285
Layne, Abner A., 102–103
leasing
  automobile, 63–66
  boxcar, 244
  computer, 243–244
legacy, convertible securities in, 141
letter stock funds, 168, 296–297
leverage
  in cattle programs, 242
  in real estate investment, 111–113
  in securities investment, 157
liabilities
  in estate planning, 259
  net worth and, 28, 32
life cycle insurance, see adjustable life (AL) insurance
life expectancy, 192–193
life income option, as payout plan, 274
life insurance
  adjustable (AL), policy for, 206–207
  annuities and, 215–219
  borrowing on, 82, 196, 310
  costs of, 209–211
  coverage, adequate, 193, 197–202
  after death, 280
  disability policies of, 196–197
  divesting, 213–215
  for education payment, 75–76, 80
  family needs of, 211–213, 263
  fixed expenses and, 10
  glossary for, 219, 221
  insurance trusts and, 252–253
  from investment companies, 166
  IRS section 79 program for, 205–206
  minimum deposit insurance (MDI) for, 203–204
  mortgage, 277
  payout plans for, 273–274
  in personal retirement plans, 101–102
  purposes of, 192
  split (SLI), policy for, 207–208
  split-dollar insurance (SDI) for, 204–205
  straight, vs. term, 193–196
  variable (VLI), policy for, 208–209
  wills and, 277
lifestyle, 20–21
  changing, in U.S., 4, 14
  employment changes and, 22–25
  financial planning and, 19, 25–27, 90
  see also standard of living
limited tax bonds, 232
liquid asset funds, 168–169
living trusts, 81, 248, 249–250
  insurance trust as, 252–253
  Schroder Trust Co. and, 257
loans
  credit and, 46, 47
  education, 68, 70
  installment, 10
  as last resort, 311
  leasing and, 64
  mortgages as, 49–50, 53–59
  passbook, 82
  against stock owned, 136
  tuition-aid, 77, 80
long-term performance bonus, 297
lump-sum payout, for life insurance, 273–274

MacGregor, Ian, 13–14

managed funds, 237
market letters, 288–289
market value, fair, 64
Master Products, 157–158
Medicare, 13
Meeting College Needs, 73
Melville Corp., 155, 160, 161
metals, precious, as investment, 184–186
minimum deposit insurance (MDI), 203–204
Missouri, aid for education in, 72
MIT/Harvard Joint Center for Urban Studies, 11
mobility, 13
money
　credit and, 47
　domination of life by, 20
　instruments, 186–188
　as medium of exchange, 2
　power of, 15
　as product, 46
　time value of, 160
money market funds, 168–169
money-purchase plan, 98–99
　compared with other plans, 100
money-related futures contracts, 186–188
Moody's Investors Service, 141, 235
mortgage(s)
　amortization of, 56, 113
　clauses in, 133
　closing costs and, 59, 60
　as fixed expense, 10
　futures, 186
　income and, 49
　on income-producing property, 122, 125
　insurance, 277
　investment in, 131–133
　obtaining, 53–54
　payments, 55, 57
　prepayment of, 61
　principal on, figuring, 55–57
　refinancing, 61–62, 82, 310
　second, 82, 310
　types of, 54–55, 57–59
Mortgage Consultants, Inc., 119
moving averages (MAs), 183
municipal bonds
　after-tax yield of, calculating, 233–235
　funds, 236–237
　selecting, 235–236
　types of, 231–233
mutual funds, 32, 290
　gold as, 185
　see also investment companies

NAIC, 171–172
National Association of Investment Clubs (NAIC), 171–172
National Committee for Manpower Policy, 23
National Service Life (insurance company), 310
National Shawmut Bank (Boston), 77, 80
National Society of Exchange Counsellors, 130
net worth
　allocations of, 33
　calculation, 28–32
　in estate planning, 259
　growth of, 34
　planning, 37
　projected, 308
　tables, 27–32
New Jersey Turnpike, 232
New York City, municipal bonds of, 232, 235
New York Post, 188
New York State Power Authority, 232
New York Stock Exchange (NYSE), 6, 149, 153, 156, 287, 291
　calls on, 157
　films from, 171
New York Times, The, 22
1976 Tax Reform Act, *see* Tax Reform Act of 1976
nonprofit institutions, pensions in, 101
North Carolina Municipal Power Agency Catawba Electric Revenue Bonds, 233
Nuveen, 237

Oakland Financial Group, 26–27
oil and gas programs, as tax shelter, 239–242
Oklahoma Natural Gas, 161

Omni-Exploration, Inc., 240, 241–242
Oppenheimer Industries, 115, 242–243
options
  calls and, 156–157
  stock, as incentives, 296–297
  writing, rules for, 158–159
Outlook (Standard & Poor's), 288
overdrafts
  automatic, 47
  charges for, 48
Over-the-Counter Market (OTC), 290

Paine Webber Jackson & Curtis, 184
partnerships, limited, 120–123
  guidelines for, 124–126
  syndicates as, 123–124
  for tax savings, 228–229
  tax shelters and, 239, 241
payout plans, for life insurance policies, 273–274
payroll deduction plans, 76
pensions, 105
  checks on, 96
  corporate, 12, 16, 84–85
  elements of, 92–95
  ERISA provisions for, 91–92
  IRA plans and, 103–104
  for nonprofit institution employees, 101
  Social Security and, 88, 202
P/E ratios, 153–154, 174
perks, 299, 301
perquisites, executive, 299, 301
"phantom" stock programs, 298
planning, financial, *see* financial planning
Platte River Power Authority, 232
points, mortgages and, 54
pooled income fund, 272
population
  affected by women in workforce, 22
  real estate affected by, 111, 113
  trends, and inflation, 12–13
pourover trusts, 254
PR, 143, 144–145
preferred stock, 139–140
  fund, 140–141
  junior, 140

premiums, 157, 158–159
  on child life insurance, 212–213
  on life insurance, 193, 203–209 *passim*
prepayment plan (insurance loans for education), 80
price/earnings (P/E) ratios, 153–154, 174
private debt funds, 167–168
probate, 254, 275
productivity, inflation and, 11
professional corporation plan, 97–98
  investment and, 102–103
  Keogh plan and, 99, 101
profit rate (PR), 143, 144–145
profit-sharing
  defined-contributions plan and, 98–99, 100
  in retirement planning, 93–94
projection
  of inflation, 8–9, 10
  of investment value, 9, 10
  in zero-base budgeting, 41
Proposition 13, 12
PRO Services, Inc., 206, 291, 293
prudent man rule (ERISA), 291
puts, *see* options
pyramiding, 112

QDP II, 140–141
qualified dividend portfolio II (QDP II), 140–141

racehorses, as investment, 188–189
Railcar, Inc., 244
rate of return
  "rule of 72" for calculating, 6
  on shareholder's equity, 144–145
  target, in writing options, 158
  see also interest
raw land, 111, 113–114
real estate
  annual review of, 126–128
  depreciation and, 116–117, 123
  in estate planning, 261
  exchanging, 129–131
  farms as, 115
  glossary on, 134

as income-producing asset, 117–119
inflation and, 110, 113
joint ventures in, 120–126
leverage in, 111–113
mortgages and, 122, 125, 131–133
raw land as, 111, 113–114
taxes and, 225
timber as, 114–115
two-family house and, 119–120
see also house; mortgage(s)
real estate investment trusts (REITs), 129, 130, 131
registered representative (RR), *see* stockbroker
regulated investment companies, 140–141
REIT, 129, 130, 131
renting
  apartments, 52–53
  automobiles, 63–66
  see also leasing
Research Institute of America, 224
residence trusts, 255
restricted stock plans, 297
retirement, 12
  bonds, U.S., 163
  glossary on, 108–109
  income, assured, 14
  inflation and, 35
  investment and, 15–16, 98, 102–103, 105–108
  life insurance in plans for, 101–102
  net worth goals at, 33
  pension plans for, 16, 84–85, 91–96
  plan, personal, 16–17, 84–87, 96–101
  plan managers, 291, 293
  Social Security and, 88–89, 90–91
  see also pensions
retirement income insurance policy (RIIP), 101–102
revenue bonds, 232
  environmental control, 233
revocable trusts, 248, 249
rewards, balanced against risks, 5, 21–22
Richard Blackman & Co., 287
riders, guaranteed insurability, 213
RIIP, 101–102
risks, balanced against rewards, 5, 21–22

rollovers, 103, 104
  in cattle programs, 242
  as short-term tax strategy, 231
Rothschild, Baron de, 155
Rudy, William, 188
"rule of 72," in rate of return calculation, 6

salary
  deferred compensation plans and, 298–299
  increases, erosion of, 10
  inflation and, 1–2
  pension plans and, 16
  projecting, 3
Saphire, Lawrence, 189, 190
savings
  annuities, 217–218
  borrowing against, 82
  certificates, long-term, 7, 305
  for education costs, 76
  individual, 14
  as investment, 135
  in nonprofit institution pensions, 101
  in personal budget, 38, 306
  plans, 169, 229
  for retirement, 89–90, 102–103
  straight life insurance and, 193
  tax, calculating worth of, 225–226
scholarships
  corporate, 82–83
  in financial planning, 71
  from government, 73, 74
  from private sources, 75, 77–79
Schroder Trust Co., 257
Schumpeter, Joseph, 13
SEC, *see* Securities and Exchange Commission
securities
  bank buying and selling, 291
  borrowing against, 82
  buying, analysis for, 149–154
  common stock as, 136, 137–139
  convertible (CVs), 141, 156
  for education costs, 76
  incentive plans and, 297–299
  inflation and, 138, 159–162
  options and, 156–159, 296–297

securities (cont.)
  preferred stock as, 139–141
  rating of, 142–143
  retirement investment in, 102–103
  selection of, 143–148
  selling, 154–156, 310
  taxes on, at death, 265
  tax exempt-, 231–237
  tax loss and, 225–226
  trusts and, 256–257
  U.S. government debt, 162–164
Securities and Exchange Commission (SEC), U.S., 123, 184, 240
  investment advisers and, relations of, 289
  rules on stock options of, 298
Select Information Exchange, 288
self-interest transactions, 102–103
"shadow" stock programs, 298
Shearson Hayden Stone, 183, 184
Smith, Glenn O., 206
Social Security, 2, 4, 11, 14, 20, 302
  benefits, 263
  counsulting, after death, 280
  deductions, 51, 303
  education aid from, 72
  elimination of payments to, as saving in estate, 261
  Keogh plans and, 99
  life insurance and, 198, 202
  payments, anticipated, 307
  in pension computation, 88, 92, 94
  population affecting, 12, 13
  in retirement, 88–89, 90–91
Social Security Administration, 29
South Africa, 185–186
special assessment bonds, 232
split-dollar insurance (SDI), 204–205
split life insurance (SLI), 207–208
spreads, in futures investments, 187
sprinkling trusts, 253–254
Standard & Poor's, 142, 143, 159, 161
  500 Stock Price Index, 257, 294
  Outlook, 288
  Price Indices, 290
standard of living
  improving, 2
  in U.S., 3–4, 13

see also lifestyle
stock appreciation rights, 297–298
stockbroker
  as investment adviser, 288–289
  selection of, 287–288
Stock Guide (Standard & Poor's), 143, 159
stockholder's equity, 143–144
stock market, 136
  50% rule in, 4
  fundamental analysis of, 153–154
  technical analysis of, 149–153
stocks, *see* securities
Stolper, Michael, 29, 294–295
Stolper & Co., 294–295
straight life insurance, 193–196, 198, 201, 209
  guaranteed insurability riders on, 213
  interest-adjusted cost concept and, 211
  switching from, 214–215, 216
straight-line depreciation, 116, 117
subchapter S corporation, 124
sum-of-digits depreciation, 116, 117
syndicate(s)
  art speculator, 190
  cattle, 242–243
  guidelines for real estate, 124–126
  racehorse owner, 188, 189
  real-estate, 123–124

tax(es)
  accountant selection and, 285
  on annuities, 216
  on art, 191
  on automobiles, 64, 66, 67
  credits for education, 4, 68, 72, 73
  deductions, 237–238, 270, 302–303
  deferred compensation and, 298–299
  estate, 99, 249, 250, 260, 263–266, 277
  -exempt bonds, 231–237
  gift, 264, 271–272
  glossary on, 222
  home purchase and, 51–53, 55, 61
  inflation and, 9–10
  IRA plan and, advantages of, 104
  laws, 223–224

liens, 111
  on life insurance policies, 205,
    208–209
  on options, 159
  partnerships for saving on, 228–229
  planning, 230–231
  on racehorse ownership, 189
  on real estate, 110, 121, 123, 130
  record keeping and, 238
  on retirement plans, 15, 85, 97,
    106–108
  savings, calculating, 225–226
  on savings plans, 169, 229
  on securities, 137, 140–141
  on trust funds, 17, 80, 82–83
  trusts and, 248
  in 21st century, 12
  see also income tax; Internal Revenue Service; tax shelters
Tax Information on Investment Income and Expenses (IRS), 172
Tax Reform Act of 1976, U.S., 223–224
  estate taxes affected by, 263–266
  wills and, 278
tax shelter(s), 80–81, 115, 223, 245–246
  cattle as, 242–243
  common stock as, 137
  equipment leasing as, 243–244
  oil and gas, 239–242
  QDP II as, 140–141
  racehorses as, 189
  savings annuities and, 217–218
  terminations, early, 244–245
Teleprompter, 291
term life insurance, 193–196, 198, 201
  at age 65, 214
  decreasing, 202–203
  interest-adjusted cost concept and, 210
testamentary trusts, 248, 249
timber, 114–115
Tobin, James, 12
Totten trusts, 252
Trainor, D. Bruce, 241
Treasury bills, U.S., 162, 163, 168, 305
  futures, 187
  mixed with commodities, 183
Treasury bonds, U.S., 162, 163
  futures, 186–187

Treasury notes, U.S., 162, 163
trend line, on stock charts, 151, 154,
  155, 174
Truman Scholarship Foundation, 72, 74
trustee, 274–257 *passim*
  bank as, 291
  as executor of estate, 261, 269
  fiduciary as, 105
  lawyer as, 285
trust fund(s)
  common, 164
  for education, 80, 82–83, 251
  one-time, 17, 18
  short-term, 81, 251–252
trusts
  alimony, 255
  bank, 256–257
  benefits of, 248, 264
  charitable, 256, 272
  charitable remainder annuity, 272–273
  Clifford, 291
  diamond investment, 188
  family equity, 256
  glossary on, 257–258
  indirect installment sales and, 228
  installment sale, 255
  insurance, 252–253
  irrevocable, 248, 250
  land, 124
  living, 248, 249–250
  pourover, 254
  real estate investment (REITs), 129
  residence, 255
  revocable, 248
  short-term, 251–252
  sprinkling, 253–254
  testamentary, 248, 249
  Totten, 252
  unit, 236–237
Tucson Gas & Electric Co., 233

unemployment
  insurance, 4, 11, 20
  Kahn on, 13
  as problem, 4
unified tax credit, in Tax Reform Act
  (1976), 264–265

Uniform Gifts to Minors Act, U.S., 252
Uniform Premium Table, 206
U.S. Post Office, 94
unit trusts, 236–237
utilities, 139
   junior preferred stock of, 140
   tax-exempt bonds and, 231–233

Vanguard Group funds, 218, 257
variable life insurance (VLI), 208–209
variable rate mortgage (VRM), 59
vesting, 92
Veteran's Administration, 280
Veteran's Administration (VA) mortgage, 54, 55, 60
   GNMA certificates and, 162, 163, 186
   prepayment and, 61
Veterans of Foreign Wars (VFW), 280

Wachovia Individual Capital Management, 131
Walsh, Charles H., 99, 101
Washington University, 72

Wellington Management Company, 218–219
West Virginia Turnpike, 232
will(s)
   community property and, 279–280
   at death, 280–281
   estate distribution in, 260–261
   in estate planning, 259–260, 270
   joint tenancy and, 275–276
   pourover trusts and, 254
   preparation of, 276–279
   review of, 279
   trusts and, 248–252 *passim*
Winnipeg Commodity Exchange, 185
women, role of, in business, 22–23
Wright, John Winthrop, 225
Wright Investors' Service, 143

Yale University, 12, 69, 70
yield on cost, 160

zero-base budgeting (ZBB), 38, 41, 43
Ziegler, Richard S., 259*n*.